Administrative Law
and Government Action

Administrative Law and Government Action

The Courts and Alternative Mechanisms of Review

GENEVRA RICHARDSON
and
HAZEL GENN

CLARENDON PRESS · OXFORD
1994

Oxford University Press, Walton Street, Oxford OX2 6DP

Oxford New York
Athens Auckland Bangkok Bombay
Calcutta Cape Town Dar es Salaam Delhi
Florence Hong Kong Istanbul Karachi
Kuala Lumpur Madras Madrid Melbourne
Mexico City Nairobi Paris Singapore
Taipei Tokyo Toronto
and associated companies in
Berlin Ibadan

Oxford is a trade mark of Oxford University Press

Published in the United States
by Oxford University Press Inc., New York

British Library Cataloguing in Publication Data
Data available

Library of Congress Cataloging in Publication Data
Administrative law and government action: the courts and alternative
mechanisms of review / [edited by] Hazel Genn and Genevra
Richardson.
p. cm.
Includes index.
1. Judicial review of administrative acts—Great Britain.
2. Administrative law—Great Britain. 3. Great Britain—Politics
and government—1979- I. Genn, Hazel G. II. Richardson, Genevra.
KD4902.A93 1994
342.41'06—dc20   94-29641
[344.1026]
ISBN 0-19-876276-3
ISBN 0-19-876277-1 (Pbk)

Typeset by Cambrian Typesetters Frimley, Surrey
Printed in Great Britain
on acid-free paper by
Biddles Ltd., Guildford and King's Lynn

Contents

Contents

Contributors

Robert Baldwin is Reader in Law at the London School of Economics and Political Science.

Alan E. Boyle is Professor of Public International Law at the University of Edinburgh.

Paul Brown is a Barrister whose chambers are in 4–5 Gray's Inn Square, London.

Roger Cotterrell is Professor of Legal Theory at Queen Mary and Westfield College, London.

Ross Cranston is Cassel Professor of Commercial Law at the London School of Economics and Political Science.

Hazel Genn is Professor of Law at University College London.

Cosmo Graham is H. K. Bevan Professor of Law at the University of Hull.

Ian Loveland is Lecturer in Law at Queen Mary and Westfield College, London.

Genevra Richardson is Reader in Law at Queen Mary and Westfield College, London.

Roy Sainsbury is Senior Research Fellow at the Social Policy Research Unit, University of York.

The Hon. Mr Justice Stephen Sedley is a Justice of the High Court.

David Williams is Price Waterhouse Professor of International Business Taxation at Queen Mary and Westfield College, London.

Ian Yeats is Senior Lecturer in Law at Queen Mary and Westfield College, London.

Table of Statutes

Table of Cases

OMBUDSMAN CASES

Table of Cases

INVESTIGATIONS

Introduction

The unprecedented expansion of administrative law over the last two and a half decades has inspired a rich academic literature. Writers have analysed the changes from a variety of perspectives. Some have produced detailed analyses of the law of judicial review,[1] while others have urged a wider approach to the subject with greater emphasis on alternative mechanisms for the regulation of government action.[2] At the same time the theories and assumptions underlying the judicial role have been subjected to extensive scrutiny[3] and the literature on specific techniques of regulation has been expanded.[4] Any student of administrative law wishing to acquire a comprehensive view of the subject must therefore consult a wide variety of sources and grapple with a sometimes bewildering range of approaches.

This book is designed to meet some of the difficulties raised by this diversity. It does not attempt to provide a comprehensive text but offers a collection of essays on important and often contentious aspects of administrative law. The individual contributions, which are informed by a wide variety of theoretical perspectives, are drawn together by certain common themes: the constitutional role of judicial review, its efficacy as a mechanism for the regulation of government decision-making, and the scope and impact of alternative mechanisms. All of the contributions address issues of current significance and, while some develop a broad conceptual analysis, others rely on a more internal critique. Each contributor sets out both to provide an accessible synthesis of existing literature and to develop his or her own critical approach. Considerable emphasis is also placed on the results of relevant empirical research where available. Many of the contributions, particularly those in Part II, draw on recent research and case-study material in order to illuminate the more theoretical debate.

The volume falls into two parts. Part I is concerned primarily with

---

[1] H. W. R. Wade, *Administrative Law* (7th edn. Oxford, 1994); M. Supperstone and J. Goudie (eds.), *Judicial Review* (London, 1992).

[2] C. Harlow and R. Rawlings, *Law and Administration* (London, 1984).

[3] T. Prosser, 'Towards a Critical Public Law' (1982) 9 *Journal of Law and Society* 1; I. Harden and N. Lewis, *The Noble Lie* (London, 1986); P. Craig, Administrative Law (2nd edn. London, 1989); id., *Public Law and Democracy in the United Kingdom and the United States of America* (Oxford, 1990); M. Loughlin, *Public Law and Political Theory* (Oxford, 1992).

[4] R. Baldwin and C. McCrudden (eds.), *Regulation and Public Law* (London, 1987); P. Birkinshaw, I. Harden, and N. Lewis, *Government by Moonlight: The Hybrid Parts of the State* (London, 1990); J. Baldwin, N. Wikeley, and R. Young, *Judging Social Security* (Oxford, 1992); K. Hawkins, *The Uses of Discretion* (Oxford, 1993).

judicial review and its appropriate constitutional role, while Part II
discusses alternative mechanisms for the regulation of governmental
action. Any serious discussion of the proper role of the judiciary in the
supervision of government is bound to reveal a broad range of opinion in
reflection of the participants' personal views on such issues as the role of
the state, the competence of the judiciary, and the value of democratic
accountability. The discussion contained within Part I is no exception. The
six chapters reveal a wide variety of approaches, priorities, and political
preferences. Nevertheless they all address, in one way or another, the
same central questions: what is the proper relationship between the
judiciary and the other arms of the state within a Western democracy? And
how far does the mechanism of judicial review enable the courts
adequately to fulfil their particular role? In the variety of the views they
express the individual chapters complement one another and together
provide a balanced picture of a complex and controversial topic.

In Chapter 1, 'Judicial Review and Legal Theory', Cotterrell reminds us
that the debate about the proper place of judicial review does not exist in
isolation; it reflects wider concerns about law and the nature of
government. He identifies two broad views of judicial review within the
legal literature. One sees courts as performing, from within government,
the technical role of monitoring and safeguarding the rule of law, while the
other views the court as an outsider to the process of government and as
serving a variety of independent values, some of which might even buttress
democracy. Cotterrell relates these two views to the two contrasting
images of society suggested by legal philosophy: *imperium* and community.
While the traditional and internal, rule of law, approach to judicial review
is easily understood in terms of *imperium*, the alternative 'principled'
approach cannot be so readily accommodated and tends to reflect instead a
community image of society. However, according to Cotterrell, although
recent academic writing on judicial review may reflect an image of
community, the dominant practice of judicial review in the courts adheres
closely to the image of *imperium*. While such an analysis might disappoint
those who wish to strengthen the position of the court as a legitimate
promoter of independent values, Cotterrell is at pains to stress the limits of
the legal image of community. As reflected in legal philosophy the image is
not of a 'vibrant community that makes its values and its law', but 'rather
an image of a population dependent on experts to speak for it—perhaps to
tell it what its values really are (or ought to be)'. It is not, it seems, the
vehicle for the introduction of democratic values. In conclusion Cotterrell
suggests that the debate on the role of judicial review has been constrained
by the dominant images of community and *imperium* and has been shaped
by their limitations in vision and scope. Most significantly, neither
community nor *imperium* 'provides the means of envisaging ·an adequate

democracy', and any consideration of judicial review modelled upon them, whether consciously or unconsciously, must reflect a similar failure.

While Cotterrell's chapter serves to place the judicial review debate within the wider context of legal theory and to draw lessons from that literature, Sedley looks more specifically at the role of the judiciary within the UK constitution, at how this role has evolved, and at what alternatives there might be to the hegemony of the courts. In Chapter 2, 'Governments, Constitutions and Judges', Sedley charts the rise in the power of the judiciary since the Second World War. Significantly this expansion of judicial might has occurred in the absence of a written constitution: the courts in the UK enjoy no expressly protected status, yet with the passive acquiescence of Parliament they have achieved what Sedley describes as 'nothing less than a refashioning of the UK's constitution'. As possible reasons for this judicial success Sedley suggests the autonomy of the judicial notion of fairness, which permits the courts on occasion to 'swim up the political rapids', a less myopic view of expediency than that possessed by government, and popular support for judicial control of an otherwise unaccountable executive. While Sedley recognizes that judicial review, the main vehicle for the exercise of judicial power, remains limited in scope and impact, he suggests that the powerful constitutional role adopted by our judiciary has 'so far been beneficial'. Despite his faith in the judiciary, however, Sedley concludes by cautioning against the use of a written constitution to present the judges with power to review primary legislation: 'A judiciary which can become as powerful a constitutional actor as ours can become the master, not the servant, of a written constitution.'

The tone of Cranston's chapter, 'Reviewing Judicial Review', is much more overtly critical of the judicial role. Where Sedley sees the courts as a necessary, albeit imperfect, mechanism for the control of an otherwise unaccountable executive, Cranston emphasizes the importance of allowing government to govern: 'It is just as much in the public interest that public authorities exercise their power as that they exercise it lawfully.' In a wide-ranging analysis of recent developments in the scope, grounds, and procedure of judicial review, Cranston challenges what he sees as the modern orthodoxy: the expansive view of judicial review which tends to welcome every extension of the court's power to control government action. In addition to his scepticism about the value of certain juris-prudential developments, Cranston voices a more general concern both about the ability of the courts to understand and to reflect the realities of the administrative task, and about the practical impact of judicial review. He concludes by discussing some principles which might be developed by the courts in order to encourage an appropriate level of 'judicial modesty'. While Sedley and Cranston differ quite significantly in their attitudes towards the judiciary, they both stress the dangers inherent in judicial power. Sedley sees the potential threat in broad constitutional terms and cautions against any formal extension of judicial might, while Cranston is more concerned with the implications for administrative authorities of what he regards as already too immodest a judiciary.

In his chapter 'Sovereignty, Accountability, and the Reform of Administrative Law', Boyle specifically addresses some of the misgivings voiced by Cranston and considers whether recent European developments will eventually lead our home-grown judicial review beyond its traditional constitutional limitations. Boyle describes developments in the field of administrative law over the last few decades and considers how far they have met the widely held reservations about the efficacy of judicial review. He concludes that, by working within the orthodox constitutional framework, institutional reform in the form of tribunals and ombudsmen has failed to create any mechanism capable of exercising any real control over the executive. On the other hand, freed from its procedural limitations judicial review has shown greater vitality and, spurred on by the demands of Europe, is beginning 'to assume the role of a constitutional remedy'. Nevertheless, for Boyle, as for Cranston, judicial review remains too peripheral and selective to provide a useful means of challenging the decisions of public bodies. However, unlike Cranston, Boyle envisages a strong role for judicial review and considers the actual and potential impact of the European Convention on Human Rights on both its substance and its structure. Boyle's analysis thus serves to confirm Sedley's claim that, even without the benefit of a written constitution, the judiciary are both willing and capable of extending their constitutional role.

The final two chapters in Part I address more directly the specific grounds of judicial review. In 'The Legal Regulation of Process' Richardson examines the various justifications offered for the imposition of process requirements by the common law. She reviews the existing literature and case-law and concludes that the current judicial attitude, which is strongly influenced by orthodox constitutional theory, reflects a narrow view of the court's role in the regulation of process. Richardson argues that significant consequences arise from this prevailing attitude which both limit the potential of process regulation and bring the courts perilously close to conflict with orthodox constitutional principle. Reflecting less faith in government and existing channels of political accountability than Cranston, Richardson suggests an alternative basis for the court's role which, being grounded in the pursuit of democratic principles, addresses some of the concerns expressed by Cotterrell. Such an approach, she argues, would both expand the scope of common law procedural regulation into the policy-making process itself and move the court's role beyond the reach of any orthodox constitutional criticism.

In his chapter 'Findings of Fact: The Role of the Courts' Yeats provides a detailed analysis of the courts' practice with regard to the review of determinations of fact on the part of public bodies. While the courts' willingness to review errors of law may derive from an orthodox top-down vision of the legal system, Yeats suggests that the current approach to the review of fact is much more pragmatic: 'grander issues of the constitutionality of judicial review bear only peripherally' on the review of fact. He sees the courts' reluctance to question findings of fact by inferior bodies as a means of both preserving a manageable work-load for the reviewing courts, and maintaining a division of labour between the courts and the subordinate agencies which appropriately reflects their respective areas of expertise.

Together the six chapters in Part I provide a varied and outspoken discussion of one of the most important questions facing public law today: what is or should be the role of the judiciary in the oversight of governmental action? Reflecting as they do very different attitudes to judicial power they reach no consensus, but by helping to identify the central issues they provide instead a useful base from which further analysis can spring. One such issue clearly to emerge is that of the value of alternative mechanisms. Many of the chapters in Part I allude to the peripheral nature of judicial review, its selectivity, and its lack of practical impact. Whatever the preferred role of judicial review it cannot alone provide for the comprehensive oversight of public decision-making. Alternative mechanisms are essential. In Part II the performance and the potential of a variety of such mechanisms is discussed with reference to both theoretical analyses and empirical data.

Judicial review in its present form is primarily concerned with the *ex post* regulation of government decision-making. It is designed to measure the legality of a decision against existing common law principles. Ever since the work of K. C. Davis in the 1960s the potential for *ex ante* regulation through administrative rule-making has given rise to extensive and sometimes heated debate. The first four chapters in Part II all address different aspects of the process of administrative policy formulation in general and, in some cases, the phenomenon of rule-making in particular.

In 'Governing with Rules: The Developing Agenda' Baldwin provides an overview of the area. He discusses the case for the employment of rules in preference to other possible devices for the achievement of governmental purposes and suggests five measures for judging the legitimacy of rules. According to Baldwin the use of governmental rules in the UK is most readily justified by reference to claims to expertise and efficiency, which inevitably increases the significance attaching to enforcement. Drawing on existing empirical data Baldwin examines the difficulties arising from the need to design rules which are conducive to effective enforcement and considers how the demands of enforcement can be reconciled with the possibly conflicting demands of requirements such as accountability. Finally, Baldwin considers the form of secondary and tertiary rules within the European Community and assesses the extent to which they meet his five measures of legitimacy. His overall analysis, which is widely informed by the results of empirical research, is critical of many of the prevailing assumptions concerning rules and their use.

In 'Self-Regulation' Graham examines one particular mechanism increasingly employed by government for both the formulation and implementation of detailed policy. Graham defines self-regulation as 'the delegation of public policy tasks to private actors in an institutionalised form' and is concerned to judge self-regulatory arrangements against the essentially procedural principles of openness and accountability. Referring back to Cotterrell's analysis, Graham suggests that the government's increased use of self-regulation has developed as a partial response to the limitations of imperium methods of policy delivery. He charts the rich variety of arrangements adopted and critically examines the mechanisms provided to ensure both internal and external accountability, *ex ante* and *ex post*. His conclusions reveal a generally pragmatic and unprincipled growth in self-regulation, except possibly in the area of financial services, and a marked lack of effective accountability. More attention must be paid to the constitutional principles according to which self-regulation should be both selected and judged.

The question of enforcement, raised by Baldwin, is studied in depth by Loveland in 'Irrelevant Considerations? The Role of Administrative Law in Determining the Local Connection of Homeless Persons'. Loveland claims that administrative law typically fails to understand the realities of the administrative process and he examines this claim through an empirical account of the implementation of Part III of the Housing Act 1985. Loveland presents data from a study of three housing authorities which demonstrate that the decision-making processes in all three were 'in varying degrees unlawful'. According to Loveland, however, this does not automatically imply that they were also illegitimate. In his view the growing body of empirical evidence which highlights the gap between legal formality and bureaucratic reality should encourage administrative lawyers to reassess their traditional attitudes. They must decide whether to continue the pursuit of the ideal rule to be imposed from without, or to engage in a dialogue between legal principle and bureaucratic practice.

From their various perspectives the first three chapters in Part II are all critical of the particular mechanisms for the implementation of public policy with which they are concerned. From a constitutional point of view problems of accountability and public participation arise in relation to rule-making and self-regulation, while the problems of enforcement identified by both Baldwin and Loveland attest to the very real difficulties faced by the implementation of structures modelled on *imperium.*

In 'The Influence of European Union Law upon United Kingdom Administration' Williams expands on the European dimension of the debate, introduced by Baldwin, by examining the implications for the processes of UK policy formulation and implementation which flow from our membership of the European Union. Taking the administration of taxation and social security Williams describes the significant influence now exercised by European Union law. In some cases the Union law has direct effect while in others it requires specific implementation. In all cases administrators can be faced with a dilemma when trying to identify the rules, principles, and standards which define the legality of their actions. Williams describes how these dilemmas arise and the various means which have been adopted for their resolution to date. Drawing from the experience of two specific areas of rule-making and policy implementation, Williams reaches conclusions very similar to those reached by Boyle. The European influence over our domestic administration, which is already strong and set to grow stronger, has the potential to effect major, and possibly welcome, change within our established administrative legal order.

While the questions addressed in the four chapters concerning administrative rule-making and other policy formulation techniques concentrate on the *ex ante* regulation of government action, the final three chapters deal with mechanisms designed primarily for the *ex post* review of administrative decision-making. In 'Tribunal Review of Administrative Decision-Making' Genn examines the factors that are traditionally regarded as distinguishing tribunals from courts, and discusses the philosophical and practical arguments that have underpinned the growth of statutory tribunals in the twentieth century. According to Genn there exists among administrative lawyers a somewhat uncritical support for tribunals as efficient and straightforward means of challenging administrative decision-making, and this support typically tends to ignore issues which require empirical validation. In a bid to redress the balance Genn presents the results of a research study designed to look at tribunal processes, and particularly to assess the effect of representation on the outcome of tribunal hearings. Genn argues that the data emerging from this research serve to challenge the orthodox assumptions held concerning the cheapness and accessibility of tribunals and the value of their informality for tribunal applicants. Genn concludes that there are considerable limits to the effectiveness of tribunals as a check on administrative decision-making and that these limitations stem at least in part from the design of tribunals and the low levels of representation at them. In order for tribunals to act as an *effective* means of review, those who appear before them must be capable of establishing their entitlement according to regulations and of providing relevant evidence to the tribunal, largely without the benefit of advice or representation. Genn argues that there is a need to reconsider the procedures and standards of adjudication in tribunals, and to address the problems that arise when attempting to provide simplified tribunal procedures that are capable of delivering substantive justice.

In recent years increasing use has been made of internal reviews either as a substitute for or as a supplement to tribunal hearings. In 'Internal Reviews and the Weakening of Social Security Claimants' Rights of Appeal' Sainsbury examines the part played by internal reviews within the first-tier appeal arrangements operating in the area of social security. He identifies the defining characteristics of 'ideal-type' reviews and tribunal appeals. In their ideal type reviews are speedier and cheaper than tribunal appeals, while tribunals offer independence, and hence impartiality, greater participation, and a deeper experience of adjudication. Having compared the ideal types with existing arrangements, Sainsbury concludes that mainstream social security adjudication conforms most closely to the ideal, while housing benefit, the social fund, disability benefits, and child support all depart from it in varying degrees. Sainsbury argues that the increased injection of internal review between administration and appeal has reduced the rights of claimants to participation and impartial decision-making, and expresses concern that such developments can go unremarked.

The creation of the Parliamentary Commissioner for Administration in 1967 presented Britain with its first ombudsman and introduced a further mechanism for the resolution of disputes between individuals and government. In 'The Ombudsmen: Remedies for Misinformation' Brown presents the results of research into one aspect of the ombudsmen's work: the investigation of complaints that individuals have been misled by information given by a government body. He explains that the area was chosen because it raises problems for which the courts have yet to find a solution. According to Brown the ombudsmen have been able to break away from the *ultra vires* strait-jacket which so constrains the courts in this area, and have endeavoured to return the complainant to the position he or she would have enjoyed had correct advice been given from the outset. The research findings serve to demonstrate the value of extra-judicial remedies and to support Cranston's contention that judicial review should not invariably be regarded as the most appropriate means of seeking redress against a public body.

The last three chapters together provide a wealth of empirical data about the way that alternative mechanisms for the resolution of grievances against public authorities operate in practice. Genn and Sainsbury, in particular, challenge some of the assumptions which typically underlie the claims made for the value of both tribunals and internal review to the interests of those affected by administrative decisions. These chapters clearly indicate the need for the value and impact of alternative review mechanisms to be empirically assessed.

PART I

The Courts

1

Judicial Review and Legal Theory

Roger Cotterrell

At the heart of much of administrative law—and certainly of the practice of judicial review of administrative action—stand fundamental and seemingly intractable theoretical questions about the role of courts in government. What, if anything, gives judges the general authority to review governmental action? What is sought from such review and what can it achieve? How, if at all, is it compatible with ideas of democratic government, lawmaking, and policy implementation? In common law systems, courts have ultimate authority to interpret law, including administrative law. Equally, administrative law is assumed to provide an essential legal framework for most routine governmental activity. Thus, in this environment, the most basic and inescapable question becomes: what is the relationship between courts, polity, and society? More specifically, how do courts that apply administrative law relate to the state, on the one hand, and the regulated population of individual citizens and varied social groups, on the other?

Different kinds of answer to this last question can be sought. Some may be primarily prescriptive, considering, perhaps in terms of some theory of desirable forms of government, what courts properly can or should do. Other approaches may seek to describe or explain the activity of courts in relation to government. They may be historical, institutional, or socio-logical, seeking to show empirically what the actual position of courts within the political structure or culture of a particular society is or has been; or what contribution courts actually make to social or political order or change; or how the activity of courts historically has related to the development of government and administration. This chapter adopts an analytical approach that cuts across yet relates closely to many of the kinds of inquiries just mentioned. It is less concerned with judicial activity than with the ideas used to justify or criticize this activity. It seeks to bring to light general currents of thought or belief about the nature of law and society that shape the way in which the political place of courts, specifically in the United Kingdom context, has been understood. Debates about what has been called the 'mighty problem' of judicial review[1]—its very

---

[1] M. Cappelletti, *The Judicial Process in Comparative Perspective* (1989), ch. 4.

legitimacy—do not, after all, exist in isolation. They reflect much broader ideas about law, and about the nature of government. Often these broader ideas are implicit, but they are sometimes made explicit, when arguments about what courts should or should not do are presented. Equally, they may inform interpretations of the actual practice of courts in relating to government and administrative spheres.

This analytical approach is not, as such, prescriptive. It is a means of trying to clarify the intellectual foundations of debates in Britain around judicial review and the place of courts in government. It seeks to trace back judicial practices and discussion of them to fundamental ideas in order to gain a clearer view of what is at stake in the arguments. But such an approach may help to dispel illusions about what different approaches to judicial review of administrative acts might achieve. and it may help to explain the climate of thought that has coloured modern British forms of judicial review.

Where might these broad components of intellectual context be found? In the following discussion I try to identify some of them in the literature of legal philosophy; a storehouse of lawyers' speculation which is drawn on increasingly and explicitly in support of some contemporary prescriptive arguments in administrative law. However, ideas from this literature are treated as potentially useful, for the purposes of this chapter, not because of any direct influence legal philosophy may have on practical debates, but because it tends to reflect and express over time—at least in its most influential theories—some widely shared and important general views of lawyers about law and its social and political environment.[2]

JUSTIFYING JUDICIAL REVIEW

That there is a need to re-examine broad intellectual foundations of judicial review is hardly in doubt. Administrative law's definitions often present, according to one commentator, a 'bottomless pit of ambiguity and uncertainty'.[3] The relationship between courts and the authority of Parliament is 'the central unresolved problematic in traditional accounts of the constitution'.[4] Judicial review in the United Kingdom is more limited than in some other Western societies since it excludes review of legislation and parliamentary legislative processes. It encompasses only the review of administration; that is, subordinate rule-making and other governmental

---

[2] See generally R. Cotterrell, *The Politics of Jurisprudence* (1989), for an attempt to interpret main currents of modern Anglo-American legal philosophy in these terms.

[3] D. Oliver, 'Is the *Ultra Vires* Rule the Basis of Judicial Review?' [1987] *PL* 543, 545.

[4] I. Harden and N. Lewis, *The Noble Lie: The British Constitution and the Rule of Law* (1986), 190.

administrative action. Nevertheless in all its forms judicial review is an 'enigmatic institution. It operates principally in states with democratic philosophies, yet it claims to frustrate, in certain situations, the will of the majority.'[5] It purports to control acts of democratically elected decision-makers and rule-makers, or of their agents and delegates. 'How can one solve the theoretically insoluble contradiction that an "undemocratic" institution [an unelected judiciary] is used to safeguard us and our liberties against the abuse of power, and thus against undemocratic perversions?'[6]

Despite these dilemmas, judicial review of administrative (and, in some nations, legislative) acts has expanded greatly in many Western countries during the twentieth century so that it 'must reflect a deeply felt need of contemporary Western societies'.[7] While some see the development in Britain of a more active judicial review of administration as a modern revolution of profound significance in which courts have asserted the need for principle as a basis of governmental activity,[8] others consider that 'the impact of the law on the administrative process is marginal. The rhetoric is far removed from the reality'[9] and 'judicial review is apparently of little or no account in major matters'.[10] These diverse views suggest, if nothing else, that many different kinds of expectations exist in this field, with widely varying criteria of success or significance being applied.

What is required is a clear conception of the position of the judiciary (or that part of it concerned with administrative law) in relation to the machinery of state as a whole; a specification of the place of judges in the whole structure of government. Are judges agents of government in the sense of being no less a part of the state hierarchy of authority and powers than other governmental agencies and institutions, executive or legislative? If so, can judicial functions be clearly distinguished from executive and legislative functions? The claim that judicial and executive roles can hardly be clearly separated in practice is an old one in the modern literature on legal frameworks of administration in Britain.[11] But can the separation of powers have meaning as a theoretical if not as a practical matter? For many observers it is obvious that courts 'are arms of established government . . . vital cogs in the wheels of a well-oiled vehicle of stable government'.[12] 'The question is not "when, if at all, should judges step into the political arena?"

---

[5] Cappelletti, *Judicial Process*, 149.   [6] Ibid., p. xvii.   [7] Ibid. 154.

[8] See e.g. B. Schwartz, *Lions over the Throne: The Judicial Revolution in English Administrative Law* (1987).

[9] A. C. Hutchinson, *Dwelling on the Threshold: Critical Essays on Modern Legal Thought* (1988), 86.

[10] P. McAuslan, 'Administrative Justice: A Necessary Report?' [1988] *PL* 402, 409.

[11] See e.g. W. A. Robson, *Justice and Administrative Law: A Study of the British Constitution* (3rd edn. 1951), ch. 1.

[12] L. Blom-Cooper, 'Lawyers and Public Administrators: Separate and Unequal' [1984] *PL* 215, 235.

but what should they do there, for they are never not in the political arena.'[13]

A standard answer, if courts are seen as an integral part of government, is that judges should police the rule of law, the requirement that governmental decision-making be carried out within the framework of legal rules and stable procedures. Accordingly, a special governmental function for courts is founded on their ability to determine whether the decisions of other agencies of government have been made within the terms of those agencies' legal authority or whether necessary principles of natural justice have been complied with in decision-making. The acceptability of this special position of courts within the state structure seems to depend, however, on three somewhat insecure claims. The first is that, while courts are only one kind of governmental decision-making agency among others, they are *uniquely* capable of establishing what should count as fairness in decision-making for all other governmental agencies, despite the immense variety of the latter and the great range of contexts in which they operate and of types of decision-making with which they are charged. Secondly, although judges are servants of the state, the purposes and demands of the rule of law and the means of fulfilling them can be known and determined by courts in an inherently more *independent and reliable* manner than can be done by any other state institutions or agencies. Thirdly, courts as agencies of the state, staffed by unelected officials, can properly control the actions of other agencies of state, *including elected authorities*: this is neither undemocratic (since courts merely apply objective principles of which they alone have expert understanding) nor is it a sham (because the objective principles that courts apply always prevail over any contrary demands on courts loyally to support the actions of other governmental authorities).

A sense that these justificatory claims are not unassailable may explain why the 'obvious' idea that courts are arms of established government operating in a political arena is often viewed with great ambivalence. For many commentators (and judges) the idea is acceptable rhetorically but wholly to be rejected in its implications. 'Judges have nothing to do with either policy making or the carrying out of policy.'[14] The uneasy governmental role of the judiciary is often defended by being portrayed as extremely modest and strictly limited. Judicial review is held not to challenge (but to fulfil) parliamentary sovereignty, the prerogatives of democratic government, and the needs of policy-making and implementation. This is because it merely ensures that the law, which represents the democratic will expressed through parliamentary processes, is carried into

---

[13] Hutchinson, *Dwelling on the Threshold*, 91.
[14] *Laker Airways Ltd.* v. *Department of Trade* [1977] 2 WLR 235, 267 (per Lawton LJ).

effect according to its terms.[15] Judicial review is just a 'logical consequence of the fact that it is the very function of judges to interpret the law'.[16]

For many observers, however, judicial review of administration obviously entails much more than this 'modest underworker' image suggests. Whatever the basis of other judicial activity, the rules of natural justice applied in English courts are generally considered to have their source in common law developed independently by the courts. Thus, the 'objective' principles applied in judicial review are often traced to the character of courts not as agencies of the state, nor as servants of the parliamentary will, but as guardians and pronouncers of *values anchored in society and culture*, outside structures of government as such. Mauro Cappelletti writes of judicial review in its varied forms in Western societies (including review of both administrative and legislative acts) as a protection against 'the mutable whims of passing majorities', a means of protecting minorities in democracies and expressing enduring values, 'the permanent will, rather than the temporary whims, of the people'.[17] On this view judicial authority is 'deeply rooted in society's daily needs, grievances, aspirations and demands'.[18] In Britain in recent years it has been argued that judicial review of administrative action is founded on a need to control abuse of power and to protect individuals;[19] to balance public purposes against the interests of individual citizens;[20] or to promote individual rights.[21] The search underlying such claims is for values or commitments which courts can and do consistently serve, and which are not merely a reflection of the priorities, policies, or outlook of regimes in power. The specific source of these commitments is often treated as the common law tradition itself, as in the case of the rules of natural justice. More ambitiously, efforts have been made to claim a general grounding for judicial controls on government in a 'shared political morality' that is presupposed by and may even impose limits on parliamentary sovereignty.[22]

The appeal to independent judicially protected values as a basis for judicial review is especially interesting when it is used to try to solve the problem of the democratic legitimacy of judicial involvement in government. In contrast to the modest underworker approach which seeks to portray the activity of judicial review as so limited that it slips by unnoticed as part of the orderly machinery of government, the appeal to judicially protected values seems to follow the strategy that attack is the best form of

---

[15] See e.g. D. J. Galligan, *Discretionary Powers: A Legal Study of Official Discretion* (1986), 235.   [16] Cappelletti, *Judicial Process*, p. xv.
[17] Ibid. 131, 206, 210.   [18] Ibid. 44.
[19] Oliver, 'The *Ultra Vires* Rule', 543.
[20] See discussion and references cited in Hutchinson, *Dwelling on the Threshold*, 92.
[21] T. R. S. Allan, 'Pragmatism and Theory in Public Law' (1988) 104 *LQR* 422.
[22] T. R. S. Allan, 'The Limits of Parliamentary Sovereignty' [1985] *PL* 614, 621.

defence. Thus it is argued 'that democracy means more than simply majority rule, that it connotes a relationship between each individual and the majority, within which the individual is guaranteed certain protections, and that these in turn may constitute fetters upon majority rule. The argument is that the values inherent in this fuller sense of democracy might be tapped by the courts in exercising review.'[23] According to this view, courts do not merely avoid intruding on democratic processes. Nor do they meekly follow the will' of the democratically empowered regime. They positively help to secure values that make democracy a worthwhile system for all citizens, and not only for those whose interests are directly promoted by those in power.

An alternative claim is that democracy requires popular participation in and access to public decision-making and courts help to provide this. Potentially, they can do this in at least two distinct ways. First, they can enforce procedures in governmental decision-making that allow popular input into decision-makers' deliberations.[24] Secondly, they can supplement administrative processes with judicial hearings, which provide different kinds of opportunity for influence on administrative matters by citizens as litigants. Courts are relatively open to public view, accountable (through appeal systems), and in some sense participatory. They not only allow, but normally require opposing voices to be heard. Hence some writers have suggested that they actually embody democratic values or have the potential to do so.[25]

However, the fact remains that, in centralized judicial systems staffed by state-appointed judges, neither the decision-makers, nor the processes of decision-making in courts, are democratically controlled. Equally, it is not possible to argue that participation in or access to these courts is uniformly available to all citizens. Again, it cannot be said that courts actually promote participation in administrative processes in any consistent or comprehensive way.[26] If courts operated under different conditions from those that typically prevail and with different principles of organization their relation to democratic practice might be transformed. But the 'democratic' argument for judicial review seems to come down to one of

[23] Galligan, *Discretionary Powers*, 236.

[24] See e.g. Harden and Lewis, *Noble Lie*, 213–14, 303–5, and P. P. Craig, *Public Law and Democracy in the United Kingdom and the United States of America* (1990), 160–92, both arguing that this judicial role exists in embryonic form and should be extended greatly. The issue is taken further in Richardson's chapter below. In the very different context of justification of judicial review of legislation in the United States the argument that judicial review serves the value of promoting participation has exerted considerable influence. See especially J. H. Ely, *Democracy and Distrust: A Theory of Judicial Review* (1980).

[25] H. Collins, 'Democracy and Adjudication', in N. MacCormick and P. Birks (eds.), *The Legal Mind: Essays for Tony Honoré* (1986); and see Cappelletti, *Judicial Process*, 45.

[26] Craig, *Public Law and Democracy*, 160–2, and see Ch. 3 below.

aspiration. The claim is not that judicial practice enshrines democracy or promotes it but that courts have a potential to articulate democratic principles that are immanent in the organization of collective life and reflected imperfectly in other institutions of government. State institutions are thus to be understood in the light of fundamental democratic values of the community as a whole. Judges can express these values and impose them on governmental processes even if courts do not serve directly as conduits for democratic participation.

In very broad terms, two different kinds of outlook on courts can be identified in the wide range of views on judicial review that have been sketched above. One kind assumes courts to be an integral part of the state apparatus or merely servants of the state's own law, which provides a structure of legality for the entire governmental process. Courts thus have a special technical role inside government, overseeing, correcting, and facilitating the activity of other state agencies. They are, in this context, a specialist arm of government entrusted with monitoring and safeguarding the rule of law. The other kind of outlook tends to treat courts in relation to the administrative process as, in some sense, outsiders to this process, in so far as it is to be seen as directive and policy oriented. Courts, in this view, serve independent values of various kinds, which are in some sense rooted in culture or society and which serve as an essential matrix for evaluation of governmental practices.

COURTS AND GOVERNMENT: IMAGES FROM LEGAL PHILOSOPHY

These two contrasting orientations reflect a more general and very important dichotomy in broad currents of thought about law, government, and society. It is a dichotomy clearly expressed in the literature of Anglo-American legal philosophy and, in this context, legal philosophy can serve as a resource for bringing to light its nature and significance. Legal theories propose general conceptions of the nature of law or of legal ideas, legal interpretation, legal relationships, or legal reasoning. In theorizing about law, jurists convey images of law's place in society and of the way a legally ordered society is regulated and structured. Legal theories often express or imply ideas about the fundamental character of the society that law regulates, in so far as this character is assumed to define the possibilities, limits, justification, and orientation of regulatory tasks.

Anglo-American legal philosophy, at least in its dominant, most influential forms, suggests two sharply contrasting images of society. The first can be called an image of *community*; an image of a morally cohesive association of politically autonomous people. It suggests a horizontal relationship of natural, spontaneous, or freely chosen association between individuals and between social groups on the basis of values held in common. The second image can be called one of *imperium*; an image of individual subjects of a superior political authority. It suggests a vertical relationship of domination between a political authority (which may be conceived as concrete and personal or as highly abstract) and each subordinate person. In this latter image, subordinates do not necessarily hold any values in common but may share only their recognition (for whatever reasons) of a common superior authority.

These images can be traced through a great deal of the modern literature of legal theory.[27] The image of community, in the sense described above, is present in classical common law thought of the seventeenth and eighteenth centuries, with its ideal of a form of legal reason or wisdom distilled from the entire history or ancient origins of the community for which the common law judges are considered to speak.[28] In more modern times the image of community surfaces in Roscoe Pound's view of law enshrining the values of the time, expressing principles and balancing interests in a largely homogeneous polity;[29] in Lon Fuller's defence of case-law as a means of continuing the search for reason in time-honoured common law methods[30] and defining 'a body of common morality';[31] and especially in Ronald Dworkin's view of law as the practical interpretations, made by the members of a 'community of principle', of the entire structure of political values crystallized in historical practices and precepts which are their shared legacy and which they seek to continue.[32]

By contrast, the *imperium* image is conveyed most simply in John Austin's nineteenth-century legal philosophy, built on the foundation of Bentham's ideas and treating as central the sovereign–subject relationship. Austin's image of society is that of a mass of subjects rendering submission to an essentially centralized state, but one in which sovereign power is extensively delegated through subordinate agencies.[33] In H. L. A. Hart's modern legal philosophy the authority of the sovereign is replaced with that of secondary rules—ultimate legal rules accepted as controlling the manner in which other rules of law are created, modified, enforced, or

---

[27] R. Cotterrell, 'Law's Images of Community and Imperium', in S. S. Silbey and A. Sarat (eds.), *Studies in Law, Politics, and Society: A Research Annual*, 10 (1990); id., *Politics of Jurisprudence*, 225–8. See also R. Cotterrell, *Law's Community: Legal Theory in Sociological Perspective* (forthcoming 1994), ch. 11.

[28] G. J. Postema, *Bentham and the Common Law Tradition* (1986), ch. 1, 63–76.

[29] See e.g. R. Pound, *Social Control through Law* (1942).

[30] L. L. Fuller, 'Reason and Fiat in Case Law' (1946) 59 *Harvard LR* 376.

[31] L. L. Fuller, *The Law in Quest of Itself* (1940), 137.

[32] R. Dworkin, *Law's Empire* (1986).

[33] J. Austin, 'Centralization' (1847) 85 *Edinburgh Review* 221.

destroyed.[34] But, despite Hart's ridiculing of Austin's 'threadbare'[35] top-down conception of law as command, his own theory ultimately also suggests an image of *imperium*, though of a different character. The decisively rejected image of domination by a personal sovereign gives way to an image of domination by impersonal rules—the rule of law. Yet it is significant that the social processes by which law is created or changed are not, in themselves, portrayed as theoretically fundamental in this picture. All that is necessary is that these processes be rule governed. In Hart's portrayal of a legal system law is created, interpreted, and applied by officials; and law governs society. The image is not that of society (in the form of a morally cohesive community) controlling and determining law. Law is not seen theoretically as an expression of the values of a community, or a population which in some way is the collective author of its law. It consists of the rules that confer, limit, and organize authority in a polity. In this image of a working legal system the only contribution that ordinary citizens (as opposed to officials) must make to the existence of the system is obedience (for whatever reasons) to the primary rules of law, those aimed directly at social control.[36]

Both of these contrasting legal images of society in terms of community or *imperium* can embrace representative democracy though it appears differently in each. The community conception implies that democratic practice is an inadequate expression of values that unite society, which are assumed to be more intricate, profound, and enduring than the result of a popular vote.[37] The judicial wisdom of classical common law thought, for example, is clearly not the opinion of a democratic majority but the expression of timeless or evolving communal values. In this image of community there is often a sense that mere governmental authority—even if democratically structured or supervised—is not to be accepted without question. For Dworkin, individual rights are best understood as grounded in the complex of values that structure a political community. Hence they can be asserted against the will of democratic majorities; they are dependent on principle and not transient policies. Further, individual citizens no less than judges are entitled to interpret law, and act on their interpretations within the limits of their responsibility as citizens within the community.[38] Law is not to be monopolized by technical experts or the politically powerful, even when they possess democratic authority. Each

---

[34] H. L. A. Hart, *The Concept of Law* (1961), 91–6.
[35] H. L. A. Hart, *Essays in Jurisprudence and Philosophy* (1983), 59.
[36] Hart, *Concept of Law*, ch. 6.
[37] See e.g. R. Dworkin, 'Philosophy and the Critique of Law', in R. P. Wolff (ed.), *The Rule of Law* (1971), 152; Dworkin, *Law's Empire*, 211.
[38] R. Dworkin, *Taking Rights Seriously* (1977), ch. 8.

citizen is properly a legal interpreter by virtue of being a *member of the community* whose law is interpreted.

Again, in classical common law conceptions of judicial law-finding, it is accepted that even eminent judges may make legal rulings that can properly be ignored as lacking all legal force; judicial decisions—even if they possess all the political weight of a prestigious royal court—are not precedents if judges mistake or misstate the community's law.[39] The authority of judges resides in their capacity to find the meaning of law in its intangible historical and communal sources; not in their political power. And, for Roscoe Pound, the unconstrained popular will—'King Demos'[40]— untempered by wisdom and expertise, was always a matter for suspicion. Thus Pound sees the guiding values of legal development not as those that democratic legislators import into law but as the professionally developed values of common law—the 'jural postulates' of the time and place.

Most importantly, however, this image of community is ultimately not an image of a population that participates actively and directly in the development of law. For the classical common lawyers, law may have been the reason or wisdom of the community, past and present, but it was also, crucially, an 'artificial reason' accessible only to the lawyer because, as Coke noted, it required 'long study and experience, before that a man can attain to the cognisance of it'.[41] And while Dworkin asserts the citizen's entitlement to engage in contests of legal interpretation, even when the opposing players are judges of the supreme court of the land, he—like almost all jurists—devotes virtually his entire effort as a theorist to considering lawyers' and judges' professional interpretation of law and the contexts of this interpretation. Civil disobedience is the only means Dworkin suggests by which a individual citizen can act positively on his or her honest, but dissenting, interpretation of legal principle.[42] Thus, the

---

[39] Postema, *Bentham*, 9–11, 194–5.

[40] Cf. D. Wigdor, *Roscoe Pound: Philosopher of Law* (1974), 199, 227, 230.

[41] *Prohibitions del Roy* (1608) 12 Co. Rep. 63, 65.

[42] R. Dworkin, *A Matter of Principle* (1985), ch. 4; *Taking Rights Seriously*, ch. 8. Recently Dworkin has related the composition of a political community to its 'formal political acts'; that is, the acts of its government through its legislative, judicial, and executive institutions. The community is composed of those who 'play some role' in the decisions produced by these institutions 'and are most directly affected by them'. See R. Dworkin, 'Liberal Community' (1989) 77 *California LR* 479, 496. But this explains little about the nature or extent of a political community. What is 'some role' and who are 'most directly affected'? The formulation seems symptomatic of Dworkin's ambivalence about the character or significance of participation in such a community. How much influence over 'formal political acts' is necessary before it becomes meaningful to consider oneself a member of the community? Does this require the ability to sit in a legislature; or ownership of a giant corporation or a string of newspapers, or merely the legal entitlement to vote in elections; or a desperation great enough to produce rioting on the streets? What is the community membership status of those who, like many homeless people, are affected by government decisions—for example, on welfare provision—but have no political voice at all? Are 'playing some role' and being

image of community rarely shows citizens shaping law. More often, the rhetoric of community obscures the reality that when judges and politicians purport to determine law by appealing to the values of 'the community' they almost invariably invoke values they ascribe to such a community rather than any that its members are known actually to share.[43]

What of the image of *imperium*? Despite Austin's suspicion of and later hostility to democracy, he recognized that the sovereign could be the electorate of a democracy. But essentially democracy appears only at the periphery of the *imperium* conception. What is central in this imagery is a clear hierarchical structuring of government. For Austin, political institutions, including courts and local government, are defined in essence by their location within such a hierarchy. All derive their authority from above, by delegation from ultimate sovereign power. Hence courts, in this conception, are not representatives or voices of a community but servants of a sovereign power expressing itself through all the institutions of the state. It is not theoretically important for Austin's image of a legally structured society whether its law derives from representative democratic processes of law creation or not. Only at the highest levels of authority in the centralized state may the issue of democratic accountability—to an electorate that is part or the entirety of the sovereign power—arise. Otherwise the structures of regulation are to be understood as structures of command. Their legal authority is never considered to depend, even in part, on popular accountability or on congruence with communal values.

Hart's effort to sweep aside almost the entire Austinian legacy in legal philosophy has not made this kind of legal imagery of society and government redundant. The replacement of the concept of sovereignty with that of a government of rules effects less of a change than is sometimes supposed. Legal philosophy's focus is still on a hierarchy of powers, though now structured by rules rather than validated as the direct or indirect expression of a sovereign's will. The hierarchy is now conceived in abstract, impersonal terms: in Hart's terminology, secondary rules control the creation, validation, application, or alteration of primary rules of law. But the fundamental conceptual structure of authoritarian (even fascist) legal systems would not be significantly different, in terms of Hart's central theoretical preoccupations, from those of democratically based ones.[44]

'directly affected' alternative or interdependent marks of membership? Whatever the answers, it seems that specifications of practical political participation are not a high priority in defining the character of Dworkin's liberal community.

[43] Cf. R. D. Chesler, 'Imagery of Community, Ideology of Authority: The Moral Reasoning of Chief Justice Burger' (1983) 18 *Harvard Civil Rights-Civil Liberties LR* 457; L. Newton, 'The Rule of Law and the Appeal to Community Standards' (1976) 21 *American Journal of Jurisprudence* 95.

[44] Hart, *Essays in Jurisprudence and Philosophy*, 72–8; id., *Concept of Law*, 195–207.

Law for Hart, no less than for Austin, is positive law; posited on the basis of a hierarchy of authority. It is 'top-down' law, even if inspired by elected governments and legislators. It does not acquire its authority as the expression of the life conditions of a community.

JUDICIAL REVIEW AND *IMPERIUM*

What relevance do these legal images of society have for discussions of the place of judicial review in a British context? I have tried elsewhere to demonstrate through a study of aspects of the legal rhetoric of judges in English higher courts that the image of *imperium* is far more often implied in this rhetoric than is that of community; by contrast, in the modern opinions delivered by justices of the United States Supreme Court the opposite seems to be the case.[45] It is perhaps significant that most (though not all) 'of modern legal philosophy's images of community come from American sources, while the dominant forms of legal philosophy produced by British jurists (especially in the tradition extending from Bentham, through Austin to Hart) have conveyed the imagery of *imperium*. It is beyond the scope of this chapter to explore differences in legal culture that might be relevant here, or indeed to consider the relationship between judicial review and legal philosophy's images of society beyond a specifically British context. But debates on the nature and legitimacy of judicial review of administrative action in Britain seem indirectly (and occasionally directly, with explicit borrowing from the arguments of legal philosophers) to mirror the dichotomy between the images of *imperium* and community. Can those debates be clarified in any way in the light of legal philosophy's imagery and its theoretical elaborations?

The image of *imperium* makes it natural to think of courts as part of, and limited by, the hierarchy of political authority within the state. In an Austinian conception judges are delegates of the sovereign power. This is not, of course, to suggest that they are mere servants of a parliamentary legislature. Whatever the problems of identifying Austin's sovereign in the United Kingdom (he wrote of it as the monarch, the members of the House of Lords, and the electorate of the House of Commons),[46] Parliament as such is seen by Austin as one of the agencies or institutions expressing sovereign power, not as its locus as such. Hence courts, like legislators, are part of a hierarchical structure of government unified by a sovereign will.

Dicey, however, modified and simplified the Austinian idea of sovereignty, which he considered in any case to be merely a deduction from

---

[45] Cotterrell, 'Law's Images'.
[46] J. Austin, *The Province of Jurisprudence Determined* (1955 edn.), 230–1.

familiar English constitutional ideas.[47] He wrote of *parliamentary sovereignty* as indicating ultimate authority *within* the legal system. By contrast, Austin's concern had been with the sovereignty of monarch, Lords, and electorate of the Commons as a *foundation* for the legal system. The broader Austinian idea of a social foundation of sovereignty underpinning the entire constitutional framework (including courts and Parliament) appears to metamorphose into Dicey's particular conception of the rule of law—a kind of guarantee, expressed through the mechanisms of judge-made common law, that all participants in the polity (all those whom Austin would have included as part of the sovereign) would be treated as having a full claim to be taken fairly into account in the exercise of governmental power. Thus, through what can be seen as transformations of Austin's particular image of *imperium*, Dicey combined the idea of courts as an integral part of the structure of government, and indeed as handmaids to Parliament's will, with the idea that all institutions and agencies of state are to operate under the rule of law.

It remains, in this theoretical picture, by no means apparent why or in what way courts should monopolize supervision of the requirements of the rule of law in government. Indeed, not only is the concept of rule of law largely absent from Austin's legal philosophy,[48] but he ridicules the idea of the separation of powers as unrealistic and contrary to historical experience and contemporary practice.[49] Courts are portrayed in the Austinian tradition simply as elements within the complex hierarchies of government; one set of agencies among many others discharging the governmental tasks of direction and control in a complex society. This tradition of thought may partly explain why the special responsibilities of courts for maintaining the rule of law in government were initially treated by English judges as extensions of the historically established role of courts as agencies for resolving private disputes in accordance with law, or for interpreting law (the Austinian sovereign's commands) in specific contexts of private relationships. Such a judicial outlook would help to preserve the courts' prerogatives as specialist agencies for the processing of individual claims and the ordering of individual rights. At the same time it could help to keep at bay the encroachments of other agencies of the state on these preserves of individual claims and disputes.[50]

In so far as the Austin–Dicey tradition suggests that courts have a special role beyond this 'private law model'[51] in overseeing the actions of other agencies of government, this appears as the role of monitoring the

---

[47] A. V. Dicey, *An Introduction to the Study of the Law of the Constitution* (10th edn. 1959), 72–3.   [48] Cf. Cotterrell, *Politics of Jurisprudence*, ch. 3.
[49] Austin, *Province*, 235–7.   [50] Cf. Craig, *Public Law and Democracy*, 27.
[51] Cf. Galligan, *Discretionary Powers*, 222.

technical delegation of sovereign power. Thus, judicial review of administrative acts is treated as a matter of giving effect to Parliament's implied
intentions;[52] courts 'perform an indirect power-allocation function'[53] and
the doctrine of *ultra vires* is the primary means of defining the nature of
each level of delegated authority within the state structure. But it is clear
that within this tradition of legal thought there are no sources, external to
the state structure itself, of judicial authority from which enduring, stable
principles of judicial review can be derived. Judicial review can be *nothing
more than the application of the state's law (primarily legislated by
Parliament) to the state itself.* Although Austin clearly recognizes that
judges can and should themselves create law on the sovereign's behalf as its
delegates, there is nothing in the Austinian tradition to provide a
justification for imposing this judicially developed law on other agencies of
government.

Hart's legal philosophy does not produce any fundamentally different
outlook on the matter. Hart's image of *imperium* is one of structures of
rules, many of which give powers to officials (including judges) and
ordinary citizens. But in so far as judges act creatively—that is, they seek
principles or policies to inform their application or interpretation of rules—
they are considered by Hart to exercise governmental 'choice' or
discretion.[54] In other words, they behave in *this* respect in essentially the
same way as does any other responsible administrative decision-maker
within the state apparatus. Thus, in so far as judicial decisions are not
wholly bounded by the given (legislative) law of the state, or by established
judicial precedents, judges act essentially as governmental policy-makers
or administrative policy-interpreters. It would seem self-evident that,
acting in this capacity, they have no special *judicial* mandate or authority to
control the acts of other administrative officials. The role of judge is, in
such a situation, no different in essential character from that of other
decision-making officials within the state apparatus. Equally, it appears
that Hart's legal philosophy cannot suggest that the common law as a body
of principle provides any special authority for judicial review. This is
because common law itself must be understood, according to the logic of
his legal theory, as the crystalization of numerous specific instances of the
application of judicial discretion.

In so far as these images of *imperium* dominate the background of legal
thought within which debates on judicial review take place in Britain it
seems clear that they help to create an outlook in which (1) judicial review
that amounts to anything more than a process of purely literal statutory
interpretation is extremely suspect, if not illegitimate, and (2) no sources of

---

[52] Galligan, *Discretionary Powers*, 235.
[53] P. Cane, *An Introduction to Administrative Law* (2nd edn. 1992), 343.
[54] *Concept of Law*, 123–5.

principles available to judges in the exercise of judicial review are considered to exist outside legislation itself and the necessary practicalities of its implementation. If judges purport to invoke principle they act merely as governmental decision-makers, possessing no greater inherent authority than such decision-makers operating elsewhere within the state structure.

A BASIS FOR PRINCIPLED REVIEW?

It is clear, however, that in Britain today judicial review is not thought of in such negative and limited terms. In a host of ways judicially developed principles are imported into the practice of review. They include the idea of so-called *Wednesbury* 'unreasonableness',[55] the notions of fiduciary duty, 'irrelevant considerations', and 'improper purposes', and the various ideas expressed in the doctrines of natural justice. To a limited extent some of these principles can be interpreted, in conformity with the image of *imperium*, merely as necessary incidents of the effective delegation of governmental powers in accordance with the rule of law or the will of the Austinian sovereign. But their source is usually located either, vaguely, in common law or, more specifically, in values of fairness, reason, or accountability. And not only does judicial practice import such principles but many commentators advocate their further explicit development, supplementation, and rationalization in terms of still broader values such as fundamental rights of equality of treatment, themselves associated 'with those independent principles of justice that are appropriate for judicial application in all other areas of the common law'.[56]

In some of these extensions of the idea of judicial review beyond that suggested by legal philosophy's image of *imperium* there are clearly suggestions of a very general cultural source of principles available for judicial control of government. The still controversial principle of proportionality has been welcomed in some quarters with the comment that it is 'characteristically English'.[57] This form of advocacy hints at the sheer difficulty of finding a rigorous grounding for principle in a climate of legal thought dominated by the image of *imperium*. It also seems to appeal to some notion of shared culture or community as a source of governmental morality. Plainly *imperium* is not enough for many commentators on public law. 'Without principles, there is no basis for constitutional analysis to do more than map the location of power.'[58] Thus, extending beyond some

---

[55] *Associated Provincial Picture Houses Ltd.* v. *Wednesbury Corporation* [1948] 1 KB 223.

[56] J. Jowell and A. Lester, 'Beyond *Wednesbury*: Substantive Principles of Administrative Law' [1987] *PL* 368, 382. [57] Ibid. 375.

[58] I. Harden, 'The Constitution and its Discontents' (1991) 21 *British Journal of Political Science* 489, 500.

writers' cautious advocacy of more imaginative, varied, or rigorous principles of and approaches to judicial review, are broader constitutional arguments for interpreting the whole governmental and legislative structure of the state in terms of principles founded in a general political morality that unites the entire regulated society—the Dworkinian 'community of interpretation'.[59]

Some public law commentary in this country does, therefore, seem to reflect clearly legal philosophy's image of community. But the dominant practice of judicial review in the courts can be seen as very definitely consistent with the image of *imperium*. The appeal to common law in, for example, principles of natural justice does not evoke the image of an active community associated with classical common law thought. It draws on a common law inhibited, confined, and formalized by legal positivism, and subordinated by the doctrine of parliamentary supremacy. More generally, the invocation of values in judicial review appears typically what the image of *imperium* would suppose it to be—a cloak for the exercise of judicial discretion, the activity of judges as essentially political actors. In so far as judges make *substantive* judgments of one kind of another (for example, judgments of 'reasonableness') about the exercise of power by other agencies of the state (local authorities, government agencies, ministers, or departments), they appear, more often than not, to be putting forward their own discretions alongside or in competition with those of other governmental decision-makers. Where values are invoked these seem to lack clear definition, scope, and grounding, since the image of community is foreign to the dominant climate of legal thought.

The reflection of the *imperium* image in judicial review is apparent. Since the image of law is entirely a 'top-down' image, the democratic quality of regulation is, despite the hopes of some commentators,[60] ultimately unimportant to judicial review. The parliamentary process appears merely as the formal authoritative source of regulation of many different kinds poured into the funnel of the state administrative structure through which it runs by means of various delegation processes finally to affect the population of individual citizens. Consequently, it is unsurprising that, as Dicey noted, 'the courts will take no notice of the will of the electors. The judges know nothing about any will of the people except in so far as that will is expressed by an Act of Parliament.'[61] In so far as there is a consistent view of democracy among the senior judiciary it is apparently that of democratic élitism, which 'restricts public participation to a periodic take-it-or-leave-it choice between competing political elites, freeing the elected group to do much as it will between elections'.[62]

---

[59] See e.g. Allan, 'Limits of Parliamentary Sovereignty', and 'Pragmatism and Theory'.
[60] See sources cited in n. 24, above.   [61] *Law of the Constitution*, 74.
[62] D. Feldman, 'Public Law Values in the House of Lords' (1990) 106 *LQR* 246, 247.

The effects of this outlook are clear when questions of local democracy are in issue. While the democratic mandate of Parliament is considered virtually absolute and unquestionable, that of local authorities is usually accorded only very limited weight. The input of democracy to local government (which Austin, for example, saw as government delegated from the central authority of the state[63]) comes at too low a level in the governmental hierarchy to be seriously considered. The Greater London Council's 'Fares Fair' policy for reduced fares on public transport was the outcome of a major campaign commitment of the political party that won the Council elections. The policy was held by the House of Lords, on judicial review, to be unlawful.[64] In so deciding, the Law Lords evaluated the overall interests of the local population in relation to the statutory requirement that the Council operate an integrated, efficient, and economic service. Some of the judges plainly considered that in any such evaluation they were not bound to recognize the overriding force of a local democratic mandate but could and should substitute their own interpretation of appropriate balances of interests between members of the local population. In conformity with the image of *imperium* this interpretation is treated by the judges merely as objectively giving effect to Parliament's intention expressed in the words of the controlling statute. If this explanation fails to convince, however, the decision is bound to be seen, in a climate of thought dominated by the *imperium* conception, as a straightforward exercise of discretion; a decision by judges acting as unelected politicians imposing their decision in place of that of elected politicians.[65]

To avoid such a conclusion an appeal is made to principle by the Law Lords in the *GLC* case. The principle of a fiduciary duty to ratepayers, adopted in some earlier cases,[66] is invoked. In terms of the image of *imperium* this cannot be recognized as judicial principle, of course, but only as a variety of governmental policy. The image of community, however, provides an independent source of principle in community values. Hence, if the idea of fiduciary duty is to be a convincing non-political ground of decision, it needs to be justified as a partial expression

---

[63] Austin 'Centralization', 223.

[64] *Bromley London Borough Council* v. *Greater London Council* [1983] 1 AC 768.

[65] In some cases, invoking a democratic mandate may be a means of trying to avoid the 'mighty problem' (see n. 1 above) of the court substituting its discretion for that of an official of the elected government. In *Secretary of State for Education and Science* v. *Tameside Metropolitan Borough Council* [1977] AC 1014 an incompatibility between the local electorate's mandate and central government action in relation to the locality concerned was treated by the House of Lords as a partial justification for declaring the action invalid in judicial review.

[66] See e.g. *Roberts* v. *Hopwood* [1925] AC 578; *Prescott* v. *Birmingham Corporation* [1955] 1 Ch. 210.

of these values, 'the permanent will, rather than the temporary whims, of the people'.[67] It might be said that such values as fairness, accountability, and participation require an overall view of the benefits, burdens, opportunities, and involvements of all members of the local community (including, for example, ratepayers as well as those who voted for the party in power) arising from decisions of government made on their behalf. A majority decision is not necessarily legitimate if it ignores these wider considerations.

Some speeches of the Law Lords in the *GLC* case suggest an appeal to communitarian reasoning of this kind. But legal philosophy's fuller elaboration of the image of community and its implications show clearly the difficulties and weaknesses of this kind of thinking. As noted earlier, the image of community is not an image of an actively participating population, collectively constructing or negotiating values and infusing them into its law. Rather, community values tend to be products of the professional lawyer's 'artificial reason' of common law, or the legal philosopher's confident attribution of values to a population and its law. Sometimes these may link together. In this regard it is interesting to note Lord Scarman's comment that some judicially developed principles of fairness (which he appears to approve) in administrative law are 'not too far removed' from the principles enshrined in the philosopher John Rawls's theory of justice.[68]

In general, when courts invoke judgments of 'irrelevance', 'improperness', 'unreasonableness', and related criteria of administrative propriety it is apparent 'how relative to changing political and social views' such judgments can be.[69] But these changing social and political views are those of judicial decision-makers, legal experts, and other opinion-forming élites; not the feelings or wishes of an active, participating community which might work collectively to realize values expressing shared conditions of life and an equitable distribution of benefits and burdens, opportunities, and influence; that is, values that all can share with positive commitment. In a climate of thought dominated by the image of *imperium*, judges are not likely to engage in a search for values of these kinds. Nor are they likely, despite the urging of some commentators, to be able to give reliable content to any 'determination to call decision-makers to an adherence to standards of integrity and reason in which a distinction between substance and procedure is misleading and out-of-date'.[70] Instead, in such a climate,

---

[67] Cappelletti, *Judicial Process*, 131.

[68] Lord Scarman, 'The Development of Administrative Law: Obstacles and Opportunities' [1990] *PL* 490, 492–3; and see G. Maher, 'Natural Justice as Fairness', in MacCormick and Birks (eds.), *The Legal Mind*.   [69] Cf. Cane, *Introduction*, 156.

[70] Cf. J. G. M. Laws, 'The Ghost in the Machine: Principle in Public Law' [1989] *PL* 27, 31.

courts may upset administrative or governmental decisions in judicial review because judges genuinely believe that the decisions are not within the terms of the legal mandate given to the decision-maker. In this sense courts act to preserve the legitimacy of government. In extreme cases judges may, as governmental decision-makers, pit their own political judgments about the appropriateness of administrative decisions against the judgments of other officials or agencies of the state. In doubtful cases, however, they are likely to give the benefit of the doubt to central government and its agencies.

Because, even under conditions of parliamentary sovereignty, common law courts can still appeal to an independent source of their authority in the tradition of the common law, they do possess means of constructing stable principle as a subordinate expression of their authority in judicial review. In general, however, in so far as the climate of legal thought and practice is dominated by the image of *imperium*, principle will be used merely to aid the efficiency of government. Hence the principle of *audi alterem partem* is, from one viewpoint, a sensible device for ensuring adequate fact-finding and wise deliberation in administrative decision-making, and for easing the acceptability of decisions on the part of those affected by them. But as English administrative law shows, the fair hearing principle gives way in many situations where it is considered administratively inappropriate; for example where a hearing would be too expensive or more generally because of a recognition that different kinds of decision-making in widely varied contexts should be regulated by standards appropriate to the particular setting.[71] Again, imposition of the principle of natural justice requiring the exclusion of bias—that the decision-maker not be a judge in his or her own cause—can be seen, in terms of the image of *imperium*, not so much as a necessary protection for those subject to the decision but rather as a prerequisite for wise and efficient decision-making by officials acting in the interests of the administrative system in general, rather than their own. In requiring that administrators, no less than judges, act without bias, courts can be seen as treating administrators as fellow servants of good administration within the state.

There may, however, be some warrant for saying that where regulation within limited social groups, rather than the whole politically organized society, is in issue courts are prepared to exercise independent principles more forcefully, as if recognizing the group concerned as a specific community whose values are to be expressed and protected.[72] We have already noted that this kind of approach may explain aspects of the reasoning in local government cases such as the GLC 'Fares Fair' decision. It may also help to explain why rules of natural justice seem to be imposed

[71] Cane, *Introduction*, 163–7.   [72] Cf. Cotterrell, 'Law's Images', 15.

in a relatively uncompromising way in cases involving decisions of 'domestic tribunals' such as those of trade unions, private licensing bodies, or disciplinary bodies. The context is not necessarily that of an agency operating within the hierarchy of the state system. Judges may consider that through judicial review they are actively protecting the values that help local agencies of decision to provide integrity for professional, occupational, or local groups treated as cohesive communities uniting autonomous individuals. By contrast, where the review is of decisions in an essentially hierarchical relationship, as in employment cases, the tendency seems to be to loosen greatly fair hearing requirements, as though courts treat the context merely as one of 'private government' compatible with the image of *imperium*.[73]

COMMUNITY AND DEMOCRACY

Finally, it is necessary to make a more definite assessment of what an appeal to independent principle or cultural values in judicial review can achieve. Here, the important point is that legal philosophy's elaboration of the image of community—an image which seems recognizable behind much academic (and some judicial) urging for a different, more ambitious, and more principled approach to judicial review—suggests that expectations should not be raised too high. We have seen that the image of community is not an image of popular participation in determining legal regulation. We have noted that the appeal to community values, whether in courts, in the writings of legal philosophers, or in the consciousness of political leaders and opinion-makers, is likely to be an appeal to those values that the person making such an appeal ascribes to the community. Indeed, the very idea that the regulated population constitutes a community holding shared values may be merely a construction by the advocate of community values. The particular image of community that is elaborated in legal philosophy and reflected in much legal thought is not that of political society as a living community of people having the practical institutional means to establish and elaborate beliefs they can share and conditions of both interdependence among themselves and independence of each other. It is not an image of the structure of a community that enables all its members to express complex concerns in ways that must be heard—a vibrant community that makes its values and its law. It is rather an image of a population dependent on experts to speak for it—perhaps to tell it what its values really are (or ought to be).

It may well be that legal philosophy—as an expression of much more

---

[73] Cf. Cane, *Introduction*, 174–6.

diffuse currents of legal thought—has not created an image of an active, vibrant community because ultimately law and community in this sense are incompatible: 'Law seems to bespeak an absence of community, and law grows ever more prominent as the dissolution of community proceeds.'[74] Law is familiar as a structure of hierarchical authority and coercion. If so, perhaps we should not expect legal thought to present images of society that define its regulatory structures in terms of popular participation. Perhaps, indeed, the very idea of community or cultural values as some kind of existing shared foundation of government should be dismissed as myth-making. But be this as it may, legal thought's image of *imperium* is no more satisfactory than its image of community. We have seen that the image of *imperium* often presupposes democracy but in fact attaches little real significance to it. Democracy tends to be seen as no more than the theoretical justification of certain technical means of producing most of the regulation fed into the governmental process at the top of the hierarchy of legal authority. In legal philosophy's image of *imperium* it is this hierarchy of authority that is fundamental. If law's image of community offers no real communal underpinning of principle to guide regulation, the image of *imperium* presents *no possibility of principle at all*; all that it shows as existing is governmental policy, and law as a means of efficiently implementing this.

We can conclude that debates on the justifications and foundations of judicial review have been unsatisfactory because ultimately, in reflecting the broader dichotomy between law's images of community and *imperium*, they have also reflected the limitations of vision and scope that seem to be built into these images. Progress might be made by recognizing clearly these limitations in the ideological bases of legal thought and debate and by trying consciously to transcend them with a different kind of discourse. The argument of this chapter is not that judicial review is unimportant practically or symbolically. Neither is it denied here that debate about judicial review may resolve important problems about its scope and operation. But a prerequisite for greater clarity in these debates is that the nature and implications of the two legal images of society often presupposed in them be recognized.

Above all, it is necessary to recognize that neither the imagery of community nor that of *imperium* in legal thought provides the means of envisaging an adequate democracy. Dicey sought to reconcile his recognition of the absence of judicially supervised legal controls on parliamentary democracy with his claims that lawmaking through Parliament was responsive to, and represented, the interests and will of the entire electorate. He was able to convince himself that this reconciliation had

---

[74] D. J. Black, 'The Social Organization of Arrest' (1971) 23 *Stanford LR* 1087, 1108.

been achieved because he assumed, in the context of his times, that representative democracy worked to express the popular will in some direct and fair manner.[75] Legal thought has, on the whole, made a generally similar assumption throughout the period since Dicey wrote. But now, if we assert a pressing need for responsive lawmaking, which represents in some way the interests and complex network of values and aspirations of the entire polity, we are increasingly doubtful that this can be achieved under present conditions.

The problem is not merely one of electoral arrangements. It is also and more fundamentally that of the essentially hierarchical, non-participatory, 'top-down' conception of government and administration that is reflected in legal thought in the dominant image of *imperium*. A more fully democratic polity would be one in which the aspirations, interests, values, and beliefs of all citizens could be asserted fully, in all their richness and variety, in many different kinds of processes of deliberation and decision producing the regulation under which these citizens must live. In such a democracy the dichotomy between community and *imperium*—between reason, values, and negotiated consensus, on the one hand, and authority, power, and hierarchical control, on the other—might even disappear. We are far from achieving any such state. Consequently, the search for judicial principle in the legal control of government is an appropriate part of a second-best effort to improve an insufficiently responsive and accountable political system. But ultimately it is not a substitute for a radical rethinking of what democracy means in Britain today and for a serious effort to envisage in new ways the building of structures of community within our inherited institutions of *imperium*.

---

[75] Dicey, *Law of the Constitution*, 73: 'the arrangements of the constitution are now such as to ensure that the will of the electors shall by regular and constitutional means always in the end assert itself as the predominant influence in the country.' See generally Craig, *Public Law and Democracy*, ch. 2.

2

Governments, Constitutions, and Judges

The Hon. Mr Justice Stephen Sedley

The phrase 'an unwritten constitution' is something of a confidence trick. In the context of the United Kingdom it suggests that we manage without the need of a real constitution: we know how to govern ourselves and do not have to write it down; common sense and tradition tell us what to do; written constitutions are for nations which have to work out how they should be governed. But unpacking these subjectivities reveals rather more. If there are no prior written rules, someone has to ascertain what the unwritten rules are. Since the organic nature of an unwritten constitution makes it typically descriptive rather than prescriptive, rules will be ascertained only as occasion demands. This being so, the demands of the occasion are likely to have an influence at least as powerful as that of received principle in determining what the rule is to be. And the perception of exactly what the occasion demands may well vary with the limb of the state which is taking—or thinks it is taking—the decision. All of this is comfortably lumped together as the pragmatism of the British, and so it is; but it is a mistake to imagine that pragmatism cannot be an efficient vehicle for legal and political theory.

For example, ministers have historically relied on their civil servants to do most of their work and much of their thinking for them. By the 1940s this was well established, but no statute or doctrine of common law had ever sanctioned it, and executive and prerogative powers were always (as they still are) vested by law in ministers alone. Intra-departmental delegation, theoretically underpinned by ministerial responsibility, was an accepted convention, but when in 1943 its lawfulness was challenged[1] the Court of Appeal found itself compelled to elevate departmental practice into a doctrine of law. Since the whole immunity of the state from tort actions rested on the theory that civil servants were servants not of their minister but of the Crown, so that the minister was legally no more than first among equals, an entirely heterodox concept of the civil servant as the minister's *alter ego* was enunciated. It violated all the common law rules against unauthorized delegation, but it perfectly adequately described

---

[1] *Carltona Ltd.* v. *Commissioners of Works* [1943] 2 All ER 560.

what went on and could not conveniently be stopped, and it has done service ever since as a principle of constitutional law.[2]

The separation of powers, to which no serious overt challenge of principle is offered today, in Britain vests primary lawmaking powers in not one but two places, Parliament and the courts. This in itself is a major artefact of the organic constitution: instead of a legal system confined to the interpretation and application of legislation, and able at best to create judge-made islands in a sea of prescriptive statute law, Britain enjoys a legal culture in which statutes form parliamentary islands in a sea of common law. While the proliferation of primary and delegated legislation has turned some of the statutory islands into land masses, the constitution remains essentially part of the ocean of common law. The privileges of Parliament, of which the courts take judicial notice, are Parliament's own common law; but the courts' deference to it is marginal in comparison with Parliament's deference to the courts. Both in the construction of legislation and in the establishment of the ambit of the common law the constitutional shots can be, and in the post-war era have been, called almost unimpeded by an alert and active judiciary. In the first area, legislative construction, Parliament is accustomed to accepting from the judges that it meant things which may never have crossed its collective mind and were certainly not meant by the departmental authors and parliamentary draftsmen.[3] In the second area, the common law, I want to suggest in what follows that the judges have in the last thirty years changed the face of the United Kingdom's constitution. Both areas exemplify something which coexists with and underpins British legal pragmatism—legitimism, the belief that what the courts hold to be the law is right in a sense that calls for no further debate. I do not suggest that for this reason the relationship of government to the courts is antithetical. Governments need courts to confer legitimacy on their legislative progeny; but legitimacy is a gift which the courts can bestow on other children, their own included.

A written constitution is, or at least tries to be, prescriptive and even proactive. It may well have an educative role in setting civic and legal standards. It may also, and more importantly, have a validating role in giving credence and legitimacy to social movements which set out to require delivery of promised rights: the US civil rights movement of the 1950s and 1960s is a prime example of this kind of popular constitutionalism. But a written constitution is not self-implementing. For those who want to challenge the constitutionality of what the authorities are doing, courts and

---

[2] See *R.* v. *Secretary of State for the Home Department ex p. Oladehinde* [1991] 1 AC 254.

[3] It remains to be seen to what extent the decision of the House of Lords in *Pepper* v. *Hart* [1993] AC 593 changes this picture. It is an oddity that the best evidence of legislative intent, the Notes of Clauses which are the departmental brief to the draftsman, become generally available only under the thirty-year rule. Usually, but not always, ministers' explanations in the House will be derived from them.

judges are needed, and it is their word which is the last word on what such a constitution means.[4] For this reason it is also the last word on what rights the constitution is actually going to deliver and—most important of all—to whom. The process thus all but converges with the reactive and organic process of lawgiving under an unwritten constitution, for in both situations hegemony passes to the courts.

A state which puts in writing a series of legal standards by which government itself is to be governed, and which hands them to judges to interpret and enforce, may find that it has changed nothing or that it has provoked a constitutional revolution. If it turns out to be the latter, it cannot decently complain. The US Constitution and Bill of Rights did not overtly hand ultimate power to the judiciary. It was the Supreme Court itself which, early in the life of the Constitution, pronounced itself all-powerful;[5] and it says much for the esteem in which the law is held that neither people nor president nor Congress has seriously tried since then to take the courts' power away. In Canada, where in 1982 the Trudeau government patriated the constitution and enacted a Charter of Rights and Freedoms which expressly abdicated power to the Supreme Court,[6] the same thing is now happening at high speed: the sovereignty of parliament has yielded to the sovereignty of the judiciary, and what were once politics have become a battleground and gold-mine for lawyers. The Canadian Supreme Court has already declared itself to be above the prescriptive law of the Charter; it has upheld a court injunction which interfered with the Charter right of free expression on the ground that the Charter restrains only acts of 'the legislative, executive and administrative branches of government', and that the judicial system is not part of government for Charter purposes and so not bound by its prescriptions.[7]

This is not, however, the inevitable order of things. Canada had actually had a written constitution since 1867 and a Bill of Rights since 1960, both of which the judiciary had declined to use for anything more exciting than maintaining an equilibrium of power between Ottawa and the provinces. Long spells of US history witnessed similar abstentionism on the part of the Supreme Court, punctuated by political *laissez-faire* decisions that obstructed social legislation. Nixon's and Reagan's appointments to the Supreme Court were explicitly made in an effort to reverse a later phase of judicial activism and in pursuit of an abstentionist bench which would defer to presidential and congressional power. Yet in recent decades something has stirred in the judicial bowels on both sides of the Atlantic. In the USA, judges appointed to keep their hands off have embarked on hands-on

---

[4] As Chief Justice Hughes of the US Supreme Court said in the 1930s: 'The constitution is whatever the judges say it is.'   [5] *Marbury* v. *Madison* 1 Cranch. 137 (1803).

[6] Constitution Act 1982 (Can.), s. 32, subject to express legislative override (s. 33).

[7] *Dolphin Delivery* v. *Retail & c. Union* [1986] 2 SCR 573; (1986) 33 DLR (4th) 174.

decision-making, and not always of a consistently illiberal kind. In Canada, the sceptical expectation that the Charter would gather dust with its predecessors has been blown away by an explosion of judicial activism. And in the UK, by a process which I suggest is not dissimilar, the judiciary over a rather longer period has secured a commanding position from which it can now direct withering fire on executive and local government, using ordnance designed not by Parliament but by the judges themselves.

What has mattered in each of these cases has not been whether the judges had in their hands a written constitution but whether they had the will to intervene. Absent the will, there has been little or no intervention, written constitution or not. Given the will, as has happened in our generation on both sides of the Atlantic, the judiciary has picked up the ball and run with it regardless of whether or not written rules gave it the right to do so. It no doubt tells us something about Britain and its pragmatism that this is how both rugby football and modern judicial review originated.

The outcome, at least for the present, is that our unwritten constitution has in the course of a generation enhanced and consolidated the status of the judiciary within the separation of powers. It has not happened spontaneously. Although Parliament and the executive do not seem to have woken up to what was going on until it was all but accomplished, from the early 1950s a handful of policy-conscious senior judges were staking out their claims in territory hitherto occupied without serious contest for generations by government.

It is typical of the ahistoricism of lawyers that they treat as a landmark the *Wednesbury* case,[8] decided in 1948, in which the Master of the Rolls in an off-the-cuff judgment rehearsed a number of doctrines which had been perfectly familiar to the Victorian judges who devised and developed them, and proceeded to refuse relief in a case which today might well be regarded as disclosing an abuse of power by a cinema licensing authority. But while *Wednesbury* invented nothing and clarified little, it was the *Northumberland* case[9] four years later which opened the judicial counter-offensive on the new corporate state. A hospital board secretary, denied proper compensation on the absorption of his job into the new NHS, was met with the state's claim that there was nothing the court could do about the state's abuse of power. Denning and Goddard L JJ deployed against the executive the battery of review mechanisms developed in earlier periods to control the lower courts upon which central government had formerly depended for its local administration. Now it was the local and central state's turn. Planning lawyers, the only ones whose clients had

---

[8] *Associated Provincial Picture Houses* v. *Wednesbury Corporation* [1948] 1 KB 223.
[9] *R.* v. *Northumberland Compensation Appeal Tribunal* [1951] 1 KB 711 (DC); [1952] 1 KB 338 (CA).

money to stake on doubtful outcomes, were the earliest to exploit the new mood which the *Northumberland* case had signalled.[10] Then in 1963 the law lords, presided over by Lord Reid, stopped the Brighton Watch Committee, which was in no accepted sense a judicial body, sacking the Chief Constable without a proper hearing. To do it, they pulled down the old fence separating judicial from administrative acts of government, exposing both to the cold winds of judicial review. Three years later a divisional court containing Diplock LJ held that the Criminal Injuries Compensation Scheme, which had been carefully set up by government under prerogative and not statutory powers, was within the grasp of the courts. Diplock percipiently described the prerogative as the last disputed prize of the seventeenth century's constitutional conflict; by spotting and claiming it the judges appropriated it almost two decades before their victory was openly announced in the *GCHQ* case.[11] Two years later, in the *Anisminic* case,[12] the Lords opened up to judicial review effectively every error of law, far beyond strict jurisdictional error, committed by governmental bodies.

In the course of this brief account I have named the three judges who, I believe, planned and executed the constitutional raid on the fiefdoms of ministers and public authorities: Lords Reid, Denning, and Diplock.[13] To these names it is necessary to add that of Lord Scarman, whose expositions of the judges' modern constitutional principles have been consistently elegant in language, panoramic in scope, and scholarly in conception: he has been, perhaps, the ideologue of the movement. It was Lord Diplock, however, who in 1982, when the new boundaries were well settled and executive and local government becoming accustomed to kissing the judicial rod, took the opportunity of a judgment on *locus standi* to boast quietly of what had been accomplished:

The rules as to standing for the purpose of applying for prerogative orders, like most of English public law, are not to be found in any statute. They were made by judges, by judges they can be changed; and so they have been over the years to meet the need to preserve the integrity of the rule of law despite changes in the social structure, methods of government and the extent to which the activities of private citizens are controlled by governmental authorities, that have been taking place, sometimes slowly, sometimes swiftly, since the rules were originally propounded. Those changes have been particularly rapid since World War II.[14]

---

[10] e.g. *Pyx Granite* [1960] AC 260.

[11] *R. v. Criminal Injuries Compensation Board ex p. Lain* [1967] 2 QB 864; *Council of Civil Service Unions v. Minister for the Civil Service* [1985] AC 374.

[12] *Anisminic Ltd. v. Foreign Compensation Commission* [1969] 2 AC 147.

[13] Their respective roles are considered in John Griffith, *Judicial Politics since 1920* (Oxford, 1993).

[14] *R. v. Commissioners of Inland Revenue ex p. National Federation of Self-Employed and Small Businesses* [1982] AC 617, 639–40.

Lord Diplock, who never uttered a syllable without some carefully thought-out purpose, was by 1982 a dominant judge in the House of Lords, and the passage repays close reading. He starts from the lawyer's credo that the rule of law is a pole star of unchanging values in an inconstant political firmament. To this constancy he counterposes never-ending social and political changes, noting that they have occurred at varying speeds over the years but at high speed since 1945, a point to which I shall return in a moment. And he singles out among these changes the extent of government control of private citizens' activities. The rules made and adapted by the judges for citizens' access to remedies against the state he then characterizes as a bridgehead from the unstable world of civil society and politics to the safe haven of law. And he makes it clear that the rules will be changed in the future if social and political change threatens the rule of law.

This is a revealing account, though not necessarily a comprehensive evaluation, of the modern development of public law in Britain. The end of the Second World War, accurately identified by Diplock as a turning-point, saw the capture of the commanding heights of government by a political interest which was regarded by its opponents as inimical to the freedom of private citizens to order their own affairs. As the Northcote–Trevelyan Report had correctly anticipated almost a century earlier, electoral reform had placed the command of executive government within the reach of radicals. Long before the first, nervous Labour government had taken office a career civil service was in place, owing no further debt to political patronage and bearing values and standards which, in its own mind, stood above party and class.[15] But it was constitutionally impossible to cut the executive free of ministerial hegemony, and after 1945 departments of state were required by ministers to carry through measures restricting the activities of private citizens in favour of social welfare and economic control. Many of these ministers had, however, held office in the wartime coalition and there was no precipitate judicial reaction, much less sabotage, directed against their measures.[16] In administrative law, the courts at first barely stirred from the sleep of two generations which had descended on the Victorian judicial activists as the Northcote–Trevelyan civil service settled into running the country and the empire with professionalism and aplomb.

It is therefore much less easy to see the judicial process as one of reaction to a particular government's policies than as a response to the growth of a corporate state in which the executive, far from exercising restraint, was itself heavily interested. In this sense the post-war growth of

[15] See Peter Hennessy, *Whitehall* (London, 1989).
[16] See e.g. Leslie Zines, *Constitutional Change in the Commonwealth* (Cambridge, 1991), 36–7.

judicial review has mimicked its earlier, mid-Victorian development in response to the first great wave of regulatory governmental institutions.[17] That first historic response of legal doctrine had provided the judges with a purchase on the executive, and they started in the 1950s to use it in the ways I have attempted to sketch. The barely fictional Sir Humphrey Appleby, servant and scourge of ministers, began to find his power trumped by a more potent constitutional actor, the judiciary. By 1983 the judges' confidence in their new system of public law had reached the point at which the law lords felt able to reject the use of any alternative form of litigation to secure redress against the state: judicial review was to be the only way.[18]

If this picture is even broadly right, it represents nothing less than a refashioning of the UK's constitution. By the time the Thatcher government took power in 1979 the job was done and ministers began to feature in growing numbers on the casualty list as the judges contined to deploy against an unconventionally innovative central government the doctrines of abuse of power which were now firmly in place. The reasons for the judges' success can be debated, but I believe they include at least these. First, legal reasoning and the judicial sense of what is fair and unfair have a significant measure of autonomy. They can and do swim up the political rapids on occasion, most of all when something a government department has done offends a judge's sense of fair dealing. Secondly, even when the court is looking for an expedient outcome, its view of what is expedient is often less myopic than that of government. For example, a court will often do something in the interests of consistency, and hence of the law's own long-term credibility, which is inimical to the short-term aims of government. Both limbs of the state may be acting on policy grounds, but their sectional interests can pull in opposite directions. Thirdly, there is considerable public support for judicial control of an otherwise unaccountable executive, or of unresponsive local authorities. Administrations of all colours may have themselves to blame for a popular consciousness which, at least occasionally, casts them in the role of dragons and the judiciary in the role of St George.

There remains considerable leeway for arbitrary government in the sublegal regions of constitutional convention. This is at present a no man's land, regulated neither by parliamentary privilege nor by the common law, but capable both of invading the democratic process and of infringing legal norms of good government. It may yet become an area in which public law has to take an interest.

---

[17] See H. W. Arthurs, *Without the Law: Administrative Justice and Legal Pluralism in Nineteenth-Century England* (Toronto, 1985).
[18] *O'Reilly* v. *Mackman* [1983] 2 AC 237.

Meanwhile public law continues to be a source of anxiety to administrations of all political sorts in town hall, county hall, and Whitehall. This is a long way, however, from saying that judicial review has necessarily had an improving effect on them. A dawning awareness that public interest immunity does not apply to every file in a department has led in some places to the true reasons for decisions not being recorded; and forms of defensive public administration have developed, in which fireproofing decisions against judicial review take priority over conscientious decision-making. This is something for which lawyers are rightly blamed; but the blame is shared equally with administrators who react negatively to what are in principle positive demands for fair and open dealing. As always, it is the more vulnerable sections of the public on whom the fall-out of this conflict lands. But there is an encouraging up-side too: well-led administrations take more careful decisions than before, paying regard to legal principles and reviewing their own decisions when a legal challenge is made.

One of the benefits of a satellite picture of these shifts in Britain's organic constitution, to which legal practitioners are often too close to see the pattern, is that it emphasizes something which is true equally of systems with written constitutions: that a constitution is a process rather than a set of arrangements, and that its history and development are principally determined by the skills and motivation of the major players, whom the theoretical separation of powers is powerless to keep apart. Reducing the intended arrangements to writing is more often than not a symbolic act dictated by a moment of history and a widely shared sense of change. The subsequent reality of constitutional government is in no true sense determined by the written instrument: what the instrument becomes and achieves will itself be determined by the social and political events of which it and the courts' jurisprudence will form a part.

Once it is understood that a constitution is not only a process but a heterogeneous and conflict-ridden process, it becomes necessary for a society to argue out what it wants the reality of its constitution to be. To allow lawyers and judges to dictate it, whether it happens by degrees as in Britain or by an open handover of constitutional power as in Canada, has major implications for political democracy. But there is no simple alternative, and some of the easy options can be readily seen to be snares and delusions. Parliament has no way and no hope of supervising, through ministerial accountability, the myriad activities which in increasing volume it delegates to the executive. The judges at least listen to reasoned argument in public and attempt to decide issues according to known and accepted principles.

There has so far been a single point at which Whitehall has intervened in the process of modern judicial review: section 31 of the 1981 Supreme

Court Act introduced a provision which tended to prioritize administrative convenience over justice where the two came into conflict. It would be unwise to forget that a written constitution which redefines the boundaries and balance of power between the limbs of the state will offer an opportunity to executive government if not to reverse forty years of judicial invigilation then to put a brake on further developments in judicial review.

Are we therefore looking in constitutional terms at a choice of dead ends—an unresponsive legislature, an impenetrable executive, or an autocratic judiciary? The period of constitutional history we are living through, for the most part so intimately that it is hard to recognize it as more than another day's news, is full of indicators of the complexity, but not necessarily the insolubility, of our constitutional problems. My focus on the judicial role, dictated possibly by what happens to be my job, attempts to pick out the largely unacknowledged role of the limb of the state which I contend has been the major actor in our recent constitutional history. Again perhaps for venal reasons, I am inclined to argue that this role has so far been beneficial. But judicial sovereignty is a dangerous blueprint for the future. In considering what might one day go in place of this organic growth I have no prescription to put forward—only considerations of the complexity of what too many proponents of constitutional reform regard as a straightforward business. A written constitution which hands to the British judiciary what the US Supreme Court (and recently the Australian High Court[19]) has had to take for itself, the power of life and death over primary legislation as well as over acts of executive government, is making assumptions about the disinterestedness of judicial values which Australian, Canadian, and American experience shows to be false. A judiciary which can be as powerful a constitutional actor as ours can also become the master, not the servant, of a written constitution.

There seems little doubt that Western and other democracies[20] are in a period in which autonomous judiciaries are both willing and able to fill some of the deficits in political democracy. This may be inevitable; it may well be beneficial; but it is a constitutional development which needs to be understood and evaluated. Instead, a combination of popular legitimism and common law interventionism is offering us the open-ended syllogism that because the law is by definition what the judges say it is, so is the constitution.

---

[19] *Nationwide News Pty. Ltd.* v. *Wills* (1992) 66 ALJR 658; *Australian Capital Television Pty. Ltd.* v. *The Commonwealth* (1992) 66 ALJR 695.　　　　　　[20] Notably India.

3

Reviewing Judicial Review

Ross Cranston

The tone of this chapter is a rather unfashionable one. The modern orthodoxy in the courts and the commentaries takes an expansive view of judicial review: judicial review is necessary to keep government in check and as an avenue for the redress of grievances against it in an era when executive government is strong, Parliament weak, and the Opposition unsuccessful at national level. This chapter does not address these premisses but it does interrogate the orthodoxy built upon them. Let me nail my colours to the mast at launch by briefly outlining the argument.

The chapter begins by examining the scope of judicial review, questioning whether there is a principled basis for its current boundaries and for some widely canvassed proposals for their extension. It then turns to the grounds and procedures for judicial review. It is commonly remarked, and no doubt true, that the grounds of judicial review go beyond mere statutory interpretation and constitute a mode of intervention based on judge-made law. That being the case the chapter contends that the courts should tread more warily than they sometimes have in applying and extending the grounds of judicial review. On the procedural side, the chapter accepts that the procedure for judicial review should not be the tail wagging the substantive law dog, but expresses doubts as to the reasons usually given for expanding traditional tests of standing.

The chapter then moves beyond the law to look at issues of institutional competence and impact. It argues that administrators can develop an expertise in, and a detailed overview of, an area which the courts may never acquire. While some courts are willing to defer to this greater expertise of administrators, often there seems to be a failure to acknowledge the delicate balance between the need to protect individual interests on the one hand, and the need for effective administration on the other. The chapter then turns to the impact of judicial review, which has scarcely received attention. Yet in many areas of administration courts act as nothing more than a very exceptional avenue for review of decision-making. Even in areas which have been comparatively well litigated, judicial review remains sporadic in impact and administrators retain considerable scope to disregard the import of judicial decisions. Since judicial review is insufficiently systematic and continuous to provide effective control over administration, other mechanisms need to be introduced. The chapter concludes by outlining some principles which put a gloss on the modern orthodoxy and, it is suggested, render it more acceptable in modern democratic society.

BOUNDARIES OF JUDICIAL REVIEW

Judicial review puts governmental power centre-stage. Virtually no consideration has been given to why the exercise of other power in society should not be subject to review given that its effects for individuals may well be comparable in result. Lord Woolf has been one of the few to recognize this and has observed:

The interests of the public are as capable of being adversely affected by the decisions of large corporations and large associations, be they of employers or employees, and should they not be subject to challenge on *Wednesbury* grounds if that decision relates to activities which can damage the public interest? Members of large companies [have] the power to make decisions which at times not only affect the company . . . but the national interest. Should it not be possible for the court to intervene if the decision has been reached without a relevant consideration being taken into account or if the decision has been taken on the basis of some irrelevant consideration in the same way as it does in the case of a public body? Powerful bodies, whether they are public bodies or not, because of their economic muscle may be in a position to take decisions which at the present time are not subject to scrutiny and which could be unfair or adversely affect the public interest.[1]

At present privatization is one factor putting the existing boundaries of judicial review under strain—are institutions reviewable one day to be immune the next because they have been privatized? And if not why should companies which have always been private be at a competitive advantage over privatized companies by not being subject to judicial review? For the purposes of the argument, however, we need not stray far from well-trodden ground—the scope of present day judicial review.

Scope of judicial review

Although governmental powers are the focus of judicial review, in some instances they are not reviewable. In other instances non-governmental bodies exercising powers which are governmental in nature are reviewable. The conceptual foundations on which these non-reviewable governmental powers, and reviewable non-governmental powers, are based are muddy indeed. Policy—perfectly justifiable policy in the main—explains how the law has developed but in the process principle has been given short shrift.

---

[1] Sir H. Woolf, 'Public Law—Private Law: Why the Divide?' [1986] *PL* 220, 238.

The main non-reviewable governmental powers fall into three categories—government acting as employer, government acting as contractor, and government acting as maker of commercial or property decisions. Review is by no means totally excluded from these areas, although the boundaries between reviewable decisions and non-reviewable decisions seem to be as malleable as play dough.

The first area is fairly clear: in relation to personnel claims by an employee against government as employer, it has been held that it is generally unnecessary and normally inappropriate to seek judicial review. The employee proceeds in the normal way to make a claim. Yet judicial review *may* be triggered—for example by the existence of a disciplinary tribunal for government employees, or where as a matter of policy government has taken action affecting its employees generally, as in the *GCHQ* case, where membership of trade unions was banned on national security grounds.[2] As a matter of policy the floodgates argument seems to be an entirely plausible basis for limiting judicial review for public employees; possibly also there is the reason that public employees should be no better off than private employees. Whatever the dividing line between review and non-review in this area, we have an instance of where the criteria, as two experts describe them, are 'haphazard, unpredictable and produce illogical results'.[3]

Government as contractor has generally escaped judicial review primarily, it has been said, because contract is a purely private law matter.[4] This is not very enlightening. An emerging requirement seems to be that there should be some public law element to a contractual decision— whatever this means—before review can be justified.[5] Yet sometimes contracting decisions are reviewed; the judicial motivations for this in several of the leading cases are close to the surface.[6] From the point of view of policy we should expect the increasing use of contracting out of government services to push out the boundaries of review in the coming years.

The third area of non-reviewable governmental decisions involves commercial and property matters. The cases are few. *R. v. National Coal*

---

[2] *Council of Civil Service Unions v. Minister for the Civil Service* [1985] AC 374. See *McClaren v. Home Office* [1990] ICR 824, 836–7.

[3] S. Fredman and G. Morris, 'Public or Private? State Employees and Judicial Review' (1991) 107 *LQR* 298, 315.

[4] *R. v. East Berkshire Health Authority ex p. Walsh* [1985] QB 152; *R. v. The Lord Chancellor ex p. Hibbit and Saunders*, The Times, 12 Mar. 1993.

[5] See S. Arrowsmith, 'Judicial Review and the Contractual Powers of Public Authorities' (1990) 106 *LQR* 277.

[6] e.g. *Wheeler v. Leicester City Council* [1985] AC 1954; *R. v. Lewisham LBC ex p. Shell UK Ltd.* [1988] 1 All ER 938.

Board ex parte National Union of Mineworkers[7] is illustrative. There the Board had closed a colliery contrary to a recommendation of an independent review body. The court held that the decision was not reviewable because it involved an executive, business, or management decision in exactly the same category as a decision in similar circumstances made by a company. On the surface this justification is sensible but is undermined somewhat by the fact that an equally plausible categorization of the decision would have led to review. Again we are bereft of principle.

What of the non-governmental powers which are reviewable? The *Datafin* case[8] was hailed as a great advance by the proponents of modern judicial review.[9] Previously courts had looked at the source of a body's power and, if it lay in statute or some other governmental act, public law was prima facie applicable. Even this test, liberally construed, is expansive because not many private bodies are untouched by statutory regulation. *Datafin* moved beyond the source test for judicial review—was the source of power statutory or otherwise governmental?—to encompass as well the nature of the power being exercised. The wide area opened up was evident in the view of Sir John Donaldson MR that possibly the only essential elements 'are what can be described as a public element'[10] and the exclusion from review only of bodies whose sole source of power is a consensual submission to their jurisdiction.

The *Datafin* test was explosive because a public element can be found in mòst walks of life. Some saw it as sanctioning review whenever a body exercised such a *de facto* monopoly over an important area of public life that an individual had no effective choice but to comply with its rules, regulation, and decisions in order to operate in that area.[11] But in the particular case of the Takeover Panel, frequent judicial intervention would wreck havoc with the regulatory mechanism. (The tactical application for judicial intervention in take-over battles is a well-known phenomenon in jurisdictions such as the United States and Australia.[12] Its only

---

[7] [1986] ICR 791. That the applicants in this case were in bad odour cannot have helped their cause. See also *R. v. Independent Broadcasting Authority ex p. Rank Organisation PLC*, The Times, 14 Mar. 1986 (share transaction); *Page Motors Ltd. v. Epsom and Ewell BC* (1981) 80 LGR 337 (property case).

[8] *R. v. Panel on Take-overs and Mergers ex p. Datafin PLC* [1987] QB 815.

[9] e.g. M. Beloff, 'The Boundaries of Judicial Review', in *New Directions in Judicial Review* (London, 1988). Financial opinion was more sceptical: *Accountancy*, 100 (July 1987), 42; *The Economist*, 301, 6 Dec. 1986, p. 19. cf. *Financial Times*, 8 Dec. 1986, p. 16. And see Lord Alexander of Weedon QC., 'Judicial Review and City Regulations' [1989] 52 *MLR* 640, 647 ('I sense a concern in the City as to uncertainty as to how the Courts will interfere with decisions'). [10] at 838. See also 848, per Lloyd LJ.

[11] D. Pannick, 'Who is Subject to Judicial Review and in Respect of What? [1992] *PL* 1, 3–4.

[12] R. Cranston, *Law, Government and Public Policy* (Melbourne, 1987), 61–2.

justification is that occasionally it throws sand into the wheels of undesirable corporate restructuring—albeit that it also provides a useful benevolent fund for some lawyers.) The Court of Appeal itself recognized this and emphasized that the courts would as likely as not defer to the decisions of the Panel, a point made more concrete in the subsequent *Guinness* decision.[13] Hard on the heels of the *Datafin* and *Guinness* cases came decisions extending review to the self-regulatory organizations established under the Financial Services Act 1986 and to the Advertising Standards Authority, which, like the Takeovers Panel, is a body established by the industry itself with little statutory support.[14]

To limit *Datafin* subsequent courts began using the test of whether government would have assumed the powers being exercised itself were they not exercised by the non-governmental body in question.[15] That test requires of judges a greater perspicacity and insight into governmental intentions than most politicians and civil servants would claim. Now a recent decision of the Court of Appeal reverts to a source test, or at least limits review to instances where governmental, rather than public, functions are being exercised.[16] Judicial abnegation was also evident a few months previously, when a two-judge Court of Appeal held that Lloyd's insurance market was not subject to judicial review in relation to its members' contracts; even though Lloyd's performed public functions, its powers 'are derived from a private Act which does not extend to any persons in the insurance business other than those who wish to operate in the section of the market governed by Lloyd's.[17]

These recent decisions certainly gel with a more limited role for judicial review. Yet one important conceptual problem is how to reconcile them with the group of cases outside public law, where courts have supervised the decisions of private bodies such as sports associations, political parties, and trade unions.[18] Supervision is sometimes justified in these cases on the basis that the requirements of natural justice are implied into the contract which is constituted by the rules of the body involved. That is too simplistic, given the test of implied terms in contracts, and in any event

---

[13] *R.* v. *Panel on Take-overs and Mergers ex p. Guinness PLC* [1990] 1 QB 146. See J. Jowell, 'The Take-over Panel: Autonomy, Flexibility and Legality' [1991] *PL* 149.

[14] e.g. *R.* v. *Life Assurance and Unit Trust Regulatory Organisation Ltd. ex p. Ross* [1993] QB 17; *R.* v. *Advertising Standards Authority Ltd. ex p. Vernons Organisations Ltd.* [1992] 1 WLR 1289; *R.* v. *Advertising Standards Authority Ltd. ex p. Insurance Service PLC* [1990] COD 42.

[15] *R.* v. *Chief Rabbi ex p. Wachmann* [1992] 1 WLR 1036; *R.* v. *Code of Practice Committee of the British Pharmaceutical Industry ex p. Professional Counselling Aids Ltd.* [1991] COD 228.

[16] *R.* v. *Disciplinary Committee of the Jockey Club ex p. Aga Khan* [1993] 1 WLR 909.

[17] *R.* v. *Lloyd's of London ex p. Briggs* [1993] 1 Lloyd's Rep. 176, 185, per Leggatt LJ.

[18] e.g. *Breen* v. *Amalgamated Engineering Union* [1971] 2 QB 175; *Nagle* v. *Fielden* [1966] 2 QB 633.

does not explain how unsuccessful applicants to these bodies, denied natural justice, can take advantage of a contract to which they never become a party. Quite rightly, the contract justification was to Lord Denning a fiction and judicial intervention occurred because 'the truth is that the rules are nothing more nor less than a legislative code—a set of regulations laid down by the governing body to be observed by all who are, or become, members'.[19] While refreshingly honest, this does not take us any further down the road of principle.

Justiciability

The scope of judicial review is characterized in some jurisdictions in terms of justiciability. English courts have never refined their ideas of justiciability at the level of principle. Historically opinions as to what is justiciable have varied. The majority reaoning in *Liversidge* v. *Anderson*[20] is now, rightly, discredited,[21] but in 1942 Sir William Holdsworth approved, arguing that the minister's decision to intervene 'was not a justiciable but a political or administrative issue'.[22] These days judicial review is not inclined to see boundaries to its estate. Prerogative powers are now firmly under control, although the scope of review of the prerogative seems to be narrower than with other powers.[23] The modern tendency to review governmental powers, irrespective of their source, means that many of the older cases insulating certain types of decision-making are of doubtful authority.

However, the courts still decline jurisdiction over certain categories of issue. The famous *CND* case is illustrative.[24] The Official Secrets Act 1911, section 1, created the offence of entering a prohibited place for any purposes prejudicial to the safety or interest of the state. CND wished to argue that they were acting in the interest of the state by attempting to immobilize an airfield occupied by the United States air force. The House of Lords held that the disposition and armament of the armed forces was

---

[19] *Enderby Town Football Club Ltd.* v. *Football Association Ltd.* [1971] Ch. 591, 606. Contrast the restrictive view of Megarry, VC: 'I think that the courts must be slow to allow any implied obligation to be fair to be used as a means of bringing before the courts for review honest decisions of bodies exercising jurisdiction over sporting and other activities which those bodies are far better fitted to judge than the courts.' *McInnes* v. *Onslow-Fane* [1978] 1 WLR 1520, 1535.   [20] [1942] AC 206.

[21] *R.* v. *Inland Revenue Commissioners ex p. Rossminster Ltd.* [1980] AC 952, 1011, per Lord Diplock. But see A. Carroll, 'The Gulf Crisis and the Ghost of Liversidge v. Anderson' (1991) 5 *Immigration and Nationality Law and Practice* 72.

[22] (1942) 58 *LQR* 2, quoted G. Marshall, 'Justiciability', in A. Guest (ed.), *Oxford Essays in Jurisprudence* (Oxford, 1961), 268.

[23] *Council of Civil Service Unions* v. *Minister for the Civil Service* [1985] AC 374; *R.* v. *Secretary of State for the Home Department ex p. Northumbria Police Authority* [1989] QB 26.

[24] *Chandler* v. *Director of Public Prosecutions* [1964] AC 763. For the aftermath of the case: C. Harlow and R. Rawlings, *Pressure through Law* (London, 1992), 171–2.

not justiciable. It was said by Lord Reid to be a political question, which could not be raised before the courts.[25]

Identifying such parameters of justiciability is no easy task. The classification of a function as legislative, judicial, or administrative is now seen as unhelpful. Neither does institutional delineation fit the cases except possibly for the immunity of the parliamentary process. Certainly some matters are by tradition guaranteed a quarantine from judicial review—the conduct of foreign policy, decisions on macro-economic and monetary policy, and matters of national security are examples.[26] In some cases it has been said that it is high policy-making which is insulated from review; the several cases challenging accession to the European Economic Community fall perhaps into this category,[27] although there is some authority that treaty-making can in some circumstances be reviewed.[28] Clearly high policy-making reduced to the specfic can lead to decisions which are reviewable in the ordinary way. Another test, Lord Wilberforce's distinction between the planning and operational levels of government, has suffered a sad fate, not simply because policy and administration are inextricably linked.[29] (The courts' reluctance to interfere with the criminal process, by granting a civil remedy, ought also to be noted here.[30])

Although it would render considerable assistance there is no doctrine of 'political questions' in English law.[31] If put to them directly the courts will say that they will not be used for political purposes dressed up as points of law.[32] But there are several recent examples where the courts have

---

[25] at 791.

[26] See J. Evans, *de Smith's Judicial Review of Administrative Action* (4th edn. London, 1990), 286–90, 499–509. For a recent case on macro-economic policy see *R. v. Secretary of State for the Environment ex p. Hammersmith and Fulham LBC* [1991] 1 AC 521, where it was said (pp. 593, 597): 'What is the appropriate level of public expenditure and public taxation is, and always has been, a matter of political opinion . . . The formulation and the implementation of national economic policy are matters depending essentially on political judgment. The decisions which shaped them are for politicians to take and it is in the political forum of the House of Commons that they are properly to be debated and approved or disapproved on their merits.' Cf. *R. v. Secretary of State for the Home Department ex p. Ruddock* [1987] 1 WLR 1482, where Taylor J boldly rejected the argument that he should decline jurisdiction because of the supposed detriment to national security.

[27] *Blackburn* v. *Attorney-General* [1971] 1 WLR 1037; *McWhirter* v. *Attorney-General* [1972] CMLR 882.   [28] *Ex p. Molyneaux* [1986] 1 WLR 331.

[29] *Anns* v. *Merton LBC* [1978] AC 728. See P. Bayne, 'The Court, the Parliament and the Government: Reflections on the Scope of Judicial Review' (1991) 20 *Federal LR* 1, 7–10.

[30] *Gouriet* v. *Union of Post Office Workers* [1978] AC 435; *Attorney-General* v. *Able* [1984] QB 795; *R. v. Manchester Crown Court ex p. Director of Public Prosecutions* [1993] 2 WLR 846.

[31] G. Sawer, 'Political Questions' (1963) 15 *Univ. Toronto LJ* 49.

[32] e.g. *R. v. Greater London Council ex p. Kensington and Chelsea Royal Borough*, The Times, 7 Apr. 1982, per Neill, J.

intervened in issues having a definite party political character—issues
better left alone. One is *Wheeler* v. *Leicester City Council*,[33] where the
question was whether a local authority with a very large number of its
inhabitants from ethnic minorities could temporarily ban from use of its
recreational ground a local rugger club which declined to condemn a South
African tour and declined actively to discourage its members from
participating. Forbes J said yes, the majority of the Court of Appeal
agreed, but to the surprise of many sensitive to the need to promote better
race relations the House of Lords held that the local authority had acted
unreasonably, in the *Wednesbury* sense, or irrationally.

The decision is even more difficult to understand when contrasted with
Nottingham City Council v. *Secretary of State for the Environment*.[34] There
the House of Lords refused to apply the *Wednesbury* principle to a decision
of the Secretary of State, approved by the House of Commons, which, it
was said, would result in disproportionate disadvantages to some local
authorities in the money they received from central government. Lord
Scarman said that it was a decision in the field of public financial
administration which inevitably required a political judgment on the part
of the Secretary of State. There may well be a justiciable issue in the
construction of the legislation, and examination by the court may be
justified if the Secretary of State had acted in bad faith, for an improper
motive, or absurdly. But otherwise, said Lord Scarman, it was not
constitutionally appropriate to intervene on the ground of unreasonableness, given the separation of powers, the approval by Parliament, and the
subject-matter—in this instance a tax burden falling on either general
taxpayers or local ratepayers.[35]

Nothing could be more party political than election manifestos, which
set out the policies which political parties place before the voters. Of
course it can hardly be said that a political party which takes power after an
election, even with a majority, has majority support for each and every
policy in the manifesto. On that basis alone it is difficult to argue that
manifestos should be absolutely binding on political leaders, still less that
their proposals should not be modified in the light of changed circumstances
and wider consultation. Lord Wilberforce's sensible statement, that a local
authority was 'entitled—indeed in a sense bound—to carry out the policy
on which it was elected'[36] encapsulates a judicious balancing of these

---

[33] [1985] AC 1054. See also *R.* v. *Derbyshire CC ex p. The Times Supplements Ltd.* [1991]
COD 129.   [34] [1986] AC 240.
[35] esp. at 250. See also *R.* v. *Secretary of State for Trade ex p. Anderson Strathclyde PLC*
[1983] 2 All ER 233, 243 (whether the Secretary of State should accept the advice of the
Monopolies and Mergers Commission 'a matter of political judgment, not a matter of law').
[36] *Secretary of State for Education and Science* v. *Tameside MBC* [1977] AC 1014, 1051.

different considerations. So especially worrying is Lord Diplock's suggestion that when a political party wins power it should consider all manifesto
proposals afresh, without feeling committed to them.[37] This overlooks
completely the important role which manifestos play internally within
political parties, the extent to which they are used as a monitoring device
by other political parties, the press, and the public, and the fact that they
distil policies developed by political parties after what is often long and
expert consideration.

GROUNDS, STANDING, AND PROCEDURE

The scope of judicial review is, then, a jumble of rules in search of some
principles. What of the grounds and procedures according to which review
may be granted? Surely, here we are on a firmer base. Possibly, although
at the outset we find that the underlying premiss of judicial review is not
entirely clear. Upholding the rule of law and preventing abuse of power are
high on the litany of judicial comment.[38] In this sense the judges echo
Dicey, who argued that the preservation of the rule of law was dependent
on the judges. The contention is that it is the judicial task to ensure that
public authorities exercising functions under legislation (and also in some
cases the prerogative) do not exceed or abuse their power. In its extreme
formulation the notion is that without judicial review public authorities
would take dictatorial powers.[39] This assumption that power needs to be
controlled typically discounts or ignores completely the point that power
has a beneficent face. Citizens need protection against the activities of the
state, as indeed against the activities of corporations, but they also need
the state to act in their interest. It is just as much in the public interest that
public authorities exercise their powers as that they exercise them lawfully.

Remedying individual grievances against the state features as another
justification for judicial review.[40] This is not surprising since a concern with
individual grievances is part and parcel of the role of the courts. When
individual liberty is threatened the standard of judicial scrutiny is quite
rightly higher than in other cases: concern with individual liberty should

---

[37] *Bromley LBC* v. *Greater London Council* [1983] AC 768, 790, 829. Cf. at 853. See also
R. v. *Waltham Forest LBC ex p. Baxter* [1988] QB 419, which held that if councillors voted for
a resolution in council not because they favoured it but simply because of party loyalty or
policy that would be a breach of duty—an approach touchingly remote from political realities.

[38] e.g. *R.* v. *Inland Revenue Commissioners ex p. National Federation of Self-Employed
and Small Businesses* [1982] AC 617, 641; *R.* v. *Knightsbridge Crown Court ex p. International
Sporting Club (London) Ltd.* [1982] QB 304, 315; *Nottinghamshire CC* v. *Secretary of State
for the Environment* [1986] AC 240, 249.

[39] Sir W. Wade, *Constitutional Fundamentals* (London, 1980), 65.

[40] e.g. *R.* v. *Secretary of State for the Environment ex p. Norwich CC* [1982] QB 808, 826.

outweigh any difficulties which are faced by public authorities in the administration of their tasks. But remedying an individual grievance is rarely costless. Time, effort, and resources devoted, say, to rehearing one person may be at the expense of the services which could be provided to others. Indeed in public law one person's remedy is often another's injury. A pupil obtains a place in a school as a result of judicial review, thereby excluding another just as deserving. A final point to note is that the notion of remedying individual grievances sits ill with the underdevelopment of damages as a remedy in public law.

These justifications for judicial review do not point inevitably to the courts as the only, or even the major, means of their accomplishment—of preventing abuse of power or remedying individual grievances against the state. Public authorities are held to account as much, if not more so, through other mechanisms such as parliamentary select committees, investigations of the ombudsmen, or the activities of official audit bodies. These institutions may be as appropriate as the courts in reviewing the legality of a public authority's action and will have a greater expertise in deciding on other matters, for example, financial accountability. In some circumstances the political process itself will be a more effective and desirable avenue of accountability or redress. The despised MP, for example, is often able to obtain satisfaction for an aggrieved constituent.[41] And there is the important role of the media. Internal procedures within public authorities are also vital in ensuring that their activities are carried out within the limits of the law and that the position of individuals dealing with them is protected.[42]

Grounds of review

If we turn to examine more specifically the grounds of judicial review we find at the base the *ultra vires* doctrine.[43] Built on this are the traditional grounds of review—substantive *ultra vires*, abuse of discretion, errors of jurisdiction, procedural *ultra vires*, and natural justice.[44] In particular the courts have said that in exercising discretion public authorities must not act for an improper purpose; must not act so unreasonably that no reasonable public authority would act in that way (*Wednesbury* unreasonableness);[45] must take relevant considerations into account; and must not have

[41] See R. Rawlings, 'The MP's Complaints Service' (1990) 53 *MLR* 22; (1990) 53 MLR 149.

[42] e.g. R. Cranston, *Legal Foundations of the Welfare State* (London, 1985), 252–74.

[43] cf. D. Oliver, 'Is the *Ultra Vires* Rule the Basis of Judicial Review?' [1987] *PL* 543.

[44] Given well-established categories Lord Diplock's idiosyncratic catalogue—illegality, irrationality, and procedural impropriety—is best ignored: *Council of Civil Service Unions* v. *Minister for the Civil Service* [1985] AC 374, 410.

[45] *Associated Provincial Picture Houses Ltd.* v. *Wednesbury Corporation* [1948] 1 KB 223. Unreasonableness does not constitute a ground upon which a decision approved by

regard to irrelevant considerations.[46] Public authorities may—possibly must—develop rules and policies to guide discretion, but these must be consistent with the legislative scheme and be applied flexibly (i.e. not fetter discretion).[47] If these conditions are met, the exercise of discretion should not be reviewed on the merits.[48]

All this is hornbook law. Yet merely stating the grounds of review brings home how thin the line is between *ultra vires* (reviewable) and merits (supposedly non-reviewable). In practice, of course, it is a line which has frequently been crossed. Viewed over recent decades these grounds have facilitated a rapid expansion of judicial review, at the initiative of the courts. The grounds of review have acquired an expansive quality. *Wednesbury* unreasonableness, for example, is a reliable long stop when nothing else fits.[49] But, as two leading commentators put it, because the courts are reluctant to articulate the grounds on which an act may be considered to be unreasonable, the suspicion is encouraged that 'prejudice or policy considerations may be hiding underneath *Wednesbury's* ample cloak'.[50] Occasionally, however, the courts draw back. So the principle of proportionality—that there must be a reasonable relationship between the objectives sought to be achieved and the means used—was recently held not to be an independent ground of review but an aspect of *Wednesbury* unreasonableness.[51] Ironically the justification given was that if it were the courts would move in the direction of assessing merits.

Legitimate expectations

It is impractical here to examine each of the grounds of judicial review.

Parliament can be challenged: *R.* v. *Secretary of State for the Environment ex p. Hammersmith and Fulham LBC* [1991] 1 AC 521. The opposite conclusion would be an extraordinary attack on democratic theory.

[46] *Padfield* v. *Minister of Agriculture, Fisheries and Food* [1968] AC 997 is a leading case on improper purpose and irrelevant considerations.

[47] *British Oxygen Co. Ltd* v. *Board of Trade* [1971] AC 610; *In re Findlay* [1985] AC 318. A fettering case with heavy political overtones is *R.* v. *Hammersmith and Fulham LBC ex p. Beddowes* [1987] QB 1050 (see esp. the dissent of Kerr, LJ).

[48] e.g. *R.* v. *Secretary of State for Trade and Industry ex p. Lonrho* [1989] 1 WLR 525, 535: 'The judgements of the Divisional Court illustrate the danger of judges wrongly though unconsciously substituting their own views for the views of the decision-maker who alone is charged and authorised by Parliament to exercise a discretion. The question is not whether the Secretary of State came to a correct solution or to a conclusion which meets with the approval of the Divisional Court but whether the discretion was properly exercised.' Judicial review must of course be distinguished from appeal.

[49] e.g. *West Glamorgan CC* v. *Rafferty* [1987] 1 WLR 457 (council acting unreasonably in evicting travellers without first making provision for alternative accommodation). Cf. *R.* v. *Avon CC ex p. Rexworthy* [1988] 87 LGR 470.

[50] J. Jowell and A. Lester, 'Beyond *Wednesbury*: Substantive Principles of Administrative Law' [1987] *PL* 368, 372.

[51] *R.* v. *Secretary of State for the Home Office ex p. Brind* [1991] 1 AC 696. Proportionality is an independent principle of European Community law.

(Not even one so rash as the present author could accommodate the editors' initial wish for a chapter reviewing the scope, rationale, grounds, and remedies of judicial review.) Illustrative of current trends, however, is the doctrine of legitimate expectations. Legitimate expectations now play an enhanced role in administrative law, not just in obliging a public authority to consult before it significantly changes its position (the procedural aspect), but also in preventing it from acting inconsistently with statements made or long-standing practice (the substantive aspect).[52]

The duty in relation to the procedural aspect extends beyond legal rights to the 'new property', at least where persons already enjoy a benefit or advantage, for example a licence, and this is being withdrawn.[53] On their face, however, some of the decisions are difficult to reconcile: thus the bleak contrast between the decision that there was no duty to consult in advance residents at an old people's home about its closure, even though they would be greatly distressed;[54] and the decision that, before withdrawing a grant for rail freight, the Secretary of State was obliged to give the recipient the chance to make representations.[55]

In the various cases both the demands of the 'new property' and the practices of the public authority seem to be relevant to the duty to consult. Whether the concept of legitimate expectations adds anything in the case of the former is often doubtful; if the circumstances of the 'new property' interest call for consultation then it adds little to invoke the concept. As to the latter there seems some merit in saying that prima facie a public authority which gives an assurance that it will consult ought to keep its word—but surely not as a matter of legal obligation if there are plausible grounds for it reversing its policy. Otherwise the public authority which commendably says that it will try to consult will be held to generate legally enforceable expectations. The failure to consult on a departure from existing practices, plausibly grounded, should not be reviewable. The remedy should be a political one.

The modern orthodoxy is that consultation is uniformly a good. The reality is more complex. There is the ever present danger in courts ordering consultation of placing particular persons or groups at an unfair advantage over others. Thus those with the 'new property' must be consulted but not those without, even if the latter will be profoundly affected by its disposition and use. Moreover the political process usually results in wide

[52] *Council of Civil Service Unions* v. *Minister for the Civil Service* [1985] 1 AC 375; *Attorney-General of Hong Kong* v. *Ng Yuen Shiu* [1983] 2 AC 629. See P. Craig, 'Legitimate Expectations: A Conceptual Analysis' (1992) 108 *LQR* 79; R. Baldwin and D. Horne, 'Expectations in a Joyless Landscape' (1986) 49 *MLR* 685.
[53] e.g. *R.* v. *Liverpool Corporation ex p. Liverpool Taxi Fleet Operators' Association* [1972] 2 QB 299.
[54] *R.* v. *Devon CC ex p. Baker*, *The Times*, 20 Oct. 1992.
[55] *R.* v. *Secretary of State for Transport ex p. Sheriff & Sons*, *The Times*, 18 Dec. 1986.

consultation involving elected representatives and officials, and while it is far from perfect lawyers should be slow to assume that it fails to operate and that their conception of consultation is better.

The substantive doctrine of legitimate expectations is still in its infancy and its metes and bounds uncharted. At present the substantive doctrine seems to include conduct equivalent to breach of contract, or persons acting in reliance to their detriment or changing their position.[56] This is a good place for the courts to stop. Why should a person be able to found a case on a statement or conduct in public law when that could not be done in an analogous situation in private law? The courts seem to have realized, moreover, that they are ill equipped to weigh the ingredients—to take two litigated examples,[57] in licensing and prosecution policy—so as to say that a person has a legitimate expectation in a licence being renewed or a prosecution not being brought.

It would be quite wrong for any substantive doctrine of legitimate expectations to stand in the way of policy changes by public authorities. Fundamental to public law is that a public authority cannot fetter its discretion. A policy must always be capable of change whatever may have been said in the past. The Court of Appeal recognized this in *R. v. Secretary of State for Health ex parte United States Tobacco International Inc.*,[58] where the company claimed that its legitimate expectation had been denied because the government had decided to ban a particular tobacco product. The company had built a factory to produce that product following numerous discussions with the government. The Court of Appeal held that the government could not be fettered by any moral obligation to the company despite its earlier favourable treatment of it. 'It would be absurd to suggest that some moral commitment to a single company should prevail over the public interest,'[59] a statement with which one can but whole-heartedly agree.

The fact is that changes in government policy often occur as economic, political, or social circumstances change. There is thus an important public benefit in the general right of government to change its mind, although surprisingly the courts do not always acknowledge this.[60] Perhaps one

[56] *R. v. Inland Revenue Commissioners ex p. Preston* [1985] AC 825; *R. v. Jockey Club ex p. Ram Racecourses* [1990] COD 346; *R. v. Inland Revenue Commissioners ex p. MFK Underwriting Agencies* [1990] 1 WLR 1545, 1569, per Bingham, LJ. Cf. *R. v. Secretary of State for the Home Department ex p. Ruddock* [1987] 1 WLR 1482.

[57] *R. v. Birmingham CC ex p. Sheptonhurst* [1990] 1 All ER 1026; *R. v. Torbay BC exp p. Cleasby* [1991] CID 142, cf *R. v. Inland Revenue Commissioners ex p. Mead* [1993] 1 All ER 772.

[58] [1992] QB 353.   [59] at 369, per Taylor LJ.

[60] Cf. Lord Diplock: 'Administrative policies may change with changing circumstances, including changes in the political complexion of governments. The liberty to make such changes is something that is inherent in our constitutional form of government.' *Hughes* v. *Department of Health and Social Security* [1985] AC 776, 788.

reason is that, while they are used to identifying individual injustice, the same cannot be said of the complex issue of the public benefit. Yet remedying what seems an individual injustice may do untold harm to unidentified others. For this reason redress in this respect lies best in the political not the judicial sphere. To argue that a public body must adduce evidence of an overriding public benefit in order to change its policy is to transfer to the courts the debates which should occur in the political arena. And it is to shackle government when business is free to roam.

Standing

Let us turn to the procedural prerequisites to invoking judicial review. First, standing. Private rights are of course enforceable by the private citizen but, absent a sufficient interest, enforcement of public rights is committed to the Attorney-General (or other bodies entrusted by statute with the task). In the leading case, the House of Lords said that whether a person has a sufficient interest cannot be decided separately from the merits of the application but turns on a consideration of the full legal and factual context of the power or duty involved and the unlawfulness alleged.[61] On one interpretation this means that when a matter is heard the issues of standing and substance merge; tests of standing only apply at the leave stage when hopeless cases are filtered.[62] However, standing can still act as a block on proceedings, the most notable recent example being the *Rose Theatre* case,[63] where a trust company set up with the objects of preserving the remains of the Rose Theatre and making them accessible to the public was denied standing to challenge a decision of the Secretary of State refusing its application to schedule the remains as an ancient monument.

Despite the *Rose Theatre* case, it is fair to say that in recent decades the courts have been notably liberal in granting standing. Many of the barriers have come down. Admittedly some of the case-law is at first blush difficult to fathom or only understood in non-legal terms. Generally ratepayers have standing to challenge their local authority, but not taxpayers to challenge the government.[64] In the late 1960s and early 1970s, those seeking to enforce standards of traditional morality did well in obtaining standing (in a few cases simply being a citizen seemed to constitute

---

[61] R. v. *Inland Revenue Commissioners ex p. National Federation of Self-Employed and Small Businesses* [1982] AC 617.

[62] The Law Commission, *Administrative Law: Judicial Review and Statutory Appeals*, Consultation Paper no. 126 (1993) 56.

[63] R. v. *Secretary of State for the Environment ex p. Rose Theatre Trust Co. Ltd.* [1990] 1 QB 504.

[64] See Ackner LJ on the illogicality: [1980] QB 407, 433.

standing[65]). In the last decade so too have those advocating welfare rights and equal opportunities.[66] And counterbalancing the *Rose Theatre* case are a number of recent decisions where courts have accorded community groups standing to challenge planning-type decisions.[67] *R.* v. *Felixstowe JJ. ex parte Leigh*[68] is an especially liberal case, where a journalist was given standing to challenge a decision of justices that their identities must not be disclosed. The court held that the journalist had a seriousness of purpose on a matter of national importance to justify a declaration, although not mandamus for disclosure in the particular case. Watkins LJ emphasized 'the importance to the community at large of open justice and the role of the press as guardian and watchdog of the public interest in this matter'.[69]

In adopting a liberal doctrine of standing the courts seem to justify it mainly on rule of law grounds. Denying standing, and hence access, means that the violation of legal rights goes unchecked and administrative abuse continues with impunity.[70] In the light of the concern with the rule of law, however, it is ironical that this approach in practice has resulted in rules of standing which are largely discretionary.[71] It behoves the courts to develop a principled approach to standing especially if judicial intervention is to be justified on the ground of ensuring adherence to the rule of law.

Certainly some of the traditional, pragmatic arguments for preserving restrictive rules of standing no longer carry great weight. The need to screen out those whose claims are futile can probably be met by the rules against vexations, frivolous, or oppressive claims. The notion that the ideologically motivated will not present as convincing or helpful an argument as others does not hold water.[72] We must also put to one side the use of standing as a regulator of the volume of matters which the courts handle; if there is a case for limiting judicial review then this should be done explicitly. However, while the traditional floodgates argument is

---

[65] e.g. *R.* v. *Commissioner of Police of the Metropolis ex p. Blackburn* [1968] 2 QB 118; *R.* v. *Commissioner of Police of the Metropolis (No. 3)* [1973] QB 241; *Attorney-General ex rel. McWhirter* v. *Independent Broadcasting Authority* [1973] QB 629. Cf. *R.* v. *Independent Broadcasting Authority ex p. Whitehouse, The Times*, 4 Apr. 1985, where Mrs Whitehouse's standing was left open.

[66] e.g. *R.* v. *Secretary of State for Social Services ex p. Child Poverty Action Group* [1990] 2 QB 540; *R.* v. *Secretary of State for Employment ex p. Equal Opportunities Commission* [1992] 1 All ER 545, 556.

[67] e.g. *Covent Garden Community Association* v. *Greater London Council* [1981] JPL 183; *R.* v. *Hammersmith and Fulham LBC ex p. People Before Profit Ltd.* (1981) 80 LGR 322; *R.* v. *HM Inspectorate of Pollution ex p. Greenpeace*, Independent, 30 Sept. 1993.

[68] [1987] QB 582. [69] Ibid., at 597.

[70] See *National Federation of Self-Employed* [1982] AC 617, at 644, per Lord Diplock, at 654, per Lord Scarman. [71] Ibid. 642.

[72] L. Jaffe, 'The Citizen as Litigant in Public Actions: The Non-Hohfeldian or Ideological Plaintiff' (1968) 116 *Univ. Pennsylvania LR* 1033.

sometimes disparaged it would seem to have at least some support in the recent increase in the number of cases where judicial review has been sought.[73]

Sir Konrad Schiemann has referred to the uncertainty which would result if anyone could challenge a decision at any time and the cautiousness in administration which might result.[74] These concerns have been dismissed by the Law Commission, which states that uncertainty is more appropriately addressed by other mechanisms, particularly time limits. It acknowledges that over-cautiousness in decision-making is a factor to be considered but contends that that should be a consideration when deciding whether an act is invalid not who has standing to challenge it.[75] This response does not join issue with the concerns which Schiemann J has advanced. Multiplying the instances in which decisions may be challenged must add some uncertainty to administration even if some of these fall out of time. Greater caution in decision-making would be a not unnatural result if there were many more opportunities for administrative arrangements and political balances to be upset.

There are also issues of principle. If declaring an act or decision unlawful will affect a particular individual or group of individuals, and if none of them decides to challenge it, there is a heavy onus to discharge in arguing that someone more remote from the act or decision ought to be able to do so.[76] A more liberal test of standing in this situation would undermine individual autonomy and expectations. The fact is that persons who have rights may choose not to exercise them for a variety of reasons. In private law a party to a contract may choose to condone its breach, or someone injured by a tortious act may choose not to sue. A person's failure to activate the judicial process may have nothing to do with the cost of litigation but may turn on a desire to maintain good relations with another (the contract example) or an intention to use non-legal methods to seek a remedy (the tort example). Similarly, if those more directly affected by an act of government choose not to seek judicial review, to enable others to sue may be acting against the interests and wishes of the former. The desirable aim of promoting good government is certainly a factor which must go into the balance as well, but later in the chapter I express scepticism as to whether to any great extent it is either possible or desirable to attempt to promote good government through judicial review.

In some instances more liberal tests of standing can threaten expectations. To take a particular example, why if government has decided to act in a certain way in relation to a particular individual should someone else be

---

[73] M. Sunkin, L. Bridges, and G. Meszaros, *Judicial Review in Perspective* (London, 1993).
[74] Sir K. Schiemann, 'Locus Standi' [1990] *PL* 342, 348.
[75] Law Commission, *Administrative Law*, 64.
[76] See *R.* v. *Legal Aid Board ex p. Pateman* [1992] 1 WLR 711; [1992] 3 All ER 498.

able to seek judicial review of the decision. Why, for example, should the person cautioned rather than prosecuted suddenly find that someone else is taking the matter to court. Why, for example, should a person suddenly find that his or her tax assessment is challenged as legally invalid because it is too low?[77] These are matters of principle which cannot simply be brushed aside.

Finally, it is sometimes suggested that if in private law a litigant may initiate action unhindered, why not in public law? The premiss of this argument is shaky. Certainly standing is not an issue which arises in many private lawsuits, since the question of a plaintiff's standing to sue merges with the question whether he or she has a cause of action on the merits. In general the law does not countenance the possibility that a person not possessed of a legal right should be able to claim.[78] But it should not be forgotten that standing does operate in areas of private law. The rule in *Foss* v. *Harbottle*[79] has given sustenance to generations of company law students—and honest work for many a company law teacher. Whether a 'NIMBY' (not in my back yard) can enforce a restrictive covenant from an earlier time in order to block development (or preserve the environment) turns on standing.[80] In a recent decision the question was whether a medical authority was the appropriate person to ask the court for a declaration of the legality of deciding to discontinue life support to an insensate patient.[81] In summary standing is a feature of both public and private law; in particular circumstances there may well be good reasons for limiting access to the courts. Liberal standing rules cannot always be justified.

Procedure

'English law fastens, not upon principles, but upon remedies,' as Lord Wilberforce sagely observed on one occasion.[82] Nowhere is this more so than in public law. The results have been unfortunate for a clear development of the law. Two examples are illustrative.

Order 53 of the Rules of the Supreme Court was supposed to bring some rationality to the procedure for seeking the remedies of administrative law. Henceforth the principal orders (*certiorari*, prohibition, mandamus) were only to be obtainable on an application for judicial review under the Order, which abolished an accretion of peculiarities to their scope and

---

[77] Cf. *R.* v. *Attorney-General ex p. Imperial Chemical Industries PLC* [1985] 1 CMLR 588.
[78] A. Chayes, 'The Supreme Court: 1981 Term-Foreword: Public Law Litigation and the Burger Court' (1982) 96 *Harvard LR* 4, 8–9.   [79] (1842) 2 Hare 461.
[80] *Emile Elias & Co. Ltd.* v. *Pine Groves Ltd.* [1993] WLR 305.
[81] *Airedale NHS Trust* v. *Bland* [1993] 2 WLR 316.
[82] *Davy* v. *Spelthorne BC* [1984] AC 262, 276.

procedure. An injunction and declaration could still be sought by writ or originating summons. So far so good—until *O'Reilly* v. *Mackman*,[83] which held that it was an abuse of process in certain circumstances to secure a remedy in a public law matter other than by way of an application for judicial review. Arguably this procedural exclusivity had never been intended by the drafters of Order 53.[84] There must also be doubt whether the judges would have had the authority to make an Order having such an effect.

The procedural exclusivity said to be mandated by Order 53 was at one time justified in the interest of good administration—to 'protect from harassment public authorities on whom parliament has imposed a duty to make public law decisions'[85]—and of the third parties who might be indirectly affected if there were to be uncertainty as to whether a decision was valid.[86] But if the courts now acknowledge that *O'Reilly* v. *Mackman* has given rise to a 'procedural minefield',[87] and have sought to avoid the strait-jacket of procedural exclusivity,[88] much needless litigation over procedural issues has still not clarified the tests for whether a case involves public or private law issues or whether a matter falls within the so-called collateral issue exception. In fact the distinction between public and private smacks of true essences and leads to sterile litigation. Clearly there is nothing in the argument that procedural exclusivity ensures judicial expertise which, if it is needed, should turn on subject, not procedural specialization. Procedural exclusivity should be abolished.

A second example relates to leave. In recent times the leave procedure for those seeking judicial review has generated a great deal of debate. It has been justified as a way of weeding out trivial and misguided actions and removing the uncertainty in which public authorities might be left as to whether they can safely proceed with administrative action while proceedings for judicial review are pending.[89] Of course trivial and misguided complaints may be winnowed in any event by dint of the legal process. Moreover, the evidence is that a significant number of applicants who on first attempt are denied leave are granted it on a second or subsequent attempt.[90] Also worrying is the variation between different judges in

---

[83] [1983] 2 AC 237.

[84] Report of the Committee of the JUSTICE/All Souls Review of Administrative Law in the United Kingdom, *Administrative Justice: Some Necessary Reforms* (Oxford, 1988), 150.

[85] *Cocks* v. *Thanet DC* [1983] 2 AC 286, 294. See also *Wandsworth LBC* v. *Winder* [1985] AC 461, 510. [86] *O'Reilly* v. *Mackman* [1983] 2 AC 237, 284.

[87] *Roy* v. *Kensington and Chelsea and Westminster Family Practitioner Committee* [1992] 1 AC 624, 653.

[88] J. Beatson, 'Public and Private in English Administrative Law' (1987) 103 *LQR* 34.

[89] The *National Federation of Self-Employed* case [1982] AC 617, 643.

[90] A. Le Sueur and M. Sunkin, 'Applications for Judicial Review: The Requirement of Leave' [1992] *PL* 102, 112.

granting leave and that certain categories of case—for example those concerning homeless persons and immigration applicants—seem to be subject to more stringent tests at the leave stage than others.[91] Leave is not required to seek judicial review in other jurisdictions, although a directions hearing may be required to identify issues and to encourage settlements. This seems a much more sensible approach.

THE CONTEXT OF JUDICIAL REVIEW

A fuller assessment of judicial review requires a consideration of its context. One aspect is that of institutional competence. The function of courts historically has been to declare and enforce the private rights of individuals and to settle disputes concerning those rights. The judicial process has been refined with that end in view. By contrast public authorities are concerned with the development and application of public policy. Particular public authorities develop an expertise in, and a detailed overview of, an area. It is in the practical administration of legislation that its purposes often become manifest. Yet too often in deciding on the legality of administrative action the courts bring an orientation towards individual rights, rarely deferring to administrative expertise, or acknowledging the sometimes delicate balance between the need to protect individual interests on the one hand and the need for effective administration on the other.

In some respects the courts are not even the best instrument to enforce individual rights in relation to administration. Because of the nature of litigation, the courts are only an exceptional avenue for individual redress. Not only is there the obvious barrier of cost, but there is also the nature of the remedies which the courts grant in cases of judicial review. Compensation is rarely awarded where persons have suffered loss as a result of administrative activity, although from the point of view of the individual compensation is probably a more appropriate remedy in many cases than the quashing of a decision or the ordering of its reconsideration.

Another issue is that of effectiveness. If a court overturns a decision that might be all that the applicant desires. If he or she wants a new decision, it is a matter of reapproaching the decision-maker: courts do not substitute their own decision for the original decision. But the decision-maker may then make a decision along the lines of the original but in a judge-proof way. Moreover, judicial review is sporadic in terms of the total volume of decision-making, even in areas which are heavily litigated. There is

---

[91] *Puhlhofer* v. *Hillingdon LBC* [1986] AC 484, 518; *R.* v. *Secretary of State for the Home Department ex p. Swati* [1986] 1 WLR 477.

considerable scope for public authorities to disregard the import of judicial review. Unfortunately we must rely largely on anecdotal evidence as to whether judicial review has had an impact on the quality of administration. Since effective control over administration needs to be systematic and continuous we may hypothesize that that provided by judicial review is not great.

Two cultures?

Polycentric decision-making

Public authorities and the courts work on different assumptions. Public authorities are concerned with administrative efficiency, policy, and the 'public interest'.[92] In recent times public authorities have also had to come to terms with new management techniques and market approaches. Estimation and probability are used by public authorities as a means of generalizing.[93] Judgments are made that particular policies can only be partly accomplished. The need to retain managerial flexibility to meet new circumstances is highly prized. Law is not seen as central to the enterprise. Viewed positively, it may be seen as a set of pegs on which to hang policies; viewed negatively it may be seen as a series of hurdles to be jumped.[94]

By contrast, the legal process is particularistic. Facts are systematically gathered and law is applied to them. The process is not unsubtle. There is a dialectic as legal principle and the concrete case interact; it is in the concrete case that principle is applied and refined. The judicial investigation in any particular case may be time-consuming and expensive, with the aim being to secure a definite result and not to reach approximation. Broad policy is generally eschewed in judicial decision-making and individual rights regarded as paramount.

This cultural cleavage between public authorities and the courts leads to misunderstandings and in some cases tension.[95] Public authorities are apt to express surprise when decisions are struck down on judicial review:

[92] D. Rosenbloom, 'Public Administrators and the Judiciary: The "New Partnership" ' (1987) 47 *Public Administration Review* 75; P. Cooper, 'Conflict or Constructive Tension: The Changing Relationship of Judges and Administrators' (1985) 45 *Public Administration Review* 643.

[93] As Mr Justice Brennan notes: 'Some administrative action is not based upon the existence of a fact but on the apprehension of the possibility that the fact exists': 'The Purpose and Scope of Judicial Review', in M. Taggart (ed.), *Judicial Review of Administrative Action in the 1980s* (Auckland, 1986), 20.

[94] Harlow and Rawlings, *Pressure through Law*, 45. Law hardly features, if at all, in public administration texts: e.g. I. Taylor and G. Popham, *An Introduction to Public Sector Management*, (London, 1989); C. Pollitt and S. Harrison, *Handbook of Public Services Management* (Oxford, 1992); L. Metcalfe and S. Richards, *Improving Public Management*, (2nd edn. London 1990).

[95] See Sir M. Kerry, 'Administrative Law and Judicial Review: The Practical Effects of Developments over the Last 25 Years on Administration in Central Government' (1986) 64 *Public Administration* 163, 168.

decisions which seem reasonable to those taking them are treated as unreasonable (in the *Wednesbury* sense); discretion of a broad character necessary to handle the diversity of problems is taken as having been exercised for an improper purpose; and policies which have evolved after consultation with, and the balancing of, interests are said to have been based on irrelevant considerations. One particular source of tension is that judicial review does not act in a clearly normative way, indicating to public authorities what they must do. This is because the grounds of judicial review are not sufficiently precise to guide public authorities in their daily operations. Another source of tension is that courts have been slow to recognize that the issues in public law litigation are much wider than in private litigation—beyond the identifiable parties before the court are others who may be affected by a decision. In other words the issues on judicial review are polycentric compared with private law litigation and also touch more directly on political, social, and economic issues. As Pannick concludes in relation to the *Fares Fair* case:

All the Law Lords emphasised the financial consequences to ratepayers if the GLC policy were to be upheld. But there is a paucity of reference to the social impact of the GLC's policy and the consequences of holding it unlawful: reduced passenger flow leading to even higher fares; an increase in road traffic causing more road accidents and greater pollution; a less frequent public transport service; and less jobs for London Transport staff. Nor is there any reference to the transport systems of other major cities in Europe, the subsidy of which was no doubt in the mind of Parliament in 1969.[96]

Finally, public authorities resent it when courts seem to be oblivious to the budgetary constraints which they all face and which prevent them from fully carrying out their statutory and other duties.

Yet the two cultures could be bridged; there are obvious areas where the courts could take account more sympathetically of the ways in which public authorities operate and the problems they face. One example relates to the rules which public authorities inevitably develop to enable them to administer discretion routinely. These rules may be brief or detailed, written or unwritten, sophisticated or simple, and they may or may not have legal effect.[97] They may take the form of standard operating procedures within a public authority.[98] How do the courts treat them?

[96] D. Pannick, 'The Law Lords and the Needs of Contemporary Society' (1982) 53 *Political Quarterly* 318, 322. See generally P. McAuslan, 'Public Law and Public Choice' (1988) 51 *MLR* 681.

[97] As a matter of policy when rules are formulated they should be made public, subject to consultation and consistent with their statutory mandate—matters beyond the scope of the present chapter.

[98] e.g. in *Government Accounting*, (London, 1989), which is an official guide on accounting and financial procedures for the use of government departments, annex 35.1 contains an algorithm for dealing with overpayment to individuals.

Rule-making

Since the classic statement in *Ex parte Kynoch*,[99] the courts have required that, whatever administrative rules may provide, decision-makers must consider each matter as an individual case. Stated in extreme form, this non-fettering rule means that an applicant is 'entitled to put forward reasons urging that the policy should be changed, or saying that in any case it should not be applied to him'.[100] Less extreme is Lord Reid's approach in the *British Oxygen* case,[101] that a public authority with a multitude of similar cases will almost certainly evolve a policy, so precisely that it could be called a rule, which is unobjectionable 'provided the authority is always willing to listen to anyone with something new to say—of course I do not mean to say that there need be an oral hearing'.[102]

Just how the more extreme version of the non-fettering rule can be justified is a puzzle, especially when the courts themselves convert their own discretion into rules and treat those rules as precedent (although admittedly there is less tendency these days to pretend that the law is always as it has been). It is not especially persuasive to say that when Parliament confers a discretion it intends the decision-maker to retain its latitude to make individual choices. It adds little to argue that Parliament has legitimized the non-fettering rule because it has not expressed its disapproval. In fact the origin of the rule seems to be the judicial model of decision-making, that decisions are made after considering the circumstances of particular cases. Yet it is as likely that the assumption of public authorities is correct—that once policy is formulated with care and after consultation while it has to be tailored to each particular case there is no reason why it also has to be reconsidered each time.

The other side of the coin of the non-fettering rule is the trend of modern decisions, that if public authorities have formulated rules they must be taken into account as a relevant consideration.[103] Where rules are intended to be enforced, and are capable of enforcement, there seems nothing objectionable to holding a public authority to them, especially if they have been relied upon by individuals. But where in the rule the decision-maker retains an overall discretion—which it might well want to do, for example because a policy is in its infancy or operates in a relatively complex area—it

---

[99] *R. v. Port of London Authority ex p. Kynoch Ltd.* [1919] 1 KB 176, 184. Closely related to the non-fettering principle is that public authorities must not act under dictation: *R. v. The Mayor, Alderman and Councillors of Stepney* [1902] 1 KB 317. But what is the objection to one public body relying on the superior expertise of another public body?

[100] *Sagnata Investments Ltd. v. Norwich Corp.* [1971] 2 QB 614, 627, per Lord Denning MR.   [101] *British Oxygen Co. Ltd. v. Board of Trade* [1971] AC 610.

[102] at 625.

[103] e.g. *R. v. Secretary of State for the Home Department ex p. Asif Mahmood Khan* [1984] 1 WLR 1336. Cf. *Din v. Wandsworth LBC* [1983] 1 AC 657.

seems difficult to justify judicial review simply because a new factor (not mentioned in the rule) is taken into account, so long of course as the new factor falls within the legislative mandate. The fact is that incremental decision-making is necessary, nay praiseworthy in particular contexts even though it means that similar cases may be treated differently.

Administrative structures

Delegation is of course the essence of administration. It is simply impossible for ministers and senior officials to exercise all the discretion conferred upon them by statute. With central government departments the judiciary is not 'blind to the well-known facts' applicable to the workings of government, as Lord Shaw put it in *London Government Board* v. *Arlidge*.[104] In that case Viscount Haldane LC said:[105]

The Minister at the head of the Board is directly responsible to Parliament like other Ministers. He is responsible not only for what he himself does but for all that is done in his department. The volume of work entrusted to him is very great and he cannot do the great bulk of it himself. He is expected to obtain his materials vicariously through his officials, and he has discharged his duty if he sees that they obtain these materials for him properly. To try to extend his duty beyond this and to insist that he and other members of the Board should do everything personally would be to impair his efficiency. Unlike a judge in a Court he is not only at liberty but is compelled to rely on the assistance of his staff.

Viscount Haldane's approach is enshrined in the *Carltona* principle[106] although juridically the courts regard the issue as not strictly one of delegation but of an official acting as the *alter ego* of the minister.[107] Inklings of a less sympathetic approach to delegation are evident in a recent immigration decision where the House of Lords suggested that the *Carltona* principle may not operate if delegation would conflict with or embarrass the officials in the discharge of duties specifically conferred by statute, or if the decision so conferred was not suitable for the grading and experience of the officials involved.[108] The first qualification need not constitute a disabling factor in administration if it means only that officials should not act when statute clearly intends them not to, or when they would be in breach of long-accepted principles of good administration. But the second qualification is a direct contradiction of what Lord Greene MR said in *Carltona*—'if for an important matter he selected an official of such junior standing that he could not be expected competently to perform the work, the minister would have to answer for that in Parliament.[109] If taken

---

[104] [1915] AC 120.
[105] At 133.   [106] *Carltona Ltd.* v. *Commissioners of Works* [1943] 2 All ER 560.
[107] *R.* v. *Skinner* [1968] 2 QB 700.
[108] *R.* v. *Secretary of State for the Home Department ex p. Oladehinde* [1991] 1 AC 254, 303.
[109] At 563.

seriously, *Oladehinde* opens up for judicial investigation the whole question of the allocation of departmental functions, a matter which one would have thought is both non-justiciable and beyond the immediate ken of the judiciary.

Outside central government the courts have said that on other than purely administrative matters delegation needs statutory authority and cannot be justified on grounds of the difficulty or impracticality of the body or person mentioned in the statute acting itself. Statutory bodies and local authorities have also fallen foul of the maxim of statutory interpretation against delegation in a number of cases where committees have relied on the recommendation of a subcommittee without considering a matter themselves.[110] Legislation has been necessary to overcome the insuperable problems for public authorities which would otherwise have arisen from so strict an approach.[111]

The context of administration

In considering whether to grant judicial review, the courts do sometimes take into account the practicalities of administration. For example, there are cases where they have gone out of their way to acknowledge the boundaries set by financial and time constraints. Except when an absolute statutory duty has to be fulfilled, it seems that they will permit public authorities to have some regard to financial considerations in the exercise of their discretion.[112] Time constraints are less amenable to judicial indulgence, but in one recent case the Court of Appeal took into account the exceptional pressures of time to which the Home Secretary was subjected.[113]

The courts also have some regard to administrative context when exercising their overall discretion to grant a remedy once the grounds of review have been made out. For example in considering whether a remedy ought to be granted in *Ex parte Argyll Group*[114] the Court of Appeal dwelt on a range of factors entering good administration.[115] Similarly, in another commercial case, this time involving the Takeovers Panel,[116] the Court of Appeal said that it would use its discretion in granting remedies to underpin, not undermine, the Panel's operations. It will be evident from

---

[110] *Jeffs* v. *New Zealand Dairy Production and Marketing Board* [1967] 1 AC 551; *R.* v. *Preston BC ex p. Quietlynn Ltd.* (1984) 83 LGR 308.

[111] e.g. Local Government Act 1972, s. 101.

[112] *R.* v. *Brent LBC ex p. Connery* [1990] 2 All ER 353.

[113] *M.* v. *Home Office* [1992] QB 270.

[114] *R.* v. *Monopolies and Mergers Commission ex p. Argyll Group PLC* [1986] 1 WLR 763.

[115] Esp. at 774–5. See also at 778–9; 782–3. Legislation requires consideration of good administration in whether leave should be granted in the event of delay: *R.* v. *Dairy Produce Quota Tribunal for England and Wales ex p. Caswell* [1990] 2 AC 738.

[116] *R.* v. *Panel on Takeovers and Mergers ex p. Datafin PLC* [1987] QB 815, 842.

the argument so far that my view is that courts ought always to have an appreciation of the administrative context when deciding whether and how to grant judicial review.

Impact of Judicial Review

To their shame public lawyers have taken little interest in the impact of judicial review. Yet surely it is the different aspects of this issue which are central to the whole enterprise. Has an applicant actually obtained substantial benefit as a result of successful judicial review? What of others in the same position or a similar position? Are standards of administration in the relevant public authority better for having been exposed to judicial gaze? Has there been any improvement in the standards of government in general following this and other instances of judicial review?

Without the benefit of empirical inquiries our knowledge of the impact of judicial review is patchy. Where successful judicial review has involved a very specific issue, and has attracted publicity, its impact may be traceable. The more diffuse an issue, however, the more likely its impact will not be visible on cursory investigation. If a court decision is implemented, there may be no further cause for complaint, but the vagaries of litigation are such that even if the cause of judicial review persists the matter may not again see the light of judicial day.

We know the sequels to several of the high profile, leading cases on judicial review. After the House of Lords decision in *Padfield*,[117] which established that ministers' discretionary powers are subject to review, the minister referred the matter of milk marketing to a committee of inquiry (thus reversing his original decision not to refer). Although the committee recommended in favour of the complainants, the minister still decided that the pricing structure of the milk marketing scheme should remain unchanged.[118] No doubt *Padfield's* aftermath is not unusual: complainants win reconsideration after successful judicial review only to find a public authority adhering, lawfully, to its original view.

What of decisions on liability, since it is sometimes assumed that the imposition of liability will influence administrative behaviour? *Dorset Yacht*[119] was a House of Lords case imposing liability on a public authority, in that case the Home Office for four young offenders who had escaped from custody, causing damage to property. Subsequently it was difficult to discern any operational changes as a result of the decision. Any tightening of prison security was for other reasons; standing orders of the prison

---

[117] *Padfield* v. *Minister of Agriculture, Fisheries and Food* [1968] AC 997.
[118] HC Deb., vol. 780, cols. 46–7, 31 Mar. 1969.
[119] *Dorset Yacht Co. Ltd.* v. *Home Office* [1970] AC 1004.

service continued to remind governors of penal establishments (without
specific reference to young custody establishments) of the need for care in
conducting the type of scheme which enabled the youths in the *Dorset
Yacht* case to escape; and the Home Office continued to say in its policy
documents that compensation for loss or damage caused by absconders was
paid *ex gratia*, not as a result of a duty in tort (as established by the
decision). Blom-Cooper contends that the absence of any impact of the
Dorset Yacht decision is explained on the ground, as he puts it, that it was
'made, with respect, on wholly inadequate knowledge, or indeed appreciation, of policy considerations relating to prison administration'.[120]

A decision that a public authority reconsider a matter, or a decision on
liability, may not have an immediate discernible impact on the substance of
decision-making. Yet sometimes the legislative framework and particular
outcome of judicial review are such that the public authority must either
take implementing action or stand in defiance of the law. *R. v. Secretary of
State for the Environment ex parte Norwich City Council*[121] was such a case.
Tenants were having difficulty in exercising the right to buy their council
houses in Norwich, the Secretary of State intervened, and the council
challenged this. The Court of Appeal upheld the Secretary of State's order
but expressed the hope that the council would speed up the procedure so as
to avoid further complaints. In fact following the Court of Appeal's
decision the council co-operated with the Department, notably by taking
on more staff to process tenants' applications, and eventually the Secretary
of State withdrew his threat of intervention. It has been said that success in
the courts strengthened the Secretary of State's hand in relation to other
authorities and enhanced the Department's knowledge.[122]

Legislative reversal of the effects of particular decisions on judicial
review is at once both a tribute to its potency but also a reminder that at the
end of the day parliamentary power trumps judicial power. *Anisminic*[123]
was followed by the Foreign Compensation Act 1969; *Malloch* v. *Aberdeen
Corporation*[124] by the Education (Scotland) Act 1973; *Burmah Oil*[125] by
the War Damage Act 1965; and *Puhlhofer*[126] by section 14 of the Housing
and Planning Act 1986. These are House of Lords cases, but legislative
reversal is not confined to decisions of the highest court. The upshot of *R.*

---

[120] L. Blom-Cooper, 'Lawyers and Public Administrators: Separate and Unequal' [1984]
PL 215, 233. Contrast the probable impact of *Egerton* v. *Home Office* [1978] Crim. LR on one
aspect of prison reform: G. Richardson, *Law, Process and Custody* (London, 1993), 89.
   [121] [1982] QB 808.
   [122] R. Forrest and A. Muries, *An Unreasonable Act? Central–Local Government Conflict
and the Housing Act 1980* (1985), 129–30, quoted S. Bailey, B. Jones, and A. Mowbray
(eds.), *Cases and Materials on Administrative Law* (London, 1992), 113.
   [123] *Anisminic Ltd.* v. *Foreign Compensation Commission* [1969] 2 AC 147.
   [124] [1971] 1 WLR 1578.
   [125] *Burmah Oil Co. Ltd* v. *Lord Advocate* [1965] AC 75.
   [126] *R.* v. *Hillingdon LBC ex p. Puhlhofer* [1986] AC 484.

v. *Secretary of State for Social Services ex parte Stitt*[127] was additional government expenditure of £10,000,000 on the Social Fund, but amending legislation was quickly enacted to reverse the long-term effects of the decision.[128] Another example of legislative reversal in the social welfare area involved the Board and Lodgings Regulations. These were introduced in 1985 and constrained claims to social security by those living in bed and breakfast lodgings, hostels, private residential care, and nursing homes. The regulations were attacked in the courts on various procedural grounds. In *Cotton*[129] the Court of Appeal held that the original regulations were *ultra vires* since the Secretary of State did not have the power to fix the cost and time limits contained in them. The challenge was apparently successful because of inadequate preparation by the Department. The regulations were then redrafted and further applications for judicial review were unsuccessful.[130] Legislative reversal, as in other cases, indicates the centrality of rule-making in the modern state.[131]

It is sometimes said that *Cotton* is the only instance in the social security area where judicial review has had any profound impact on the practices of the Department of Social Security. This may be true, but it is speculation. Unfortunately few public lawyers have conducted systematic studies of the complex impact of judicial review on bureaucracies. Loveland is an exception and his excellent empirical research on the homelessness legislation throws some light on the matter.[132] He found that the key determinant in decision-making under the Housing (Homeless Persons) Act 1977 in particular local authorities was the availability of empty properties for allocation to the homeless. When it occurred, judicial review may have had a short-term effect on the perception of senior officers within

---

[127] [1991] COD 68; [1990] COD 288.
[128] HC Deb., vol. 170, col. 22, 26 Mar. 1990. *Annual Report by the Secretary of State for Social Security on the Social Fund 1990–91*, Cm. 1580 (1991), para. 3.3–3.8; *Annual Report by the Secretary of State for Social Security on the Social Fund 1989–90*, Cm. 1157 (1990), para. 3.4–3.5; Social Security Act 1990, s. 10 (3).
[129] *R. v. Secretary of State for Social Services ex p. Cotton*, The Times, 14 Dec. 1985.
[130] G. Stewart, R. Lee, and J. Stewart, 'The Case of the Board and Lodgings Regulations' (1986) 13 *J. Law and Society* 371, 391.
[131] C. Harlow, 'The Justice/All Souls Review: Don Quixote to the Rescue', (1990) 10 *Oxford JLS* 85, 87. Other examples of legislative reversal are collected in C. Harlow, 'Administrative Reaction to Judicial Review', [1976] *PL* 116, 119, 123; Cranston, *Legal Foundations of the Welfare State*, 321–2; P. McAuslan and J. McEldowney, 'Legitimacy and the Constitution: The Dissonance between Theory and Practice', in P. McAuslan and J. McEldowney (eds.), *Law, Legitimacy and the Constitution* (London, 1985), 28–31.
[132] I. Loveland, 'Legal Rights and Political Realities: Governmental Responses to Homelessness in Britain' (1991) 16 *Law and Social Inquiry* 249; id., 'Administrative Law, Administrative Processes, and the Housing of Homeless Persons: A View from the Sharp End' (1991) 10 *J. Social Welfare and Family Law* 4; id., 'Irrelevant Considerations? The Role of Administrative Law in Determining the Local Connection of Homeless Persons', Ch. 9 below. See also P. Birkinshaw, 'Homelessness and the Law: The Effects and Response to Legislation' (1982) 5 *Urban Law and Policy* 255, 285.

a local authority, but it had little if any on day-to-day decision-making. Even at the higher level the concern was to avoid the costs and unfavourable publicity associated with judicial review rather than anything positive. Within the constraints posed by reasons, the motor of day-to-day administration was driven by a range of factors such as inter- and intra-agency relations, conceptions of morality, and expediency. Law rarely became relevant but when it did it was something to be manipulated to reach desired ends.

One of the few systematic studies focusing specifically on the impact of judicial review involves the controversial *Fares Fair* case.[133] That was the decision of the House of Lords holding that the Greater London Council had acted *ultra vires* and in breach of its fiduciary duties to ratepayers with regard to a reduction of fares by the London Transport Executive. The reasoning was that the LTE was obliged to conduct its operation on ordinary business principles and that it and the GLC were acting *ultra vires* with the Fares Fair policy. The breach of fiduciary duty which the House of Lords discovered was said to be because the loss of fares had to be made up from the rates and because the charging policy resulted in a loss of rate support grant.

General incredulity, coupled with disenchantment, greeted the decision both in London and in other local and transport authorities.[134] The response of some authorities was to implement the decision and either to increase fares on public transport or at least not to reduce fares as planned. In other authorities, however, transport policies were devised on legal advice to achieve the level of fares desired.[135] Generally as a result of the case authorities changed the way they made decisions (although not necessarily the decisions themselves). There was a closer involvement of lawyers, especially outside lawyers—sometimes local authorities shopped around for the legal advice they wanted. Cosmetic changes were made to decision-making processes; authorities adopted procedures which would enable them to demonstrate (if challenged) that all relevant factors had been taken into account. As one officer put it:

. . . we generate a lot more paper. . . . there is more, longer writing down of relevant factors and irrelevant factors in decisions. We are now setting down many

[133] *Bromley LBC* v. *Greater London Council* [1983] 1 AC 768.

[134] L. Bridges, C. Game, D. Lomas, J. McBridge and S. Ranson, *Legality and Local Politics* (Aldershot, 1987), 28–9, 39–40. Surprise was especially because of the way the House of Lords construed the legislation: J. Dignan, 'Policy-Making, Local Authorities and the Courts; The GLC Fares' Case' (1983) 99 *LQR* 605; J. Griffith, 'Judicial Decision Making in Public Law' [1985] *PL* 564, 577–9.

[135] In London itself see *R.* v. *London Transport Executive ex p. Greater London Council* [1983] QB 484. See also *R.* v. *Merseyside CC ex p. Great Universal Stores Ltd.* (1982) 80 LGR 639.

things that were previously implicitly understood . . . the lack of acceptance of experience and tacit understanding, all contrive to lengthen and complicate the decision process.[136]

It is very difficult to characterize these changes as an advance. Indeed judicial review in this as with other matters may have had adverse consequences for goals such as accountability and good government. Lawyers may have acquired an undemocratic veto over decisions (or at least provided an excuse for inertia) inasmuch as they can say that a decision will not pass muster if judicially reviewed; bureaucracy may have increased; and more paperwork may actually have confused the elected members. The legalization of issues is not necessarily a step on the road to good government.

The reaction to the *Fares Fair* case illustrates that judicial review may be conceived of as something to be avoided if possible, not something to be welcomed and responded to positively as contributing to good government and administration. This seems to have been the reaction in the central departments of state as a result of increasing judicial review in the 1970s and 1980s. Judicial review has generally been regarded as a nuisance and departments have taken steps to avoid challenge. An official in the planning department of the Department of Environment put it this way:

Much time must now be spent in a painstaking checking operation to make sure that every fact has a clear source in the report and relates to a matter which has been argued at the inquiry . . . decision makers . . . must now do a check on the 'mechanisms' of the decision making process instead of just concentrating on the planning merits.[137]

This reaction is symbolized by the well-known pamphlet *The Judge over your Shoulder*, which is a guide to judicial review prepared by the Treasury Solicitor's department in conjunction with the Cabinet Office. In the course of outlining the basic principles of judicial review, and giving practical advice as to how to avoid it, the pamphlet talks of the increasing willingness of the judges to intervene in the day-to-day business of government, their 'imaginative interpretation of statutes', and the flexibility they have in substituting their own views if there is a decision they do not like.[138] The rather provocative tone of such statements in the pamphlet, however accurate, was wrongly exaggerated by some lawyers into an attack on the rule of law.[139]

The inter-departmental group of senior officials and lawyers, which led to the drafting of *The Judge over your Shoulder*, concluded that there was

---

[136] Bridges *et al.*, *Legality and Local Politics*, 106.
[137] Quoted Harlow and Rawlings, *Law and Administration*, 465.
[138] (London, 1987), 2, 3, 6, 15.
[139] A. Bradley, 'Comment' [1987] *PL* 485.

an urgent need to reduce the risk of successful legal challenge to governmental decisions by more careful drafting, by raising the legal awareness of officials, and by improved training. The only empirical study of the impact of judicial review on central government—a small pilot study—found that the reaction of officials to judicial review was generally tentative and ambivalent. The overall impression was that if the new ethos of judicial review was having an effect it was 'to encourage officials to become more cautious in their work and more aware of the need to explain and justify action.'[140] A Home Office administrator was quoted in this study as opiniong that decision-making was becoming more careful, but not necessarily higher in quality.

In de Smith's aphorism judicial review has only a sporadic, peripheral, and temporary impact on government policy.[141] Without more empirical work we must treat this as an hypothesis rather than a conclusion. But in some respects we should not be surprised if generally this were to be the case. First, there are the characteristic features of how the courts operate, which constrains their power as instruments of social change. The system of precedent, for one, precludes too many bold steps. Of course the courts also have a limited capacity to implement policies (for example of good administration), even if they were inclined to do so; they lack direct power of enforcement; and their moral authority may not be strong in the area of judicial review, which flows against the tide of political legitimacy.

Undeniably judicial review can have an impact benefiting a particular applicant and sometimes a group in the same position as the applicant. In exceptional cases the impact is so significant, at least in the eyes of government, that judicial review prompts legislative reversal. But in general the weight of the evidence, such as it is, is to support de Smith's aphorism. For we know that in many areas the incidence of judicial review is exceptional and its history recent. We have also seen that in many cases judicial review simply mandates the reconsideration of a matter—the public authority may then reach an identical decision, and even if it modifies or reverses the original decision this need have no general impact on how it conducts its business. Finally, judicial review must rank low in the priority of those in the driving seats of public authorities.[142] Implementing departmental policy, working to a tight budget, and coping with the work-load must all rank as more pressing concerns.

More difficult to assess without further empirical inquiry are the 'radiating' effects of judicial review. To what extent have public authorities changed their general practices as a result of the spate of cases since

---

[140] M. Sunkin and A. Le Suer, 'Can Government Control Judicial Review?' [1991] *Current Legal Problems* 161, 174–5.   [141] Evans, *De Smith's Judicial Review*, 3.
[142] A point reflected in the public administration literature: e.g. Pollitt and Harrison, *Handbook of Public Services Management*, 5, 7–15.

Padfield? Answering that question requires some knowledge of the range of signals which public authorities read into public law decisions. As we have seen it also requires detailed study of how these have fashioned the values, procedures, and decision-making of public administrators. It may be that, instead of seeing judicial review as a catalyst for good administration, public authorities may have regarded its shadow as an ominous intrusion, to be side-stepped if at all possible.[143]

A NEW AGENDA

The argument of this chapter is that judicial review is confused about its principles and largely ignorant of its impact. As to the latter I have said that if one's concern is with promoting good government or redressing grievances the courts are not the best avenue for achieving this. As to the former I reject the seductive and popular arguments for judicial imperialism. The underlying theme of this chapter is that the courts should tread warily in granting judicial review if a proper balance is to be maintained between the elected representatives of the people and the judiciary. Any intrusion on to the politically sensitive cannot but sap the courts' moral authority. As regards the substantive grounds of review, their interpretation is already so expansive that the lay person sees what is supposedly eschewed—review on the merits. The legitimacy of the courts' involvement in this way is open to question.[144] If, as I would contend in this chapter, there is a need for judicial modesty, what principles might inform it? The following should be part of the agenda.

Justiciability

The notion that justiciability is a matter of discretion, or can be dealt with on a case-by-case basis, is not especially helpful.[145] A more principled approach to justiciability would focus on the nature of the decision-maker, the political context of the decision, and the decision's analytical character.

The first is straightforward in theory, although not necessarily so in practice. Certainly one institution which should attract an immunity is cabinet; for two centuries it has been regarded as the primary executive organ of government. Its centrality to governmental policy-making, to the

---

[143] *Rowling* v. *Takaro Properties Ltd.* [1988] AC 473, 502.

[144] The matter is expertly canvassed in R. Cotterrell, 'Judicial Review and Legal Theory', Ch. 1 above.

[145] See D. Williams, 'Justiciability and the Control of Discretionary Power', in Taggart (ed.), *Judicial Review*.

political process, and to expressing the political will make judicial review inappropriate.[146] Of course cabinet's decisions once implemented may produce legislative or administrative acts which are properly reviewable. (In theory a particular problem in immunizing cabinet decisions from judicial review is the temptation to interpose cabinet in the decision-making process, even if only as a rubber stamp. Whereas in effect the ultimate decision-maker is the minister or civil servant, decisions are presented as having come from cabinet.[147] In practice this does not seem to be a problem. In any event distinguishing substance from form is a recurrent problem for the law and would not seem to be any more difficult here than in other areas.)

The second aspect of justiciability is the political context of the decision. Judicial restraint is prudent in matters of political controversy, not least because involvement may undermine the authority of the courts.[148] Lord Wilberforce hinted at this in *Gouriet* when he noted that the 'very fact, that . . . decisions are of a type to attract political criticism and controversy shows that they are outside the range of discretionary problems which the courts can resolve'.[149]

Moreover, some matters are obviously best left to elected persons, acting on the advice of officials, and some rights are best protected by the political, rather than the judicial process. Partly this is because political bodies have a wide fact-finding and policy-making capacity, partly because of the diverse backgrounds of their members, and partly also because an issue may have many facets associated with it. Perhaps the extreme example occurred in *Essex County Council* v. *Minister of Housing and Local Government*,[150] where Plowman J rightly accepted the minister's argument that the question of whether, when, and where there should be a third London airport was 'a question of national policy to be resolved in the political arena', and that the applicant council was 'trying to turn a political matter into a justiciable issue'.

Finally, justiciability turns on whether decisions are suitable for adjudication. That depends primarily on whether they are made in accordance with set standards so that the parties may adduce arguments and proofs about their interpretation and application.[151] But, as we have seen, policy decisions of administrators are often concerned with the formulation of general standards for application to an indeterminate

[146] M. Harris, 'The Courts and the Cabinet: Unfastening the Buckle?' [1989] *PL* 251, 279–80, 294–6.
[147] Cf. *Teh Cheng Poh* v. *Public Prosecutor, Malaysia* [1980] AC 458.
[148] Cf. Lord Ackner, 'Judicial Review: Judicial Creativity at its Best' (1987) 61 *Australian Law Journal* 442, 451.
[149] *Gouriet* v. *Union of Post Office Workers* [1978] AC 435, 482.
[150] (1967) 66 LGR 23.
[151] D. Galligan, *Discretionary Powers* (Oxford, 1986), 240–51.

number of future uses and arguments are about the public benefit of one standard over another. Moreover, discretionary decisions of administrators may only be loosely related to general standards since for good reason these are changed in their application. As suggested earlier polycentric decision-making falls outside what can sensibly be reviewed.

If these factors weigh against judicial review of much administrative decision-making what can be reviewed? Most importantly there are the issues of whether a decision-maker has the legal authority to make a decision, if so whether the decision reasonably relates to any purposes contained in that legal authority, and whether in making the decision proper procedures have been adhered to. But it is only such limited matters which should be justiciable.

Exhaustion of remedies

Exhaustion of remedies as a doctrine is less sophisticated in England than in other jurisdictions. Partly this is because the alternative avenues available for appeal are in important respects underdeveloped, inefficient, or subject to time limits.

There are areas such as university administration and wardship where the courts have refused to review because of alternative avenues for redress (the visitor and the statutory child care procedure respectively).[152] In granting judicial review elsewhere, the courts supposedly take account of the alternative remedies available to an applicant. The rule is that, if the alternative remedy is available by way of appeal to a specialized body or a court, the courts will not exercise jurisdiction save in exceptional circumstances.[153] In practice, however, the courts readily exercise jurisdiction, even when an alternative remedy is available, justifying this course because in their view the appeal may not resolve the question fully and directly, or is slower than the procedure by way of judicial review.

In particular cases one can sympathize with the court's approach. Take *Leech* v. *Deputy Governor of Parkhurst Prison*.[154] The Home Secretary had power to remit a disciplinary punishment but not to quash a decision, which still remained on the prisoner's record. The House of Lords held that such an alternative remedy was inadequate and granted judicial review. It was influenced by the fact that disciplinary decisions were handled on the papers alone, and for this reason as well held that the procedure was inadequate since breaches of natural justice were in issue

---

[152] *Thomas* v. *University of Bradford* [1986] Ch. 381; *In re W (Minor)* [1985] AC 791.
[153] *R.* v. *Chief Constable of the Merseyside Police ex p. Calveley* [1986] QB 424; *R.* v. *Secretary of State for the Home Department ex p. Swati* [1986] 1 WLR 477. See C. Lewis, 'The Exhaustion of Alternative Remedies in Administrative Law', (1992) 51 *Cambridge LJ* 138.
[154] [1988] AC 533.

and the appellate authority lacked power to order discovery and could not resolve disputed issues of fact.

However, at least three considerations point in favour of a more developed doctrine of exhaustion of remedies. The first is the purely practical consideration that pursuing the alternative remedy may resolve a matter quickly and inexpensively when compared with a High Court action for judicial review. There is the related point that, when the alternative remedy is available from a special appellate body, that body may have advantages, for example, it may be able to handle factual disputes and may have built up a considerable expertise about the subject-matter of the disputes before it. Finally, there is the point that the exhaustion doctrine is an expression of the constitutional position of the courts. As Lord Donaldson MR said in the *Guinness* case, if Parliament has sanctioned an appeal procedure then it is not for courts to usurp its functions.[155]

Much needs to be done to develop the exhaustion doctrine. It cannot be an absolute rule. Attention needs to be given to the efficacy of the alternative remedy, although it would be too high a standard to demand an equivalence to judicial review of any alternative remedy. That would yet again constitute cultural arrogance on the part of the courts.

Judicial deference

Justiciability is concerned with the institutional role of the courts. It is self-regarding in the sense that it reflects the courts' perception of their role. For that reason it is closely related to the principle of judicial deference— that the courts should, in appropriate cases, defer to decision-making by public authorities. Even if a matter is justiciable, it may still be the case that it is more appropriate that its resolution be handled elsewhere than in the courts.

There are conflicting strands of authority here. In one, no account seems to be taken of the expertise which public authorities or specialist tribunals may acquire, least of all in legal matters such as the interpretation of legislation. Lord Diplock conjured an important constitutional principle that the issue of the construction of both primary and secondary legislation is for the courts and not for others 'however specialised and prestigious they may be'.[156] By contrast there is a strand of deference to public authorities. In *Chief Adjudication Officer* v. *Foster*[157] a social security commissioner concluded that the relevant income support regulations were *ultra vires*, the Court of Appeal held that this issue was a matter for it

---

[155] [1990] 1 QB, at 177.

[156] *Energy Conversion Devices Inc.'s Application* [1983] RPC 231, 253. See also *R.* v. *Local Commissioner for Administration for the South ex p. Eastleigh BC* [1988] 1 QB 855, 866–7.

[157] [1993] 1 All ER 705.

alone, but the House of Lords held that the commissioners did have such jurisdiction. Lord Bridge (with whom the others agreed) gave as one reason for this conclusion the 'great "expertise" of the commissioners in this somewhat estoeric area of the law'.[158]

This strand of deference has sometimes operated in relation to local authorities because of the 'respect which the law requires to be paid to the decisions of elected bodies made within their lawful procedures on matters entrusted to them'.[159] Deference to local authorities can be traced back to the judgement of Lord Russell of Killowen CJ in *Kruse* v. *Johnson*,[160] where he said that when courts are called upon to consider their bylaws they

ought to be approached from a different stand point. They ought to be supported if possible. They ought to be, as has been said, 'benevolently' interpreted, and credit ought to be given to those who have to administer them that they will be reasonably administered. . . . Surely it is not too much to say that in matters which directly and mainly concern the people of the country, who have the right to choose those whom they think best fitted to represent them in their local government bodies, such representatives may be trusted to understand their own requirements better than judges.[161]

This strand of deference seems to have faded in recent times. However it equates to that in the United States, where certainly since the 1940s the tradition of judicial deference to administrative policy has been a central platform of administrative law. Deference extends to questions of legislative interpretation: courts accept any reasonable reading of legislation and do not seek to substitute the 'right' construction. In a leading decision, the Supreme Court of the United States emphatically endorsed judicial deference, giving as reasons that courts should respect the legislative decision to entrust administrative responsibility to agencies, and that policy choices should be made by persons answerable to the political branches rather than by unelected judges.[162] In addition to these considerations based on notions of legitimacy, the argument that administrative agencies are likely to do a better job often features in support of the doctrine.

Judicial deference on United States lines may not be appropriate in other constitutional contexts, but it does give pause when considering the modern orthodoxy in England about judicial review. An intermediate

---

[158] At 712. See also *R.* v. *Secretary of State for the Home Department ex p. Zamir* [1980] AC 930, 948–9. cf. *R.* v. *Secretary of State for the Home Department ex p. Khawaja* [1984] AC 74.

[159] *West Glamorgan CC* v. *Rafferty* [1987] 1 WLR 457, 473. See also authorities cited there and *Dowty Boulton Paul Ltd.* v. *Wolverhampton Corporation (No. 2)* [1976] Ch. 13, 26–7.

[160] [1898] 2 QB 91.   [161] At 100.

[162] *Chevron USA, Inc.* v. *Natural Resources Defense Council, Inc.* 467 US 837 (1984). See also *Young* v. *Community Nutrition Institute* 476 US 974 (1986).

position would accord deference if earned: this would depend on factors such as the public authority's expertise and experience, whether its position is consistent and plausible, whether its position has been formulated thoroughly and in detail, whether the issue is a technical one, and whether (when the matter is one of construction) the public authority participated in the drafting of the measure.

Conclusion

Sedulous and lordly are the proponents of modern judicial review. Without it, to put their argument in a nutshell, the political executive would be in undisputed command of society and individual rights would be trampled. I beg to differ, not because I am unconcerned with individual rights or government wrongs (although it happens that I think politicians and civil servants are often the easy targets for others' failings, including our own). Rather, I am troubled by the constitutional implications of some of the more extreme ambit claims advanced for judicial review; concerned about the inconsistencies and absences of principle in its doctrines; and exasperated that the songs of praise for its beneficent effects and founded on faith rather than hard evidence. Perhaps most importantly I object that the attention lawyers lavish on judicial review diverts their gaze from more fundamental, if less glamorous, mechanisms to redress citizens' grievances and call government to account. These need urgent legal thinking for they must be revamped and supplemented. But explication of that agenda, which strays well beyond judicial review, is for another day.

4

Sovereignty, Accountability, and the Reform of Administrative Law

Alan E. Boyle

INTRODUCTION

In the previous chapter Ross Cranston warns against developments which have given judicial review more prominence within contemporary English administrative law, to the detriment of effective administration. His arguments are those of a long and distinguished tradition among English administrative lawyers, which includes Robson, Griffiths, McAuslan, and more recently Prosser, Loughlin, Harlow, and Rawlings. The essential features which all these scholars have in common are a distrust of judges interfering in government, and a preference for other institutional approaches to the problem of accountability and values in administrative law.

It is this perspective which influenced much of the early concentration on structural and institutional reform of administrative law, involving resort to tribunals, inquiries, and ombudsmen of various kinds, rather than to courts.[1] Together, these reforms, which are considered below, have significantly increased the opportunities for citizens to seek redress against government for maladministration, injustice, and illegality. But, though important in redefining 'the right relationship between the citizen and the State', they have not of themselves fundamentally changed the place of administrative law within British politics and the constitution. Nor, despite its renewed vitality, has judicial review changed the basic assumption that the merits of administrative decisions and policies are political matters, for which government is accountable to Parliament and not to courts, inquiries, ombudsmen, or tribunals. On this view, the scope of administrative law is limited by the same sense of constitutional deference to parliamentary sovereignty that precludes courts from reviewing or rewriting legislation; some notion of a separation of powers, though scarcely

---

[1] See the Donoughmore Committee on Ministers' Powers, Cmd. 4060 (1932); the Franks Report on Tribunals and Inquiries, Cmnd. 218 (1957); JUSTICE, *The Citizen and the Administration* (London, 1961); and the Law Commission's most recent working paper, *Administrative Law: Judicial Review and Statutory Appeal*, Consultation Paper no. 126 (London, 1993).

articulate, has acted as a constitutional restraint and, it could be said, is necessary in a parliamentary democracy where governments, but not courts, are ultimately responsible to the people.

The challenge now posed by European developments, however, is whether and how far the present system of administrative law, and in particular judicial review, will move beyond its past constitutional limitations and take on forms and functions more typical of constitutional review in other jurisdictions. Put another way, how should English administrative law respond to the demands placed on it by European Community law, with its doctrine of legal supremacy,[2] and by the European Convention on Human Rights,[3] with its commitment to certain fundamental values? How above all will the courts respond to a situation in which two external legal orders require English courts to provide effective remedies for rights that may be inconsistent with English law?

What European law has done, both in its EEC form and through the European Convention on Human Rights, is to alter for the first time the historic notion of parliamentary sovereignty and consequently the role of the courts within our constitutional order. Even if one does not yet accept MacCormick's argument that sovereignty in these fields has shifted to the European organs,[4] decisions of the House of Lords in *Factortame (No. 2)*,[5] *Brind*,[6] *Derbyshire County Council*,[7] and the *Equal Opportunities Commission* case[8] reveal something of the extent of the change which has occurred. In this chapter therefore we are concerned with indicating and exploring some important trends and influences on contemporary administrative law whose significance has only gradually become fully apparent. At their most far-reaching they foreshadow nothing less than a revolutionary shift in the balance of power between judges and the state which has persisted since the constitutional settlement forged in the seventeenth century.

The extent and character of this subtle erosion of the notions of parliamentary sovereignty and political accountability contrast with the limited character of earlier reforms in administrative law. It is this emerging European perspective which poses the greatest challenge to Cranston's arguments for judicial restraint. But it also begins to answer some of Cotterrell's concerns about judicial values and the need for a

---

[2] Case 26/62, *Van Gend en Los* v. *Nederlandse Administratie der Belastingen* [1963] ECR 1; Case 70/77, *Simmenthal* v. *Administrazione Finanze dello Stato* [1978] ECR 1453.

[3] UKTS 71 (1953), Cmd. 8969, in force Sept. 1953.

[4] N. MacCormick, 'Beyond the Sovereign State' (1993) 56 *MLR* 1.

[5] *R.* v. *Secretary of State for Transport ex p. Factortame (No. 2)* [1991] 1 AC 603.

[6] *R.* v. *Secretary of State for the Home Department ex p. Brind* [1991] AC 696.

[7] *Derbyshire County Council* v. *Times Newspapers* [1993] AC 534.

[8] *R.* v. *Secretary of State for Employment ex p. Equal Opportunities Commission* [1994] 2 WLR 409.

rethinking of what democracy means in Britain today. The implications of change do not merely relate to the role of judges, but affect the institutions of administrative and constitutional law as a whole, and point to the need to locate reform of administrative law within the context of Cotterrell's arguments for a new political order.

INSTITUTIONAL REFORM: THE FAILED PROMISE OF TRIBUNALS, INQUIRIES, AND OMBUDSMEN

Perceived at the time of their introduction as significant reforms, the Tribunals and Inquiries Act of 1958 and the Parliamentary Commissioner Act of 1967 were symptomatic of an era in which judicial review was largely moribund. The purpose this legislation served was still seen largely in terms of the legitimization of an existing decision-making structure rather than as extending the boundaries of accountability. The citizen was given new opportunities to be heard, and to make complaints of maladministration, but not to challenge government policies or to appeal on the merits of a decision. Tribunals, inquiries, and ombudsmen have remained underdeveloped and relatively static elements in a system of administrative law which since the late 1960s has seen the role of judicial review expanded out of all recognition, partly in response to the limitations of these other institutions. These limitations are easily identified.

Tribunals

The Franks Report on Tribunals and Inquiries saw tribunals as alternatives to courts, not as part of the administration. Their role was to be judicial, their task the application of rules after a more or less formal procedure involving a hearing of the parties and the giving of reasons. Their guiding philosophy, and their main justification in preference to decision-making by administrators, was to be their 'openness, fairness and impartiality'. This model still left policy and administration firmly in the hands of the administrators, where, despite the emergence later of a few semi-independent policy-making tribunals like the Civil Aviation Authority,[9] they have since remained. Moreover, with their own rules of procedure and evidence, tribunals have tended to become markedly more judicial-ized,[10] and to operate in a mainly adversarial way, although some do have features closer to the Continental inquisitorial systems. Their main

---

[9] Civil Aviation Act 1971. See *Laker Airways* v. *Department of Trade* [1977] QB 643, and R. Baldwin, 'A British Independent Regulatory Agency and the "Skytrain" Decision' (1978) *PL* 57.

[10] C. Harlow and R. W. Rawlings, *Law and Administration* (London, 1984), 95.

differences compared to courts are a relative informality, the absence of an automatic right to legal representation, and the fact that they tend to be faster and cheaper.

As institutions, tribunals were thus marginalized by Franks, confined to ensuring the correct application of rules whose content and object were decided elsewhere, but facilitating the exercise of governmental power by affording the citizen the opportunity for a fair hearing. It is in that sense that they have had an effect on administrative procedure. Franks could not guarantee even this limited role for tribunals, however; as one later report noted, 'no consideration was given to the question whether any discretionary decisions which do not at present come under the tribunal system could, with advantage, be brought within it'.[11] Once again, the use of a tribunal was essentially selective, and it was left to governments to make the selection on whatever criteria they chose.[12] In practice only certain areas of governmental decision-making have been surrendered into the hands of independent tribunals: these include aspects of social security, immigration, pensions, transport licensing, and other parts of social and economic policy.[13]

Most tribunals are thus concerned with adjudicating on the application of rules—whether a claimant for social security is or is not entitled to some benefit, whether an immigrant is or is not entitled to enter the country, and so on. With some few exceptions they cannot question the policy or legislation on which their decision rests. Some tribunals are appellate bodies, however: the Immigration Appeals Tribunal[14] is one such example. Here, the tribunal does have power to substitute its decision for that of the initial administrator. Moreover, section 13 of the Tribunals and Inquiries Act provides a right of appeal from a tribunal to a court of law, but only on points of law, not on the merits of the decision. No attempt has been made, however, to establish a general appeal tribunal, a reform long ago advocated by JUSTICE in its 1961 Report *The Citizen and the Administration*. This omission, and the lack of any wider provision for administrative appeals, is perhaps the most obvious structural weakness of our present administrative law.

Inquiries

Inquiries, by contrast, were more clearly viewed by Franks as adjuncts of administration, intended to collect information for the minister by offering a hearing to citizens affected by certain kinds of administrative decisions or

---

[11] JUSTICE, *The Citizen and the Administration*.
[12] G. Ganz, 'Allocation of Decision-Making Functions' (1972) *PL* 215 and 299.
[13] See H. W. R. Wade, *Administrative Law* (6th edn. Oxford, 1988), ch. 23.
[14] Immigration Act 1971.

policies. For the most part, the inquiry system envisaged by the Tribunals and Inquiries Act applied to planning decisions affecting the use of property, such as the construction of new roads or nuclear power plants. Although, increasingly, the inspector conducting an inquiry has become a quasi-independent or even judicial figure, the essential limitation of this process is that the final decision remains the responsibility of the minister. An inquiry is thus only advisory, although in judicial review cases courts have placed a significant burden on ministers of justifying decisions which depart from those recommended by the inquiry inspector.[15]

Inquiries offer a platform which is liberally available to a wide range of individuals and groups interested in the decision at issue. They have given environmental bodies in particular the opportunity to make their case in a public forum and seek in this way to influence through open debate the process of government.[16] But, in practice, Franks's view of inquiries concealed the same basic weaknesses as his concept of the tribunal system: it left the choice of when to use an inquiry in the hands of government, and allowed little or no scope for challenging the policy or decision itself. You could not in most cases argue the need for a motorway or an airport; you could only argue that it should be in someone else's garden, not your own. This limited role was confirmed by the House of Lords in *Bushell* v. *Secretary of State for the Environment*,[17] where their Lordships declined to overrule the inquiry's refusal to consider the accuracy of traffic forecasts and so undermine the Department's case for building new motorways. Procedure at inquiries is very much a matter for discretion for the Minister or the inquiry inspector; no fixed rules are laid down by the 1971 Act. Moreover, as *Bushell* illustrates, in reviewing their operation, the courts have been reluctant to impose too highly judicial a model of due process. Failure to allow cross-examination of witness is thus not regarded as *per se* unfair in this context, and this consequently limits the possibility of real scrutiny of government policy or decision-making.

By the 1970s the public was refusing to play the game of participation in inquiries on these restricted rules, which had become counter-productive as instruments for securing the implementation of policy. Giving back to Parliament the role of conducting an inquiry into the Channel Tunnel was merely an acknowledgement of what had always been the case: that the real decisions were political and the only real power lay with Parliament,

[15] *Coleen Properties Ltd.* v. *Minister of Housing and Local Government* [1973] 1 WLR 433; *Murphy and Sons Ltd.* v. *Secretary of State for the Environment* [1973] 1 WLR 560; *Iveagh (Earl)* v. *Minister of Housing and Local Government* [1964] 1 QB 395; *Bushell* v. *Secretary of State for the Environment* [1981] AC 75.

[16] See generally P. McAuslan, *The Ideologies of Planning Law* (London, 1980), chs. 1–2; Harlow and Rawlings, *Law and Administration*, at chs. 14–15.

[17] [1981] AC 75. Compare *R.* v. *Secretary of State for Transport ex p. Gwent County Council* [1988] QB 429.

which in practice meant with the government. For both tribunals and inquiries the Franks model of the 'right relationship' between authority and the individual left authority a large measure of autonomy from external checks and gave the individual only very restricted possibilities for challenging the decision-makers.

The 'ombudsman' system

The Labour politicians who took office in 1964 could not be expected to foresee their later role as guinea pigs for the development of judicial review. Instead they had their own ideas for keeping the state at bay. Inspired by an appreciation of the limitations of Franks and by the 1961 JUSTICE Report, which identified the absence of any formal machinery outside Parliament for dealing with complaints against discretionary decisions and acts of maladministration as 'a gap in the British Constitution', Parliament in 1967 enacted the Parliamentary Commissioner Act. Pioneered in Sweden and first transplanted to the common law world in New Zealand, the ombudsman concept was intended to be yet another 'important step forward in restoring the balance between the individual and the State'.

Unlike the courts, the ombudsman's methods were to be inquisitorial, not adversarial; he was given privileged access to departmental papers not normally available in judicial proceedings, and, as former administrators, the early ombudsmen were well versed in the ways of Whitehall. These advantages could have been the basis for a radical innovation in the institutions of administrative law. In practice this was not to be, and the ombudsman system has failed to fulfil the aspirations of its founders. One reason, identified by Bradley, is that 'the scheme was notable . . . for erring on the side of caution and for insulating the Ombudsman from the complainants'.[18] Limited to the investigation of individual complaints passed to him through an 'M.P. filter', the parliamentary ombudsman could not seriously conduct systematic inquiries on his own initiative into the quality of the administrative process. Nor, even when broadly construed, did the concept of 'maladministration' allow him to go very far or permit inquiry into the merits of decisions. Few decisions, however questionable, were 'so thoroughly bad in quality' that they could be overturned on that ground alone and the ombudsman was otherwise largely relegated to the investigation of a relatively trivial range of procedural matters such as delay, misrepresentation, and rudeness. Even here, there was increasing overlap with the grounds of judicial review. In several cases, most notably *Congreve* v. *Home Office*,[19] the courts proved

[18] A. W. Bradley, 'Sachsenhausen, Barlow Clowes—and then?' (1992) *PL* 353.
[19] [1976] QB 629.

more willing to remedy abuse of discretionary power than the ombudsman.

Another reason for the ombudsman's marginal impact is described by Harlow: 'parliamentary attachment to ministerial responsibility dictated that the PCA probe only the administrative activities of government and not the exercise of its policy-making or political powers.'[20] This was not a necessary limitation, nor are the reasons for it convincing. Unlike tribunals or the courts, the ombudsman is not an independent decision-maker. He reports to Parliament and relies on parliamentary pressure to ensure that ministers heed his reports. He is not divorced from the parliamentary process but is an integral part of it. There is no reason why he could not equally well report on the merits of administrative decisions and policies, giving Parliament the benefit of a detached viewpoint while leaving to MPs the decision how far to press ministers to think again. This would not be inconsistent with ministerial responsibility, but would complement and strengthen the present select committee system. In confining the ombudsman to investigating maladministration, we can see again a reluctance to create institutions capable of exercising any real control over the executive even when, as here, they are designed to operate within the parliamentary system.

Returning to the point made in the introduction to this chapter, the development of these institutions has posed no challenge to orthodox theories of parliamentary sovereignty and political accountability, and offered no novel constitutional departures for administrative law. What then of 'judicial review'?

REFORMING JUDICIAL REVIEW

The availability of judicial review

Judicial review until the 1970s was a subject in which the substance of the law was still subordinated to the procedure for obtaining individual remedies and thus plagued by technicality. The litigant did not have to have a bad case to lose; he was just as likely to fail because he had chosen the wrong remedy or the wrong proceedings. Private law remedies and prerogative orders were not available from the same court: they overlapped but were not interchangeable. Time limits and other procedural hurdles limited the availability of prerogative orders, whose use was inadvisable in any case likely to turn on disputed or undisclosed issues of fact. Declaration as a remedy avoided these difficulties, but had a narrower test of *locus standi* and would not quash decisions. It could thus only be effective against decisions taken without jurisdiction, and even after

[20] *Law and Administration*, at 201.

Anisminic v. *FCC*[21] it was not clear that all decisions tainted by error of law could fit within this category. For these reasons declaration could not entirely supplant the prerogative orders as an all-purpose remedy, and to allow it to do so would have deprived public authorities of the procedural benefits they enjoyed in prerogative order cases.

These problems were clearly identified by the Law Commission in a report on remedies in administrative law issued in 1976.[22] Implemented first by amending the Rules of the Supreme Court,[23] and then by legislation,[24] the Law Commission's recommendations have produced important procedural reforms, the key to which lies in their fusion of public and private law remedies. By making prerogative orders and private law remedies available in the same proceedings—the application for judicial review—the courts are now able to choose whichever remedy is most appropriate to doing justice in the case before them. And, following the House of Lords' decision in the *National Federation of Self-Employed*[25] case, standing is now available on more liberal terms for all remedies.

These reforms have for the first time given English administrative law some of the characteristics of Continental legal systems. Most notably, a system of public law, distinct and procedurally separate from private law, has emerged. Though partly inspired by the Law Commission's report, this system is largely a judicial creation. The procedural separation of public and private law, which is its most novel and controversial feature, was brought about by the decision of the House of Lords in *O'Reilly* v. *Mackman*.[26] It was neither recommended by the Law Commission nor considered by Parliament. The effect of the separation can be seen in *O'Reilly* and in *Cocks* v. *Thanet District Council*.[27] All judicial review applications against public bodies would now be brought within the procedural mould of Order 53; applications to the Chancery Division or to the county court for declarations would no longer be possible, save in exceptional cases. This did not quite turn the Divisional Court into an Administrative Court, still less a Conseil d'État, but to some extent it has produced a body of High Court judges specializing in administrative law. Moreover, the new procedure has allowed the courts to choose appropriate remedies according to considerations of substance, unhindered by earlier technical

---

[21] [1969] 2 AC 147.

[22] *Remedies in Administrative Law*, Cmnd. 6407 (London, 1976).

[23] Rules of the Supreme Court 1978, Order 53.

[24] Supreme Court Act 1981, ss. 29–31.

[25] *R.* v. *Inland Revenue Commissioners ex p. National Federation of Self-Employed and Small Businesses* [1982] AC 617. But compare *R.* v. *Secretary of State for the Environment ex p. Rose Theatre Trust* [1990] 1 QB 504, and *R.* v. *Secretary of State for Employment ex p. the Equal Opportunities Commission* [1994] 2 WLR 409.

[26] [1983] 2 AC 237.   [27] [1983] 2 AC 286.

or conceptual limitations.[28] Instead of manipulating concepts like jurisdiction, voidness, and voidability to produce the desired result, a process characteristic of the old administrative law, they are now freer to concentrate on developing the policies and principles on which judicial review is based.[29] For litigants, access to judicial review is in some respects easier than before, and, although the point should not be exaggerated, its use has significantly increased, though mostly in cases concerned with homelessness and immigration.[30] For the administrator the same procedural devices—time bars and the need for litigants to obtain leave of court— are supposed to provide protection from late or unmeritorious applications regardless of the remedy sought. The boundaries of this sytem of public law have expanded into areas formerly beyond judicial control, such as the exercise of prerogative powers,[31] or the self-regulatory functions of certain private bodies which control economic activities in accordance with government policy.[32]

But the new Order 53 and the exclusivity principle introduced by *O'Reilly* v. *Mackman* have also brought problems that are once again the subject of a Law Commission inquiry.[33] The most substantial criticisms are that a separate public law procedure with its own rules is unnecessary, that it is difficult to draw the line satisfactorily between public and private law, and that litigants still face the risk of losing, not because their case is bad, but because they began the wrong proceedings. Moreover it is clear that a concentration of all judicial review cases in the High Court, to the exclusion of the cheaper and more accessible county courts[34] and administrative tribunals,[35] is not beneficial, both because its hinders litigants, and because it has contributed to an inexorable rise in High Court

---

[28] See e.g. *Chief Constable of North Wales* v. *Evans* [1982] 1 WLR 1155.

[29] Sir Harry Woolf, 'Judicial Review: A Possible Programme for Reform' (1992) *PL* 221.

[30] See M. Sunkin, L. Bridges, and G. Meszaros, *Judicial Review in Perspective* (London, 1993), who stress that the problem in other contexts is 'certainly not one of over-use'.

[31] *Council of Civil Service Unions* v. *Minister for the Civil Service* [1985] AC 374; R. v. *Secretary of State for Foreign and Commonwealth Affairs ex p. Everett* [1989] QB 811; R. v. *Secretary of State for Foreign & Commonwealth Affairs ex p. Rees-Mogg* [1994] 2 WLR 115.

[32] *R. v. Panel on Takeovers and Mergers ex p. Datafin PLC* [1987] QB 815; R. v. *Advertising Standards Authority Ltd. ex p. Insurance Service PLC* (1990) 2 Admin. LR 77; R. v. *Code of Practice Committee of the British Pharmaceutical Industry ex p. Professional Counselling Aids Ltd.* [1991] COD 228. See D. Pannick, 'Who is Subject to Judicial Review and in Respect of What?' (1992) *PL* 1. Whether this extension of judicial review has enabled the courts to keep pace with the Thatcherite revolution in the structure of government and the devolution of power inherent in the policy of economic deregulation is more questionable: see I. Harden, *The Contracting State* (Milton Keynes, 1992).

[33] Above n. 1.   [34] See e.g. *Cocks* v. *Thanet District Council* [1983] 2 AC 286.

[35] *Chief Adjudication Officer* v. *Foster* [1991] 3 All ER 846, on which see A. W. Bradley, 'Administrative Justice and Judicial Review: Taking Tribunals Seriously?' (1992) *PL* 185; D. Feldman, 'Review, Appeal and Jurisdictional Confusion' (1992) 108 *LQR* 45. The House of Lords, [1993] AC 754, has since held that social security adjudicators and appeal tribunals do have jurisdiction to consider the *vires* of delegated legislation.

judicial review cases with consequential delays in the availability of justice.[36] While the House of Lords has responded to some of these criticisms by seeking to limit the exclusivity principle to cases which directly raise only issues of public law,[37] this has added to the inherent uncertainty of the distinction without addressing the more fundamental problems that the division of public and private law procedures has caused. And although the courts have also been more flexible in allowing applications for judicial review outside the normal time limit of three months, the Law Commission rightly poses the question why so short a limit should be necessary.

The new system's fundamental weakness is thus seen by the Law Commission as being its uncertainty and unpredictability for litigants. If the logic of *O'Reilly* remains unassailable, in that it makes no sense to allow the special procedural rules of Order 53 to be circumvented,[38] there is nevertheless a perception that the present system has failed to give satisfactory weight to the interests of litigants against the needs of public administration and that the principle of exclusivity has been applied with excessive rigour in areas where it is quite inappropriate. The fact that opportunities are so limited for appeal against administrative decisions to a court or tribunal adds to the pressure on judicial review and makes the limitations of that procedure more acute.[39]

Order 53 and European law

The limitations of Order 53 may not matter if one accepts Cranston's thesis about the role of the courts in facilitating effective government. From this point of view, such procedural devices can be seen as yet another facet of the constitutional deference to parliamentary sovereignty and political accountability we considered earlier in this chapter. But Cranston's thesis assumes that the boundaries of judicial review are primarily dictated by the ultimate accountability of government to Parliament. His arguments for judicial restraint are less compelling once the courts take on the role of providing constitutional and legal safeguards in a European political and legal system. In this context their task is not necessarily to guarantee accountability *to* Parliament; it may, if necessary, involve addressing the

---

[36] See M. Sunkin, 'The Judicial Review Case Load, 1987–89' (1991) *PL* 490; Woolf, 'Judicial Review', 221; and for a review of trends in the use and operation of judicial review see Sunkin, Bridges, and Meszaros, *Judicial Review in Perspective*.

[37] *Roy* v. *Kensington and Chelsea Family Practitioner Committee* [1992] 1 AC 624; *Davy* v. *Spelthorne BC* [1984] AC 262; *Wandsworth LBC* v. *Winder* [1985] AC 461; *DPP* v. *Hutchinson* [1990] 2 AC 783; *Chief Adjudication Officer* v. *Foster* [1993] AC 754.

[38] Woolf, 'Judicial Review', at 231.

[39] Law Commission, *Administrative Law*, para. 2.15.

accountability *of* Parliament in order to give effective redress to those relying on EEC law.[40]

This point can be observed in a series of House of Lords cases involving the relationship between UK statutes and EC directives.[41] For the courts, acknowledging the duty to give effect to EC law has entailed increasingly radical departures from orthodox constitutional law, 'including the granting of injunctions against the Crown, suspending the operation of statutes, and effectively rewriting provisions of national legislation'.[42]

Despite judicial assertions to the contrary, the purposive construction of legislation undertaken by the courts in these cases in order to comply with EC directives is only one indication of the tension between parliamentary sovereignty and the judges' evolving constitutional role as guardians of community law. The most remarkable indication of this evolution can be seen in *R. v. Secretary of State for Transport ex parte Factortame (No. 2)*[43] and in *R. v. Secretary of State for Employment ex parte the Equal Opportunities Commission.*[44] Together, these decisions of the House of Lords are among the most important constitutional cases in many years.

Factortame (No. 2) involved an application for an interim injunction to restrain the Crown from enforcing an Act of Parliament against Community nationals on the ground that it would be contrary to Community law to do so. Following the House of Lords' initial refusal to grant an interim injunction against the Crown, the European Court of Justice had held on an Article 177 reference that the supremacy of Community law required the grant of interim relief by national courts where necessary to protect the applicant's Community law rights. The House of Lords thereupon granted the relief sought, Lord Bridge observing that 'in the protection of rights under Community law, national courts must not be inhibited by rules of national law from granting interim relief in appropriate cases'.[45] The earlier rule that the Crown was immune from injunctive relief was simply ignored.

The *Equal Opportunities Commission* case raised the question whether judicial review is an appropriate procedure for securing a declaration that UK legislation is incompatible with Community law. Following *Factortame*, the House of Lords refused to allow technical arguments about the

---

[40] See G. de Burca, 'Giving Effect to E. C. Directives' (1992) 55 *MLR* 215; C. Lewis and S. Moore, 'Duties, Directives and Damages in European Community Law' (1993) *PL* 151; N. Gravells, 'European Community Law in the English Courts' (1993) *PL* 44.

[41] See e.g. *Duke* v. *Reliance Systems Ltd.* [1986] 1 All ER 626; *Pickstone* v. *Freemans PLC* [1989] AC 66; *Litster* v. *Forth Dry Dock and Engineering Co. Ltd.* [1990] 1 AC 546; *Webb* v. *Emo Air Cargo Ltd.* [1993] 1 WLR 49; and for relevant EC cases see Case 14/83, *Von Colson and Kamann* v. *Land Nordrhein-Westfalen* [1984] ECR 1891 and Case C106/89, *Marleasing SA* v. *Comercial Internacional de Alimentación SA* [1990] ECR I-4135.

[42] De Burca, 'Giving Effect to the E.C. Directives', at 227.

[43] [1991] 1 AC 603.   [44] [1994] 2 WLR 409.   [45] [1991] 1 AC 603, at 659.

availability of remedies in judicial review proceedings to determine the outcome of the case. Having concluded that the provisions of the Employment Protection (Consolidation) Act were incompatible with Community law, they granted the Equal Opportunities Commission a declaration accordingly. Lord Keith observed that 'The Divisional Court is the only English forum in which the E.O.C., having the capacity and sufficient interest to do so, is in a position to secure the result which it desires,' even though it might not be appropriate to grant a prerogative order in a case involving primary legislation.

Here, for the first time, we can see an English court in effect grappling with the constitutionality of primary legislation and finding itself forced to rewrite the law of remedies in cases involving the Crown so as to give effect to rights conferred by EC law but denied by Parliament. This is taking judicial review into areas uncharted by English law, using existing remedies and procedures to challenge legislation, in a manner for which they were never designed. Moreover, determining the compatibility of national legislation with EEC law may also require national judges to make value judgments about whether that legislation is necessary and proportionate to its own objectives, and whether those objectives are themselves justifiable under EEC law.[46] These are novel questions for English judges to address whether within the procedure of Order 53 or elsewhere. In the *Equal Opportunities* case we can see how far-reaching this process may be. In effect, the Secretary of State was required to justify the exclusion of certain categories of part-time workers from legislation concerning redundancy pay and employment protection. His argument that exclusion promoted more part-time employment was dismissed by Lord Keith for want of evidence. In coming to the conclusion that the Act's provisions could not objectively be justified, Lord Keith took account of several European Commission reports, a report of the House of Commons Employment Committee, and the practice of other EEC Member States. What is most noteworthy in all of this is not simply the Court's liberal resort to relevant social studies, but its refusal to accept the implicit judgment of Parliament or the explicit opinion of the Secretary of State. It is a rather new constitutional phenomenon for ministers to have to justify primary legislation to judges, and a measure of how far we have departed from the traditional deference to political accountability. This does not mean that political judgments are irrelevant, as Lord Keith's reference to select committee reports shows, but rather indicates that they must be rationally and explicitly made, at least where matters affecting European law are involved. The interplay of judicial and political judgment which

---

[46] See e.g. *Stoke on Trent City Council* v. *B & Q PLC* [1993] AC 900, per Advocate-General Gerven (ECJ), and A. Arnull, 'What Shall We Do on Sunday?' [1991] 16 ELR 112.

these cases entail also makes all the more important the House of Lords' decision in *Pepper* v. *Hart*[47] to allow judicial reference to Hansard if the statute does not disclose the legislative intention.

Nor are the changes which *Factortame (No. 2)* makes to the law of remedies necessarily confined to cases with an EEC law element. In *M.* v. *Home Office*[48] the former Home Secretary, Kenneth Baker, was held by the House of Lords to have acted in contempt of court in his official capacity by contravening an undertaking that M, an applicant for asylum, would not be removed from the jurisdiction. Their Lordships went on to hold that there was power in judicial review cases to grant interim and final injunctions against officers of the Crown, based on section 31 of the Supreme Court Act 1981. This Act, of course, does not say so explicitly; their Lordships' interpretation of it reflects a decision in principle that officers of the Crown should not be in a different position as regards remedies from other respondents, notwithstanding section 21 (2) of the Crown Proceedings Act and earlier cases. The accountability of government ministers to the courts has never before been so firmly stated, or placed on such explicit terms. Though the outcome is unsurprising, it should be seen as part of a broader trend affecting the relationship between the courts and the executive.

Like the emerging influence of European law on the public law of tort,[49] *Factortame (No. 2)* and the *Equal Opportunities* case are only the beginning of what may eventually be a profound change of direction for the courts in English public law. These cases show how the procedure of judicial review is now beginning to assume the role of a constitutional remedy which it enjoys in other systems which possess a formal written constitution and a legislature with limited power answerable to courts. In this important sense, it has moved closer to the position described by Sedley in Chapter 2 above, and away from the interpretation favoured by Cranston.

The limitations of judicial review

Where then do these developments leave judicial reivew? Shorn of its former procedural limitations, it has displayed a far greater vitality than institutions created by earlier reforms. But, as Cranston observed in the previous chapter, judicial review remains, despite these changes, a

---

[47] [1993] AC 593.   [48] [1993] 3 WLR 433.

[49] See *Garden Cottage Foods Ltd.* v. *Milk Marketing Board* [1984] AC 130; *Bourgoin SA* v. *Ministry of Agriculture* [1986] QB 716; *Kirklees MBC* v. *Wickes Building Supplies Ltd.* [1992] 3 WLR 170; and *Francovich and Bonifaci* v. *Italy* [1992] IRLR 84 (ECJ), on which see also R. Carranta, 'Governmental Liability after Francovich' (1993) 52 CLJ 272; M. Ross, 'Beyond Francovich' (1993) 56 *MLR* 55.

fundamentally restricted way of challenging decisions. It is not a system of appeal, nor, in principle at least, a way of attacking the merits of a decision. There remain limits, even if it is not always easy to identify where they are. Those limits are not revealed by simple articulation of the grounds of judicial review. Attractive though Lord Diplock's trilogy of illegality, irrationality, and procedural impropriety may seem,[50] it is deceptively simple, concealing the reality that however described, the principles of review have been, and doubtless always will be, used in a flexible, selective way. The art lies not in defining the principle, but in determining when and how it will be applied. It is in this amorphous fashion that the limits of judicial review have to be determined.

In *R.* v. *Hillingdon LBC ex parte Puhlhofer*,[51] the House of Lords demonstrated the essential selectivity of judicial review by refusing to review a local authority's interpretation of what constituted accommodation under the Housing (Homeless Persons) Act 1977. This was a matter of fact, according to their Lordships, of which Parliament had intended the local authority to be the judge, not the courts. Now the correct meaning of 'accommodation' could just as easily have been treated as a question of law requiring strict interpretation by courts, which is what happened with the Foreign Compensation Commission's construction of the words 'successor in title' in *Anisminic* v. *FCC*.[52] However we explain *Anisminic*, and the position of tribunals like the Foreign Compensation Commission, it is clear that the different approach in *Puhlhofer* indicates a determination to leave local authorities a larger measure of autonomy in administering a difficult social problem, and that much turns in each case on the nature of the institution, and of the power, being reviewed.

Behind cases like this lies an assumption that the limits of judicial review are ultimately constitutional, that a separation of powers between the executive, Parliament, and the judiciary is at issue. In *R.* v. *Secretary of State for Environment ex parte Notts. CC*,[53] Lord Scarman makes these points explicitly. Here the House of Lords refused to review guidance on grant-related expenditure issued to local authorities by the Secretary of State with the approval of the House of Commons. To Lord Scarman, the case concerned a matter of political judgment with which the courts had no right to interfere. Of necessity, the minister's discretion would be exercised on political grounds; only if he had misconstrued the statute or deceived Parliament through bad faith or improper motives could judicial review take the place of political accountability.

---

[50] *Council of Civil Service Unions* v. *Minister for the Civil Service* [1985] AC 374.
[51] [1986] AC 484. See also *R.* v. *Secretary of State for Home Department ex p. Khawaja* [1983] 1 All ER 765; *R.* v. *Secretary of State for Home Department ex p. Bugdaycay* [1987] AC 514.   [52] [1969] 2 AC 147.   [53] [1986] AC 240.

This may seem an obvious and necessary limit on the scope of judicial review; judges are after all not suited to making the political judgments which Parliament and government are elected to make. But what is it which makes political judgment a necessary and legitimate part of the minister's decision in *Notts.*, where in *Padfield*[54] and *Bromley*[55] the same exercise of political judgment merited judicial review? The different outcome is not the product of different principles of review; rather it illustrates again the selectivity of that process, in which the result turns on the judge's view of the scope and purpose of the power in question. Cranston is correct to argue that this is essentially unpredictable and that what is justifiable in one case may not be in another. Nevertheless it is a limit of sorts; judges cannot simply substitute their view of what is right for the decision-maker's.

Nor it seems can judges substitute judicial review for other more appropriate remedies, where these are available. A feature of recent case-law is the emergence of a principle precluding the use of judicial review unless alternative remedies have been exhausted. In *R. v. IRC ex parte Preston*[56] the House of Lords allowed judicial review of a decision of the Inland Revenue Commissioners, but only after making it clear that where Parliament provides an appeal 'it will only be very rarely that the courts will allow the collateral process of judicial review to be used to attack appealable decisions'. And in *R. v. Secretary of State for the Home Dept. ex parte Swati*[57] this reasoning led the Court of Appeal to refuse leave for judicial review to immigrants denied permission to enter the UK. Since an appeal procedure existed, judicial review should not be used unless there was an exceptional case requiring it. Fearful perhaps of the growing tide of judicial review cases, these decisions show judicial review in a strictly confined role. Only if there is no other suitable remedy, and only if the case raises a justiciable issue of law, will judicial review be a useful means of challenging decisions of public bodies. Like the institutions considered in the previous section, it too is ultimately peripheral, an indirect and artificial remedy of little real interest to many of those who have to use it. What most litigants actually want, but cannot get, save in the few cases where appeal tribunals exist, is a means of challenging and changing decisions whose substance they do not like. Even in its most developed form judicial review is no substitute for this.

But here too, traditional assumptions of this kind now face conflicting European influences, most notably from the European Convention on

---

[54] [1968] AC 997.
[55] [1983] 1 AC 768. Cf. P. McAulsan, 'Administrative Law, Collective Consumption and Judicial Policy' (1983) 46 *MLR* 1.   [56] [1985] AC 835.   [57] [1986] 1 WLR 477.

Human Rights, in terms both of the institutional arrangements it requires, and of the scope of review.

THE IMPACT OF THE EUROPEAN CONVENTION ON HUMAN RIGHTS

Human rights as a basis of judicial review

The European Convention on Human Rights[58] is simply a treaty to which the United Kingdom is a party; it does not have the force of statute and it lacks the legal status in the United Kingdom that EEC law possesses by virtue of the European Communities Act 1972. Failure to comply with the Convention is, however, a matter for which the United Kingdom may be held responsible before the European Court of Human Rights, not merely in interstate cases,[59] but also as respondent to individual applicants alleging they are victims of a violation.[60] In the latter respect it differs from other treaties to which the United Kingdom is a party. The obligation to ensure compliance with the Convention applies to courts as well as to governments;[61] not only does this affect the interpretation of statutes, but where a breach of the Convention is established it becomes incumbent on the United Kingdom to bring its law and practice into conformity with the Convention as interpreted by the European Court of Human Rights.[62] Where necessary, settled rules of common law must be changed, if not by the courts themselves, then by legislation.[63] Thus, although not formally part of English law, the Convention cannot be ignored by either Parliament or the courts. Despite its unenacted status, it does have an impact on English law.

Human rights standards are already a basis for judicial review in European Community law, and elsewhere in European systems of public law. Their explicit adoption by English courts would give English administrative law a radically wider scope of judicial review, no longer limited to essentially technical questions of procedure, reasonableness, and interpretation. Statutory incorporation of the Convention into English law would thus represent a major reform of far-reaching significance for administrative law. But non-incorporation does not mean that it cannot be a basis for judicial review.

The decision of the House of Lords in *R.* v. *Home Secretary ex parte*

---

[58] Above n. 3.   [59] e.g. *Ireland* v. *UK* (1978) 2 EHRR 25.
[60] Convention, Art. 25.   [61] e.g. *Sunday Times* v. *UK* (1979) 2 EHRR 245.
[62] Convention, Arts. 1, 53, 54, 57.
[63] e.g. *Malone* v. *UK* (1984) 7 EHRR 14; *Sunday Times* v. *UK* (1979) 2 EHRR 245.

Brind[64] shows only that their Lordships were unwilling in that case to allow judicial review to be governed explicitly by the European Convention in the absence of statutory incorporation. By rejecting any presumption that a statutory discretion must be exercised in accordance with the Convention they in effect limited the possibilities for invoking its provisions in judicial review proceedings to cases where the statutory power in question was ambiguous but capable of bearing a construction which complies with the Convention, or to those where the decision to interfere with human rights either ignored the Convention altogether or lacked sufficient justification and was therefore unreasonable on *Wednesbury* grounds. In *Brind* itself, the applicants would thus have had to show that there was no material on which a reasonable Secretary of State could reasonably conclude that interference with freedom of expression was necessary and proportionate to the harm it was sought to prevent.[65] But the courts would not simply substitute their own view on this question for that of the Secretary of State.

Brind was arguably a weak case on which to base an attempt to broaden the scope of judicial review, since the Convention itself leaves national authorities a significant 'margin of appreciation' to decide how far to go in restraining freedom of expression.[66] But the reasoning in the case remains fundamentally flawed. By limiting their own role to the resolution of ambiguities and review based on *Wednesbury* unreasonableness, the House of Lords in effect left it to judges of the European Court of Human Rights to substitute their view of what is necessary and proportionate under the Convention. This disparity between the powers of review of the ECHR on the one hand and English courts on the other means that their Lordships' approach will not necessarily be enough to escape condemnation in Strasbourg and legislative intervention. Once it is appreciated that the courts must themselves provide an adequate and effective remedy to ensure conformity with the Convention,[67] the inadequacy of the reasoning in *Brind* becomes apparent.

That human rights *are* part of English common law is shown by the decision in *Derbyshire County Council* v. *Times Newspapers*.[68] This was the case in which a local authority thought it could suppress critical comment by suing for libel. The House of Lords had no doubt that democratically elected public bodies should be open to uninhibited public criticism free from the fetter of civil actions. Without expressly relying on the European Convention, they observed that the common law's protection of free speech did not differ from Article 10 of the Convention, and concluded that public bodies had no right to sue for libel. The futility of

---

[64] [1991] 1 AC 696.   [65] Ibid., per Lord Templeman at 750–1.
[66] See Art. 10.   [67] Art. 13.
[68] [1993] AC 534. See also *Rantzen* v. *Mirror Group Newspapers Ltd.* [1993] 3 WLR 953.

holding otherwise in circumstances where the defendant was bound to succeed before the European Court of Human Rights hardly needs stressing.

What *Derbyshire* also suggests, however, is that at least some of the rights set out in the European Convention can acquire a common law status, which the courts should protect in whatever form the proceedings may arise. This view has the support of several senior judges.[69] The House of Lords has already accepted in *Bugdaycay*[70] that the courts should be more rigorous in their scrutiny of administrative powers which contravene human rights, but to do so simply on a basis of *Wednesbury* unreasonableness still risks giving too little weight to the fundamental rights at issue in these cases. The implications of a more demanding standard of scrutiny following the *Derbyshire* case are succinctly put by Laws J: 'What is therefore needed is a preparedness to hold that a decision which overrides a fundamental right, without sufficient objective justification, will as a matter of law, necessarily be disproportionate to the aim in view.'[71] *Derbyshire* may thus have breathed new life into the concept of proportionality as a standard of judicial review in fundamental rights cases,[72] notwithstanding its apparent rejection in *Brind*, and in this way it has opened up the possibility of a very significant expansion of the substantive grounds of review. Laws J goes on to argue that the use of statutory powers to violate human rights should also be regarded as acting for an improper purpose unless the statute clearly does authorize interference with fundamental rights.

None of this erodes the sovereignty of Parliament as such, but, as with the wording of ouster clauses, it means that legislation must be very much more explicit before it can be used to limit rights the courts now wish to protect. As in the case of EEC law, it means that judges may have to alter their approach to the interpretation of statutes and make value judgments on issues such as proportionality and necessity which they would never have done before.

Moreover, in the context of EEC law, British courts are already bound to have regard to the European Convention on Human Rights, since the ECJ itself relies on the Convention to determine the legality and construction of the Community treaties and legislative and administrative

---

[69] Lord Browne-Wilkinson, 'The Infiltration of a Bill of Rights' [1992] *PL* 397; The Hon. Sir John Laws, 'Is the High Court the Guardian of Fundamental Constitutional Rights?' [1993] *PL* 59; Right Hon. Sir Thomas Bingham MR, Denning Lecture, 2 Mar. 1993.

[70] [1987] AC 514.   [71] [1993] *PL* at 74.

[72] On proportionality see J. Jowell and A. Lester, 'Proportionality: Neither Novel nor Dangerous', in J. Jowell and D. Oliver (eds.), *New Directions in Judicial Review* (London, 1988), and for application of the concept by the Court of Appeal see *Rantzen* v. *Mirror Group Newspapers Ltd.* [1993] 3 WLR 953.

acts.[73] The obligation of national courts to apply Community law will thus include an obligation where relevant to apply the ECHR, whether or not it is directly incorporated into national law.[74] As Grief also points out, 'the E.C.J.'s case law makes it clear that the Convention is at least relevant with regard to the domestic implementation of Community Law'.[75] In such cases the principle of supremacy of Community law, on which *Factortame (No. 2)* rests, will also extend, at least in general terms, to the European Convention on Human Rights.[76]

The European Convention on Human Rights and the structure of administrative law

That Convention is also relevant to the institutions and structures of administrative law, and to the availability of appeals on the merits of decisions. Article 6 (1) provides for a 'fair and public hearing' by an 'independent and impartial tribunal' in the determination of 'civil rights and obligations' or of any 'criminal charge'. A growing body of ECHR case-law[77] has applied this article to administrative law issues. Its main impact has been to require the use of appellate tribunals empowered to reconsider the merits of a decision. It thus goes further than the English concept of natural justice, which is largely concerned with *how* a decision should be made, not *who* should make it. The implications of this interpretation for English law are worth consideration here, and are further explored by Genevra Richardson in Chapter 5 below.

The European Court has construed Article 6 to require what is essentially a judicialized form of due process. The tribunal must be independent of the parties, and of the executive, it must hold its proceedings in public, pronounce its decision publicly, and ensure a fair hearing of both parties, which seems in most cases to require an oral hearing. The Court has shown some flexibility in regard to these requirements, but in substance it envisages a model of procedural due

[73] Case 136/79, *National Panasonic (UK) Ltd.* v. *Commission* [1980] ECR 2033; Case 44/79, *Hauer* v. *Land Rheinland-Pfalz* [1979] ECR 3727; Case 374/87, *Orkem* v. *Commission* [1989] ECR 3283; See also the Maastricht Treaty on European Union, Art. F of which provides that 'The Union shall respect fundamental rights as guaranteed by the European Convention for the Protection of Human Rights and Freedoms . . . and as they result from the constitutional traditions common to the Member States, as general principles of community law.'

[74] For examples, see Case 63/83, *Kent Kirk* v. *UK* [1984] ECR 2689; Case 5/88, *Wachauf* v. *Germany* [1989] ECR 2609.

[75] N. Grief, 'The Domestic Impact of the European Convention on Human Rights as Mediated through Community Law' (1991) *PL*, at 567.

[76] Ibid., at 566; Browne-Wilkinson, 'The Infiltration of a Bill of Rights', at 398.

[77] See generally A. E. Boyle, 'Administrative Justice, Judicial Review and the Right to a Fair Hearing under the European Convention on Human Rights' (1984) *PL* 89.

process very similar to that for tribunals described in the Franks Report. In *Campbell and Fell* v. *UK*[78] the Court reviewed the question whether the Board of Prison Visitors, a tribunal responsible for punishing serious misconduct by prisoners, met the requirements of Article 6 (1). It held that in assessing the independence of a tribunal regard should be had to the manner of appointment of members, the duration of their term of office, the existence of guarantees against outside pressure, and the appearance of independence. It found that the Board members were in practice, though not in law, irremovable, and acted independently despite the short duration of their appointment, and their involvement in the general supervision of the prison. Although the Board did not hold its proceedings in public, the Court was prepared to find that this did not contravene Article 6 (1) provided its decision was pronounced in public. Most British tribunals would thus be very likely to pass scrutiny under Article 6 (1).

But what about those cases where Enlgish law affords no right to an independent tribunal? It is here that Article 6 (1) is important, since its primary effect, as we have seen, is to guarantee the right to a tribunal. Leaving decisions entirely in the hands of government ministers, or their departments, cannot satisfy this requirement. No constitutional principle exists in English law to determine whether a tribunal must be established; by focusing on decisions which affect 'civil rights and obligations', Article 6 (1) has come close to supplying such a principle. That the Convention does require a full appeal before an independent tribunal on the merits and not just judicial review of the legality of the decision can be observed in the cases of *Sporrong*[79] and *Le Compte*.[80] Here the availability of judicial review was held to be insufficient to satisfy the requirements of Article 6. It is true that large areas of discretionary decision-making by public bodies are excluded from Article 6 (1) by the narrow interpretation given by the Court to 'civil rights and obligations', and its distinction in this context between private rights to which the Article does apply and public rights to which it does not. But decisions affecting liberty, property, employment, or family are undoubtedly about 'private' rights.[81] Moreover, in subsequent cases, including *Benthem*,[82] *Feldbrugge*,[83] and *Deumeland*,[84] the Court has

---

[78] (1982) 5 *EHRR* 207.   [79] *Sporrong and Lonnroth* v. *Sweden* (1982) 5 *EHHR* 35.
[80] *Le Compte, Van Leuven and De Meyere* v. *Belgium* (1981) 4 *EHHR* 1; *Albert and Le Compte* v. *Belgium* (1982) 5 EHRR 533.
[81] Boyle, 'Administrative Justice', at 90–7, and see *Eriksson* v. *Sweden* (1990) 12 EHRR 183; *Fredin* v. *Sweden* (1991) 13 EHRR 284; *Hakansson* v. *Sweden* (1991) 13 EHRR 1; *Wiesinger* v. *Austria* (1993) 16 EHRR 258.
[82] *Benthem* v. *The Netherlands* (1985) 8 EHRR 1; see also *Tre Traktörer Aktiebolage* v. *Sweden* (1991) 13 EHRR 309.
[83] *Feldbrugge* v. *Netherlands* (1986) 8 EHRR 425, on which see A. W. Bradley, 'Social Security and the Right to a Fair Hearing' (1987) *PL* 3.
[84] *Deumeland* v. *Germany* (1986) 8 EHRR 448; Bradley, 'Social Security'.

given a broader interpretation to this phraseology than hitherto and applied Article 6 to decisions which involve the licensing of business activities, and entitlement to sickness benefit and pensions.

Thus, for English law, Article 6 (1) stands as a potential basis for the creation of a wider range of appeal tribunals, and possibly a more general appeal tribunal. No case has yet raised this lacuna directly in England, but a comparable example, based not on Article 6 (1), but on Article 5, is the case of *X*,[85] in which the United Kingdom was obliged to establish an independent tribunal to review the continued detention of mental patients. This is the first of several cases in which the Convention has required institutional reform of administrative procedures dealing with different forms of detention in the UK.[86]

Another possibility is that, instead of creating new tribunals to meet the needs of Article 6, the jurisdiction of courts could be extended beyond the traditional confines of judicial review by giving them a wider appellate jurisdiction in appropriate cases. Such a development would bring English courts closer to the French Conseil d'État or the Australian Administrative Appeals Tribunal in reviewing the merits of administrative decisions.

ADMINISTRATIVE LAW AND CONSTITUTIONAL REFORM

As we have seen, administrative law in the United Kingdom has traditionally faced certain structural constraints. These can be summarized as the limited role of judicial review, uncertainty surrounding the use of independent tribunals, and the failure to develop a stronger system of administrative appeals. These weaknesses are partly the consequence of certain basis assumptions about the structure of government within the British constitution. Most importantly, the concept of governmental accountability to Parliament has generally been thought to preclude the exercise of independent political authority by courts, tribunals, or other bodies not accountable to democratic control. This is a strong argument of principle, which differentiates the United Kingdom from federal systems such as the United States or Germany. A more pragmatic argument against change is that British judges are by training exclusively lawyers: they do not for example enjoy the mixture of legal and administrative training that members of the French Conseil d'État possess. Those who decide administrative law cases are simply common lawyers with the same

---

[85] *X* v. *United Kingdom* (1981) 4 EHRR 188.
[86] *Weeks* v. *UK* (1987) 10 EHRR 293 and *Thynne, Wilson and Gunnell* v. *UK* (1991) 13 EHRR 666 have led to changes in the powers of the Parole Board under the Criminal Justice Act 1992; see G. Richardson, 'Discretionary Life Sentences and the European Convention on Human Rights' [1991] *PL* 34.

background and career structure as other judges. Thus the argument has been put that they are unsuited to making judgments on the merits of governmental decisions, and should confine their role to adjudicating questions of legality: to judicial review, rather than administrative appeal.

Nevertheless, experience in other common law jurisdictions with closer similarity to the British legal system does suggest that these objections are not insurmountable. In Australia, an Administrative Appeals Tribunal[87] has been established to hear appeals on a range of decisions concerning immigration, discretionary benefits, customs and excise, health and welfare, and other matters. This tribunal has three distinctive features. Like British tribunals, its membership is drawn from a range of backgrounds and is not limited to those with legal skills, although it is presided over by a judge. Unlike most British courts and tribunals, it has adopted a more inquisitorial style of operation in some cases. What differentiates it most from the UK, however, is its power to substitute the 'right or preferable' decision for that of the administrator, and, if necessary, to depart in doing so from government policy. This is a genuine appellate function on the merits of individual decisions. Though sparingly exercised, it is much more extensive than judicial review, and goes beyond what most British tribunals are permitted to do. Although the AAT is not accountable to Parliament for its decisions, it remains open to the legislature to change the law if dissatisfied with the outcome of any particular case. The merit of this system is that it provides a cheap and easy way for the citizen to have his case fully reconsidered by a body with a wider experience than the average judge. It also provides a means of improving the quality of decision-making in government and complements parliamentary scrutiny of the executive.

Proposals have been made for similar reforms in the United Kingdom. At least one senior judge has called attention to the merits of developing the tribunal system on the Australian model as a means of reducing the work-load of the High Court and improving the quality and accessibility of administrative proceedings. In his view 'the way forward over a period of time should thus involve creating a unified system of tribunals for resolving administrative disputes, with the High Court and Court of Appeal required to resolve only difficult problems of law and points of principle and policy of high importance to the development of administrative law.'[88]

---

[87] Administrative Appeals Tribunal Act 1975. See generally M. Kirby, 'Administrative Review: Beyond the Frontier Marked Policy' (1981) 12 *Federal LR* 121; id., 'Administrative Review on the Merits: The Right or Preferable Decision' (1980) 6 *Monash Univ. LR* 171; A. N. Hall and R. K. Todd, 'Administrative Review before the AAT: A Fresh Approach to Dispute Resolution' (1981) 12 *Federal Lr* 71 and 95; G. Osborne, 'Inquisitorial Procedure in the AAT' (1982) 13 *Federal LR* 150.   [88] Woolf, 'Judicial Review', at 230.

More radical schemes of constitutional reform would have a more profound impact on administrative law. The Institute for Public Policy Research has published a draft constitution for the United Kingdom which would incorporate a Bill of Rights based on the European Convention on Human Rights and the International Covenant on Civil and Political Rights.[89] Persons whose rights or freedoms have been infringed would be entitled to damages, injunctions, and other appropriate remedies, without prejudice to their right to judicial review. Judicial review would be regulated by statute, and its scope would also be much expanded by incorporation of a Bill of Rights. An independent Director of Civil Proceedings would be empowered to bring proceedings *inter alia* for judicial review, contravention of the Bill of Rights, or other provisions of the constitution. A Commission for Public Administration would replace the Parliamentary Commissioner for Administration, local government ombudsmen, and the Council on Tribunals, but its powers would be left to Parliament to determine, and it would not necessarily have the appellate function envisaged by an earlier SDP proposal.[90]

Reforming administrative law has been seen by some as an essentially technical process of making modest improvements in the existing procedures for obtaining judicial review, the powers of ombudsmen, and the operation of tribunals and inquiries. The Report of the JUSTICE/All Souls Review of Administrative Law has taken this approach,[91] and the Law Commission's Consultation Paper no. 126 follows in the same vein. However, this chapter has sought to argue that the problem cannot be seen as one of administrative law and procedure alone. It is part of a wider debate about the forms of political and legal accountability and the reform of the British constitution within a European legal and political setting.[92] Thus we return to our starting-point: administrative law is about the exercise of power in society; it cannot be divorced from broader political choices about the structure of government and the constitutional order.

When that constitutional order is changing, as it may be, at present, in the United Kingdom, alterations in the relationship of government, Parliament, and the courts are inevitable. Many of the most recent developments we have observed in administrative law are not the product of any organized endeavour of constitutional reform; rather they show judges responding in individual cases to the demands of a new European

[89] IPPR, *The Constitution of the United Kingdom* (London, 1991).
[90] See Social Democratic Party, *Taming Leviathan: Towards Fairer Administration* (1983), commented on by A. E. Boyle, 'Reforming Administrative Law' (1984) *PL* 521.
[91] Report of the Committee of the JUSTICE/All Souls Review of Administrative Law in the UK, *Administrative Justice: Some Necessary Reforms* (1988).
[92] On constitutional reform see in particular N. Johnson, *In Search of the Constitution* (London, 1977), and D. Oliver, *Government in the United Kingdom: The Search for Accountability, Effectiveness and Citizenship* (London, 1991).

constitutional order, in a piecemeal, *ad hoc*, but surprisingly consistent way. As *Marbury* v. *Madison*[93] reminds us, no constitution, whether written or not, is ever static. In the present context, British judges are simply acting to fill the empty spaces between Parliament and Europe, where British notions of political accountability have given way to much stronger forms of judicial supervision. Those who do not like judges in this void must find some other way of filling that gap. Those who want to reform Order 53 must bear in mind the major constitutional role that procedure is now beginning to assume. If there is a pressing need to reduce the increasing volume of litigation Order 53 faces, then it is time to think again about the role of tribunals, inquiries, and ombudsmen, and about the conventions of parliamentary accountability which have historically limited their roles and generated so much pressure on judicial review as a surrogate for the inadequacy of the rest of our system of administrative law. But it is important not to take too narrow or blinkered a view of the role of judicial review; remedies will continue to exert the profound influence they have always had on the development of English law, whether public or private.

---

[93] 5 US (1 Cranch.) 137 (1803).

5

The Legal Regulation of Process

Genevra Richardson

The purpose of this chapter is to examine the possible justifications for the involvement of the common law in the regulation of process within the public law sphere. Two preliminary points must be made. In the first place the notion of process requires some explanation. At its widest process, within the context of public law, can cover both the structure and the procedure of all the bodies involved in the evolution and the application of policy. It thus includes not only process in the narrow sense of the procedures adopted by administrative and judicial bodies when applying policies to individuals, but also the structure and constitution of these policy-applying bodies together with both the structure and the procedures of the bodies responsible for formulating the initial policy itself.[1] Secondly, for the purposes of the present discussion it is necessary to adopt a very simple classification of public decision-making: policy formulation, policy application, and policy validation. The first two categories are self-explanatory, if not mutually exclusive: a decision to apply a policy in a particular way to a specific set of circumstances may act as a precedent to guide future application decisions, thus constituting policy formulation in addition to application. Policy validation occurs when an application, or possibly a formulation, decision is challenged. Thus process in its broadest sense covers both the structure and the procedures of decision-making bodies at all three stages of policy implementation. However, for reasons which will be considered below, the common law has traditionally confined itself to the regulation of process in the narrow procedural sense and has directed most of its energy to application and validation decisions at the possible expense of policy formulation.

The discussion which follows will fall into four main sections. At the outset a very brief description will be provided of the ways in which the law can become involved in the regulation of public process, and the justification for that involvement in terms of orthodox constitutional principle. The second section will consider the main approaches adopted by the legal literature to the common law's involvement in the regulation of

---

[1] For a discussion of process in this broad sense, see L. Tribe, *Constitutional Choices* (Cambridge, Mass., 1985), and P. Craig, *Public Law and Democracy in the United Kingdom and the United States of America* (Oxford, 1990).

process in the narrow sense. In the third section current judicial practice will be examined in the light of the conceptual approaches outlined in the previous section, while in the fourth section consideration will be given to alternative and broader approaches to the law's involvement in process and the practical implications of such alternatives.

THE LAW'S INVOLVEMENT IN PROCESS AND ITS PLACE IN ORTHODOX CONSTITUTIONAL THEORY

As will be suggested below, much of the law's current involvement with process can be explained by reference to orthodox constitutional principles. Although the United Kingdom has no written constitution, constitutional lawyers have identified certain fundamental principles which are said to govern the relationship between public bodies and between individuals and public bodies. Briefly stated these principles which, as Cotterrell suggests above in Chapter 1, are strongly influenced by the *imperium* image of society, include: the legislative supremacy of Parliament, the separation of powers, and the rule of law. At the heart of the system lies the supremacy of Parliament.

Process broadly defined

In order to set the law's involvement in process in its orthodox constitutional context it is important to appreciate the implications of these constitutional principles for the role of the courts. Process in its broad sense, encompassing both the structure of policy-applying bodies and the structure and procedure of policy-formulating bodies, will be taken first.

With regard to Parliament, the ultimate policy formulator, the courts perform a very limited role. Although the composition of Parliament is to some extent regulated by the law and supervised by the courts through the rules governing the electoral system, the ordinary law has little influence within the Houses of Parliament themselves. According to established legal doctrine no court can inquire into the procedures adopted by the legislature during the conduct of a bill through the two houses of Parliament.[2] Parliamentary process itself is therefore outside the jurisdiction of the ordinary courts. Secondly, when Parliament sets up a decision-making structure no court can challenge the lawfulness of that structure. Thus, if Parliament wished to exclude the accused from the criminal trial or to insist that the parole board be comprised exclusively of prisoners serving life sentences, no domestic court could object. Parliament is legislatively supreme: it expresses the will of the people.

---

[2] *Edinburgh and Dalkieth Railway* v. *Wauchope* (1842) 8 Cl. and F. 710.

Thus, ostensibly at least, the courts have to accept the process requirements provided by Parliament. The position is different in international law where Parliament has ratified our adherence to an international convention, as is the case with the European Convention on Human Rights. Thus in *X* v. *United Kingdom* a mentally disordered offender, compulsorily detained in hospital, was able to challenge the structure provided by the Mental Health Act 1959 to govern decisions concerning his discharge.[3] Subsequent to the ruling of the European Court that domestic law failed to comply with the obligations imposed by the European Convention, the relevant statutory provisions were changed.[4] Most typically, as in *X*, the process requirements imposed by the European Convention involve the prescription of adjudication where domestic law relies on some form of executive or administrative decision-making, and the imposition of more stringent procedural safeguards before existing adjudicatory bodies. However, the requirements of the Convention do also relate to the way in which the law itself is articulated and they have been used to impose conditions of certainty and publicity on administrative rules.[5]

Once Parliament has created the basic structure of decision-making the High Court, in the exercise of its supervisory jurisdiction, has the power to intervene to ensure that the empowered bodies perform the tasks allotted to them. The common law doctrine of *ultra vires* enables the High Court to strike down a decision that it considers to be outside the powers of the inferior body. It is a very expansive doctrine that can impinge on questions of process, broadly defined, in a number of ways. In the first place, in its substantive guise the doctrine of *ultra vires* requires that a public body act within its powers: it must make only those decisions it is empowered to make and must not act unreasonably or irrationally. The application of these rules, despite the substantive label, can touch on matters of process. In *Ex parte Handscomb* the court held that the Home Secretary's policy of delaying, for three to four years, consultation with the trial judge over the earliest date for the release of a life sentence prisoner was unreasonable.[6]

Secondly, a body which is vested with discretionary powers must exercise those powers itself; it cannot delegate them to another body, nor can it fetter itself by adopting a preordained, inflexible policy. If it does so it is acting *ultra vires*, it is failing to use a discretion given to it.[7] In *Re*

---

[3] (1981) 4 EHRR 181.   [4] See Mental Health Act 1983, Part V.

[5] See *Silver* v. *United Kingdom* (1980) 3 EHRR 473. The imposition of procedural requirements by the European Convention is discussed further in Ch. 4 above.

[6] *R.* v. *Secretary of State ex p. Handscomb* (1987) 86 Crim. App. R. 59.

[7] *British Oxygen Co. Ltd.* v. *Board of Trade* [1971] AC 610. See Ch. 3 above, for a critical discussion of these common law rules.

Findlay an attempt was made to challenge the Home Secretary's introduction of a new parole policy on the ground that the new policy, by applying a restrictive attitude to certain categories of prisoner, constituted an unlawful fetter on the Home Secretary's discretion.[8] In the event the House of Lords rejected this contention and upheld the policy.

Traditionally the application of the common law doctrine of *ultra vires* by the High Court has been justified by reference to all three fundamental principles listed above. In the first place, the legislative supremacy of Parliament suggests that any inferior body that seeks to extend its powers beyond those granted to it by Parliament is defying Parliament's legislative monopoly. It is seeking to empower itself. Secondly the rule of law in its traditional form demands that a public body act within the law, within the powers given to it by Parliament, and it is for the courts not the public body itself to provide the definitive statement of the law's requirements. Similarly, the separation of powers suggests that it is for Parliament to empower the public body, for the body to exercise those powers, and for the courts to ensure that it does so within the law. If the body itself were entitled conclusively to interpret the extent of its powers it would be assuming the functions of the legislature.

Process narrowly defined

The involvement of the law wih process more narrowly defined is extensive. The criminal trial provides a clear example of the direct legal regulation of process. The rules concerning procedure and evidence have perhaps been more highly developed in the context of a criminal trial than for any other forum. Criminal procedure is largely covered by statute, while criminal evidence, that is the rules which determine what facts may be proved in a trial and what evidence may be called to prove those facts, has been developed by the common law and significantly codified by statute.[9]

Outside the criminal trial the law is also involved in the direct imposition of procedural requirements on numerous decision-making bodies operating at all three stages of policy implementation, even though the requirements imposed may vary greatly in their stringency and specificity. Commonly this procedural regulation will be achieved through delegated legislation. The direct imposition of procedural requirements in this way by statute or delegated legislation is entirely justifiable in orthodox constitutional terms by reference to the supremacy of Parliament. It can also be said to promote

---

[8] *Re Findlay* [1985] AC 318.

[9] The Police and Criminal Evidence Act 1984, for example, replaces the common law on improperly obtained evidence, s. 78, and confessions, s. 76, while at the same time retaining the court's power to exclude evidence in its discretion, s. 82 (3).

the rule of law by helping to ensure that the relevant agencies fulfil their functions in a rational, non-arbitrary manner. To demand that reasons be given, for example, as is the case for tribunals governed by the Tribunals and Inquiries Act, should encourage a decision-maker to ensure that proper grounds exist for the decision.[10]

In addition to the direct imposition of procedural requirements by statute the High Court, in the exercise of its common law supervisory jurisdiction, can ensure that public boides meet the requirements of natural justice and the duty to act fairly. These requirements may be applied both where there are no statutory provisions as to procedure and where the High Court considers the statute to be either adequate or in need of clarification. The rules of natural justice, and more recently the duty to act fairly, have been evolved gradually by the supervisory courts.[11] In the earlier part of this century natural justice was applied mainly to quasi-judicial bodies and the rules tended to reflect an adjudicatory model of decision-making, occasionally emulating the criminal trial. In recent years the requirements have been extended to apply to more 'administrative' decision-making and some attempt has been made to break away from the adjudicatory model. The wide use of the term 'duty to act fairly' rather than 'natural justice' reflects this development. Whatever term is used, however, the common law procedural requirements are notoriously flexible and will vary significantly according to the nature of the body, the context in which it is operating, the function it is performing, and the interests at stake. They encompass the right to a fair hearing and the rule against bias. In very broad terms the former involves the right to be given notice of the decision, either the criteria to be met or the charges to be faced, the right to know the nature of the evidence, to respond and to put your own case, and the right to a decision based on that evidence. At present there is no general common law right to reasons. The rule against bias provides the right to an impartial decision-maker who neither has nor appears to have a personal interest in the outcome of the decision.

It is perhaps harder to find a justification in orthodox constitutional theory for the imposition of common law procedural requirements, whether through the doctrine of substantive *ultra vires* or by the imposition of the duty to act fairly, than it is for any of the other forms of the law's involvement in process. In the case of the duty to act fairly the courts are prepared to impose requirements in excess of those demanded by the

---

[10] For further discussion see G. Richardson, 'The Duty to Give Reasons: Potential and Practice' (1986) *PL* 437.

[11] For an account of the evolution of natural justice, see M. Beloff and P. Elias, 'Natural Justice and Fairness: The Audi Alteram Partem Rule', in M. Supperstone and J. Goudie (eds.), *Judicial Review* (London, 1992).

statute: the statute may be entirely silent on the question of procedure or may impose procedures which the judges then amplify.[12] In either case the courts could be seen as usurping the functions of Parliament despite their assurances that they will not act to frustrate the purposes of the legislature. In answer to such fears reliance is sometimes placed on the concept of an implied statutory requirement that the rules of natural justice be followed. In some cases such a concept may be persuasive, but when rapidly evolving common law rules are applied to venerable statutory structures it becomes less plausible. The application of relatively stringent common law principles to the decisions of prison boards of visitors on the back of very scant statutory requirements arguably provides an example of judicial activism which is hard to reconcile with strict constitutional orthodoxy.

The application of the principles of substantive *ultra vires* can leave the courts similarly vulnerable to orthodox constitutional challenge. The courts have effectively assumed the right to determine when a public body is acting unreasonably or irrationally, arguing that there is an implied statutory requirement that power be exercised reasonably. However, when the Divisional Court in *Ex parte Handscomb* held that the Home Secretary's delay of three to four years was so unreasonable as to render his decision unlawful, it might be argued that it was acting unconstitutionally by imposing limits to the Home Secretary's discretion where Parliament had imposed none.

The above argument is not intended to suggest that there can be no justification for the court concerning itself with the Home Secretary's delay or with the detailed procedures adopted by boards of visitors. The suggestion is merely that the constitutional doctrines of parliamentary supremacy and the rule of law in its narrowest sense are insufficient on their own to provide such a justification. Indeed these doctrines might suggest that such interference on the part of non-elected judges is positively anti-democratic. While alternative constitutional approaches grounded in notions of democracy have been considered elsewhere[13] and are referred to further below, the following section will concentrate on that body of literature which has sought to justify the regulation of process on other grounds. In the fourth section an attempt will be made to suggest links between this latter endeavour and the more constitutional debate.

---

[12] For a discussion of the courts' recent practice in this regard see ibid. 168–74. The courts will not supplement the requirements of the statute if to do so would frustrate the purposes of that statute, *R. v. Birmingham City Council ex p. Ferrero* [1993] 1 All ER 530. See also the discussion in Cotterrell, Ch. 1 above.

[13] See: Craig, *Public Law and Democracy*; J. Ely, *Democracy and Distrust: A Theory of Judicial Review* (Cambridge, Mass., 1980); G. Richardson, *Law, Process and Custody: Prisoners and Patients* (London, 1993); and Cotterrell, Ch. 1 above.

EXISTING APPROACHES TO PROCESS IN
ADMINISTRATIVE LAW

Broadly speaking, there are two basic approaches within the literature. The first, which comes in a wide variety of guises, views the insistence on 'fair' process as justified primarily by reference to the beneficial effect of process on the direct outcome of the decision. Thus strict procedural requirements can be justified if they encourage accurate decisions. The second sees 'fair' processes as justified in so far as they protect values which exist independently of the direct outcome of the decision.[14] For example, my right to be heard before a decision which affects me is taken is essential in order to protect my personal dignity and autonomy, and is thus justified irrespective of the impact of my participation on the ultimate decision.

Instrumentalism

The first approach emphasizes the link between process and direct outcome. Thus, assuming it is possible to identify the 'correct' outcome, a procedural requirement is justified to the extent that it encourages such an outcome. So, if the sole purpose of the criminal trial is to reach an accurate finding of guilt or innocence, then any procedural requirement that encourages accuracy is justified and any which fails to do so is not.[15] Procedures are not, however, free and if an efficiency objective is introduced the ideal level of procedural regulation will be that which minimizes both the cost of the procedure itself (direct costs) and the costs of reaching a wrong, e.g. inaccurate, decision (error costs). Any attempt to calculate this ideal level, however, is likely to encounter major difficulties.

In the first place, as implied above, it is not always relevant to talk in terms of correct outcomes. Even in the context of application and validation the policies to be applied may often involve standards requiring interpretation, judgment, and opinion. There may be no uniquely correct outcome. Further, while the facts may be agreed, the precise implications of the policy in relation to them may be hotly contested. The biographical details of a psychiatric patient's background, for example, may be fully and accurately documented, but the implications to be drawn from them and the application of the statutory release criteria to them by the mental

---

[14] See the brief discussion in P. Craig, 'Legitimate Expectations: A Conceptual Analysis' (1992) 108 *LQR* 79, at 86.

[15] See e.g. J. Bentham, *A Treatise on Judicial Evidence*, ed. M. Dumont (Littleton, Col., 1981). For further discussion of Bentham's views see W. Twining, *Theories of Evidence: Bentham and Wigmore* (Stanford, Calif., 1985).

health review tribunal may be highly controversial, and hard to assess as correct or incorrect. Secondly, while the identification of direct costs may be fairly straightforward, the salaries paid to an adjudicator and the necessary clerical staff for example, the calculation of error costs can give rise to considerable difficulties. This familiar criticism of the economic approach can be usefully illustrated by further reference to the discharge decisions of mental health review tribunals, where the range of 'incorrect' decisions available is very wide. A patient who is discharged when insufficiently recovered may fail to cope with conditions within the community, and may suffer a significant reduction in quality of life until recalled to hospital, while another prematurely discharged patient may commit a serious offence of violence shortly after leaving hospital. Alternatively a patient whose discharge is inappropriately refused will suffer prolonged and significant loss of liberty. While each of these decisions can be regarded as wrong, any sensible assessment of their relative error costs will be hard to achieve.

The stark economic approach as described also fails to recognize any benefit in process beyond the facilitation of correct outcomes. Thus, in considering the role of procedures. Dworkin introduces another element to the notion of error costs.[16] Using the criminal trial as an example, he distinguishes between two types of harm, bare harm and moral harm. The innocent suspect who is mistakenly convicted and punished suffers bare harm in being sent to prison, a direct cost of the error. In addition, he or she also suffers moral harm by being wrongly deprived of the right not to be punished when innocent. It is these additional moral costs deriving from the infringement of a right which, according to Dworkin, justify greater expenditure on procedures designed to avoid wrongful convictions than on procedures designed to avoid wrongful acquittals. It seems that to deprive someone of a right is to treat that person unfairly: to have a right is to have some undertaking from society that certain interests will be protected, to breach that undertaking is to act unfairly towards the right holder. Thus with the notion of moral costs Dworkin moves beyond the bare economic analysis of process and in so doing introduces the concept of rights. For Dworkin the possession of a substantive right triggers a secondary right to procedural protection.

This is a powerful argument for procedural rights in relation to substantive rights. The corollary is, however, that there are no procedural rights in relation to bare interests.[17] The harm which may result from interference with bare interests is bare harm; there is no moral harm since nothing has been lost to which there is a right, and it is only moral harm

---

[16] R. Dworkin, *A Matter of Principle* (Oxford, 1985), ch. 4.

[17] But see D. Galligan, 'Rights, Discretion and Procedures', in D. Galligan and C. Sampford, *Law, Rights and the Welfare State* (London, 1986).

that attracts procedural protection. It seems that for Dworkin, once outside the sphere of substantive rights, procedures are essentially matters of policy with any claim to specific procedures being so weak as to be negligible.

Process values

Both the economic and the moral costs approach to process are instrumental in the sense of regarding the primary purpose of procedural requirements as facilitating correct decisions: processes are related directly to decision outcomes. The economic approach can be described as 'single value instrumentalism' and the moral cost approach as 'multi-value instrumentalism'.[18] An alternative approach is to see processes as designed to protect values which are independent of the direct outcome of the decision, such as participation, fairness, and the protection of individual dignity. While such values may contribute to correct outcomes, that may not be their primary justification. For example, respect for individual dignity may be regarded as a value worthy of protection in decision-making structures irrespective of its impact on the direct decision outcome. As Bayles describes it, in the case of the instrumental approach the causal chain from procedure to economic or moral error cost goes through the decision outcome, whereas in the process values approach the causal link from procedure to process values does not go through the decision outcome.[19]

This emphasis on the role of process as the protector of independent values is common to the dignitary approach to process which has been influential in the United States. The precise details of the approach vary. For some commentators the requirement that an individual be treated fairly is grounded in a notion of justice derived from social contract theory,[20] for others it springs from natural rights,[21] from fundamental liberal values,[22] or from Kant's injunction condemning the treatment of individuals merely as means.[23] Whatever the precise foundation of the

[18] M. Bayles, *Procedural Justice: Allocating to Individuals* (Dordrecht, 1990), ch. 6.
[19] Ibid. 128.
[20] R. Saphire, 'Specifying Due Process Values: Towards a More Responsive Approach to Procedural Protection' (1978) 127 *Univ. Pennsylvania LR* 111, and W. Van Alstyne, 'Cracks in "The New Property": Adjudicative Due Process in the Administrative State' (1977) 62 *Cornell LR* 445.
[21] J. Mashaw, 'Dignitary Process: A Political Psychology of Liberal Democratic Citizenship' (1987) 39 *Univ. Florida LR* 433.
[22] J. Mashaw, *Bureaucratic Justice: Managing Social Security Disability Claims* (New Haven, Conn., 1983).
[23] E. Pincoffs, 'Due Process, Fraternity, and a Kantian Injunction', in J. Pennock and J. Chapman (eds.), *Due Process NOMOS 18* (New York, 1977), and J. Mashaw, 'Administrative Due Process: The Quest for a Dignitary Theory' (1981) 61 *Boston Univ. LR* 885.

approach, however, the claim is made that the need to provide procedural fairness, particularly in the form of participation, springs from the obligation to respect a person's dignity and autonomy as a human being. To deny an individual the opportunity to participate in decisions affecting her is to deprive her of the conditions necessary for continued moral agency.[24] The primary justification for a claim to fair process, accordingly, lies not in the ability of such processes to achieve correct outcomes, but in the respect that they afford to the dignity and autonomy of individuals. The instrumental value of fair procedures is not denied by dignitary theorists, it is merely viewed as secondary.

Bayles has attempted to develop a means of evaluating processes that combines features of both the instrumental and the dignitary approaches.[25] Together with the dignitary theorists he assumes that process benefits exist which are independent of the direct decision outcome, but he does not derive them exclusively from the dignity and autonomy of individuals. Such benefits, according to Bayles, are those that a 'fully rational person would accept',[26] and he lists participation, fairness in the sense of equality, intelligibility, timeliness, and confidence in the decision-making process. Some of these benefits would further the instrumental accuracy objective, but their value is accepted even if they have no such effect. Thus, Bayles argues that procedures should be evaluated in terms of the extent to which they reduce error, moral, and direct costs, and promote process benefits. Bayles uses this 'norm' to evaluate the characteristics of procedural justice which he sees as impartiality, the provision of a hearing, the provision of grounds for decisions, and the principles of formal justice. Impartiality, for example, may increase accuracy, but even if it fails to do so, it will provide a process benefit in the form of an increase in confidence in the decision-making process. Thus Bayles's formula enables factors beyond the directly instrumental and those immediately related to the protection of individual dignity to be taken into account when assessing or selecting procedures, and as such it helps to widen the debate.

Three main justifications for the regulation of process, therefore, are to be found in the existing literature: the instrumental approach which regards process regulation as designed primarily to reduce direct, error, and moral costs, the dignitary approach which sees fair process as essential to the maintenance of the dignity and autonomy of individuals, and Bayles's broader, process values, approach.

---

[24] Mashaw, 'Dignitary Process'.
[25] Bayles, *Procedural Justice*.
[26] Ibid. 130.

JUDICIAL PRACTICE

As was explained above, the procedural requirements of the common law are primarily contained in what are traditionally referred to as the rules of natural justice, that is the rule against bias and the right to a fair hearing. It was suggested, particularly with reference to natural justice, that in certain circumstances the interference of the common law might be hard to justify by reference to orthodox constitutional principle. In an attempt to understand how the judges themselves view, and presumably justify, their role, judicial practice will be considered with reference to the conceptual approaches described in the previous section. The majority of the discussion will relate to the rules of natural justice but some reference will be made to those other common law procedural principles which spring more directly from *ultra vires*.

The criteria for the imposition of the rules of natural justice (or more recently the duty to act fairly) and their enforcement through public law can be said to involve two elements: interference with the right or interest of an individual and the decision of a body exercising a public function. Each requires further consideration. First it is evident from the case-law that the requirements of the common law, especially those incorporated in the right to a fair hearing, are triggered by the existence of a right or interest in an individual.

The rights or interests of individuals

Since *Ridge* v. *Baldwin*[27] and subsequent case-law it is quite clear that the protection afforded by common law procedures extends beyond the legally recognized rights of individuals: the old distinction between rights and privileges has finally disappeared. In *Council for Civil Service Unions* Lord Diplock explained that to be subject to procedural requirements a decision must affect some person, either by affecting his or her private law rights or obligations, or by depriving that person of a benefit or advantage which he or she legitimately expected to enjoy.[28] Such a legitimate expectation can arise through past practice or through a specific undertaking. The expectation may be of a substantive benefit which then attracts procedural protection, or it may refer directly to the procedure itself, as when an individual or a group is promised consultation. Thus, while the extent to which the recognition of a legitimate expectation can guarantee the receipt of a substantive benefit may be open to some doubt, the relevance of the

---

[27] [1964] AC 40.
[28] *Council for Civil Service Unions* v. *Minister for the Civil Service* [1985] AC 374, 408.

concept to the application of common law procedural protection is considerable.[29] According to Wade the concept is flexible enough to be used to trigger procedural protection 'in any of many situations where fairness and good administration justify the right to be heard'.[30] On the other hand its flexibility could just as readily allow it to be used restrictively. The court may, for example, deny the existence of a legitimate expectation in certain circumstances, as it did in *US Tobacco*,[31] or it may define the extent of the expectation very restrictively, as was arguably the case in *Re Findlay* when the House of Lords adopted a very restricted view of the legitimate expectations possesed by life sentence prisoners.[32]

Once the possession of an interest is established the court must also be satisfied that the interest stands to be *affected* by the decision. Strictly speaking this requirement exempts preliminary recommendations from procedural regulation,[33] and may partially explain the courts' slightly ambivalent attitude to the procedural regulation of statutory inquiries.[34] The courts can also be very restrictive in their identification of those 'affected' by the decision and limit such persons to the direct subject of the decision, even where the decision has an immediate effect on the very tangible interests of third parties.[35]

Thus, the application of common law procedures is triggered by the existence in an individual of a substantive interest which is deemed worthy of procedural protection and which is affected by the decision. One exception to this substantive interest requirement, however, is provided by the legitimate expectation doctrine on those occasions when it is applied, not to provide a substantive interest with some procedural protection, but directly to enforce an undertaking to follow a certain procedure: here the expectation deemed worthy of protection relates to a procedural rather

[29] For a discussion of legitimate expectations and their ability to protect substantive rights, see C. Forsyth, 'The Provenance and Protection of Legitimate Expectations' (1988) 47 *CLR* 238.
[30] H. Wade, *Administrative Law* (6th edn. Oxford, 1988), 522. See R. Baldwin and D. Horne, 'Expectations in a Joyless Landscape' 49 *MLR* 685, for a discussion of the potential of legitimate expectation as a device to encourage the judicial protection of an expectation of government largess.
[31] *R.* v. *Secretary of State ex p. US Tobacco* [1992] 1 All ER 212.
[32] [1985] AC 318.
[33] The relevant cases are discussed in Beloff and Elias 'Natural Justice and Fairness', 182–3.
[34] See e.g. *Bushell* v. *Secretary of State for Environment* [1981] AC 75 and *R.* v. *Secretary of State for Transport ex p. Gwent* [1987] 2 WLR 961.
[35] In the context of a self-regulatory body, the High Court has taken the view that the right to a fair hearing before a disciplinary tribunal resides in the subject of the decision alone and does not extend to directly affected third parties, *R.* v. *LAUTRO ex p. Ross* [1992] 1 All ER 422. While this view was discounted on appeal the Court of Appeal still concluded that the third party had not been treated unfairly, [1993] 1 All ER 545.

than a substantive benefit.[36] In such cases the common law is prepared directly to enforce the non-statutory procedures promised by public bodies.

The strong connection which, apart from the above exception, exists between the substantive interest of an individual and the procedural obligations of the decision-maker is reinforced by the rule that only the person denied the fair hearing, the person in possession of the affected interest, can sue for breach of common law procedures. So a third party with a general interest in the maintenance of fair procedures cannot challenge the validity of a decision even if it is made in clear breach of the duty to afford a fair hearing. The duty can be enforced only by those to whom the fair hearing is owed. The requirement is similar to that contained in the idea of standing, namely that an individual seeking judicial review of an agency's action must first possess sufficient interest in the matter to which the application relates, but Wade suggests the requirement is also 'inherent in the principle of natural justice itself'.[37]

In practice most of the case-law seems to reflect an instrumental approach to the role of process regulation, particularly with regard to the right to a fair hearing. The common law seeks to encourage informed and accurate decision-making by insisting that before a decision is made a fair hearing is afforded to those whose interests stand to be affected. Common law intervention is thus designed to protect the interests of individuals from interference consequent upon incorrect decisions. Orthodox judicial rhetoric, by contrast, displays an additional concern for process, possibly dignitary, values. According to this orthodoxy the reviewing courts will intervene to ensure adherence to the requirements of the common law, even if such adherence would have made no difference to the decision outcome: 'If the principles of natural justice are violated in respect of any decision it is, indeed, immaterial whether the same decision would have been arrived at in the absence of the departure from the essential principles of justice. The decision must be declared to be no decision.'[38] Such an approach would suggest a desire to ensure fair procedures which is independent of any impact on the direct outcome of the decision itself. In practice, however, the effect of this orthodoxy is often avoided either by a refusal by the court to grant a remedy for the alleged breach, or by a denial that any breach occurred.[39] Nevertheless, whatever its practical significance, the emphasis placed on process values in judicial rhetoric is still

[36] *A.-G. of Hong Kong* v. *Ng Yuen Shiu* [1983] 2 AC 629. See the discussion in Craig, 'Legitimate Expectations'.
[37] Wade, *Administrative Law*, 537, and see Beloff and Elias, 'Natural Justice and Fairness', 204.
[38] *General Medical Council* v. *Spackman* [1943] AC 627, per Lord Wright, 644.
[39] See *Fullbrook* v. *Berkshire Magistrates' Courts Committee* (1970) 69 LGR 75, and *Glynn* v. *Keele University* [1971] 1 WLR 487, for examples of the former approach, and *Cinnamond* v. *British Airports Authority* [1980] 1 WLR 582 as an example of the latter.

firmly linked to the possession by an individual of a substantive interest worhty of protection: the obligation to provide fair procedures and to treat a person with dignity may be independent of the direct outcome of the decision, but it only arises when that person's recognized substantive interests are at stake.

To some extent the judges' approach towards the rule against bias differs from their approach towards the right to a fair hearing. The rule against bias has traditionally been regarded as being more concerned with appearances than is the right to a fair hearing. It extends beyond actual to presumptive bias. No actual bias need be present. Instead the court must ask itself whether, having regard to all relevant circumstances, 'there was a real danger of bias'.[40] Thus the rule appears to be designed not only to protect the interests of individuals from interference flowing from biased decision-making, but also to safeguard process benefits through supporting the principle that justice be seen to be done. On this basis it is closer to Bayles's process values approach than to narrow instrumentalism. In line with this broader concern with the appearance, if not the reality, of the decision-making structure, a greater willingness to allow third parties to complain might be anticipated in relation to the rule against bias than exists with regard to the right to a fair hearing. To some extent the case-law does indeed reflect a more flexible approach: the decision of a biased planning authority to grant planning permission, for example, has been quashed at the instance of an interested party other than the applicant.[41] But that flexibility is very limited. Even in the example given the successful challenger had a substantive interest: he owned property neighbouring the development land. Further, the doctrine of waiver enables an individual to waive the presence of a biased decision-maker, and having done so to be barred from any subsequent challenge on grounds of bias.[42] Such a doctrine tends to reflect the narrower interest protection approach by regarding the directly affected individual as the only person properly concerned: if he or she accepts the presence of bias, so be it. It does little to support any broader concern with the fairness of the decision-making structure itself, whether apparent or real.

Thus the interpretation of the first criterion, the existence of a decision affecting the rights or interests of an individual, tends to indicate an essentially instrumental approach: fair process is required in order to encourage accurate decisions and thereby to protect the substantive interests of individuals. Further, even where a concern with process values

---

[40] *R.* v. *Gough* [1993] 2 All ER 724, 737–8. The real danger test was articulated by Lord Goff in place of the previous alternatives, 'reasonable suspicion' and 'real likelihood'.

[41] *R.* v. *Hendon Rural District Council ex p. Chorley* [1933] 2 KB 696. See Wade, *Administrative Law*, 476.

[42] *R.* v. *Secretary of State for Health ex p. Prison Officers Assoc.*, *The Times*, 28 Oct. 1991.

is expressed that concern is inspired by the presence of a vulnerable substantive interest. This is not to contend that the desire to protect substantive interests cannot be outweighed by a concern to maintain the integrity of the process itself. In *Ex parte Benaim and Khaida* the interests of the individual applicants were outweighed by the perceived need to protect the future efficacy of the decision-making process.[43] It is merely to suggest that an instrumental approach in the form of a desire to protect the substantive interests of individuals from interference as a result of inaccurate decision-making appears to dominate the case-law in practice.[44]

The decision of a body exercising a public function

The second criterion for the application of the common law procedural requirements, that there be a decision by a body exercising a public function, relates primarily to the question of remedies. While common law procedures can occasionally be imposed by private law, susceptibility to procedural regulation through public law is restricted to bodies performing a public function.[45] Within the jurisdiction of the public law itself, however, there is now little or no distinction between those bodies which are bound by the duty to act fairly and those which are not. In the days prior to *Ridge* v. *Baldwin*, even with regard to obviously public bodies, the courts had developed a distinction between administrative and judicial bodies. The latter were susceptible to procedural regulation, the former were not: a decision had not only to be public but judicial or quasi-judicial as well. *Ridge* v. *Baldwin* was thought to have destroyed that distinction, at least in so far as it affected the *application* of natural justice, and although the distinction has re-emerged on occasions since, it can only be hoped that thanks to the House of Lords' decision in *Leech*[46] it is now dead beyond all resurrection. The nature of the body and its functions will, however, continue to affect the *content* of the procedural requirements imposed on it by the common law.

Until the early 1970s the procedural requirements of the common law were described generally as the rules of natural justice. In the late 1960s, however, the courts began to develop the notion of a duty to act fairly,[47] and it is now common for the courts to talk in terms of the duty to act fairly

---

[43] R. v. *Gaming Board of Great Britain ex p. Benaim and Khaida* [1970] 2 QB 417.

[44] There is one significant exception to this trend. As mentioned above the courts will occasionally intervene to enforce a bare undertaking to provide a particular procedure, above, n. 36.

[45] See Beloff and Elias, 'Natural Justice and Fairness', 171–4, for the imposition of procedural regulation in private law, and see Cranston, Ch. 3 above, for the identification of bodies performing a public function.

[46] *Leech* v. *Deputy Governor Parkhurst Prison* [1988] AC 533.

[47] *Re HK* [1967] 2 QB 617.

in preference to the rules of natural justice. To an extent this development mirrored the whittling down of the old administrative/judicial distinction. While natural justice in its traditional form might properly apply to judicial and quasi-judicial decisions, a less formal set of requirements incorporated in the duty to act fairly might be more appropriate in a primarily administrative context. Considerable debate has surrounded the precise nature of the duty to act fairly and the implications that can be drawn from its introduction,[48] but it is at least clear that it, like its traditional counterpart, is primarily concerned with the protection of the interests of individuals. A public body may be under a duty to act fairly but such a duty will attach to its activities primarily in so far as they directly affect the interests of individuals.

The influence of adjudication

It is often remarked that the procedural requirements of the common law are closely modelled on the adjudicatory format, particularly the adversarial adjudicatory form familiar to the British courts.[49] Accordingly the common law insists, with varying degrees of formality, on adequate notice of the impending decision, an opportunity to see the evidence, an opportunity to be heard, and a decision from an impartial decision-maker which is based on the revealed evidence. Through this form of participation the vulnerable individual is given the opportunity to improve the accuracy of the decision and to facilitate informed decision-making. In the eyes of the judiciary, who are familiar with the adversarial adjudicatory model, such a procedural form may represent the most suitable process available for the protection of individual interests from the inaccurate application of public policy.[50]

Although it is true that the duty to act fairly has introduced greater flexibility into the common law, the content of the requirements still tends to derive from the adjudicatory model and their impact only rarely extends beyond application decisions. Admittedly, in recent years the courts have shown a greater willingness to entertain claims to consultation, a potentially encouraging development. As will be argued below, however, in so far as such claims relate to the common law duty to consult they tend to involve application or very specific policy formulation decisions, and to

---

[48] M. Loughlin, 'Procedural Fairness: A Study of the Crisis in Administrative Law Theory' (1978) 28 *Univ. Toronto LR* 215, and R. Macdonald, 'Judicial Review and Procedural Fairness in Administrative Law: I' (1979) 25 *McGill LJ* 520.

[49] See P. Cane, *An Introduction to Administrative Law* (2nd edn. Oxford, 1992), ch. 8.

[50] Bayles, *Procedural Justice*, and id., *Principles of Law: A Normative Analysis* (Dordrecht, 1987). For further discussion of adversarial and inquisitorial models of adjudication see Richardson, *Law, Process and Custody*.

be most successful where the alleged consultee is also the person directly affected by the decision outcome. They therefore add little either to the common law's traditional adjudicatory format or to its emphasis on application decisions.

Implications and limitations

In the light of the above discussion it is possible to argue that the common law's involvement in the regulation of process is based on a mutually supportive structure comprised of three elements: an instrumental justi- fication for involvement, an emphasis on the application and validation stages of policy evolution, and the adoption of an adjudicatory model of procedure. Without extensive research it is not possible to attribute cause and effect between these three elements, but the links between them are clear. In the first place, the attitude of the courts to the basis for their imposition of procedural requirements seems, in the main, to reflect the instrumental approach. Procedures are required in order to protect individuals', largely substantive, interests: the possession of such an interest triggers the procedural requirement. The need to protect the individual's interest may, in the result, be outweighed by the need to promote the integrity of the system, and at the level of rhetoric may be seen as secondary to the promotion of fairness, but the whole question of procedural propriety is triggered by the existence of a vulnerable interest in an individual deemed worthy of protection.[51] Secondly, the common law rules are applied predominately at the application and validation stages where these individual interests are most likely to be directly affected. Thirdly, and finally, the adjudicatory model which prevails is widely regarded as particularly well designed for the protection of individual interests from interference resulting from uninformed and inaccurate decisions.

Arguably the present character of the common law procedural require- ments imposes significant limitations on their potential. In the first place the emphasis placed on the protection of individual interests by the common law, and especially by the right to a fair hearing, has provided no incentive to extend procedural regulation beyond the application and validation stages of policy evolution and implementation. The substantive interests of individuals are most vulnerable to direct interference as a result of decisions to apply policy and by subsequent attempts to challenge such applications. With regard to policy formulation in the form of rule-making the common law has traditionally been reluctant to become involved. According to established principle, natural justice does not apply to decisions of a legislative nature. There is, for example, no general common

[51] Mashaw, 'Dignitary Process'.

law right to be heard before the making of legislation, whether primary or delegated,[52] although it may be possible to establish a legitimate expectation to such consultation.[53] A duty to consult may, of course, be created by statute in relation to delegated legislation but, while such duties are regarded as mandatory and may be interpreted quite strictly by the courts,[54] non-compliance will not necessarily lead to invalidation of the relevant regulations.[55]

With regard to administrative rule-making the position at common law seems now to be governed primarily by the doctrine of legitimate expectation. Thus, if an interest group has always been consulted in the past or has been promised consultation in the future, they can argue that they have a legitimate expectation to consultation which they should be denied only on the grounds of the strongest public interest.[56] While such a development might suggest a greater willingness on the part of the common law to regulate the processes of policy formulation, reservations remain concerning the nature of that regulation. In the first place, a close look at the cases suggests that only those who are directly affected by the decision can successfully claim a legitimate expectation to consultation.[57] The doctrine of legitimate expectation has yet to be used to impose an obligation to consult specialist or expert third parties.[58] Secondly, many of the cases involve policy-making with a very specific focus. They thus occupy the uncertain borderline between policy formulation and application, where the consequences flowing from a legitimate expectation of consultation become hard to distinguish from those which would flow from the more traditional right to a fair hearing.[59] Thus, while the recognition of a legitimate expectation of consultation may have encouraged the common law to contemplate the procedural regulation of policy formulation, it

[52] Wade, *Administrative Law*, 573. And see *Leech* v. *Deputy Governor Parkhurst Prison* [1988] AC 533, 578.

[53] See e.g. *R.* v. *Secretary of State for the Environment ex p. NALGO* [1992] COD 282, and *R.* v. *Lord Chancellor ex p. Law Society, The Times*, 25 June, 1993.

[54] See *Ex p. US Tobacco* [1992] 1 All ER 212.

[55] *R.* v. *Secretary of State for Social Services ex p. AMA* [1986] 1 WLR 1; *R.* v. *Secretary of State for Health ex p. Natural Medicines Group* [1991] COD 60; *R.* v. *NW Thames RHA ex p. Daniels, The Times*, 22 June 1993 and *Ex p. Law Society, The Times*, 25 June 1993.

[56] *Council for Civil Service Unions* v. *Minister for the Civil Service* [1985] AC 374.

[57] See e.g. *R.* v. *Liverpool Corporation ex p. Liverpool Taxi Fleet Operators Assoc.* [1972] 2 WLR 1262; *R.* v. *Secretary of State for the Environment ex p. Brent LBC* [1982] QB 593; *Council of Civil Service Unions* v. *Minister for the Civil Service* [1985] AC 374; and *R.* v. *Birmingham City Council ex p. Dredger and Paget* [1993] COD 340.

[58] P. Elias and M. Beloff, 'Procedural Rules and Consultation', in Supperstone and Goudie, *Judicial Review*, 144, take a narrow view of the basis of the legitimate expectation doctrine, and argue that it cannot be used to impose a duty to consult third parties.

[59] See e.g. *Ex p. Dredger and Paget* [1993] COD 340, and *R.* v. *Secretary of State for Transport ex p. GLC* [1986] QB 556, where the point is made on p. 587. See also Cranston, Ch. 3 above.

cannot yet be said to have developed the nature of that regulation far beyond the traditional protection of substantive interests through some modified form of adjudication. Other common law doctrines, however, have shown even less potential. The courts seem unwilling, whether through the general duty to act fairly or through the extended principles of *ultra vires*, to demand consultation where none is required by statute, by promise, or by established practice. The House of Lords, for example, had no hesitation in denying the claim, brought on behalf of affected prisoners, that the Home Secretary had a duty to consult the parole board prior to the introduction of a new policy on parole.[60]

The second major limitation derives directly from the emphasis on individual interest protection. Before the procedural requirements can be triggered, the court must recognize a substantive right or legitimate expectation in need of protection. The judicial approach thus closely resembles that of Dworkin: procedural rights are secondary to the protection of substantive interests. Admittedly, with the development of legitimate expectations the courts have signalled a willingness to go beyond Dworkin and to protect interests which do not constitute rights,[61] but they do still demand some *legitimate* expectation. This requirement immediately raises the familiar problem of selection: who selects the expectations worthy of protection and on what basis?

ALTERNATIVE APPROACHES

In the light of the limitations flowing from the traditional approaches to process as reflected in current judicial attitudes, it becomes relevant to consider whether an alternative can be found which moves beyond the secondary role typically attributed to 'rights' to fair process. Most of the literature discussed above concerning the bases for the involvement of the law in the regulation of process tends to concentrate on decisions at the application and validation stages. There is, of course, a separate and extensive literature concerned with the processes involved in the constitution of governments. In this country, however, the two debates tend to run in parallel, there is little exchange between the two.[62] As Craig has pointed

---

[60] *Re Findlay* [1985] AC 318, and *R. v. Secretary of State for the Home Dept. ex p. Cox* [1992] COD 72. See D. Oliver, 'The Courts and the Policy Making Process', in J. Jowell and D. Oliver (eds.), *New Directions in Judicial Review* (London, 1988), for an interesting discussion of the court's attitude in *Findlay*.

[61] See the discussion in Baldwin and Horne, 'Expectations in a Joyless Landscape'.

[62] But see T. Prosser, 'Democratisation, Accountability and Institutional Design: Reflections on Public Law', in P. McAuslan and J. McEldowney (eds.), *Law, Legitimacy and the Constitution* (London, 1985).

out in the context of participation, there is no satisfactory theory recognizing the possibility of participation other than as a voter or as a litigant, in the broadest sense.[63] While no attempt will be made here to provide a single such comprehensive theory, it will be suggested that a sufficiently close relationship exists between the ideas underpinning claims to participation in government and the regulation of process in the more individual context to indicate an alternative basis for the latter which moves beyond the mere protection of substantive interests.

At the centre of the argument lies the notion of legitimate authority. The decisions of officials exercising public power should comply with certain principles of justification. Typically public officials exercise their power by reference to the law, and only by establishing the authority of the law is it possible to establish the authority of the individual decision-maker operating within that law. The issue is a large one, but for present purposes it is sufficient to concentrate on one specific question: under what conditions is law authoritative, in the sense of being deserving of support and respect in more than just a formal sense?

In the interests of space it will be assumed that state intervention through law is necessary in order to achieve the co-ordination required to enable a society to function.[64] However, a government charged with co-ordinating social activities will be authoritative only if it acts in accordance with certain basic principles. While the precise identification of these principles will vary widely, depending on the overall approach taken to fundamental issues of moral and political theory, it is sufficient here to consider briefly just two alternative approaches.

Liberal pluralism

According to the first approach, which is essentially grounded in the Western liberal tradition, it is convenient to separate the 'acceptable principles' into three different categories by reference to their origins and levels of specificity. In the first place even liberals, who deny that any particular conception of the good should take automatic priority, accept that there are some principles that are so fundamental that compliance is a necessary condition of authority within any society. Amongst such principles are ideas of respect for persons and their liberty, ideas about autonomy, privacy, and personal responsibility, about the protection of individuals from harm and the provision of basic welfare. To some extent these principles reflect the primary goods considered as the bare essentials

[63] Craig, *Public Law and Democracy*, 175. But see contributions to J. Pennock and J. Chapman (eds.), *Participation in Politics* (New York, 1975).

[64] See further H. Hart, *The Concept of Law* (Oxford, 1961); J. Finnis, *Natural Law and Natural Rights* (Oxford, 1980); and J. Raz, *The Morality of Freedom* (Oxford, 1986).

by Rawls's thin theory of the good.[65] Such abstract precepts have to be interpreted and made concrete, but they are nevertheless regarded as the foundation stones of a justifiable social order.

At a second level, each community is likely to be committed to more specific values which are implicit in day-to-day life and which become embedded in its political structure, its form of government, and its legislation, administration, and adjudication. These working values might include a commitment to democratic principles, representative government, duties of care towards others, entitlements to property, and rights to welfare. Working values are discovered by examining the laws and practices of the society, so that a study of the criminal law, for example, would provide a guide to a host of values.[66] Indeed, a level of consensus about such intermediate or working values is important in securing social cohesion. The working values of a community, of course, might be repugnant and merit no support. But provided that they meet the first layer of principles and can be seen to be the historical products of a humane society, which is open to change, then there is virtue in preserving those values and in encouraging consistency between them. That virtue is expressed by Dworkin in the idea of integrity, and for Dworkin integrity is of cardinal importance in the legitimization of a legal system.[67] Part of its importance lies in the stability and certainty which flows from integrity; but part is also to be found in the way that it preserves and perpetuates a sense of community.

The third category of principle which contributes to the authority of a legal system, according to this approach, is of particular relevance to the role of process and, thus, is of special interest here. The argument is pluralist in so far as it accepts that modern societies are complex and diverse. They are complex in the sense that the task of co-ordinating their many activities cannot be forced into a single master plan: effective co-ordination will depend on more localized action, on responding to issues and disputes, on accommodating interests and groups, and on finding compromises amongst them. Societies are diverse in the sense that groups and individuals vary across a wide spectrum in their activities and interests, their values and preferences. Within such a society one of the principal liberal values must be 'the freedom of the citizen and of associations freely chosen by citizens'.[68] Such a value recognizes personal freedom and the diversity that follows from it: it allows for differing concepts of the good. In

---

[65] J. Rawls, 'The Basic Liberties and their Priority', in S. McMurrin (ed.), *Liberty, Equality and Law* (Salt Lake City, 1987). And see the discussion in Craig, *Public Law and Democracy*, 249. [66] Bayles, *Procedural Justice*.

[67] R. Dworkin, *Laws Empire* (London, 1986).

[68] P. Hirst and P. Jones, 'The Critical Resources of Established Jurisprudence', (1987) 14 *J. Law and Society* 21, 24.

addition, principles of equality, often expressed in terms of democracy, suggest that each person counts in the decisions of government. In order to satisfy these two principles of freedom and equal political significance, any exercise of government power must demonstrate that full regard has been paid to the diversity of values and interests represented within society. Co-ordination requires some subordination of individual interests to the public good; individual or group freedom cannot be absolute. But, arguably, subordination should only occur after full consideration of the plurality of interests and values at stake. A decision which evolves through such a process of consideration should reflect a broad public interest, in furtherance of which the exercise of government power is authoritative.

According to this third category of principle, therefore, legal and administrative institutions at every level of government, from legislation to individualized decisions, must be designed to ensure that all interests are represented and that none is accorded automatic priority. Through the full participation of individuals and groups and the responsiveness of public decision-makers, decisions can be reached which reflect the public interest in its broadest sense, a public interest which is refined from the wealth of group and individual interests. In this way the requirements of freedom and equal political significance carry with them implications for the process through which governmental decisions evolve, and any governmental decision which evolves through a process designed to facilitate, if not to guarantee, the full reflection of the public interest will have a further claim to authority.

In sum, according to the traditions of liberal pluralism, the principles necessary for the authoritative exercise of state power fall into three categories. The first of these principles demands compliance with fundamental moral values, the second reflects a concern for the stability and continuity of values within the system, and the third, recognizing the complex and plural nature of modern society, places particular importance on the process of public decision-making. While this third principle is not regarded as sufficient on its own to provide full authority for the exercise of governmental power, it is seen as a necessary condition. Thus, according to this approach the claim to full process, at whatever stage in policy implementation it is being made, whether it be in relation to individual application decisions or with regard to policy formulation, is grounded ultimately on the citizen's entitlement to the legitimate exercise of public power, and exists independently of any vulnerable 'substantive' interest possessed by that citizen. Further, any external mechanism, such as legal regulation through the courts, which is designed to ensure compliance with the demands of full process would be justified as serving to promote the legitimacy of governmental power. The enforcement of common law principles reflective of full process in this sense would be supportive of democracy rather than hostile to it: they would be constitutional in the most fundamental sense.

Strong democracy

There is an alternative, more radical, approach which accords process an even more central role. According to Barber's theory of strong democracy the co-ordination required within a society is achieved by way of direct participation and self-regulation. The authority of 'state' action is achieved through the 'active consent of participatory citizens'.[69] While in the more liberal approach described above the individual and the state are distinct and the relationship between the two requires a balance of control and accountability, which is often understood in contractual terms, within strong democracy there is no clear divide between individual and government: the individual as a direct participant is part of government. Further, within strong democracy there are no prior values. Conflicts will be resolved and decisions reached through a process of public deliberation, and any values that evolve will emerge from discussion between the citizens themselves. In the absence of prior individual rights, tyranny by the majority is to be avoided, not by external controls, but through the process of self-regulation.

At the heart of strong democracy lies process. It is process that protects the substance of decisions and the process through which a decision evolves is the fundamental source of its authority. The role of the law as a mechanism for ensuring the maintenance of strong democratic processes, however, is more uncertain. Ideally direct self-regulation requires no external control. However, Barber recognizes that direct participation and self-regulation will not always be possible and that certain agencies with decision-making powers will be required even within strong democracy. In relation to these agencies some external mechanism may be necessary to guarantee their adherence to the principles of participatory democracy. Further, even though the presence of prior values is denied by strong democrats, the commitment to strong democratic principles could itself, as Craig argues, be seen as such an independent value and some system of external review might be advisable to safeguard adherence to it.[70]

Conclusions

These two alternative, broader approaches to process, although coming from different traditions, share common characteristics. They both see full process as fundamental to the authority of state action, and they both recognize that participation is required at every stage of government in

[69] B. Barber, *Strong Democracy: Participatory Politics for a New Age* (Berkeley, Calif., 1984), 137.   [70] Craig, *Public Law and Democracy*, 382.

order to legitimize the decisions reached. According to liberal pluralism the individual is distinct from the state and is entitled to expect the legitimate exercise of state authority, one component of which demands that all decisions be taken in the full reflection of the public interest. According to strong democracy, on the other hand, where there is no clear line between individual and state, the authority of action is derived exclusively from the process of direct participation and self-regulation through which decisions evolve. Thus, despite the differences in emphasis, under either approach the individual, who claims a fair hearing before a policy application decision is made affecting her, is relying essentially on the same principle as that which entitles her to participate in the legislative process of policy formulation. The precise nature of the participation required at either point will depend on the stage in the process of policy implementation at which the decision occurs, but the basis of the claim remains essentially the same. It is not to protect her independent substantive interests that she participates, but to ensure the true authority of the decision. Admittedly the two approaches reflect very different attitudes towards the role of government, but both emphasize the fundamental role of process in the legitimization of governmental decisions, and thus provide an alternative view of the law's involvement in the regulation of process which could encourage the law to develop beyond the narrow parameters of interest protection set by the more traditional approaches. Most significantly a broader approach of this nature would both break the essential link between substantive interests and procedural protection, claims to fair procedures would not longer be secondary, and would carry the demands for fair process into the realm of policy formulation.

However, immediately the claim to fair process is recognized as independent of any substantive right in need of protection, the problem of rationing emerges. Under the traditional common law approach rights to procedural protection only arise when substantive interests are at stake and can be claimed only by those directly involved: the demand is strictly limited. At first sight it may be thought that the broader approach which provides no such in-built rationing mechanism must be unworkable in practice: the widest possible participation is required at every stage of policy implementation and any process failure would offend the rights of all citizens, however remote their substantive interests. In the first place, however, it is important to refine the notion of participation. The broader approach, particularly in its liberal pluralist guise, requires participation as a mechanism for ensuring the full reflection of the public interest, not merely as an end in itself.[71] The nature of the interests requiring expression

---

[71] For the practical implications of strong democracy in this context see Richardson, *Law, Process and Custody*.

will, therefore, differ according to the subject-matter of the policy and the stage within the process of policy implementation at which the decision is made: the full reflection of the public interest does not require universal participation at every stage. For the creation of national policy or guidelines it might be appropriate to provide for the reflection of individual preferences through democratic representation, and to combine that with the open consideration of technical information and the views of experts and groups with an interest at the national level. Open consultation with third parties would become essential to the policy-making process within central government. On the other hand, once it could be assumed that national policy guidelines were appropriately created, then participation in the creation of more specific and directly applicable rules should be designed to ensure that the general policy was accurately distilled in the light of 'local' circumstances, whether those be defined according to geography, institution, or subject-matter. A different range of consultees would be involved. In many cases a series of rule-making stages will be required in order to render national policy operational at a local level, but at each stage participation could be limited to those with immediately relevant interests. Similarly at the application stage, once it can be assumed that the above procedures have been followed and the relevant policy is fully reflective of the public interest, participation could be limited to those whose interests were relevant to the appropriate application of the policy in that individual case. The approach does not demand infinite participation at every stage.

Secondly, while the recognition of a right to full process possessed and enforceable by all, irrespective of their substantive interest in the decision, may conjure up the spectre of vexatious challenge, the floodgates breached; the essential justification for the broad approach to process must be borne in mind. In theory all the procedural requirements demanded by this approach should be designed to ensure that decisions are reached in the full reflection of the public interest, and if such requirements are ignored any citizen has a legitimiate claim; it is not vexatious to demand the authoritative exercise of public power. In practice if an individual, whether a third party or someone with a direct interest, sought to rely on a technical breach of procedure, the courts should continue to have the power to uphold the decision despite the breach, but only if satisfied that the procedural breach in no way affected the decision-maker's ability to assess the public interest. The courts would retain their discretion but would exercise it in furtherance of the broader aims of their procedural intervention.

In sum a broader approach to the law's involvement in the regulation of process has been suggested which grounds the justification for that involvement in the notion of legitimate authority. Its application is not limited to the present role of the common law: it provides the justification for all legal involvement, whether by legislation or common law. However, when applied to the common law it can be used to justify claims to full process in the face of legislative silence, or even hostility, at all stages of policy implementation, and is not limited in its application to the protection of individual interests. It could, therefore, equip the judiciary with a mechanism designed for the furtherance of democratic values rather than merely the protection of recognized substantive interests.

Sections of this chapter have appeared in G. Richardson *Law, Process and Custody: Prisoners and Patients* (Butterworths, Law in Context, 1993).

6

Findings of Fact: The Role of the Courts

Ian Yeats

INTRODUCTION

A public body or official charged with a duty or entrusted with a power has, even in the most routine and mechanical situations, to make some findings of fact and frequently to make some assumptions or findings about the applicable law. Those affected by the decisions of such bodies or officials may through the process of judicial review invite a court to find that some of these findings or assumptions are 'wrong', that the body or official has been guilty of 'error'. If the court always accepts such invitations and agrees to impose its own view of what is 'right' for the decisions of the agency, the court will be swamped with applications and the agency will have no worthwhile purpose. If the court always declines these invitations and always defers to the agency's conclusions, the agency will ensure an extended range of functions. Where the line is drawn between those extremes depends on the view taken of the constitutional role of agencies discharging public functions of various kinds, of the proper scope of judicial supervision, of alternative mechanisms for ensuring that agencies discharge their functions responsibly and of the amount of judicial time and effort which may properly be expended on such questions.

The jurisdictional principle and its limits

In the simplest situations, the facts which have to be found and the law which has to be determined can be presented as a series of preconditions which have to exist before the duty can be performed or the power exercised. A board is empowered (or obliged) to take some action in respect of 'dilapidated dwelling houses in Greater London'. The ability (or duty) to act in respect of a particular building depends on establishing that it is (1) in Greater London, (2) a dwelling house and (3) dilapidated. If the board finds that the three conditions are satisfied, it may (or must) proceed. If it finds that any one of them is not satisfied, then it cannot.

A disgruntled property owner invites a court to review the board's findings: the court has to decide whether, and how far, it should defer to the board's views. If the complaint is that the premises are not in Greater

London, the court is likely to intervene. The question defines in the most literal way the area in which the board has competence, can easily be resolved by a court, and is unlikely to occur frequently. The question is not about the correctness of the decision on the building's fate, but about whether the board whose decision is under review had the function of determining it. If the complaint is that the house is not dilapidated, the court will be reluctant to intervene. That is a question involving elements of judgment which naturally appears to have been remitted to the board and which it, rather than the court, has the facilities and probably the specialized expertise to answer; if the court were to agree to answer it, every decision of the board would be potentially reviewable. If the complaint is that the premises do not constitute a dwelling house, the issue is less clear-cut. The court might think it proper to impose its view, partly because the problem might be posed in a narrowly legal form, that of identifying the correct sense in which the expression 'dwelling house' was used in the legislation.

These issues could be, and often were, presented in terms of defining the jurisdiction of the subordinate body. Some matters determined or defined its area of action; its decisions on these matters were provisional, subject to ultimate resolution by a reviewing court. Other matters were assigned as the responsibility of the body itself; its decisions on these had to be respected by the court. Some errors 'went to jurisdiction' and others were 'within jurisdiction'.

The concept of jurisdiction is useful, at least when confined to situations where the subordinate agency has embarked on a decision of a kind not entrusted to it. It does represent a basis on which matters where strict judicial control is appropriate can be separated from those where it is not, but a looser (or no) supervision is called for. It does have a number of weaknesses. First, the court tends to justify its decisions by reference to the intention of the legislature; the exercise is presented as the logical one of determining the scope of the authority given to the agency and of deducing from that which questions are jurisdictional. This conceals such principled views as the reviewing court might have as to the apt level of review. Secondly, the various issues of law and fact may stand to each other and to the ultimate functions of the agency in more complex relationships than the simple list of threshold requirements in the first paragraph. Thirdly, where a court refused to review because, as it was said, the error was within jurisdiction, this gave the undesirable impression that the decision was wrong but unreviewable, that officials were getting away with blunders. Diplock LJ analysed the use of the words 'right' and 'wrong' in this context when the *Anisminic* case was before the Court of Appeal.[1] To say that a

[1] [1968] 2 QB 862.

decision was right might mean only that there was no one with authority to say that it was wrong. A decision by a subordinate agency which is neither subject to appeal nor held to be reviewable is necessarily in some sense right. To refuse to set it aside is not to countenance error but to accept that the agency is to have the ultimate say as to what is 'right'. Fourthly and most significantly, the jurisdictional analysis appears inflexible. It fastens on the characterization of the question to be decided rather than on the quality of the answer. It tends to suggest that, if the agency has blundered outside its authority, its decisions have no legal effect, but that, if it has stayed within it, its decisions are immune from judicial scrutiny. The court appears to be faced with a choice between full review and no review, between substituting its view for that of the agency and deferring to that of the agency. A court which felt that it had inadequate supervisory powers might react in two ways. It might tend to classify a question as jurisdictional for the purposes of asserting control and thereby extend or distort or vary the meaning of jurisdiction;[2] or it might develop techniques for reviewing the quality of decision-making even on matters which would traditionally be analysed as within jurisdiction, so that decisions could be reviewed if they were extremely or unacceptably wrong. The case-law afforded many illustrations of both these developments.

As a result of these developments the focus is not so much on which errors are reviewable but on whose decision is to be accepted as 'right'. Further the court has a choice between two broad levels of review: to substitute its own decision for that of the subordinate authority on the question in issue (strict review) or to intervene only if it concludes that the subordinate authority's decision falls in one of a number of ways outside the range of tenable or acceptable decisions (lax review). The court has a discretion at two levels, first to decide the appropriate latitude to allow the subordinate authority as a matter of principle and then, since the remedies are discretionary, to decide whether a remedy should be granted in the particular circumstances. The range of reviewable decisions cannot therefore be comfortably fitted within the terminology of jurisdiction. This has led some to abandon the language of jurisdiction (and even of *ultra vires*) as the basis of review of errors of law or of fact.[3]

---

[2] The difficulties are illustrated by the judgment of Eveleigh LJ in *Pearlman* v. *Keepers and Governors of Harrow School* [1979] QB 56, explaining how a county court judge who had reached the wrong decision (in Eveleigh LJ's view) on whether central heating amounted to 'structural alteration, extension or addition' had gone outside his jurisdiction by asking himself the wrong question.

[3] See particularly the account by Sir John Laws in M. Supperstone and J. Goudie (eds.), *Judicial Review* (London, 1992).

Some preliminary issues

How do these questions arise?

In the first paragraph the simple situation was identified of an administrator having to determine the existence of a series of facts as a precondition of the valid exercise of some statutory function. It is possible to set out in greater detail the variety of ways in which such questions can arise. A body has power to do *A* or to decide whether *B* is the case or it has a power or duty to do something if *P*. Will a court seized of an application for judicial review from a person with sufficient interest listen to an argument (1) that what the body is doing is not *A*, or (2) that its decision that *B* is the case is wrong, or (3) that it refused to exercise its duty or power because it wrongly found that *P* did not exist, or (4) that it did exercise its duty or power because it wrongly found that *P* did exist, or (5) that it refused to exercise its duty or power because it wrongly found that *Q*, which did not exist, was a precondition for its exercise, or (6) that it did, or alternatively did not, exercise its duty or power because it wrongly found that *R*, which did exist, required, or alternatively precluded, its exercise?

So far it has been assumed that the legal and factual matters in respect of which error is alleged were identified in a statute or other enabling document and entrusted expressly to the judgment of the decision-maker. Similar issues can however arise where the decision-maker proceeds on an erroneous assumption about the existence, non-existence, or quality of facts which he has voluntarily but legitimately chosen to take into account as relevant to the way in which a statutory discretion is exercised. A board may for example validly decide in the exercise of its discretion to make the possession of a particular qualification a relevant factor in the allocation of grants, and then proceed on the erroneous belief that an applicant does not have the stipulated qualification.

Is the decision-maker exercising a discretion?

If in a particular situation a court prefers to exercise a lax review and will interfere with a decision, for example as to whether certain facts exist, only if it was unreasonable, it follows that different decisions, indeed contrary decisions, can be accepted as in some sense 'right'. Therefore the decision-maker seems to have been exercising something in the nature of a discretion. In *Puhlhofer* v. *Hillingdon London Borough Council*[4] Lord Brightman did indeed refer to 'the existence or non-existence of a fact' as being 'left to the judgment and discretion of a public body'. There are

---

[4] [1986] AC 484, 518.

difficulties in so linking judgment and discretion.[5] Suppose that on a given question a reviewing court will not interefere with an agency's decision, whether it is *A* or *B*, because either decision would be reasonable and supported by relevant evidence. Those looking from outside as reviewing courts or as commentators can say that the agency must have had a discretion which acceptable decision to select. From the internal point of view of the agency, however, the position should be otherwise. An agency which has a true discretion (e.g. to decide whether or not to refer a complaint to a committee of inquiry) has to decide which course is in its view preferable. An agency which has to decide a question (e.g. whether someone is permanently resident in an area or homeless or married or an employee) must direct *itself* to find what it believes to be the right answer and not merely an answer from a range which will ultimately be held to be not unreasonable. In *Khawaja* v. *Secretary of State for the Home Department*[6] the immigration officer merely expressed himself 'satisfied that there are reasonable grounds to conclude that you are an illegal entrant'. Even if that had been the right test for a reviewing court to apply, the officer should certainly have asked himself whether he was satisfied that the applicant was an illegal entrant.

Conceptual categories

A court has to decide whether, and, if so, how far, to substitute its own views or to defer to those of the administrator. It can utilize different concepts to guide, or to justify, its choice.

First, it can classify the error[7] as one of law or of fact. It will be more disposed to intervene if the issue for decision or the error can be described as one of law. The court is able to claim exceptional competence in determining questions of law and constitutional propriety in holding subordinate agencies answerable for their interpretations of enabling legislation.

Secondly, the distinction between jurisdictional (or precedent) and non-jurisdictional facts is still acknowledged; its meaning and continued vitality will be considered later. The court has to decide whether a fact which has to be established is to be classified as jurisdictional or not. In the case of a jurisdictional fact (one which determines the limits of the agency's authority), the court will be able to impose its view and is not confined to deciding whether the agency reached a decision which was reasonably available.

Thirdly, if it is not dealing with a jurisdictional fact, the court has

---

[5] On the idea of discretion in the finding of facts, see D. J. Galligan, *Discretionary Powers* (Oxford, 1986), 33–7.　　　　　　　　　　　　　　　　　　　　　　　[6] [1984] AC 74.

[7] The word error is used here and elsewhere where the context so demands to mean something which is alleged by the applicant for judicial review to be an error.

necessarily a considerable latitude in deciding how easily it is to be persuaded that the decision was not one to which the decision-maker could reasonably come. The extent of this latitude may depend on the character of the question to be decided and on the characteristics of the body taking the decision.

Each of these categories will be examined further in the ensuing sections.

ERRORS OF LAW

Issues and errors of law

Some errors of law arise because the wrong answer has been given to a question of law which the subordinate authority had to decide in exercising its functions. There may be a question as to the legal sense in which a particular word or expression is used. What precise meaning should be given to the expression 'accommodation' in section 1 (1) of the Housing (Homeless Persons) Act 1977?[8] Does a statute which authorizes payment of benefits to 'widows' include in this expression a widower, or a woman who had been divorced or separated from her husband before his death? Again, there may be other questions on the interpretation of enabling or secondary legislation. In *Anisminic Ltd.* v. *Foreign Compensation Commission*[9] the respondent erred in deciding as a matter of law that the appellant was not entitled to compensation because its successor in title, an Egyptian organization, was not a British national, as in its view the regulations required. More generally, there may be questions as to the purposes and objectives for which discretionary powers may be used, or the considerations which are in law relevant or irrelevant to their exercise.

Further, an incidental question of law may also arise in the course of finding facts. In order to decide whether a particular claimant is in fact a widow under the legal definition which has been adopted, it may be necessary to decide whether or not her foreign marriage had been valid by the English conflicts rules. An erroneous answer to that legal issue may invalidate the decision.

Clearly a subordinate body which has in the court's view given the wrong answer to one of these legal questions has committed an error of law. There are however situations where the error may be classified as one of law or of fact. A court may be more willing[10] to allow review if the error is

---

[8] *Puhlhofer* v. *Hillingdon London Borough Council* [1986] AC 484. The section is now s. 58 of the Housing Act 1985 as amended by s. 14 (2) of the Housing and Planning Act 1986.
[9] [1969] 2 AC 147.
[10] Or indeed on one view able to review at all only if it is so classified.

classed as the former, or rather it may be inclined to class the error as the former if it thinks that review is appropriate. The first occurs where the question involved deciding whether a particular set of circumstances fell within a legal concept. Wrong determinations of such questions can be treated as errors of law or as errors of facts. The problem has been extensively analysed[11] and will not be further considered. The second arises because when, as explained later, a decision is struck down because it was unreasonable or because there was no evidence or insufficient evidence on which it could reasonably have been based, it is sometimes described as suffering from an error of law. In *Din (Taj)* v. *Wandsworth London Borough Council*[12] Lord Wilberforce said that a decision 'may be subject to judicial review for error in law including no doubt absence of any material on which the decision could reasonably be reached'. Problems of classification in these cases have usually arisen in contexts other than judicial review, notably where an appellate court has jurisdiction to entertain an appeal only on a point of law.[13] The proper classification is not necessarily so crucial in judicial review cases; the classification as an error of law may be adopted only to give greater constitutional respectability to judicial intervention.

Review of errors of law

The circumstances in which the courts will grant judicial review on the basis of an error of law no longer derive from a clear distinction between jurisdictional and non-jurisdictional questions. They are relevant to the scope of review for errors of fact on two grounds. First, decisions on questions of fact can, as just explained, be classified as errors of law or, as Lord Griffiths has less neutrally put it, 'all too easily be dressed up as issues of law'.[14] Secondly, many of the arguments of principle for or against permitting wide-ranging review of errors of law are applicable also to the review of errors of fact.

The courts were able by the revival of the doctrine of error of law on the face of the record[15] to control a decision vitiated by a patent and obvious error of law which did not go to jurisdiction. They also developed review on the grounds that there was no evidence[16] for the agency's decision or

---

[11] See C. T. Emery and B. Smythe, *Judicial Review* (London, 1986), ch. 3.

[12] [1983] 1 AC 657, 664. The proceedings in this case were actually in the form of an action for damages and mandatory injunction in the county court.

[13] e.g. *Edwards* v. *Bairstow* [1956] AC 14.

[14] *R.* v. *Hull University Visitor ex p. Page* [1993] AC 682, 694.

[15] *R.* v. *Northumberland Compensation Appeal Tribunal ex p. Shaw* [1952] 1 KB 338.

[16] A familiar example was *Coleen Properties Ltd.* v. *Minister of Housing and Local Government* [1971] 1 WLR 433, which concerned the statutory power of review under the Housing Act 1957.

that the evidence was insufficient to support the conclusion which had been reached. Finally the decision in *Anisminic Ltd.* v. *Foreign Compensation Commission*[17] provided an opportunity for reconsidering the scope of review for error of law.

It is not necessary to explore here whether the developments in the scope of review since then have accorded with the intentions of the judges who decided the *Anisminic* case. The outcome of these developments has most recently been examined in *R.* v. *Hull University Visitor ex parte Page.*[18] The majority and minority view acknowledged[19] that 'in general any error of law made by an administrative tribunal or inferior court in reaching its decision can be quashed for error of law'.[20] This can be expressed either, as the House seemed to prefer, in the terms that a subordinate court or body which makes an error of law acts outside its jurisdiction or at least acts *ultra vires* or more radically in the terms that jurisdiction is no longer relevant to defining the court's supervisory power where an error of law arises.

Nevertheless a majority in the *Hull University* case held that the visitor's decision could not be reviewed for alleged error in interpreting or applying the law of the university (i.e. to an error of law within jurisdiction[21]). The powers of the visitor are not created by statute; the founder of the eleemosynary charitable foundation had established his own system of law and appointed a visitor with exclusive jurisdiction to resolve disputes as to that distinctive law (which were not part of the general law). The majority justified its decision, partly on the grounds that the visitor had been held immune from review on matters within jurisdiction for over 300 years, partly on grounds of convenience in that the visitor's jurisdiction was 'swift, cheap and final',[22] and partly perhaps on the grounds that otherwise the courts might have a surfeit of such cases. The minority sought to bring even a distinctive corporation with its own law within the general scope of judicial review and the principle that the ordinary courts should be the final arbiters of questions of law.

It is not clear how the outlook of the majority might be relevant to the decisions of statutory bodies. They cite with approval the speech of Lord Diplock in *Re Racal Communications Ltd.*,[23] who referred to a presumption that Parliament does not intend subordinate agencies conclusively to determine questions of law. However, some statutory agencies administer a system of law which is distinct from the general law in a more substantial

---

[17] [1969] 2 AC 147.   [18] [1993] AC 682.
[19] Referring with approval to Lord Diplock's statement in *O'Reilly* v. *Mackman* [1983] 2 AC 237, 278.   [20] Per Lord Browne-Wilkinson at 702.
[21] The minority, Lord Mustill and Lord Slynn of Hadley, concurred in the result as the visitor had made no error of law.   [22] Per Lord Griffiths at 694.
[23] [1981] AC 374.

and less technical sense than that administered by a university visitor. A court could take the view that some kinds of subordinate agencies could be permitted to form their own views as to at least technical legal questions in their specialized areas of competence so long as their views were not unreasonable, that is to say they could be conceded a latitude even in determining issues of pure law. The Court of Appeal has thought that a body like the Price Commission might to some extent develop its own view of the applicable law[24] and extended a similar indulgence to a supplementary benefits appeal tribunal in *R.* v. *Preston Supplementary Benefits Appeal Tribunal ex parte Moore*,[25] where Lord Denning MR observed that[26] 'it is plain that Parliament intended that the Supplementary Benefit Act 1966 should be administered with as little technicality as possible. It should not become the happy hunting ground for lawyers. The courts should hesitate long before interfering by certiorari with the decisions of the appeal tribunals.' A more sweeping view of this kind was taken by the United States Supreme Court, which in *Chevron USA Inc.* v. *Natural Resources Defense Council Inc.*[27] conceded that the courts could accept reasonable administrative interpretations of the law and accept an administrative agency's reasonable interpretation of ambiguous legislation. The factors which might lead a court to interfere with or defer to an administrative agency's view of the applicable law parallel those to be considered later which influence the court's attitude to alleged errors of fact.

Review for error of law is no longer sharply based on the old concept of jurisdiction. Instead there is apparently a presumption that a subordinate agency has to observe the general law and its decisions are potentially reviewable unless (1), as has been considered, the court exercises restraint out of respect for the character of the agency or of the law which it has to administer, or (2) there are provisions or implications in the statute which displace the presumption that matters of general law and of the interpretation of legislation are for the courts.[28] This bears in two respects

[24] See e.g. *HTV Ltd.* v. *Price Commission* [1976] ICR 170.

[25] [1975] 1 WLR 624. The case was argued on the basis of an error of law on the face of the record, a category now apparently rendered obsolete by the *Anisminic* case, but there seems no reason why the approach adopted in that case should not still be relevant.

[26] At 631.

[27] 467 US 837 (1984). For a recent analysis of the case and the extensive subsequent litigation, see C. R. Sunstein, 'Law and Administration after *Chevron*', (1990) 90 *Col. LR* 2071.

[28] The majority in the *Hull University* case [1993] AC 682 also considered this and gave prominence to the dissenting judgment of Geoffrey Lane LJ in *Pearlman* v. *Keepers and Governors of Harrow School* [1979] QB 56, as approved by the House of Lords and Privy Council in *South East Asia Firebricks Sdn. Bhd.* v. *Non-Metallic Mineral Products Manufacturing Employees Union* [1981] AC 363 and *Re Racal Communications Ltd.* [1981] AC 374.

on review of errors of fact. First, as noted already, certain kinds of fact may be reviewable by being treated as errors of law. Secondly, review of errors of fact may also cease to be so dominated by the notion of jurisdiction.

ERRORS OF FACT

Introduction: constitutional factors

Actions for judicial review are heard by a relatively limited number of judges of the High Court (subject to ordinary appellate procedures), who have a general expertise in administrative proceedings and law but not necessarily in any particular area of administrative activity. They are not heard by specialist administrative tribunals or by lower courts. A guiding principle of the Civil Justice Review[29] and of the facultative provisions of Part I of the Courts and Legal Services Act 1990 (enforced by regulatory provisions and by penalties in costs) was to ensure that cases were tried by the lowest possible court, so that the most expensive proceedings and most eminent judges should be reserved for cases which were important because they were technically difficult, or of constitutional significance, or determined the destiny of large sums. Section 1 (10) of the Act provides that 'no such order shall be made so as to confer jurisdiction on any county court to hear any application for judicial review'. There are no local public law circuit judges as there are commercial circuit judges in Liverpool and Manchester. Judicial review cases do not necessarily entail difficult issues of law. The restriction to a limited number of judges of the High Court confines the judicial review process to cases which are important for other reasons. They may concern gross abuses of governmental power, touch upon issues of political controversy, give guidance on methods of decision-making, or settle fundamental points determinative of a whole range of individual cases. Courts exercising such powers have themselves a wide measure of discretion; there are advantages in general principles being developed by a collegiate body with a shared understanding of their role. An unwillingness to review findings of fact takes its place alongside a requirement of leave, restrictive standing rules, and limitations on the bodies susceptible to judicial review as a means of preserving a manageable work-load for such a body. If a burgeoning case-load forces an increase in the number of judges or in the range of courts hearing judicial review applications,[30] then the restrictive approach to review for error of fact will have to depend on other considerations.

[29] *Report of the Review Body on Civil Justice*, Cm. 394 (1988).
[30] As canvassed by the Law Commission, *Administrative Law: Judicial Review and Statutory Appeals*, Consultation Paper no. 126 (1993).

The grander issues of the constitutionality of judicial review bear only peripherally on the subject-matter of this chapter in that the courts might only indirectly appear to encroach on the political or policy-making territory of others. There is of course a choice as to whether the courts or some other public body should ultimately determine certain questions on which the rights, entitlements, or immunities of the individual may depend. The choice relates more however to the relative practical suitability of different procedures and bodies and to whether, if the courts do seem to have the edge, there is sufficient justification for the extra demands on various public, as well as private, purses. In the area of adjudication on factual questions, there are two primary purposes of judicial review. One is the constitutional role, emphasized by the courts and traditionally expressed in terms of the will of Parliament, of ensuring that subordinate bodies stick only to the tasks entrusted to them. There is further a public interest in ensuring that those powers (including incidental powers of determining facts) are so exercised as to lead to results which satisfy public expectations both in the appropriateness of individual decisions and, where the powers are exercised in respect of large numbers of individuals and/or by a range of officials, in the coherence and balance of the totality of decisions. In pursuance of this function judicial review should ensure that a decision is taken by such procedures and with such attitudes that those who are affected by the outcome will at least have the feeling that it has been properly, carefully, and responsibly made. There may also be situations in which the courts will have to intervene more directly either because the results are beyond the limits of acceptability and/or because in the particular system under review alternative procedures or bodies are lacking which would provide the necessary assurances.

Introduction: a basic distinction

In *Khawaja* v. *Secretary of State for the Home Department*[31] the House of Lords had to decide as to their own function whether 'it is limited to deciding whether there was evidence on which the immigration officer or other appropriate official in the Home Office could reasonably come to his decision [that the applicant was an "illegal entrant"] (provided he acted fairly and not in breach of the rules of natural justice), or does it extend to deciding whether the decision was justified and in accordance with the evidence?'[32] The House decided that its powers were of the latter kind, Lord Fraser of Tullybelton stating that 'an immigration officer is only entitled to order the detention and removal of a person who has entered the country by virtue of an *ex facie* valid permission if the person *is* an

---

[31] [1984] AC 74.   [32] At 97, per Lord Fraser of Tullybelton.

illegal entrant. That is a "precedent fact" which has to be established.'[33] If the court's powers had been of the former kind, it could have considered only the rationality of the decision, whether the officer had acted on no evidence or had sufficient evidence for his conclusions or whether the officer had reached a decision to which no reasonable person in his position could have come. There is therefore recent high authority for the view that, not only are there two alternative levels of review, but also the language of precedent or jurisdictional facts is apt to express them. It will be necessary to consider how this distinction is made and whether it is being obscured by current developments.

Jurisdictional facts

A subordinate agency has to remain within the confines of its authority. Typically this means that it must deal with the kind of case and subject-matter entrusted to it and observe any financial, geographical, or similar limitations. Although the limits of the jurisdiction or authority are set by the existence of certain facts, these will commonly be uncontroversial or obvious, where errors will be rare and litigation fruitless. There is therefore relatively little judicial discussion of jurisdictional facts.[34] By contrast, where matters of opinion, judgment, and assessment are involved (and litigation more likely), the matter is more likely to be assumed to be something left to the determination of the agency. Where matters other than those obviously limiting the scope of authority are regarded as jurisdictional this does not imply that there is an independent intellectual process by which they can be identified and from which consequences as to the scope of review are to be derived. Rather the circumstances are thought to demand that the court impose its own view as to what is right and for that reason the issue is said to be jurisdictional. Logically two questions ought to flow from classification as a jurisdictional fact. First, the court should correct anything which it regards as error, however small and however understandable. Secondly, as the Court of Appeal acknowledged in *R.* v. *Secretary of State for the Environment ex parte Powis*,[35] the court can consider its own evidence on the matter and is not restricted to

---

[33] Ibid.

[34] There is a curious example in *R.* v. *Tower Hamlets London Borough Council ex p. Ferdous Begum* [1993] QB 447, in which the Court of Appeal held, as one ground of its decision, that the question of whether a local authority exercising its functions under the homelessness legislation had before it an application was a jurisdictional fact; the applicants were so mentally impaired that they were unable to understand that an application had been made. The housing authority had, said Butler-Scloss LJ at 459 'to establish the precedent fact . . . that an application for housing, in however informal terms, has been made'. The authority had erred and the court had jurisdiction to substitute its own opinion. The decision on the merits was reversed by the House of Lords: see [1993] AC 509.

[35] [1981] 1 WLR 584.

scrutinizing what was before the decision-maker. If there are indeed issues to which this treatment is applied they deserve to be separately designated by such a term as jurisdictional facts for it is not simply a matter of correcting certain kinds of errors but of correcting wrong answers to certain kinds of questions.

The principal recent authority on classification as a precedent fact is *Khawaja* v. *Secretary of State for the Home Department.*[36] The central question was whether the applicants were 'illegal entrants' under section 33 (1) of the Immigration Act 1971 so that, although they had been permitted to enter and had been in the United Kingdom for some time, they might be deported. The House of Lords held that the status of illegal entrant was a precedent or jurisdictional fact whose existence had to be established to the satisfaction of the court, with the consequence, if it was not, that he was not in truth a person against whom the immigration officer could exercise the particular powers in issue. The House overruled part of its own recent decision in *Zamir* v. *Secretary of State for the Home Department,*[37] Lord Scarman holding that the House had been wrong in *Zamir* to reject 'the well-established principle that, where the exercise of an executive power depends on the precedent establishment of an objective fact, it is for the court, if there be a challenge by way of judicial review, to decide whether the precedent requirement has been satisfied'.[38] In a number of the earlier authorities in this area the subordinate decision was either clearly wrong or clearly right, so that either supervisory approach would have yielded the same result and the court did not have to choose its language with any precision. The decision was explained both on the statutory language and on the fact that the liberty of the subject was in issue.

An attempt was made to apply the reasoning of this decision to a different immigration situation in *Bugdaycay* v. *Secretary of State for the Home Department.*[39] The applicants, who had originally been admitted to the United Kingdom on other grounds, subsequently sought asylum because of a well-founded fear of persecution in their own countries. The House of Lords dismissed this argument because 'all questions of fact on which the discretionary decision whether to grant or withhold leave to enter or remain depends must necessarily be determined by the immigration officer or the Secretary of State in the exercise of the discretion which is exclusively conferred on them by s 4 (1) of the 1971 Act'.[40]

Little significance can be attached to the fact that the statute gave power to deport an illegal entrant, and did not in terms refer to a person who in the opinion of the Secretary of State was an illegal entrant or to a person

---

[36] [1984] AC 74.   [37] [1980] AC 930.   [38] Ibid., at 110.
[39] [1987] AC 514.   [40] Ibid. at 522–3, per Lord Bridge of Harwich.

who appeared to be an illegal entrant, or to the fact that the restriction to illegal entrants was an express statutory provision whereas the entitlement to claim asylum in accordance with the Geneva Convention was contained only in the immigration rules, under which the dangers which the prospective immigrant faced in another country were one of the relevant factors to be considered in granting admission to those who were on the face of the statute subject to immigration control.

A series of interrelated substantive considerations may justify the different approaches in the two cases. (1) Unless it were established that Khawaja was an illegal entrant, there was no power at all to deport him; if Bugdaycay established that he was entitled to protection under the Geneva Convention, he was merely entitled to the exercise of a discretion to permit him to enter the United Kingdom. (2) The state had to establish Khawaja's status in order to justify coercive action against him. Bugdaycay had to establish grounds which would persuade the state to confer on him some benefit. It is natural to look more strictly at the facts in the former kind of situation. In the well-known case of *White and Collins* v. *Minister of Health*[41] facts which enabled the state to interfere with property were regarded as jurisdictional: in *Puhlhofer*[42] facts which enabled the applicant to seek a benefit were not. (3) In *Khawaja* there is jurisdiction only over illegal entrants; they are the group separated from the general population over whom control can be exercised. The class of people over whom the Home Office has jurisdiction in the asylum cases are all those seeking to enter or remain in the country; each has to prove some basis on which to establish eligibility as refugees, visitors, students, returning residents, etc. Finally the volume of applications for asylum has caused concern. The Lord Chancellor told the House of Lords in July 1991 that the number of asylum seekers had increased from about 5,000 a year in 1988 to 30,000 in 1990. About 500,000 would-be refugees had applied for asylum in Europe in 1990.[43] Since a large proportion of these cases would involve disputed facts as to the status of the fugitive or his likely fate, there is an obvious disinclination to allow applicants for asylum to have a second chance by seeking to establish to the satisfaction of the court what they failed to establish to the officials of the Home Office.

Although in principle the classification of a question as jurisdictional or precedent entitles the court to substitute its own view for that of the decision-maker, this has to be qualified. First, the court may for practical reasons not be able to form its own view *ab initio* but may have to content itself with deciding whether the decision-makers on the evidence available

---

[41] [1939] 2 KB 838.   [42] [1986] AC 484.
[43] HL Deb., vol. 530, col. 912, 2 July 1991. The legislation foreshadowed in that statement is now the Asylum and Immigration Appeals Act 1993.

to or garnered by them had reached the right decision. A decision on the immigrants' status in *Khawaja* could be made only after extensive fact-finding and interviewing and assessment of the answers. This had been undertaken by the immigration authorities and could not be repeated by the court on a judicial review application. The court was therefore not finding the facts for itself but still exercising a review power by assessing the quality of the original decision-making.

Secondly, further deference to the decision-maker's conclusions was shown by the House of Lords in *R.* v. *Monopolies and Mergers Commission ex parte South Yorkshire Transport Ltd.*[44] The company contested the finding of the Commission, 'crucial to its jurisdiction', as Lord Mustill put it, that the geographical area by reference to which the existence of a merger situation had to be ascertained was 'a substantial part of the United Kingdom'.[45] Lord Mustill[46] summarized their further argument thus:

The question of jurisdiction . . . is a hard-edged question. There is no room for legitimate disagreement. Either the commission had jurisdiction or it had not, the fact that it is quite hard to discover the meaning of section 64 (3) makes no difference. It does have a correct meaning, and one meaning alone; and once this is ascertained a correct application of it to the facts of the case will always yield the same answer. If the commission has reached a different answer it is wrong, and the court can and must intervene.

But this argument was not accepted in its entirety: once the court had established that the commission had directed itself correctly as to the meaning of 'substantial', that meaning was itself imprecise and different decision-makers could reasonably come to different views as to whether an area was substantial in the context of a particular reference. This of course is precisely the reasoning which would have been appropriate even if the question had not been treated as jurisdictional. The analysis is similar to that in *Puhlhofer*. The court will ensure that the correct legal meaning is ascribed to 'substantial' or 'accommodation' but will accept a reasonable decision as to whether the facts of a particular case fall within this definition. It is not clear why Lord Mustill should appear to have accepted that the question was jurisdictional.

Non-jurisdictional facts

In principle it might be thought that (apart from facts which determined the scope of its authority) it would be for the subordinate agency to determine the facts which were expressly remitted to it or on which their substantive decisions were required to be based. In such cases their

---

[44] [1993] 1 WLR 23.   [45] Fair Trading Act 1973, s. 64 (3).   [46] At 32.

findings would be reviewable only if they resulted from inadequate evidence or were otherwise unreasonable. Such failings can be described as errors of law or sometimes as procedural shortcomings in that the decision had been based on irrelevant considerations or failures to provide a hearing. In addition there seem to be some circumstances in which a decision may be set aside because findings of fact were wrong.[47] It is therefore necessary to consider which factors (1) may make it more likely that a court will hold that a decision is wrong because of an error of fact or (2) increase the willingness of a court to hold that findings of fact are irrational.

Different kinds of facts

There are many different kinds of facts and they stand in different relationships to the ultimate issue to be decided or the ultimate function to be exercised.

Primary and secondary facts (involving inferences from primary facts) present different problems for the scope of judicial review. The former raise questions about the resources and procedures available to the body under review as contrasted with the suitability of judicial review as a mechanism for determining such factual questions. The latter are more likely to involve elements of judgment about which different reasonable people might entertain different views.

In finding some primary facts the body under review will have conducted tests or measurements, visited sites, heard the testimony of witnesses, consulted documents and records. It will then have reached a conclusion about what had been the case in the past or about what was the case at that particular time. The circumstances can never be recreated or the past circumstances recalled. A court exercising a power of review is not equipped to intervene. It must be limited to ensuring that the subordinate body had followed a procedure which was fair and appropriate in all the circumstances, that it made findings of all relevant facts, and perhaps in some cases that the finding was not wholly perverse. Other primary facts do not change and proof is as accessible to the court now as it was to the agency then. There are findings, for example, as to the distance between two places or as to whether a party or property possessed particular qualifications or characteristics. They can be demonstrated to be unequivocally wrong. It may no longer be disputed that there was an error, perhaps because the evidence actually before the decision-maker was misunderstood. A decision with such a palpable error is particularly irksome to those affected and there seems to be no reason why it should

---

[47] The matter is discussed by T. H. Jones, 'Mistake of Fact in Administrative Law' [1990] *PL* 507.

not be remedied on review if the original authority is unwilling or not empowered to reopen or revise it.[48] Such a decision, even if innocently reached, could even be called perverse, since perversity is not necessarily a conscious state, as Lord Brightman recognized in *Puhlhofer*.[49] In *Rootkin* v. *Kent County Council*[50] the council was able to rescind a decision which it had made in favour of the individual because it had been based on an error of this kind. The precise extent of this power is uncertain.[51] It may be limited to circumstances in which (in the absence of fraud or statutory provision) the error had resulted in the grant of a benefit to be enjoyed over a period of time and not to a determination of entitlement to a once and for all benefit already provided to the applicant. However, although the court in *Rootkin* did not rely on this reasoning, it is difficult not to see some relevance in the fact that what was to be determined (the distance between Helen Rootkin's home and school) was a demonstrable matter of unchanging fact and not the conclusion of an exercise of judgment. If a decision favourable to the individual can in some circumstances be set aside because based on an error of fact, so also should a decision denying some benefit to the individual. Similar reasoning lay behind the decision in *R.* v. *Northumberland Compensation Appeal Tribunal ex parte Shaw*,[52] where the error was legal but manifest, but it applies with comparable force to factual misunderstandings.

Where a reviewing court is concerned with secondary facts, the more that the issue to be decided or the concept to be applied involves elements of law, the greater is the appropriateness of judicial intervention; the more that it involves questions of policy or judgment or taste, the less appropriate it becomes. If however the crucial facts or concepts involve some technical (other than legal) specialism, then, especially if those who are primarily responsible for determining them are specialists in the appropriate area or if they are by experience in and familiarity with it able to acquire the specialist knowledge, there is much to be said for not interfering with their decisions save in the most extreme cases. Indeed, although judicial intervention is often justifiable on the grounds that it promotes consistency, spasmodic review in specialist areas may distort a coherent pattern. Where many similar cases occur, the task of determining facts, especially those involving evaluation or assessment, is easier if fact patterns become clear and comparisons can be made. This cannot be done where only the facts of an isolated case come before a reviewing court.

A decision may be alleged to have been taken in the positive but

[48] Many of the examples cited ibid. are of this kind.
[49] [1986] AC 484, 518 ('a case where it is obvious that the public body, consciously or unconsciously, are acting perversely').   [50] [1981] 1 WLR 1186.
[51] See M. B. Akehurst, 'Revocation of Administrative Decisions' [1982] *PL* 613.
[52] [1952] 1 KB 338.

mistaken belief that something existed or to have been taken in ignorance that something was the case. The latter may involve either a positive belief that something was not the case or a failure to advert at all to the possibility of its existence. The effect of any of these failures may depend on the kind of decision which ultimately has to be made. That may be a narrow one, dependent on a limited number of clearly identified facts. The ultimate decision may however be a vague or open-ended one, for instance that some other person or institution 'is acting or proposing to act unreasonably'. The range of possible facts which might bear on that is much wider, because it would include information not only on what the party immediately concerned had actually done or failed to do but on what other parties in similar situations might do or think appropriate or on what had been established by independent research as to the feasibility of a proposed course of conduct. The problem takes on a different character, namely how widely the decision-maker's net has to be cast to scoop up all available information. Finally the alleged oversight may have occurred in the context not of an obligation to reach a decision as to some particular issue, but as the basis of the exercise of a true discretion. Here the obligations of the decision-maker are more limited. He has to consider relevant and exclude irrelevant considerations, but this cannot mean that he is at fault for ignoring all possible assumptions. Suppose for instance that an authority which has power to allocate grants to students decides that it will not in general give grants to mature applicants because it believes that they are less likely to complete their courses of study successfully or that it will favour applicants for certain courses because it believes that they will be more likely to lead to employment. Is such a decision susceptible of attack if (1) there is no relevant research at all supporting such an assumption or (2) research has tended to show that these assumptions are false or (3) research has more or less conclusively demonstrated that they are false? The extent of the obligation to make accurate findings of facts must depend on the nature of the facts, the purpose of the inquiry, and the resources of the inquirer. In *New Zealand Fishing Industry Association* v. *Minister of Agriculture and Fisheries*[53] Sir Robin Cooke P held that the minister had acted reasonably in investigating complex questions relating to fishing quotas and that he was not to be expected to carry out the kind of survey which would have been expected of a royal commission examining the industry.

Two other bases of review overshadow this kind of error. The first is that there is a simple failure to have regard to all relevant considerations. Lord Diplock formulated the question to be answered in *Secretary of State for Education and Science* v. *Tameside Metropolitan Borough Council*[54] thus:

---

[53] [1988] 1 NZLR 544.   [54] [1977] AC 1014, at 1065.

'Put more compendiously, the question for the court is, did the Secretary of State ask himself the right question and take reasonable steps to acquaint himself with the relevant information to enable him to answer it correctly?' The second is the requirement of fair procedure; the deciding body must give an affected party the opportunity to submit evidence on crucial matters and must not keep the party in the dark about matters which could affect the outcome. Some burden rests on the party to apprise the body of appropriate information (so that acting in ignorance of facts which the affected party had an opportunity not properly exercised to put before it would not affect the validity of the decision), but the latter must have a duty to take proper and informed cognizance of it.

Scarman LJ[55] referred as a ground of judicial review to 'misunderstanding or ignorance of an established and relevant fact . . . The fact may be either physical, something which existed or occurred or did not, or it may be mental, an opinion.' The facts in question, professional opinion about the feasibility of selection and the attitude of head teachers, were crucial to the decision in that case. Although Scarman LJ's formulation was not precisely adopted in the House of Lords, Lord Wilberforce in an often cited passage observed, 'If a judgment requires before it can be made, the existence of some facts, then, although the evaluation of those facts is for the Secretary of State alone, the court must inquire whether those facts exist, and have been taken into account.'[56] In the *New Zealand Fishing Industry* case[57] Sir Robin Cooke P agreed with counsel 'that to jeopardise validity on the ground of mistake of fact the fact must be an established one or an established and recognised opinion; and that it cannot be said to be a mistake to adopt one of two differing points of view of the facts, each of which may be reasonably be held'. This suggests that the decision-maker must first take into account whether a body of opinion, etc. exists and then whether it is established and unassailable. An important consideration is therefore the weight to be given to the qualifying adjectives 'established' and 'material'. It is clear that the 'established' facts had to exist at the time the impugned decision was taken and that changes in circumstances or information which comes to light for the first time thereafter cannot be considered. However 'established' could mean known within the body of material actually available for consideration by the Secretary of State but apparently overlooked by him, or it could mean known at the time but not necessarily incorporated within the body of information accessible to the Secretary of State. The Court of Appeal in *R.* v. *Secretary of State for the Environment ex parte Powis*[58] treated *Tameside* as an unusual case and adopted a restrictive interpretation. A reviewing court could not range

---

[55] At 1030.   [56] At 1047.   [57] [1988] 1 NZLR 544, 552.
[58] [1981] 1 WLR 584.

beyond the material available to the reviewed authority but could consider only whether the decision was valid given the material on which it had to work. Professional opinion about selection was known by the Department of Education and Science and therefore in some sense presumed to be known by the Secretary of State. The most generous interpretation of 'established' was given by Cooke J in his judgment (the other members of the Court of Appeal relied only on a breach of natural justice) in *Daganayasi* v. *Minister of Immigration*.[59] He was prepared to treat information known to a doctor appointed by him (but not an employee of his department) to carry out an examination of the child as being established facts.

The requirement of materiality presented no problem in *Tameside*: it was clear that, if the minister had considered the particular information and had yet come to the view that the council were proposing to act unreasonably, then (given the particular meaning ascribed to the statutory adverb 'unreasonably'), even though the evaluation of the facts was for him to perform, his decision would have been struck down as unreasonable. In general does 'materiality' mean that the individual would have to establish on a balance of probabilities that, if the factual error or assumption had not been made, a decision in his favour would have been made? Is the question whether the same decision would have been made or could have been made or whether a different decision would have been made or could have been made? There is some information about how this question is decided where the argument is that irrelevant considerations were taken into account. In *R.* v. *Broadcasting Complaints Commission ex parte Owen*,[60] the Divisional Court, approving and explaining the test adopted by Forbes J in *R.* v. *Rochdale Metropolitan Borough Council ex parte Cromer Ring Mill Ltd.*,[61] held that, where the reasons for taking a particular course of action were not mixed and could be clearly distinguished, but where the court was quite satisfied that even though one reason was bad in law, nevertheless the statutory body would have reached precisely the same decision on the other valid reasons, then the court would not interfere by way of judicial review.

Different kinds of decisions

A court then may be persuaded to exercise its powers of review over a subordinate agency if (1), whether or not the question is one going to jurisdiction, the agency overlooked the existence, or misunderstood the significance of, an established and indisputable fact, or professed itself satisfied as to the existence of something which indisputably had none, (2) the agency gave in the court's view the wrong answer to a question

---

[59] [1980] 2 NZLR 130.   [60] [1985] QB 1153.   [61] [1982] 3 All ER 761.

construed as jurisdictional, or (3) the agency reached conclusions which can be characterized as unreasonable or as disclosing errors of law in one of the ways described above. The court's willingness to exercise these powers may depend on the nature of the decision or the agencies or personnel by whom it was taken.

1. The agency may have been a specialist tribunal established to administer a particular subject-matter, such as the Boundary Commission,[62] the Price Commission,[63] or the Broadcasting Complaints Commission.[64] They have been given a defined role in a distinct body of work and a too-ready interference with their decisions would deprive them of their *raison d'être*. They are likely to have or rapidly to acquire a technical knowledge of their subject and to develop a consistency of approach; so long as their overall policy and approach are consistent with the objects of the statute, individual decisions can be left as they are. They are more likely than courts to have the resources and skill to make appropriate findings of fact. The subordinate agency may however be a political body, such as a government department or a local council. Even where it has relevant expertise, it is not expressly established to deal with that subject-matter and does not have the same independence. The authority may be of a different political persuasion from the party which promoted the legislation establishing the powers. The court may defer to the rules and policies developed by such an authority so long as consistent with the overall statutory language and objectives, but its decisions on technical or factual questions are not necessarily entitled to the same respect as those of specialist tribunals. Moreover in many of these cases the determining authority will itself have an interest in the outcome, for this may require it to take some action or expend resources.

2. Decisions may be taken by a unitary body with jurisdiction over all relevant cases; or by different members of a body working in a collegiate and co-ordinated manner; or by bodies whose decisions are subject to a special appeals or review machinery. In all these situations there are strong pressures towards consistency. The power to determine the application of statutory rules to individual cases may however be vested in a series of unconnected and uncoordinated individuals or authorities. Lord Denning in *Pearlman* v. *Keepers and Governors of Harrow School*[65] expressed the danger pithily. 'When an ordinary word comes to be applied to similar facts, in one case after another, it would be intolerable if half of the judges gave one answer and the other half another. No one would know where he stood.' The apparent preference of the House of Lords in the *Hull*

---

[62] *R.* v. *Boundary Commission for England ex p. Foot* [1983] QB 600.
[63] *HTV Ltd.* v. *Price Commission* [1976] ICR 170.
[64] *R.* v. *Broadcasting Complaints Commission ex p. Owen* [1985] QB 1153.
[65] [1979] QB 56 at 66.

University case[66] for Geoffrey Lane LJ's approach is curious, since it is in that kind of case that the inconsistent application of a statutory formula by different judges (or tribunals or councils) is most disturbing, as there is no policy reasoning for applying the formula differently in different parts of the country and much to be said for a definitive ruling. The decision of a reviewing court disposes of a range of future cases. This is to be contrasted with cases where interference by the court in an individual decision of the *Puhlhofer*[67] type would settle no question of principle but would provoke other disappointed applicants to seek a second opinion on their circumstances. There is however a concealed difficulty here. *Puhlhofer* is concerned with the acceptability of an isolated decision which is acceptable if it is at a permissible point on the range of possible answers. Is it acceptable for an authority *always* to give an answer which is at one end of that range, especially where this affects its own obligations and expenditure? This depends on how far the authority is free to adopt a policy: was it intended that entitlement to housing should depend on local policy or on a uniform national standard? An authority which has a discretion to award grants is free to adopt any policy which is not unreasonable and is in accord with the statutory objectives: is an authority which has a duty to award grants to all who satisfy, say, a residence criterion entitled to adopt a policy of applying that criterion in the most restrictive way possible? If not and if each individual decision is unlikely to be amenable to challenge, the overall policy could perhaps only be reviewed if some resolution adopting it can be identified.

3. Some importance might be attached to the consequences which flow from a decision under review. If the decision affects the private rights of citizens or denies them a benefit for which they are arguably eligible, the case for review is stronger. In *Secretary of State for Employment* v. *ASLEF* (No. 2)[68] the consequence of the Secretary of State's findings was that he was empowered to order a ballot of workers before a strike was called, and the court, although asserting its rights to examine the findings on which the decision was based, thought it inappropriate to interfere with the minister's decision.

CONCLUSIONS

The bases on which a court, in judicial review proceedings, will interfere with findings of subordinate decision-makers derive from no single theory of the purposes of judicial review. The willingness to review determinations of, or other errors of, law derives from a particular conception of the role

---

[66] [1993] AC 682.   [67] [1986] AC 484.   [68] [1972] 2 QB 455.

of courts in the apparatus of state administration in what Cotterrell[69] has described as a top-down vision of the legal system. The courts' distinctive function is to give final interpretations of statutory provisions or final determinations of points of law; it is this technical expertise which legitimizes their activities in suppressing the rival interpretations of lesser bodies in an administrative hierarchy. This pivotal role is enhanced by a judicious use of two extended concepts of error of law which enable the courts to control as they think appropriate and justifiable (1) the application of rules of law to particular facts and (2) conclusions which are unreasonable or are based on no or on insufficient evidence.

Where it is alleged that an individual decision is vitiated by an error of fact, a court is less inclined to interfere for no great principles are generally at stake and a willingness to intervene is an invitation to any disgruntled participant to try his luck in the courts. Fact-finding is a distinctive activity of subordinate agencies. The judicial role here is to secure that the administrative system is likely to produce results which, in so far as this has meaning in a particular case, are correct or at least satisfying to users of the system. This is done by adopting principles of sound administrative techniques to ensure that decisions are based on all relevant information, that participants have the opportunity of contributing to the fact-finding process, and, where appropriate, that reasons are given so that erroneous assumptions or beliefs are exposed. In other words the technique is to ensure that proper procedures are in place and followed. As a further disincentive to poor administration there is the risk that the decision-maker will be held accountable for decisions which are erroneous because, despite the adoption of proper procedures, an individual decision is based on a more or less incontrovertible misunderstanding, is beyond jurisdiction, or is unreasonable. At least the second of these is also derived from a 'top-down' view of the judicial role. Review of errors of fact in some cases also secures the protection of individual rights in two ways: (1) in ensuring that individual decisions are properly considered and (2) in ensuring that state agencies do not intrude without legal justification either by using the coercive power of the state against the citizen (by invoking procedures against property rights for example) or by denying the citizen rights (e.g. to grants or benefits) which the state intended him to have.

[69] See Ch. 1 above.

PART II

Alternative Mechanisms

7

Governing with Rules:
The Developing Agenda

Robert Baldwin

Most of the major activities of government are carried out in accordance with rules that are produced by the executive rather than through the parliamentary process. These various kinds of provision can be called 'governmental' rules[1] and it is these, rather than the terms of primary legislation or judicial decisions, that dominate the day-to-day operations of state departments and agencies.[2] Governmental rules can be divided into secondary and tertiary kinds. Secondary rules are items of delegated legislation: they are made in exercise of a statutory power to issue rules of legislative force—examples are binding regulations made under the authority of an Act of Parliament. Tertiary rules, in contrast, do not create rights or duties that can be directly enforced in the courts, although legal effects may result indirectly—examples are codes of practice such as the Highway Code. As is the case with the courts,[3] it is important to examine the part played by such rules within government; to investigate the authority or legitimacy of governmental rules; to consider what, in practical terms, can be achieved by employing such rules; and to explore the European dimension of governmental rule use.

I approach these issues by looking, in the first section of this chapter, at the case for employing governmental rules as opposed to other possible devices for achieving governmental purposes. In reviewing the arguments in favour of governmental rules, it is necessary to consider how legitimate rule use can be evaluated. The second section argues that the authority or

---

[1] On primary legislation see D. Miers and A. Page, *Legislation* (2nd edn. 1990); M. Zander, *The Law-Making Process* (4th edn. 1994).

[2] On the increasing use of secondary and tertiary rules in government see e.g. G. Ganz, *Quasi-legislation: Recent Development in Secondary Legislation* (1987); J. D. Hayhurst and P. Wallington, 'The Parliamentary Scrutiny of Delegated Legislation' [1988] *PL* 547, 551; R. Baldwin and J. Houghton, 'Circular Arguments: The Status and Legitimacy of Administrative Rules' [1986] *PL* 239. On rules in general see W, Twining and D. Miers, *How To Do Things with Rules* (3rd edn. 1991); F. Schauer, *Playing by the Rules* (1991) R. Baldwin, *Rules and Government* (forthcoming, 1995).

[3] See R. Cotterrell, Ch. 1 above.

legitimacy of rules (or other governmental devices) can be assessed by making reference to a limited member of identifiable values.

In turning, thirdly, to what can be achieved by means of governmental rules, the question of enforcement is central. I consider how rules may be designed so as to contribute to effective enforcement and ask how the pursuit of effectiveness can be reconciled with the furtherance of other objectives or values.

A particular concern of this volume is the European context within which government operates and the fourth section of this chapter looks at the special problems encountered in governing through rules within the European Community.[4] To this end I examine the array of European rule-types, the problems of selecting rule-types, and the measurement and achievement of successful rule use within the Community.

RULES VERSUS OTHER GOVERNMENTAL TOOLS

Using rules of one kind or another is by no means the only way to act governmentally. Ministers or officials may choose to operate by means of a number of processes other than rules.[5] They may, for example, exercise discretion managerially, they may delegate, adjudicate, consult, act informally, leave matters to the market or to third parties, negotiate, mediate, arbitrate, or simply do nothing.

If governmental rules are resorted to, a huge menu of rule-types is available and an intimidating list of labels is encountered including: delegated legislation; subdelegated legislation; quasi-legislation; administrative rules; codes of practice; approved codes of practice; guidance; guidance notes; policy guidance; guidelines; circulars; outline schemes, and statements of advice.[6] Rules bearing such labels may, moreover, vary in a number of respects, notably: as to legal form; legal effect or force; use of different prescriptions or sanctions; degree of specificity or precision in formulation;[7] accessibility or intelligibility;[8] and scope or inclusiveness.

From an administrator's point of view, there are a number of potential governmental purposes to be fulfilled by rules and there are a number of political motives that might be expected to accompany rule use. A common governmental purpose of rules is to give effect to policies by making these public and creating new legal liabilities but there are a number of other

---

[4] For an examination of the problems faced by British administrators in dealing with rules emanating from the European Community see David Williams, Ch. 10 below.

[5] See C. Hood, *The Tools of Government* (1983).

[6] See Ganz, *Quasi-legislation*; Baldwin and Houghton, 'Circular Arguments'.

[7] See C. S. Diver, 'The Optimum Precision of Administrative Rules' (1983) 93 *Yale LJ* 65.

[8] See R. Baldwin, 'Why Rules Don't Work' (1990) 53 *MLR* 321.

functions that may be accomplished. Rules may, for example, be used to offer interpretative guidance, information, or evidence as to the meaning of statutes or the content of statutory standards. Enabling rules also play a part in the organization and management of governmental activity (as in the case of administrative rules laying down procedures for making applications or criteria for deciding prosecution priorities or the distribution of largess).[9] Instructing officials on substantive matters is another major use of governmental rules and such rules may additionally facilitate planning and encourage consistency.[10] In the regulatory field, rules may be used to further a variety of compliance-seeking strategies.

A number of supposed advantages attach to the use of rules—advantages which may or may not come to fruition according to the circumstances.[11] Thus rules have been said to allow accumulated experience and wisdom to be distilled; decisions to be placed in their broader context; a longer and more detached view to be taken when deciding issues; equal and consistent treatment to be adopted in deciding cases; decision-makers to be directed towards relevant criteria and discouraged from referring to irrelevancies; staff of low training levels to be employed in relation to complex tasks; dangers of corruption, bias, or capture to be reduced; the legitimacy of decisions to be enhanced; references to experts to be facilitated, and broad public participation to be encouraged.

Turning to political motives for rule use, governments may use rules presentationally—so as to give the appearance of taking action or in order to enhance the perceived legitimacy of decisions. Rules, furthermore, may be employed to 'routinize' decisions rather than raise the quality of those decisions or the quality of participation offered to affected parties. The effect of a rule may, indeed, be to make challenging a decision more, rather than less difficult: to reduce rather than increase efficiency.[12] What cannot be assumed is that in practice the supposed benefits of rules will prevail, rather than their disadvantages.

How, then, should choices concerning the use and design of rules be approached? A starting-point in the debate on rule use is offered by examining what might be called the legalistic case for rules as put forward by Kenneth Culp Davis.[13] Davis argued in his highly influential book

---

[9] On government largess see C. Reich, 'The New Property' (1964) 73 *Yale LJ* 778. See also R. E. Megarry, 'Administrative Quasi-Legislation' (1944) 60 *LQR* 125.

[10] See J. Bradshaw, 'From Discretion to Rules: The Experience of the Family Fund', in M. Adler and S. Asquith (eds.), *Discretion and Welfare* (1969).

[11] For a review see C. E. Schneider, 'Discretion and Rules: A Lawyer's View', in K. Hawkins (ed.), *The Uses of Discretion* (1992). On the broad case for administrative rules see K. C. Davis, *Discretionary Justice* (1969).

[12] See J. L. Jowell, *Law and Bureaucracy* (1975), ch. 5.

[13] *Discretionary Justice*; for comment see R. Baldwin and K. Hawkins, 'Discretionary Justice: Davis Reconsidered' [1984] *PL* 570.

Discretionary Justice that the greatest hope for improving justice for individuals in the governmental system lay in eliminating unnecessary discretionary power. Thus he suggested that three techniques could be applied: confining discretion by laying down statutory or administrative standards; structuring discretion by using rules; and checking its use by having one official monitor another.[14] Davis conceded the need for discretion, criticized the 'extravagant' version of the rule of law that had no place for discretion, and urged the elimination of unnecessary discretionary power.[15] In cases of doubt, however, Davis was not disposed in favour of discretion, referring to its cancerous tendency to 'stifle the portion that is a government of laws'.[16]

Davis's approach is limited in a number of respects. Notably, his yardstick for evaluating processes is that of 'justice', a notion that emphasizes individuals' rights rather than social or collective concerns. His legalistic concept of justice plays down policy considerations and focuses attention on those demands typically made of administrators by subscribers to the legal paradigm—that is the typically legal view of the world which emphasizes fairness, openness, predictability, etc.[17] It minimizes the importance in public policy-making of such factors as efficiency, adaptability, and the furtherance of public, rather than private interests; it takes too much for granted that 'justice' is an agreed, unproblematic, apolitical bench-mark. Not only may 'justice' mean different things to different individuals or groups but it is arguable that governmental processes should serve other values beyond those encompassed in such a term.

The legal paradigm puts a good deal of faith in 'the idea that openness, rationality, generality and predictability (values centrally located in the rule of law ideal) will lead to fairness'.[18] In fact, rules may often procure less satisfactory results than other modes of operation (for example adjudications or discretions that are subjected to scrutiny) and they may circumvent the interests of individuals.[19] Using rules may sometimes *increase* levels of discretion—as where administrators are given a wide choice of rules to apply.[20] Davis advocates 'the right mix of rule and discretion'[21] but offers little help in describing how the optimal mix can be identified.

A further problem with the Davis argument arises out of its legalistic notion of decision-making.[22] This view underplays the complexity of

[14] See Davis, *Discretionary Justice*, 142.   [15] Ibid. 219.   [16] Ibid. 25.
[17] N. Lacey, 'The Jurisprudence of Discretion: Escaping the Legal Paradigm', in Hawkins (ed.), *The Uses of Discretion*, 362.   [18] Ibid. 369.
[19] See A. J. Reiss, Jr., 'Book Review of *Discretionary Justice*' (1990) 68 *Michigan LR* 994.
[20] See Jowell, *Law and Bureaucracy*, ch. 5; Baldwin and Hawkins, 'Discretionary Justice', 587–8.   [21] Davis, *Discretionary Justice*, 28.
[22] See generally K. Hawkins, 'On Legal Decision-Making' (1986) 42/4 *Washington and Lee* 1161–242.

decisions and tends to see these as occurring at discrete points in the administrative process. As a result, rules are seen as capable of controlling discretion at such points. In practice, decisions often occur as processes in which inputs from various sources and of different kinds produce a cumulative result. Using a rule to control discretion at one point (e.g. using a sentencing guideline to control judicial discretion) will thus often result in displacement of the discretion to another point in the process (e.g. to the prosecutorial level). Davis exaggerates the rule-maker's ability to pin down the bead of mercury that is discretion. The feasibility, and propriety, of using rules rather than other control devices (such as schemes of accountability or scrutiny) is a further issue on which Davis offers only limited help.

If Davis begs questions by employing a notion of justice that is yoked to legalistic concerns and by making optimistic assumptions concerning the effectiveness of rules, how can a more convincing means of justifying particular methods of carrying out government business be developed?

Advancing beyond this point involves recognizing that issues of process pose a broader question than whether rules or discretions are preferable. It demands an exploration of the different values to be served by governmental processes. Richard Stewart made a significant contribution on this front six years after *Discretionary Justice* was first published. In a celebrated article Stewart contrasted different modes of justifying governmental action.[23] The 'traditional' model required that such actions be authorized by the legislature, guided by rules, applied rationally, and scrutinized judicially. Such a model saw the governmental official as a 'transmission belt' for implementing legislative directives. It was, however, no longer possible to legitimate governmental action with reference to this model since the exercise of governmental discretion was inevitably seen as a policy-laden process rather than an unproblematic and mechanical application of the legislative will.[24] Nor, said Stewart, was another basis of legitimation still convincing. This was the 'expertise' model, according to which: broad discretions were necessary for successful management;[25] administrators were not political but professional beings; and public administration was objective in nature. Faith in the expertise model had waned, said Stewart, as experience eroded the general belief in an objective public interest, in the disinterestedness of agencies, and in their ability to achieve designated goals.

The weakness of these two modes of justification made way for the 'interest representation' model which looked to the 'affirmative' side of

---

[23] R. B. Stewart, 'The Reformation of American Administrative Law' (1975) 88 *Harvard LR* 1667.   [24] Ibid. 1683.
[25] See J. M. Landis, *The Administrative Process* (1938).

government and which justified processes according to their propensity to allow the proper representation of interests. A number of objections, however, pointed to the limitations of interest representation as a benchmark for good administration: unrestricted representation would lead to chaos and deciding issues concerning the adequacy of representation was a fraught and contentious process itself. 'Who may participate and how?' was a question left to be argued out.

For Stewart, the conclusion to be drawn was that interest representation might have a useful role in evaluation but it provided no comprehensive yardstick for assessing governmental procedures. For all his clarification of the issues, Stewart had stopped short of offering a coherent basis for evaluating governmental processes.[26]

A notable example of the evaluative baton being taken up again and more recently is Denis Galligan's work on discretion.[27] Galligan rejects the notion that there should be one central idea of the values supposed to be served by laws or discretion: 'law and legal institutions are part of the political and social composition of a society; they can be made instrumental in upholding values several and diverse. What those values are depends on the political theory and practice of a society.'[28]

The task for Galligan is to identify the set of political values that is to serve as a basis for controlling discretion (and no doubt for employing rules). He argues that choice of values must 'depend on a certain degree of personal preference' but by reflecting on the 'political theories that underlie modern, democratic, liberal societies . . . four basic values suggested are: stability in legal relations, rationality in decisionmaking, fair procedures and, finally, a rather loose residual category of moral and political principles.'[29]

The difficulties with such an eclectic approach are, first, a lack of precision concerning this 'residual category' and, second, the absence of any unifying basis for such values. Why, one might ask, are *these* values rather than any others important in any system of good government? A principle for selecting certain values is difficult to discern in Galligan's account and, as a result, there fails to emerge a convincing explanation of how justifications of particular processes can be made. It is, however, possible to see the seeds of such an explanation in the idea of a series of justificatory values. Such a notion was, moreover, also involved in Jerry Mashaw's contention in 1983 that 'the justice of an administrative system . . . means simply this: those qualities of a decision process that provide arguments for the

---

[26] For further discussion see R. Stewart, 'Regulation in a Liberal State: The Role of Non-Commodity Values' (1983) 92 *Yale LJ* 1357, and comment by P. Schuck at (1983) 92 *Yale LJ* 1602.   [27] D. J. Galligan, *Discretionary Powers* (1986).
[28] Ibid. 89–90.   [29] Ibid. 90.

acceptability of its decisions . . . these justificatory structures, once identified, should appear to be ubiquitous in the legal structure of public institutions and in ordinary experience.'[30] Mashaw thus suggests that there are three types of justice argument based on the 'bureaucratic rationality' model of justice, the 'professional treatment' model, and the 'moral judgement' model. These, for Mashaw, are distinct models but highly competitive.

In such an account, however, it is the notion of acceptability that proves the residual problem. 'What', it can be asked, 'constitutes "acceptable" and "acceptable" to whom?'[31] Without further underpinning, it seems, Mashaw faces many of the objections mounted against the participatory model. Not only that but the observer might protest that the offer of various bench-marks for evaluating administration is of limited utility if insufficient guidelines are offered on which bench-marks are appropriate and when.

An explanation that employs the notion of a language of justification can, however, be offered as a response to these difficulties. Thus, it can be argued that evaluating processes involves, as a matter of language use, making reference to certain recognized values. When legitimacy claims are made or assessed those persons involved can recognize relevant and irrelevant arguments with reference to certain acknowledged values and only these. Different persons may have different views as to the best possible version of liberal democracy but each can recognize the basis of the arguments made by others. When there is talk of this or that process being acceptable or legitimate (or unacceptable or illegitimate) in the sense that certain values are said to be satisfied or left unsatisfied, reference appears to be made to five key values or justificatory arguments. These are all problematic in some respects but it is the cumulative force of the claims to legitimacy that justifies. As has been argued elsewhere[32] the various claims to legitimacy can be organized under the following headings: the *Legislative Mandate Claim* (which bases support on the existence of an authorizing mandate from a representative parliament); the *Control or Accountability Claim* (which urges support on the basis of subjection to controls by the population); the *Due Process or Fairness Claim* (which advocates support with reference to the adequacy of processes in allowing

---

[30] J. Mashaw, *Bureaucratic Justice* (1983), 24–5. For other discussions of justificatory values see e.g. J. Freedman, *Crisis and Legitimacy* (1978); G. E. Frug, 'The Ideology of Bureaucracy in American Law' (1984) 97 *Harvard LR* 1277; J. Mashaw, 'Administrative Due Process: The Quest for a Dignitary Theory' (1981) 61 *Boston Univ. LR* 885.

[31] See R. Sainsbury, 'Administrative Justice: Discretion and Procedure in Social Security Decision-Making', in Hawkins (ed.), *The Uses of Discretion*, 301.

[32] See R. Baldwin and C. McCrudden, *Regulation and Public Law* (1987), ch. 3; Baldwin, *Rules and Government*, ch. 3.

participation and recognizing the interests of affected parties); the *Expertise Claim* (which refers to the need for, and benefits of, unfettered action by specialists); and the *Efficiency Claim* (which refers to the adequacy of substantive results).

The notion of such a language offers a means of understanding the evaluation of governmental processes and one that recognizes that trade-offs are made between different values worthy of pursuit. It does not give uncontestable answers to procedural choices since different persons may weight various values differently. What it does do is offer an account of the bases for such discussions. Thus, if I assert the legitimacy of a process I make a statement that evaluates the process according to collectively established bench-marks but I incorporate a personal view as to the appropriate weighting of those bench-marks or values. My idealism in such a weighting process may have to be tempered, however. If, for example, I value efficiency extremely highly but place a very low premium on accountability, I must be wary of basing legitimacy on an extreme efficiency/accountability trade-off since the reactions of other citizens (e.g. demanding accountability and criticizing the process and its operating institution) may ensure that efficiency is not achieved as anticipated in my analysis.[33]

To summarize, evaluations of rules are unlikely to convince if made with reference solely to 'traditional' legal values, nor, it seems, are wholly satisfactory bench-marks offered by the notions of expertise or interest representation in themselves. The idea of a language-based underpinning to claims of acceptability does suggest that five kinds of claim can be combined and it does accord with the way that legitimacy is debated.[34] In answering the question 'Why use rules?' it is thus necessary to go beyond Davis's unexplored appeal to a narrow set of values and to assess the performance of rules according to the five claims discussed. Rules of different kinds should, accordingly, be used in government when, in the particular circumstances, the kind of rule proposed will be most worthy of support when judged according to potential claims made under the five headings. Such an approach can be adopted at different levels of generality—looking at particular rules or particular types of rule. In turning now to consider the issues raised by secondary and tertiary rules a generic assessment will be offered.

---

[33] On legitimation generally see D. Beetham, *The Legitimation of Power* (1991).

[34] A good example is Robert Reiner's analysis of the rise and fall of police legitimacy in *The Politics of the Police* (2nd edn. 1992), ch. 2. The eight headings Reiner employs are readily subsumable under the five used here. See also R. Baldwin, 'Why Accountability' (1987) 27 *BJ Crim.* 97–105.

THE LEGITIMACY OF GOVERNMENTAL RULES

That secondary legislation and tertiary rules are used more and more to carry out the important functions of government seems hardly disputable. Ganz has pointed to the 'exponential growth' of administrative rules[35] and Hayhurst and Wallington have commented: 'Increasingly . . . primary legislation has become a skeletal enabling framework conferring not just the functions of detailed implementation but the power to determine major policy questions.'[36] A number of statutes, such as the Social Security Act 1986 and the Education Reform Act 1988, exemplify the high levels of legislative delegation carried out through modern primary legislation.

Looking in greater detail, first, at secondary legislation, one encounters rules of various forms: for example, Orders in Council; statutory instruments, regulations, rules, orders, schemes, warrants, and directives. Uniformity of promulgating procedures is ensured for statutory instruments[37] but not for other items of secondary legislation, which may be the products of various procedures. The case for employing delegated legislation is based on a number of now familiar arguments,[38] notably: that Parliament has neither the time nor the resources to legislate on details; that technical or specialist issues are better dealt with through departmental rather than parliamentary legislation; that consulting particular constituencies is more effectively accomplished by the executive than by Parliament; and that delegated legislation is more responsive to changes and crises than primary legislation.

In terms of the five bench-marks discussed above, the case for delegated legislation is principally based on the expertise and efficiency claims—Parliament and government, it has been said, would 'grind to a halt'[39] without a system of executive legislation. Claims under the other three headings may be more problematic, however. Thus, to argue that delegated legislation generally implements the legislative mandate involves a number of difficulties. In many instances it is not clear what Parliament's will was in the first place (Parliament's inability to form a view may have been a central reason for delegating). It might be suggested that Parliament commonly lays down a framework, leaving delegated legislation to flesh out details, but in practice Parliament often legislates 'blind' and

---

[35] Ganz, *Quasi-legislation*, 1.
[36] Hayhurst and Wallington, 'Parliamentary Scrutiny', 551.
[37] See Statutory Instruments Act 1946.
[38] See e.g. B. L. Jones, *Garner's Administrative Law* (7th edn. 1989), 54–7; D. Foulkes, *Administrative Law* (7th edn. 1990), ch. 3; A. W. Bradley and K. D. Ewing, *Constitutional and Administrative Law* (11th edn. 1993), 625–6.
[39] *First Special Report from the Joint Committee on Statutory Instruments 1977–8*, HC 169, para. 37.

much of the framework itself is a product of delegated legislation. The use of so-called Henry VIII clauses, which enable a minister to modify Acts of Parliament, is a practice that undermines particularly strikingly any claims to legitimacy based on the legislative mandate rationale.[40]

It is also questionable whether those promulgating delegated legislation can make strong claims to being accountable. Control by Parliament is possible but limited in scope.[41] There are no standard rules on laying procedures nor are there general provisions on publication for such subordinate legislation as is not covered by the Statutory Instruments Act 1946. Laying procedures are thus unreliable as devices for triggering parliamentary scrutiny and the quality of any scrutiny that results has also been questioned on a number of grounds,[42] notably: that time for debate is highly restricted; that MPs give such issues low priority; and that no procedure ensures that the views of the Joint Scrutiny Committee are considered before action on an instrument is taken.[43] Since 1973 a Statutory Instrument may be considered by a House of Commons merits committee, which may discuss the instrument for up to ninety minutes but which cannot vote on the merits of such legislation. No debate can take place on the floor of the House, however, in relation to such an instrument. A further factor also militates against effective scrutiny—this is the very drift from primary to secondary legislation that has been noted above. Thus the Joint Scrutiny Committee reported in 1986 that the volume, scope, and complexity of Statutory Instruments had not only increased in the previous five years but a qualitative change had also taken place:

Instead of simply implementing the 'nuts and bolts' of Government policy, Statutory Instruments have increasingly been used to change policy, sometimes in ways that were not envisaged when the enabling primary legislation was passed. We accept that this trend is not one which it will necessarily be easy to reverse.[44]

To justify the use of delegated legislation on the basis of its being subject to effective control by Parliament is thus problematic. It might be argued, however, that the courts exercise control in a manner that compensates for Parliament's weakness. The courts can declare items of delegated legislation to be void (e.g. because mandatory procedures have not been

---

[40] The device is not beyond modern consideration: in House of Commons debates on the Queen's Speech on 18 Nov. 1993 the Opposition expressed fears that the Government, by means of its Deregulation and Contracting Out Bill, might utilize a Henry VIII clause so as to allow the repeal of primary regulatory legislation by means of secondary legislation.
[41] See Hayhurst and Wallington, 'Parliamentary Scrutiny'.
[42] See J. Beatson, 'Legislative Control of Administrative Rule-Making: Lessons from the British Experience?' [1979] 12 *Cornell Int. LJ* 199; M. Asimov, 'Delegated Legislation: United States and United Kingdom' (1983) 3 *Oxford JLS* 253.
[43] See Hayhurst and Wallington, 'Parliamentary Scrutiny', 554-5.
[44] See Foulkes, *Administrative Law*, 92.

followed or because the rules are substantively *ultra vires* the parent statute). The judges have, however, been unwilling to declare items of delegated legislation invalid on the basis of their substantive unreasonableness where political judgments are at issue and the House of Commons has approved the legislation.[45] Parliamentary control may be weak but judicial control is sporadic, not easily instigated, and cannot be said to make up for such weakness.

Under the due process rationale it might be claimed that secondary legislation generally achieves acceptability through the processes of consultation. Again, however, such processes may be widespread but they are not closely regulated and there is no general requirement of notice or consultation for secondary legislation. Particular statutes may call for notice and consultation, either generally, or with stipulated organizations or individuals, or at ministerial discretion, but the common law does not, in the absence of any legitimate expectation, impose a general obligation to hear the comments of affected parties.[46] As a matter of practice, government departments do consult extensively when legislating but there is room for contention on who is to be consulted, the nature of the consultation, the acceptability of any ensuing delays, and who should bear the costs of the exercise. As a broad legitimating device consultation is thus flawed by both the incompleteness of the duty to consult and the residual areas of contention.

Moving to tertiary governmental rules, these are, as noted, distinguishable from secondary legislation in so far as they are not directly enforceable. Again, the tendency of governments to resort to tertiary, instead of primary or secondary, rules is marked and increasing. The Joint Scrutiny Committee expressed concern that the abuse of tertiary rules as long ago as 1977: 'the Committee hope that Parliament will condemn subordinate legislation by Departmental Circular when Parliament has itself passed a parent Act which requires such legislation to be by Statutory Instrument.'[47]

Many of the arguments in favour of tertiary rules can be classified as claims under the expertise and efficiency heads. Thus, administrative rules are said to routinize the exercise of discretion swiftly and inexpensively;

---

[45] On House of Commons endorsement see *Nottinghamshire CC v. Secretary of State for the Environment* [1986] 1 AC 240 (HL). On review based on *vires* tests see *Agricultural, Horticultural and Forestry Industry Training Board v. Aylesbury Mushrooms Ltd.* [1972] 1 All ER 280; *Commissioner of Customs and Exercise v. Cure and Deeley Ltd.* (1962) 1 QB 240; *Cinnamond v. British Airports Authority* [1980] 2 All ER 368.

[46] *Council for Civil Service Unions v. Minister for the Civil Service* [1985] AC 374; [1984] 3 All ER 935. On the case for general statutory control of the rule-making process see below at text accompanying n. 50, and the discussion in Richardson, Ch. 5 above.

[47] *First Special Report from the Joint Committee on Statutory Instruments 1977–8*, HL 51, para. 12.

encourage consistency; increase the incorporation of expertise and experience into decisions; enhance publicity and participation; give a flexibility lacking in primary and secondary legislation; allow non-technical language to be employed so as to make the rules accessible; enable rules to be couched in persuasive terms rather than in the form of commands; encourage compromises to be effected between those with different interests; deal with broad policy issues in a manner not possible with more precise primary and secondary rules; and allow rules to be introduced where more formal legislation is inappropriate or of doubtful practical or political feasibility.[48]

It is clear from the discussion of Davis, above, that such virtues cannot be accepted unquestioningly. Modern governments nevertheless find tertiary rules highly useful if not indispensable on expertise and efficiency grounds. Can such rules be supported on other bases though? On examination it appears that many of the problems of legitimation that are encountered with secondary legislation apply all the more in relation to tertiary rules. Thus, to claim that tertiary rules implement the legislative mandate is problematic not simply because the mandate is generally not present in any explicit form but because the legal effects of tertiary rules are highly uncertain and the very cataloguing of tertiary rule-types is a complex task involving at least eight varieties of rule. Such difficulties have not been reduced by the judicial response to tertiary rules which is marked by a failure to develop guiding principles of real utility.[49]

As for the claim that tertiary rules can be justified on the basis that their makers are accountable, this may be weaker still. Such rules may be couched in language that is accessible but they are free from general statutory controls as to modes of promulgation. Parliamentary control is also lacking and hardly seems feasible given the constraints that already render the scrutiny of secondary legislation unsatisfactory. Massively to increase the work-load of parliamentary scrutineers would be to engage in no more than a presentational exercise and it is not realistic to look to procedural reforms in Parliament in order to make accountability more effective.

The formulation of tertiary rules is, moreover, intrinsically difficult to render accountable. Apart from their variety of forms, it is often hard to establish when tertiary rules come into existence—when, for instance, a series of decisions becomes the making of a rule. To seek to regulate such a process thus involves significant problems of selection and definition.

It might be argued that Parliament might facilitate accountability by laying down standards for tertiary rules or by turning them into secondary

---

[48] See Baldwin and Houghton, 'Circular Arguments', 19–20; Ganz, *Quasi-legislation*, 96–106.   [49] For details see Baldwin and Houghton, 'Circular Arguments'.

rules where possible. Such a technique is of limited value, however, where Parliament has neither the time nor the expertise to lay down standards and where rules are made without any pretence of delegated authority. There clearly are limits to potential parliamentary action on this front although statutes might lay down more clearly than is often the case the purposes for which rules may be made and the legal effects of any rules for which rule-making authority is given, including the implications of any breaches of those rules. Even if such suggestions were followed, however, a massive body of administratively-issued rules of various kinds would inevitably emerge from governmental activity and justifying tertiary rules on the accountability basis is liable to be a speculative process.

To claim that tertiary rules are legitimated on a due process rationale involves claiming that the interests of affected parties have been respected. Such claims, again, may be made in particular instances on the basis of consultations conducted but the absence of any general requirement to consult detracts from a generic claim for tertiary rules. Such procedures could be imposed on both secondary and tertiary rule-makers by statute. The case for 'notice and comment' procedures as set out in section 553 of the United States Administrative Procedure Act 1946 (APA) has been put forward in Britain.[50] These procedures involve *inter alia*:

- general notice of a proposed rule-making in a national published register;
- opportunity for interested persons to comment in writing and, at the option of the rule-maker, opportunity for oral argument.
- issuance, when the rules are promulgated, of a statement of their basis and purpose.

Some commentators have pointed to the propensity of administrators to bypass such controls[51] and a number of further difficulties might be anticipated were such procedures to be introduced in Britain. First, which rules would be covered? Would, for instance, interpretative rules, general statements of policy, rules of organization, procedure, or practice be covered? (They are not encompassed by the United States APA.) How might exemptions be drawn so as to exclude rules of a minor nature or instances where hearing comments on draft rules would prove impracticable, unnecessary, or against the public interest? Second, loss of flexibility and speed might attend statutory rule-making procedures and an increase in legalism and defensiveness could result from efforts to avoid legal

[50] See I. Harden and N. Lewis, *The Noble Lie* (1986), 302–5.
[51] See R. W. Hamilton, 'Procedures for the Adoption of Rules of General Applicability: The Need for Procedural Innovation in Administrative Rule-Making' (1972) 60 *California LR* 1976; Baldwin and Hawkins, 'Discretionary Justice'; S. Breyer and R. Stewart, *Administrative Law and Regulatory Policy* (3rd edn. 1992), ch. 6.

challenges to the procedures adopted. Policy fudges might, furthermore, be incorporated into rules that have to be negotiated through 'notice and comment' processes. This might well prejudice the very strength of informal rule-making—its claimed efficiency and effectiveness—without commensurate due process gains. Third, statutory procedural requirements may not produce equal participation on the ground but may unduly favour well-resourced, well-organized interests. Finally, to regulate informal rule-making uniformly across the board might detract from another positive aspect of such rules: their being produced according to procedures tailored to specific circumstances. Just as legislators are poorly-placed to lay down substantive standards for executive rule-makers, they may also be ill-suited to lay down detailed procedural requirements.

Whether or not notice and comment provisions, as envisaged, would have a beneficial effect overall would depend on whether the judges could, in reviewing specific cases, apply the statutory rules so as to achieve gains under the accountability and due process rationales yet protect administrators sufficiently to avoid the efficiency losses caused by legalism, defensiveness, and the over-inclusive application of notice and comment requirements.

The judges have to date declined to develop the common law so as to impose a general consultative duty on rule-makers.[52] As argued elsewhere,[53] they might develop a rule so as to ground review on a failure to disclose a rule that has been applied in making a decision.[54] Similarly, there seems a case for developing a common law duty to consult where failure to do so would, in the circumstances, be unreasonable.[55] Such a duty would not only contribute to due process based claims to legitimacy but, would, by encouraging a fuller consideration of relevant factors, enhance claims based on the expertise rationale.

To conclude, secondary and tertiary rules are important tools of government but it proves difficult to make clear-cut claims to legitimacy on their behalf other than on the bases of expertise and efficiency. Nor do easy or radical solutions seem feasible in relation to such rules. This does not mean that secondary or tertiary rules should not be used in government. It means, first, that, where (as has been suggested) steps can be taken to improve justificatory claims, these should be taken. Second, that expectations concerning the legitimacy of secondary and tertiary rules should not be pitched at unrealistic levels—efficiency gains do have to be

[52] *Bates* v. *Lord Hailsham* [1973] 3 All ER 1019. See A. Jergesen, 'The Legal Requirement of Consultation' [1978] *PL* 290 and the discussion in Richardson, ch. 5 above.

[53] Baldwin and Houghton, 'Circular Arguments, 275–6. See K. C. Davis, *Discretionary Justice*, (1969) 110.

[54] See Lord Goddard in *R.* v. *Torquay Licensing Justices ex p. Brockman* [1951] 2 KB 487, 781 and *Doody* v. *Home Secretary* [1993] 3 All ER 92.

[55] See Baldwin and Houghton, 'Circular Arguments', 278–80.

traded-off against lower levels of accountability and due process or fairness. To aim too high may, as was seen with the structuring of discretion, lead to displacement and may be counter-productive. Third, that since secondary and tertiary rules find their main justifications in efficiency and effectiveness, all steps must be taken to ensure that results are produced effectively. This means that enforcement must be a matter of high priority. Finally, that attention should be paid to methods of pursuing governmental purposes which do not rely heavily on rules and which may achieve superior results when judged according to the five bench-marks discussed. Thus, consideration should be given, for instance, to the use of economic power, rather than mandating rules, as a strategy of government.[56] Similarly, the alternatives to 'command and control' systems of applying prescriptive rules can be explored and 'incentive-based' modes considered—particularly in the regulatory sector. These incentive-based strategies might include exerting influence by means of the taxation and grant-giving systems, relying on market and consumer-based controls, or employing contractual provisions for governmental ends.[57] Such methods do avoid relying *primarily* on prescriptive rules and should be considered in relation to particular governmental tasks but it should be cautioned that rules are likely to be involved in implementing and enforcing many incentive-based strategies and a series of problems familiar to those seeking to legitimate governmental rules may prove difficult to avoid.

RULES AND RESULTS: THE PROBLEMS OF ENFORCEMENT

Rules do not produce compliance in a mechanical, non-problematic way. They have to be enforced and it is accordingly useful if they are the kinds of rule that lend themselves to enforcement. Research into the enforcement of health and safety rules[58] suggests that the type of rule devised by policy-makers does affect its enforceability.[59] Rules may vary, *inter alia*, according to their degree of specificity or precision; their extent, coverage, or inclusiveness; their accessibility and intelligibility; their legal status and

[56] See Terence Daintith's distinction between *dominium* and *imperium* in T. C. Daintith, 'The Executive Power Today: Bargaining and Economic Control', in J. Jowell and D. Oliver (eds.), *The Changing Constitution* (3rd edn. 1994); see also T. C. Daintith (ed.), *Law as an Instrument of Economic Policy: Comparative and Critical Approaches* (1988).

[57] On alternatives to 'command and control' modes of government and regulation see S. Breyer, *Regulation and its Reform* (1982); id, 'Analysing Regulatory Failure: Mismatches, Less-Restrictive Alternatives and Reform' (1979) *Harvard LR* 549.

[58] See Baldwin, 'Why Rules Don't Work'; on enforcement methods generally see K. Hawkins, *Environment and Enforcement* (1984); B. Hutter, *The Reasonable Arm of the Law?* (1988).

[59] On enforceability see also C. Hood, *Administrative Analysis: An Introduction to Rules, Enforcement and Organisations* (1986), ch. 3.

force; and/or their prescription or the sanction they incorporate. Rules, moreover, have to be used in accordance with a number of basic strategies that are employed by enforcers in seeking compliance. Common strategies are: use of prosecutions and administrative sanctions; persuasion and negotiation; advice; education; and promotion. The key point is that different strategies may call for different kinds of rule. If prosecution is to be the mode of application, this may call for rules that are precise (as a result they may prove lengthy and complex). If, on the other hand, compliance is to be achieved by broad promotion (where, for example, safe use of ladders is encouraged by publishing guidance) then less precise but more accessible rules are more apposite.

How, then, are rules that are conducive to effective enforcement to be designed? The above points argue in favour of a 'compliance-oriented' approach to rules, one in which rules are designed to complement anticipated enforcement strategies. As to the selection of potential enforcement strategies, this in turn requires an analysis of the kinds of regulatee being dealt with. Where those regulated are well-informed, such individuals or firms are likely to comply with rules without being prosecuted and can be negotiated with. The appropriate rules will accordingly be fairly accessible but broad in coverage. Where the well-intentioned regulatee is ill-informed and less capable of analysing complex rules (perhaps in the case of a less well-resourced firm) there is, again, no need to prosecute in order to achieve compliance. The best kinds of rule will, however, be highly accessible and conducive to negotiation, education, and promotion. If, on the other hand, the regulatee is ill-intentioned and ill-informed, it may be necessary to be able to enforce through court prosecutions and, accordingly, a precise rule will be required.

In the case of regulatees who are ill-intentioned but well-informed, the enforcer faces not only the problem of those who break the rules (and are best dealt with by prosecutions and precise rules) but of those who indulge in 'creative compliance'.[60] This is the process whereby those regulated avoid having to break the rules by using legal techniques to achieve non-compliance with the intention of the law without technically violating its content. An example would be a company's reorganizing an operation so that, though in essence it is unchanged, it no longer falls within the scope of a rule. Such creative compliers are said by Doreen McBarnet and Christopher Whelan to be commonly encountered in the tax and accountancy fields. A real difficulty, suggest these two authors, is that formalistic approaches to control, which employ clearly-defined, highly specific rules, are more prone to creative compliance then are less

---

[60] See D. McBarnet and C. Whelan, 'The Elusive Spirit of the Law: Formalism and the Struggle for Legal Control' (1991) 54 *MLR* 848.

formalistic approaches employing more flexible open-textured and policy-oriented rules.[61] In so far as this argument is accepted, it means that the designers of rules may have to make judgments concerning the likelihood of creative compliance in a particular area and may have to adjust the rule design accordingly—perhaps providing a safety-net for formalistic rules by means of more open-textured provisions.[62]

Rule-making thus calls for judgments to be made concerning the kinds of regulatee covered by a rule and the blends of enforcement strategies and rule-types that will best achieve results. This implies that rule-makers should ask (seriatim) four questions:

- What is the undesirable behaviour, or mischief, at issue?
- Who is responsible for the mischief?
- Which enforcement strategies will best influence the mischief-creators?
- Which types of rule best complement those strategies?

Designing rules with an eye to enforcement is, it is clear, a highly complex task and there are, furthermore, reasons why rule-makers tend to give insufficient attention to enforcement:[63] they are prone to a 'top-down' approach to rules (in which those policy-makers who head organizations tend to assume enforcement to be unproblematic, in which information concerning enforcement is not sought out, and in which problems and costs are passed down to enforcers); they commonly underestimate the problems associated with rule-making processes (for example the tendency of consultation processes to produce compromises and, in turn, rules of diminishing accessibility); and they are invariably subject to a variety of disruptive political pressures coming from both within and beyond the organization.

Attention to the practicalities of compliance-seeking suggests that certain efficiency-based approaches to enforcement are subject to considerable limitations. In their well-known paper 'An Economic Analysis of Legal Rulemaking'[64] Ehrlich and Posner spell out the costs and benefits associated with different choices along the scale running from specific to general rules. Their purpose in doing so is to indicate the means whereby the excess of benefits over costs can be maximized. They argue that increased precision in rules discourages undesirable conduct and encourages desirable conduct by increasing the probability with which undesirable activity is identified and punished. Higher precision allegedly improves

---

[61] On goal-oriented legislation see E. L. Rubin, 'Law and Legislation in the Administrative State' (1989) 89 *Col. LR* 369.

[62] Thus the general duties for employers that are set out in ss. 2–9 of the Health and Safety at Work Act 1984 may catch employers who creatively comply around more precisely formulated regulations on workplace health and safety.

[63] See Baldwin, 'Why Rules Don't Work'.　　　　　　　　[64] (1974) 3 JL *Stud.* 257.

deterrence and increases the returns to prosecution both by making convictions more certain and by encouraging out of court settlements. As for costs, making rules more precise is said to increase costs since more information is required to make a specific as opposed to a general rule. Formulating rules more precisely is also said to raise the costs of, for example, negotiation, consultation, and legal advice because precision sharpens the focus of value conflicts.

Ehrlich and Posner construct a model with which to assess rule-making costs and benefits but it is one that pays insufficient attention to a number of factors. Thus they focus on prosecution as the method used in achieving compliance but compliance-seekers use a number of strategies other than prosecution and, indeed, prosecution is for many compliance-seekers the last option they will select because it is so resource-intensive.[65] Nor can it be taken for granted that the kind of precise rule that is useful for prosecuting will maximize benefits over costs when associated with other compliance-seeking strategies. Their analysis, moreover, is concerned with one dimension of the rule—its precision—whereas in practice there is a series of relevant dimensions including legal form, force, types of prescription or sanction used, and accessibility, all of which bear on benefits and costs. They also take insufficient account of variations in kinds of potential compliers and mischiefs. Thus, the contention that increasing the precision of a rule increases the likelihood of apprehension, conviction, and the imposition of a penalty is problematic because (even assuming prosecution is the optimal enforce ment strategy) excessive detail can increase the costs of rule application—where, for example, the rules become lengthy, cumbersome, and require expertise to handle. When prosecution is not the adopted strategy for compliance-seeking then detailed rules may produce reduced compliance because, for instance, the self-motivated, potentially self-regulating individual or firm will not find the rule sufficiently accessible. Ehrlich and Posner offer an analysis that assumes away problems of accessibility and enforcement. In practice, precise rules may (*contra* Ehrlich and Posner) discourage desirable conduct if the costs of dealing with such rules deter potential entrants to a field.

A more sophisticated approach to the efficiency-based drafting of rules is that of Colin Diver,[66] who accepts that the degree of precision appropriate to any particular rule depends on a series of variables peculiar to the rule's author, enforcer, and addressee.[67] Diver draws attention to three different dimensions of rules: their *transparency* (formulation in words with well-defined meanings), their *accessibility* (ease of application to concrete situations), and their *congruence* with policy objectives

[65] See Hawkins, *Environment and Enforcement*.
[66] Diver, 'The Optimal Precision of Administrative Rules'.　　　　　　[67] Ibid. 76.

(whether the substance of the rule produces the desired behaviour). He then offers guidance for rule-makers by identifying a series of factors that place a particularly high premium on one aspect of a rule. Thus, for example, where the costs of misapplication of a rule are high (e.g. hanging the wrong person for a homicide offence) a very precise statement of the rule is worthwhile in pursuit of congruence. Where the costs of misapplication are low (e.g. a traffic offence with modest penalties and stigma) a more transparent but less precise rule may be more appropriate. Diver's analysis does not address the form and force of rules nor the sanction-type adopted, but it does offer a series of guidelines for balancing some common variables associated with rules. It can usefully be viewed alongside a 'compliance-oriented' approach to rule-making.

Diver's analysis is particularly useful in stressing that achieving compliance does not guarantee that the 'right' results are obtained. This will only be the case where there is congruence between the rule and the relevant policy objective. Achieving congruence is, however, highly problematic in itself and the rule that best overcomes problems of under- and over-inclusiveness may not be the rule most conducive to securing compliance. As Diver points out, considerable trade-offs may have to be made and can be guided by assessments of the priority to be given to such factors as congruence in the given situation. A concern with the effectiveness of rules in producing substantive results (and the *right* results as judged with reference to the legal mandate) should not, moreover, enjoy our exclusive attention. In assessing rules, reference should also be made to the amenability of rule-making processes to accountability, the due consideration of affected interests, and the exercise of expertise.

To summarize, the rule-maker's task is a daunting one. Choosing the appropriate kind of rule does bear on the effectiveness of enforcement but issues of design have to be faced across all the various dimensions of rules and with reference to the broad array of legitimating values. This is not to assert that a comprehensively rational approach should be adopted in rule-making but to propose that, within the bounds of feasibility, rule-makers should aim to produce rules that are worthy of support on all relevant fronts and, indeed, are more worthy of support than those strategies that provide alternatives to rules.

RULE USE IN THE EUROPEAN COMMUNITY

Governing at the Community level involves a number of particular rule-related problems[68] but here I focus on two: the selection of appropriate rule-types and how success in rule use can be measured and secured.

[68] See e.g. R. Baldwin and T. Daintith (eds.), *Harmonisation and Hazard: Regulating Workplace Health and Safety in the European Community* (1992), chs. 1, 8.

Selecting rule-types

As with domestic governmental rules, it is possible to divide those of the Community into primary, secondary, and tertiary categories[69] and my concern here is with the last two of these. The primary rules of the Community are the founding Treaties with their Annexes, Protocols, and supplementing Treaties (e.g. the Single European Act 1986). They form the basis of the Community legal order. The secondary rules comprise the lawmaking acts of the Community institutions. They derive authority from the provisions of the founding Treaties which provide for three forms of obligatory act: regulations, directives, and decisions. Regulations are deemed by Article 189 EC to be 'binding in their entirety' and are directly applicable in all Member States. They thus create rights enforceable in court directly at national or community level. They require no domestic implementing measures but derive authority from the Treaties. Regulations, accordingly, contain in their preambles references to relevant Treaty provisions but whether a rule is a regulation or not is a matter, according to the European Court of Justice (ECJ), of content and nature rather than form adopted.[70] Both the Council and the Commission may make regulations and their respective powers to do so are governed by Treaty provisions.

Directives differ from regulations in so far as, according to Article 189 EC, directives are only binding 'as to the result to be achieved'. They depend on Member States for implementation and leave to Member States 'the choice of form and methods' of achieving the result. The directive can thus be seen not so much as a method of making uniform laws across Member States but as a way of approximating (or harmonizing) laws in pursuit of common objectives. Directives are addressed to Member States, which are obliged to implement them by legally binding measures, and the Commission is empowered to enforce this duty.[71] Directives may emanate from the Council or Commission and it is usual for a time limit for implementation to be imposed on Member States. The ECJ, moreover, has ruled that a directive is capable of direct effect after expiry of this time limit if the directive is sufficiently clear, unambiguous, and unconditional.[72]

---

[69] See generally S. Weatherill, *Cases and Materials on EEC Law* (1992), chs. 1–3, 16. This chapter is concerned with EC enacted law rather than the 'common law' principles developed by the ECJ, nor does it deal with international agreements as sources of EC law.

[70] Case 250/81, *Greek Canners Assoc.* v. *EC Commission* (1982) ECR 3535.

[71] Art. 169 EC.

[72] Case 41/91, *Van Duyn* v. *Home Office (No. 2)* (1975) ECR 1337. On the direct effect of directives see J. Steiner, 'Coming to Terms with EEC Directives' (1992) 55 *MLR* 215; E. Szyszczak, 'Sovereignty: Crisis, Compliance, Confusion, Complacency?' (1990) 15 *ELR* 480; G. de Burca, 'Giving Effect to European Community Directives' (1992) 55 *MLR* 215.

Directives can only be enforced directly by individuals against the state[73] but an individual may have a right to damages against a Member State where a loss results from acts of a private party and those acts are incompatible with a directly applicable provision of a directive which the Member State has not implemented.[74] Directives have indirect effects also. Thus the ECJ requires national courts to interpret national law in the light of the purpose of directives and has even indicated that this obligation can arise before the expiry of any time limit for implementation.[75] In the *Marleasing* case[76] the ECJ went further, appearing to require national courts to give effect to the provisions of directives in actions between private parties, regardless of the terms of the national legislation being interpreted.

A decision is, in the terms of Article 189, 'binding in its entirety upon those to whom it is addressed'. It thus differs from a directive in leaving no discretion as to mode of implementation and it can be addressed not merely to Member States but also to individuals or corporations. Like the regulation or directive, the decision has to be substantiated with reference to a Treaty provision. It may be enforced by the Commission and judicially reviewed at the instance of a Member State, the Council, the Commission, or an individual. Not all decisions are, however, binding, only those constituting formal acts under Article 189. Non-binding decisions can be seen merely as administrative or political, rather than legal, acts.

Tertiary rules of the Community comprise its 'soft law'[77] and come in a number of guises. Prime examples are recommendations and opinions, which are contained within Article 189 EC's list of Council and Commission powers. This Article, however, attributes to such rule-types 'no binding force'. They have a persuasive role in relation to the interpretation and execution of Community policies but they are not formal sources of Community law. They are not directly effective but they can give rise to indirect legal effect. Thus they may have to be taken into account in interpreting national laws.[78]

Community soft law also encompasses a number of other instruments, for example, resolutions, declarations, programmes, communiqués and

[73] Case 152/84, *Marshall* v. *Southampton and South West Hampshire Area Health Authority* (1986) ECR 723.

[74] Cases C/90 and C/90, *Francovich* v. *Italian State and Bonifaci* v. *Italian State* [1992] IRLR 84. See Steiner, 'Coming to Terms with EEC Directives', E. Szyszczak 'European Community Law: New Remedies, New Directions' (1992) 55 *MLR* 690; M. Ross, 'Beyond *Francovich*' (1993) 56 *MLR* 55.

[75] Case 80/86, *Kolpinghuis Nijmegen* (1987) ECR 3969.

[76] Case C-106/89, *Marleasing* v. *La Comercial* [1990] ECR I-4135.

[77] See e.g. K. C. Wellens and G. M. Borchardt, 'Soft Law in European Community Law' (1989) 14 *ELR* 267.

[78] Case C-322/88, *Grimaldi* v. *Fond des Maladies Professionelles*, see R. Nielsen and E. Szyszczak, *The Social Dimension of the European Community* (2nd edn. 1993), 163.

conclusions, deliberations, memoranda, and guidelines. Again, these instruments may produce indirect legal effects. The ECJ thus found that the UK was obliged not to act in a manner inconsistent with the Hague Resolution on Common Fisheries Policy of 1976.[79] In contrast, however, the ECJ has treated certain resolutions as mere expressions of political intention by Member States and has not attributed legal consequences.[80] As with domestic tertiary rules, it is necessary to refer to a number of factors and principles in attempting to judge the legal consequences of Community soft law.

Given the above array of rule-types, it is not surprising that selecting the appropriate form and drafting of a rule is a complex issue. Matters are often further complicated for Community rule-makers by the need to choose the appropriate legal base for a measure. Thus it may be possible to produce a directive on a topic (e.g. machinery design) with reference to different treaty provisions (e.g. Article 100A or 118A) and these may have different Community orientations—they may, for example, be directed towards completing the internal market (as with Article 100A) or towards improving social protections (as with Article 118A). Of perhaps greater tactical importance may be the choice between a legal base requiring unanimity in Council and one such as Article 118A that allows action by qualified majority.

In relation to secondary rules, the main debates on form and design have centred on the use of directives and accordingly these devices will be focused on here. In doing so we encounter distinct developments in Community approaches to rule use.

The case for legislating by means of directives rather than regulations is strongest, not where there is need for uniformity and immediate binding effect (needs best met by regulations), but where Member States may, to Community advantage, play a positive role in implementing legislation and where flexibility is required as to the means of implementation used by the Member State. Thus, if a Community rule has to be applied through a number of different regulatory systems, organizations, and cultures, the directive device allows a degree of harmonization to be achieved whilst avoiding the need to put national variations aside.

The most significant development in the use of directives has been the move from the 'traditional' towards the 'New Approach' to technical directives.[81] The traditional strategy assumed that problems arising from the existence of different national regulatory systems could only be tackled

---

[79] Case 141/78, *France* v. *UK* (1979) ECR 2923.

[80] Case 90–91/63, *Commission* v. *Luxembourg and Belgium* (1964) ELR 625; Case 9/73, *Schlüter* (1973) ECR 1135; Case 59/75, *Manghera* (1976) 17 CMLR 1157.

[81] See e.g. J. Pelkmans, 'The New Approach to Technical Harmonisation and Standardisation' (1986–7) 25 *JCMS* 249.

by the use of uniform rules imposed by directives. Over the first two and a half decades of the European Community legislators produced a very limited number of directives on specific technical aspects of products. A serious problem, however, was that the output of national regulatory rules usually exceeded the emergence of Community 'aspect directives' and trade barriers were not reduced. The traditional approach was thus criticized, *inter alia*, as time consuming; involving excessive uniformity; requiring unanimity and so allowing Member States to veto action in sensitive areas; leading to duplication and inconsistency with the standardization process; and liable to implementation problems.[82]

A response to these difficulties came with the notion of mutual recognition. This built on the principles established in the *Cassis de Dijon*[83] case which ruled that Member States could not exclude goods lawfully marketed in another Member State even if the technical standards in the two states differed. This suggested that traditional harmonization was not the only way to remove trade barriers. The Commission took the issue up in its White Paper on *Completing the Internal Market* in 1985,[84] arguing: that Member States should recognize each other's technical standards; that legislative harmonization should be limited to 'essential safety requirements'; that the task of drawing up technical standards in conformity with directives should be entrusted to competent organizations; that these technical specifications should be voluntary not mandatory; and that Member States should be obliged to recognize harmonized standards.

The New Approach was thus intended to halt the proliferation of excessively technical, 'uniform' directives and give producers the option of either manufacturing in accordance with harmonized standards or demonstrating conformity with directives by other means. It aimed to avoid overregulation by allowing flexibility and distinguishing areas where it was essential to harmonize from those capable of being left to mutual recognition. Majority voting, as introduced by the Single European Act 1986, further facilitated the realization of the Common Market by 1992. The New Approach thus was expected to speed up the rate of secondary rule-making, reduce duplication, and reduce work-loads at the Commission.

It should be noted that the New Approach has been developed primarily in relation to Articles 100 and 100A EC, measures directed at market integration. In the case of directives based on the social protection rationale there has been a separate but parallel strand of development, one that also moves away from wholesale reliance on highly detailed directives.

---

[82] Ibid. 251.
[83] Case 120/78 (1979) ECR 649; (1979) 3 CMLR 494.
[84] COM (85) 310 final, June 1985.

Here the major change has involved the Framework Directive as exemplified in the field of workplace safety and health.[85] This kind of directive has been described as 'a most radical measure'[86] and its significance noted thus:

[it] marks a change in method on the part of the Community from adopting Directives concerning specific risks or specific sectors to adopting an overall Directive which is to apply alongside a number of individual Directives giving more details about the health and safety requirements concerning specific risks or sectors.[87]

In the particular field of workplace safety and health, the Framework Directive has been followed by a series of 'Daughter Directives' on specific risks and two other features of note have been incorporated: first, the Framework Directive allows for gradual implementation and, second, it imposes 'minimum requirements' so that Member States are left free to improve on harmonized standards with better protections for their own workers. The device thus echoes the New Approach to technical harmonization in that detailed and uniform directives are not methods of first resort. It is, accordingly, an example of differentiated and flexible integration through legislation. This flexibility is a conscious response to the problems of regulating across different governmental regimes. These problems are likely to grow as Community membership expands and three difficulties are of particular concern: first, there arises the issue of the level playing field and the need to have some degree of commensurability in practical implementation (of this more below); second, the prospect approaches of a two (or more) speed Europe, in which degrees of assistance are given from some Member States to others, and this may meet resistance; third, the technique of minimum harmonization may be seen, on the one hand, as a useful mode of reconciling disparities; on the other, however, it may be viewed as a worrying sign of the decreasing integrative force of the Community.

Both the New Approach to market-integrating directives and the framework strategy constitute attempts to effect difficult balances between the requirements of the integrated market and the needs of workers and consumers. Too much rigour and uniformity detract from market efficiency, too much flexibility can create resentments and detract from Community cohesion. Community secondary legislation, we see, is not free from the familiar tension between efficiency and fairness.

---

[85] See Nielsen and Szyszczak, *Social Dimension*; Baldwin and Daintith (eds.), *Harmonisation and Hazard*.

[86] A. C. Neal, 'The European Framework Directive on the Health and Safety of Workers: Challenges for the United Kingdom' (1990) 6 *Int. J. of Comp. Lab. Law and Ind. Relns.* 80–117.   [87] Nielsen and Szyszczak, *Social Dimension*, 237.

Turning to Community tertiary rules or 'soft laws', these may prove attractive to Community officials where there is resistance to secondary legislation. Soft law, indeed, may prove feasible where secondary legislation would be impossible to introduce. Thus the Social Charter was able to be given the status of a 'Solemn Declaration' in 1989 in spite of the UK's refusing to endorse it. Majority voting, as introduced in Articles 100A and 118A, reduces the need for soft law in some areas but there is still a case for tertiary rules where Member States require a higher degree of flexibility than even a directive will allow. Thus, in the individual relations field, considerable resistance to the use of directives might be expected from some Member States since collective agreements may not be deemed to constitute adequate implementing measures[88] yet some Member States may be reluctant to move beyond such agreements and implement with legislation.[89] A solution in such cases may be to adopt a recommendation instead of a directive.

A number of broad purposes are thus served by Community soft law: it may remove a subject area from the jurisdiction of Member States and make this a matter for Community concern;[90] it may reduce the flow of national legislation and provide a breathing space for the devising of Community measures; it may provide a justification or basis for state action as well as a framework for negotiations between states; it can create expectations and agendas for action; it can lend legitimacy to state actions in the period before final Community legislation is promulgated; and it can serve to regulate the internal operations of Community institutions. Soft law is clearly seen within the Community as having considerable utility. Whether Community tertiary rules (and secondary rules) can make strong generic claims to acceptability on other bases is a matter to be returned to below.

Measuring and ensuring success in Community rule use

The Treaties intend Community rules to be both legally and practically implemented.[91] Devising and selecting rules that can produce results effectively is, as we have seen above, difficult enough at the national level but in Europe there is the further problem of producing regulatory regimes that are even-handed across Member States. As indicated, however,

---

[88] See A. Adinolfi, 'The Implementation of Social Policy Directives through Collective Agreements' (1988) 25 *CMLR* 291.　　　　　　　　　　　　　　　　[89] Ibid.

[90] See *Commission* v. *Council* (1971) ECR 263.

[91] See e.g. Art. 5 EEC. On implementation see H. Siedentopt and J. Ziller (eds.), *Making European Policies Work: The Implementation of Community Legislation in the Member States*, i. 2 (hereafter EIPA Study); F. Snyder, 'The Effectiveness of European Community Law: Institutions, Processes, Tools and Techniques' (1993) 56 *MLR* 19.

effectiveness and evenness are objectives at tension. Thus, for example, the highest cumulative standards of performance might necessitate the use of differential standards in the various Member States. Trade-offs between effectiveness and evenness thus have to be made. Too much unevenness in the regulatory playing field may, indeed, not merely create resentment, it may affect levels of compliance and produce regulatory inefficiency. One review of road transport regulation concluded that, far from harmonizing competitive conditions across Member States, 'unequal treatment of offences is a source of friction between operators and enforcement agencies and a disincentive to enforce the Regulations generally'.[92]

The same study noted the existence of strong evidence that Member States were implementing Community rules in a manner that suited their domestic traditions and that technical ambiguities were exploited to national advantage whenever possible.[93] Not only that, but on matters of practical implementation the Commission was assessed as having a highly tentative approach: 'The Commission for the most part gives very little impression of wanting to check up on how exactly Community Directives are being applied and to what effect.'[94]

What, then, can be done to improve the evenness and effectiveness with which rules are applied in disparate regimes, to make clear the trade-offs between efficiency and evenness? On the basis of a study of health and safety regulation in Community workplaces,[95] a number of conclusions can be drawn. First, that the extent of regulatory variables across Member States is difficult to exaggerate. Thus, major differences are likely to be encountered in the governmental and legal systems of Member States; in the legal duties standards, processes, sanctions, and modes of proof adopted; and in the enforcement organizations, strategies, procedures, and resources met with. Second, that any attempt to compare with rigour with which various Member States ensure the practical implementation of Community rules is fraught with difficulty if the focus is placed on the actions of the regulators—and that this is so even if it is assumed that legal implementation has occurred. Third, that a precondition of assessing regulatory evenness and effectiveness (and of taking steps to ensure these) is the development of a strategy for measurement. Three general approaches to measuring regulatory rigour can be compared. These involve assessing (1) regulatory inputs (i.e. what the regulators do); (2) compliance costs to industry; or (3) outputs (i.e. performance). As noted, assessing inputs in the form of the regulators' efforts is highly problematic because of the variables referred to above. Comparing compliance costs is

---

[92] EIPA Study, i. 216.   [93] Ibid. 99.   [94] Ibid. ii. 665.

[95] For details of the study of six Member States and their regulatory regimes, conducted under the auspices of the Institute for Advanced Legal Studies, London University, see Baldwin and Daintith (eds.), *Harmonisation and Hazard*.

also problematic because enforcement assumptions have to be made and enterprises in different Member States may occupy very different starting-points in relation to the required standards of performance. This means that the compliance cost approach is likely to prejudice those who already approximate to the approved standards of behaviour. Measuring outputs by looking at the actual levels of performance reached in different Member States is not free from a number of difficulties—for example comparing injury and disease statistics for the purposes of evaluating health and safety controls is a complex and difficult process requiring allowances for a series of social, economic, and other influences[96]—but it remains the most promising mode of comparison.

Finally, it is clear that devising a means of measuring evenness and effectiveness in implementation is necessary but not sufficient to secure that evenness and effectiveness. Practical steps have also to be taken. One course is to opt for strong central control of practical implementation—a point on which the Commission, as seen above, has been criticized. The problem is also one of resources. The Commission does have powers to proceed in the ECJ on implementation issues[97] but the informational demands of such proceedings are severe and resources are already stretched by the process of monitoring legal implementation. To expect routine monitoring and enforcement in relation to practical implementation would be unrealistic. A more practical proposal is to establish newly-resourced and specialist monitoring units within the Commission, or free-standing Community agencies as proposed in the environmental field.[98]

These bodies might strengthen central control of practical implementation by: monitoring national action; co-ordinating levels of penalties and the use of other enforcement sanctions; establishing enforcement guidelines; providing a conduit for information on enforcement; and assisting in the training of enforcement officials. Such units or agencies would at least provide an institutional basis for addressing issues of monitoring and enforcement. This is not to say that resource problems would disappear, and some Europeans might advocate decentralized systems to avoid such difficulties. Thus it has been argued that the way forward on implementation may lie in facilitating enforcement proceedings before national courts by individuals, Member States, or Community institutions—with preliminary rulings from the ECJ where appropriate.[99] A further suggestion is to give

---

[96] See HSE, *Workplace Health and Safety in Europe* (1991).
[97] Art. 169 EC.
[98] See *OJ* (1991), 271/3. A third option is to set up Standing Committees of Experts: see B. Hepple, 'The Implementation of the Community Charter of Fundamental Social Rights' (1990) 53 *MLR* 643.   [99] See Claus-Dieter Ehlermann, EIPA Study, i. 148.

interest groups powers to compel the Commission to give reasons for not pursuing infringement actions.[100] This might be combined with increased funding for Commission enforcement actions.

Designing monitoring arrangements that involve resort to court might appear to be a way of reducing central resourcing difficulties but the reality may be that central resources are still significantly involved where the strategy involves instigation of Commission action. In addition, resource constraints affecting individuals, pressure groups, and enterprises may detract from such techniques. Such factors point to the value of attempting to establish machineries, institutions, and techniques for measuring and ensuring enforcement before the Community legislates. The tendency at present appears to be to legislate and leave implementation for future attention. It could accordingly be cautioned that Europeans should demonstrate 'a healthy disrespect of programmes which are not linked to specific executory commitments and to adequate institutional arrangements'.[101] Such disrespect might be encouraged by noting, first, that Member States tend not to think beyond their own needs to adapt to Community rules when they are negotiating such rules;[102] second, that Community machinery tends to be driven by the need to sustain levels of rule production rather than to monitor rules already made; and third, that the Community legislative system is one in which the central legislative authority is not fully responsible for the execution and practical implementation of rules.[103]

Given the array of issues discussed, how can European secondary and tertiary rules be attributed legitimacy? With reference to the legislative mandate, can such rules trace authority to a democratically legitimate body? The problem of making such claims in the Community context is that the linkages between rules and mandates are very loose. The European Communities Act 1972 may be seen as a broad delegation of authority to the Community but such is the breadth of delegation that it lacks useful content as a source of legitimation for a particular rule. Even if the Community Treaties are deemed to possess their own legitimate status, the linkage between a Treaty term and the content of, say, a directive is again likely to be loose—a general instruction at best rather than a blueprint. It tends to be the step from Treaty provision to secondary

---

[100] See Nielsen and Szyszczak, *Social Dimension*, 269.

[101] R. Bieber, R. Dehousse, J. Pinder, and J. Weiler, 'Back to the Future: Policy Strategy and Tactics of the White Paper on the Creation of a Single European Market', in R. Bieber *et al.* (eds.), *92: One European Market* (1988).

[102] See J. Lodge, *The European Community and the Challenge of the Future* (1989), 303–12.

[103] See M. Cappelletti *et al.* (eds.), *Integration Through Law* (1976), vol i, bk. 2, p. 68 (S. Krislov, Claus-Dieter Ehlerman, J. Weiler).

or tertiary rule that involves the major injection of substantive content but this step is taken by unelected Community institutions. For its part, the European Parliament neither posseses legislative power nor does it control the unelected organs in a strongly legitimating manner.

Claims for Community rules on the accountability/control basis also tend to be weak.[104] The European Parliament has been made more than advisory largely as a result of the Single European Act which introduced the co-operation procedure on 1 July 1987 and the Maastricht Treaty which instituted a new conciliation and veto procedure, set out in Article 189b EC.[105] Co-operation procedure allows the Parliament to force a change in the basis of Council voting from qualified majority to unanimity. Conciliation and veto procedure for the first time allows the European Parliament to block Council legislation. The European Parliament thus has some teeth but the above two procedures are limited in scope, Parliament does not have a right to be consulted on all Treaty-based legislation, it cannot amend legislation if the Commission is unwilling to adopt such amendments, and ordinary conciliation procedure does not guarantee that the Council will not defy the wishes of the Parliament. The Parliament thus remains particularly weak in certain areas. As for national parliaments, they have no explicit role in the Community legislative process. Legal control is exercised by the ECJ, which can review the legality of regulations, directives, and decisions that are binding. The ECJ cannot formally assess the legality of non-binding 'soft law', however, and ECJ control is limited in other respects: it focuses on legality rather than merits or substance; its interventions are sporadic rather than continuous; and the breadth of discretion enjoyed by Community institutions limits their liability to review.

The British Prime Minister, John Major, has placed a good deal of emphasis on controlling European rules by means of the subsidiarity principle. He has emphasized the potential justiciability of this principle which is to suggest that the ECJ may ensure that Community action will only be taken where desired objectives cannot be achieved at Member State level and where the proposed action will be better achieved at Community level.[106] Were this to be the case, those sceptical of Community legislative ambitions might be reassured and Community

---

[104] See S. Williams, 'Sovereignty and Accountability in the European Community' (1990) 61 *Political Quarterly* 299; C. Harlow, 'A Community of Interests? Making the Most of European Law' (1992) 55 *MLR* 331; Snyder, 'The Effectiveness of European Community Law'.

[105] See S. Weatherill and P. Beaumont, *EC Law* (1993), ch. 4.

[106] See Art. 3 (b) EC. and John Major at HC Deb., vol. 213, col. 286, 4 Nov. 1992. On subsidiarity see N. Emiliou, 'Subsidiarity: An Effective Barrier against the Enterprises of Ambition?' (1992) 55 *ELR* 383.

legislation might derive some legitimacy from its subjection to control. In reality, however, subsidiarity may remain a political rather than a legally enforceable principle. Numerous committees have been advised that subsidiarity cannot be a precise measure against which to judge legislation[107] and doubts have been expressed as to the ECJ's willingness[108] and suitability to rule on breaches of the subsidiarity principle.[109]

It is difficult to argue that accountability to other institutions, such as pressure groups, compensates for the thinness of control already noted. Increasing the openness of Community legislative processes might prove helpful on this front[110] but qualified majority voting and the increased pace of Community rule-making are factors moving in the other direction and making access to the rule-making process more difficult. These points also indicate why due process based claims to legitimacy are difficult to establish in the Community. The privatization of standards-making under the New Approach has, moreover, been criticized as a factor prejudicial to accountability and participatory interests.[111] Problems of differential access affect Community rule-making generally and especially in relation to tertiary rules, where such problems are aggravated by uncertainties as to the legal effects of such rules.

Turning to expertise, Community legislators may claim that their rules offer a distillation of expert knowledge from sources across the Community. It may well be countered, however, that a diversity of opinions tends to result from such rule making processes rather than a cumulative consensus. Such processes tend, in a Community of a dozen Member States, to produce numbers of expert judgments that differ from the judgments of the Community's own experts.

Finally, Community legislators may claim effectiveness. Unfortunately, however, developments such as the New Approach point only too clearly to the ineffectiveness of former strategies without guaranteeing innovatory success and we have seen above that there are severe difficulties, not only in measuring regulatory effectiveness and evenness, but in deciding upon the appropriate balance between these two factors. The Community has progressed in devising new means of legislating but considerable problems

---

[107] See e.g. HC Foreign Affairs Committee, *The Operation of the Single European Act: Minutes of Evidence*, 17 Jan. 1990; HL Select Committee on the European Communities, 17th Report: *Political Union: Law-Making Powers and Procedures*, Session 1990/1 (HL 80), para. 57, 90–1.

[108] See Prof. J. Usher's evidence to the HL Select Committee n the European Communities, *Political Union*, Q15.

[109] See Emiliou, 'Subsidiarity', 402–3.

[110] See Snyder, 'The Effectiveness of European Community Law', 53–4; Harlow, 'A Community of Interests?'

[111] A. McGee and S. Weatherill, 'The Evaluation of the Single Market: Harmonisation or Liberalisation?' (1990) 53 *MLR* 578, 585.

remain, notably in the area of practical implementation. In the absence of new techniques for measuring and ensuring the effectiveness and evenness of implementation, the role of secondary and tertiary Community rules is unlikely to be free from contention.

CONCLUSIONS

Some care has to be taken in drawing conclusions on the part played by secondary and tertiary rules within government, on the authority of such rules, and on what these devices can achieve in practical terms. There are so many different forms and varieties of rule that generalizing is best done under sedation. It is possible, nevertheless, to suggest criteria for assessing the appropriate part to be played by rules within government and for judging whether some kind of rule rather than another type of device is appropriate for controlling or effecting governmental functions in a particular context.

The objective of designing administrative processes is best seen not as choosing between rules and discretions but as selecting the device that best furthers a broad range of governmental values. Adopting this approach means that no special priority is given to rules and the way is open to survey all options on an equal footing. Bench-marks for evaluating governmental processes can be derived from an examination of how governmental processes are debated. This reveals that five justificatory arguments are used in relation to such processes and individual rules (or rules collectively) can be discussed with reference to the strength of their claims to legitimacy according to the legislative mandate; control or accountability; due process or fairness; expertise; and efficiency rationales.

Applying these criteria to secondary and tertiary rules, it is clear that the case for using these rules is largely based on the expertise and efficiency rationales and that claims under the mandate, control, and due process headings prove highly problematic. This is particularly so in the case of tertiary rules. Steps can, nevertheless, be taken to improve, for example, the fairness with which rules are used (e.g. by developing principles prohibiting unfair non-disclosure of rules and demanding reasonable consultation).

Since the effectiveness of rules in securing governmental purposes is central to their legitimation, it is crucial that rules be enforceable on the ground so that practical results are achieved. On looking at this third theme, however, an array of problems is encountered. If they are genuinely concerned with enforceability, rule-makers have to attempt to co-ordinate rule design with assessments of potential enforcement strategies. Such strategies have, in turn, to be derived from analyses of those regulated.

On top of this, the likelihood that creative compliers will short-circuit the rules has to be anticipated also. The approach advocated here makes heavy demands of rule-makers but it does, nevertheless, offer a means of designing enforceability into rules. It further cautions against assuming that securing compliance guarantees the desired results.

On the European stage, each of the issues reviewed above is encountered in acute form. Not only are legitimacy claims under the legislative mandate, fairness, and accountability headings problematic but those under the expertise and efficiency headings are less secure than is the case in relation to domestic governmental rules. It is difficult to claim effectiveness when methods of measuring and ensuring effective application have yet to be developed. As with domestic governmental rules, there are ways in which European secondary and tertiary rules can be rendered more democratically secure but not only have a variety of measures to be taken—for example to introduce greater accountability into the Community rule-making processes—but the issue of enforcement will have to be grasped with a resolve hitherto unknown in the Community. For enforcement officials at all levels of government an enduring concern must be the propensity of those making rules to ignore questions of practical implementation.

8

Self-Regulation

Cosmo Graham

INTRODUCTION

Most administrative and constitutional law textbooks tend to adopt one of two strategies. If they are primarily about constitutional law they discuss the 'high' constitution, for example, the structure and functions of Parliament, the influence of the European Community, and the role of the courts. Textbooks on administrative law, by contrast, often take the constitutional background for granted and concentrate on judicial review of administrative action. In both instances, the law student could be forgiven for thinking that public policy is implemented through straightforward institutional means. Legislation is passed, a public agency is given a task, which it proceeds to implement through the development of rules of various kinds which affect the legal position of private parties. The courts operate as the guardians of legality to ensure that the agencies do not overstep their remit.

Underlying this picture is, implicitly, a strict division between the public and the private sector, inherited from Dicey. The business of public law is, on this model, to tease out the legal rules regarding the regulation of the public sector and the limitations these rules place on intervention in the private sector. This, however, ignores an important phenomenon characteristic of the modern state; namely the blurring of the division between the public and private spheres. This point was perhaps first recognized in the disciplines of sociology[1] and politics,[2] where a variety of different interpretations were placed on it.

This insight has been seized upon by public lawyers who have seen it as having important implications for our constitutional expectatons. Thus, for example, Norman Lewis has argued that it is not possible for a modern administrative state to take direct responsibility for all matters in which there is a public interest.[3] He has identified a pattern of hiving off public functions to bodies which are not governmental in the traditional sense.

---

[1] G. Poggi, *The Development of the Modern State* (London, 1978).

[2] See e.g K. Middlemas, *Politics in Industrial Society* (London, 1979).

[3] N. Lewis, 'Regulating Non-governmental Bodies', in J. Jowell and D. Oliver (eds.), *The Changing Constitution* (2nd edn. Oxford, 1989).

Having identified this trend, he is concerned with the issues of democratic accountability which are raised. Daintith highlights another aspect of public/private interaction by examining how governments have sought to bring their policies into effect through the use of economic power, for example, contracts, and bargaining for the compliance of affected parties.[4] He argues that these techniques may, in particular cases, conflict with values that we feel our constitution should protect.

There are a variety of different aspects to the lack of a clear public/private divide, ranging from the creation of new public agencies, such as the nationalized industries or the new regulatory agencies, to the employment of legal techniques in imaginative ways, such as the use of government's contracting power to accomplish public policy ends. In this essay I want to concentrate on one development, namely the use of 'self-regulation' to accomplish public policy ends.

DEFINITION

For the purposes of this chapter I shall follow Birkinshaw *et al.* and define self-regulation as the delegation of public policy tasks to private actors in an institutionalized form. When so defined, self-regulation becomes a means for government to accomplish particular policy ends. This definition does need to be narrowed because, as presently constituted, it covers all of 'corporatism', as defined by Birkinshaw *et al*:

corporatism is a mode of political representation and state intervention involving the attribution of public status to interest groups and other organizations involved in *regular* relations with the state. These relations will be expressed within stable formal or informal institutional contexts whereby the groups or organizations are charged to some extent with the formation and/or execution of public policy.[5]

However, they distinguish between using corporatist mechanisms to organize markets, using them to replace the market, and using them to regulate markets.[6] We will primarily be concerned with the last sense; the regulation of markets by participants within them.

Thus corporatism is the genus, while self-regulation is the species. But this creates some further definitional problems as the notion of 'regulation' is by no means free of problems. Daintith identifies four meanings of the word.[7] The first defines regulation as simply governing according to rules.

---

[4] T. Daintith, 'The Executive Power Today: Bargaining and Economic Control', in Jowell and Oliver (eds.), *The Changing Constitution*.

[5] P. Birkinshaw, I. Harden, and N. Lewis, *Government by Moonlight: The Hybrid Parts of the State* (London, 1990), 3.   [6] Ibid, 72–3.

[7] T. Daintith, 'A Regulatory Space Agency?' (1989) 9 *Oxford JLS* 534.

The second, chiefly associated with economics, opposes regulation to markets and employs the former term to describe all activity of the state which determines or controls or alters the operation of markets. The third use, found mainly in policy implementation literature, sees regulation as one of a variety of instruments for the furtherance of state policy. It is distinguished from instruments such as subsidies and taxation by its 'command and control' characteristics. In its fourth sense, lawyers are concerned with the legal rules and measures which express such command and control arrangements.

It is in the fourth sense that regulation is used here, with an important difference, namely, that the responsibility for implementing these command and control measures has been delegated from the state to the private interests concerned, who may make their own arrangements for the implementation of regulatory decisions. This delegation may be explicit, as under the Financial Services Act, or it may be implicit, through the state declining to intervene on the grounds that the existing arrangements are perfectly satisfactory. The National Consumer Council (NCC) put it thus:

In essence, self-regulation means that rules which govern behaviour in the market are developed, administered and enforced by the people (or their direct representatives) whose behaviour is to be governed. The extent to which those people control those rules can, in fact, vary considerably.[8]

THEORETICAL ISSUES

Why is self-regulation significant? At one level all that is involved is the adaptation of our constitutional values to new means and institutions of governing. Whilst not underestimating such a task, it is in one sense perfectly straightforward. However, more far-reaching claims are made about the use of self-regulation in the theoretical literature; but these will not be discussed here.[9]

The problem with assessing self-regulation against constitutional principles is that, in Britain, there are no generally accepted constitutional principles which can be used. Dicey's two principles of the constitution, Parliamentary Sovereignty and the Rule of Law, are of limited relevance to

---

[8] National Consumer Council, *Self-Regulation* (London, 1986), 1.

[9] See, for discussion, G. Teubner, 'Substantive and Reflexive Elements in Modern Law' (1983) 17 *Law and Society Review* 239; E. Blankenburg, 'The Poverty of Evolutionism: A Critique of Teubner's Case for "Reflexive Law" ' (1984) 18 *Law and Society Review* 273; N. Reich, 'Reflexive Law and Reflexive Legal Theory: Reflections on Post-Modernism in Legal Theory', Discussion Paper ZERP-DP 3/88, Zentrum für europäische Rechtspolitik, University of Bremen, 1988; I. Harden, 'Regulated Autonomy and the Concept of "Public" and "Private" ' (1990) unpublished paper.

our area of concern. Recent attempts to retheorize our constitutional principles have, however, been highly controversial and it would be impossible to survey this literature and produce a convincing argument within the compass of this chapter.[10] Nevertheless, a position has to be taken, especially if it is believed that inquiry cannot be conducted independently of theoretical positions and in a value-free manner.[11] Hence the following statement of my preferred constitutional principles is simply stipulative, for the purposes of this chapter alone.

As might be expected from a member of the 'Sheffield school',[12] my preferences are to judge self-regulatory arrangements against the principles of openness and accountability. These are essentially procedural principles, working from the premiss that recipients of delegated public power should be obliged to explain and justify their actions. This is not to say that self-regulation does not raise what might be considered issues of substantive constitutional rights. For example, both the British Board of Film Classification and the arrangements for the press clearly have implications for substantive rights regarding freedom of expression. This chapter will not seek to measure the performance of self-regulation against a constitutional theory of entitlements to those rights. Instead, we will look more generally at issues of openness and accountability.

One problem is that openness and accountability are very broad concepts which need to be made more precise. I hope, in the course of this chapter, to discover what principles are inherent in the self-regulatory arrangements adopted, somewhat as Daintith recommends.[13] However, it is worth producing a preliminary idea of how these principles might be put into effect. In the mid-1980s the NCC discussed what characteristics a self-regulatory scheme ought to have before they were prepared to support it. Their thoughts provide us with a useful check-list. The requirements were that:

i) The scheme must be able to command public *confidence*. (This might be linked to some form of 'public approval' procedure . . .)

ii) There must be strong *external involvement* in the design and operation of the scheme.

iii) As far as practicable, the operation and control of the scheme should be *separate* from the institutions of the industry.

---

[10] See, for some attempts to do this, T. Prosser, 'Towards a Critical Public Law' (1982) 9 *J. Law and Society* 1; I. Harden and N. Lewis, *The Noble Lie* (London, 1986); T. Daintith, 'Political Programmes and the Content of the Constitution', and N. Walker, 'The Middle Ground in Public Law', both in W. Finnie, C. Himsworth, and N. Walker (eds.) *Edinburgh Essays in Public Law* (Edinburgh, 1991); M. Loughlin, *Public Law and Political Theory* (Oxford, 1992).

[11] See M. Hollis, *Models of Man* (Cambridge, 1977), for some discussion of these issues.

[12] Daintith, 'Political Programmes'.　　　　　　　　　　　　　　　　[13] Ibid.

iv) Consumers and other outsiders should be fully *represented* . . . on governing bodies of self-regulatory schemes.

v) The scheme must be based on *clear statements of principle and standards*— normally a code.

vi) There must be clear, accessible and well-publicised *complaints procedures* where breach of the code is alleged.

vii) There must be adequate and meaningful *sanctions* for non-observance.

viii) The scheme must be *monitored and updated* in the light of changing expectations and circumstances.

ix) There must be a degree of *public accountability*, such as an Annual Report.[14]

In addition, any such scheme must be organized within a basic statutory framework.

Bearing these requirements in mind, the remainder of the chapter is organized as follows; first, I consider the reasons for adopting a self-regulatory scheme as opposed to using state regulation. Then we examine the legal form adopted for self-regulatory bodies. Questions of external accountability are then taken up; notably consultation, availability of information, checking devices, and performance review. Because of its topicality and importance the Financial Services Act arrangements are described independently, as a case-study. Finally, the lessons of the chapter are brought together in a short conclusion. For reasons of space, professional regulation is excluded.

Reasons for choosing self-regulation

Daintith suggests that when government wishes to solve policy problems its major difficulty is to get other people to change their behaviour.[15] The reason for this is what Hood has famously called *The Limits of Administration*,[16] in other words that governments have limited resources with which to change the world and that failure to recognize this is to invite policy failure. In the British system this acts as a pragmatic restraint on the legal principle of parliamentary sovereignty. Daintith says that one way of changing people's behaviour is to use the command of law, what he calls *imperium*.[17] We can see this as producing a legislative scheme which may involve the delegation of tasks to a public body.

The first point to notice is that a legislative scheme involves the mobilization of significant government resources, in terms of both civil service and parliamentary time. From the first extra-parliamentary consultations to putting an Act on the statute book probably takes about

---

[14] NCC, *Self-Regulation*, 15. [15] Daintith, 'The Executive Power Today'.

[16] C. Hood, *The Limits of Adminstration* (Chichester, 1976).

[17] Note here Cotterrell's distinction, in Ch. 1 above, between 'community' and '*imperium*' images of society. Self-regulation may be viewed as an attempt to find a middle path between these two.

two years on average. Because of this, a legislative scheme will be relatively inflexible and difficult to alter. Admittedly there are exceptions, for example the Dangerous Dogs Act 1991, and there may be provision for the modification of statutes by statutory instrument but these are, I should emphasize, exceptions. An additional problem is that a legislative solution may be impracticable. For example, Daintith points out that, if government wants to improve the standard of insulation in houses, it would be better to offer grants than impose a duty to insulate.[18] Poorer householders might simply be unable to afford insulation so that a coercive policy can only be 'enforced' by imposing fines which further reduce their capacity to buy insulation.

Given these problems there is an increasing tendency to use framework legislation, to delegate the issue to a public body, and to set only minimum standards in the legislation, as Baldwin points out in his chapter. It is frequently argued that the response of affected bodies to minimum standards in legislation is often to treat them as, in effect, maximum standards. An example of this is the first set of Guaranteed Service Standards for the Water Industry, enshrined in a statutory instrument, which no water company sought to improve on. Given the inflexibility of legislation this is a particular problem if government is aiming for a gradual improvement in standards or attempting to regulate a fast-changing area, such as financial services.

Delegating the task to a public body does not solve all the problems. The difficulties with a legislative framework remain. In addition, the creation of a new public body may involve additional costs on the public purse, although they may be funded by a levy on the industry. More seriously a public body will have information problems in regulating an industry. Breyer sees this as the central problem for a standard-setting process.[19] Additionally, as Breyer points out, there are problems in enforcement of the standards. He point out that it can be very difficult to produce tests which are enforceable and equitable.

These difficulties make self-regulation and bargaining with interest groups seem an attractive alternative. By reducing reliance on statute, self-regulation offers a speedier, more flexible means of solving problems. By harnessing the expertise of those involved in the industry, government is able to overcome the information problems and standards can potentially be set higher than in a statutory scheme.

Against these positive aspects, there are four major drawbacks. First, a self-regulatory scheme may not cover all the firms in an industry.[20] The

---

[18] Daintith, 'The Executive Power Today', 199.

[19] S. Breyer, *Regulation and its Reform* (Cambridge, Mass., 1982), 109.

[20] For some details on Office of Fair Trading approved Codes of Practice see N. Lowe and G. Woodroffe, *Consumer Law and Practice* (London, 1991), ch. 9.

NCC has argued that those who have not agreed to follow the self-regulatory scheme tend to be the main source of consumer problems.[21] Secondly, self-regulation can lead to restrictive practices which discourage competititon and innovation and work to the detriment of the consumer. This may not be peculiar to self-regulation,[22] but it is a problem of potential importance. Thirdly, the negotiation and bargaining necessary to establish a self-regulatory scheme may take place without input from third parties.[23] Fourthly, self-regulation may not be effective. Consumers may fail to see it as sufficiently independent, it may not be well known, a limited degree of sanctions may be available, and the rules may be very loose.

This discussion has focused on essentially pragmatic issues; what we lack is any discussion of the constitutional principles to which self-regulatory schemes should adhere. Characteristically, the debates over the setting up of self-regulatory schemes do not address constitutional issues. There seem to be two major circumstances which impel resort to self-regulation. The first is where an industry decides that, for some reason or another, regulation is needed. A good example of this is the British Board of Film Classification (BBFC). Its origins lie in worries by the early cinema industry about the loss of reputation due to activities of 'fringe' operators and that local authorities would set up a confusing array of local controls which would hinder development of the industry.[24]

Much more commonly self-regulation is a response to the threat of legislative controls imposed by government. This is true of, for example, advertising, the press, the banks' and building societies' Code of Practice, and the insurance industry's Statements of Insurance Practice.[25] The classic statement of this reasoning was contained in the first edition to the Takeover Code, which presented the choice as being between 'a system of voluntary discipline, based on the Code and administered by the City's own representatives or regulation by law enforced by officials appointed by Government'.

Self-regulation may not always be possible. The industry concerned may be too diverse and it may be impossible to obtain the level of agreement

[21] NCC, *Self-Regulation*, 6.

[22] See Breyer, *Regulation and its Reform*, 115–16.

[23] See I. Ramsay, 'The Office of Fair Trading: Policing the Consumer Market-Place', in R. Baldwin and C. McCrudden (eds.), *Regulation and Public Law* (London, 1987), 191; Breyer, *Regulation and its Reform*, 179.

[24] See B. Williams, *Report of the Committee on Obscenity and Film Censorship*, Cmnd. 7772 (London, 1979), app. 2.

[25] See, respectively, R. Cranston, *Consumer Law* (London, 1984), 48; T. Gibbons, *Regulating the Media* (London, 1991), 158–63; R. Jack, *Banking Services: Law and Practice Report by the Review Committee*, Cm. 622 (London, 1990), ch. 16; *Banking Services: Law and Practice*, Cm. 1026 (1990); J. Birds, 'Self-Regulation and Insurance Contracts', in F. Rose (ed.), *New Foundations for Insurance Law* (London, 1987).

necessary. A good example of these difficulties is in estate agency, where the Office of Fair Trading has been trying to encourage the industry to take voluntary measures but with little success[26] until the formation of the Ombudsman for Corporate Estate Agents, which, however, only covers half the industry. As a result, various legislative measures have been taken.[27]

Legal form and internal accountability[28]

Self-regulatory organizations do not, by definition, have their legal basis in statute. That said, there is no legal form in existence which is tailor-made for self-regulatory organizations. Within English law, the mere fact that a group of people form an association does not mean that they have legal personality. It is quite possible for them to form an unincorporated association, the legal basis of which is a contract between the members. This is not always convenient as the members and executive will be personally liable for the debts of the association and, not having a legal existence separate from its members, such an association cannot sue or be sued in its own name.

Nevertheless, self-regulatory institutions may use such a form or may use even less clear forms of legal status. A striking example is the 'independent' steering committee set up by the banks and building societies to oversee the implementation of the Code of Banking Practice. The Committee's Terms of Reference include satisfying itself that sufficient consultation has taken place with consumer and other interests and keeping the Code under periodic review. Its legal status is mysterious. This matters because it is not clear who makes the appointments to the Committee, how its Terms of Reference are arrived at, and who decides on its working methods. All of this raises questions as to the extent to which the Committee is truly 'independent'.

It is usual for self-regulatory organizations to take the form of a company limited by guarantee (or even an unlimited company). This gives them legal personality and a basic constitutional structure in the shape of the memorandum and articles that all companies must possess. The memorandum and articles must be registered at Companies House, which means that they become public documents, thus giving a limited form of accountability.

In the case of non-commercial companies the articles and memorandum will usually specify appropriate classes of members and the constitutional organs. Thus, for example, membership of the Banking Ombudsman

[26] Office of Fair Trading, *Estate Agency* (London, 1990), 26–7.
[27] In particular the Estate Agents (Provision of Information) Regulations 1991, SI 1991/859, and the Property Misdescriptions Act 1991.
[28] Generally see Birkinshaw *et al.*, *Government by Moonlight*, ch. 6.

Bureau is restricted to banks, and only senior officers of banks may be members of the board. Voting rights are proportional to the amount of levy paid to finance the scheme. The articles set out the responsibilities of the Board in relation to the Council, which serves as a buffer between the industry and the Ombudsman. The articles also detail the Council's basic responsibilities. However, the Companies Acts do not put any limitation on what may or may not be included in the articles and memorandum. It has been said that 'the legal form really is an almost empty vessel into which an enormous variety of internal constitutional arrangements can be poured'.[29]

Often what is important is not the formal arrangements, as set out in the articles, but the working relationships established. For example, the Advertising Standards Authority (ASA),[30] which deals with complaints about the advertising Codes of Practice and keeps them under review, is a company limited by guarantee. The ASA is controlled by a Council whose chair is appointed by the Advertising Standards Board of Finance Limited (ASBOF), which was established by the main organizations representative of those involved in advertising. ASBOF makes this appointment after consulting the existing members of the Council and obtaining their agreement, as well as informal consultation with the Secretary of State. The chair chooses the members of the council. The Code of Advertising Practice is not drawn up by the ASA but by the Code of Advertising Practice Committee (CAP), a body comprised solely of industry represent-atives. However, the ASA has the right to override CAP decisions and must approve the text of the Code and any proposed alterations. As can be seen this is a complicated system and what will be important is the relationship between its constituent elements. Although the OFT did think the self-regulatory system was, in general, effective in 1978, it did recommend certain changes such as wider consultation on appointment of Council members and for revisions of the Code.[31] What this suggests is that relationships between the constituent elements of a self-regulatory scheme need to be placed on a public record.[32]

EXTERNAL ACCOUNTABILITY

There are a number of means of accounting to a wider public. The literature does tend to draw a distinction between *ex post* and *ex ante*

---

[29] Ibid. 198.

[30] See Office of Fair Trading, *Review of the UK Self-Regulatory System of Advertising Control* (London, 1978). [31] Ibid., paras. 4.15, 4.17.

[32] For the Insurance Ombudsman see J. Birds and C. Graham, *Complaints against Insurance Companies* (Sheffield, 1992), 9–12, 68–9.

accountability, that is, accountability before and after the decisions are made. Let us begin with *ex ante* accountability, more specifically the consultation of interests outside the regulatory body. Overall, this seems to vary quite substantially. We have seen how the OFT criticized the CAP for not consulting more widely when revising the Code of Practice. The same criticism has been levelled at the OFT's practice in the past when negotiating Codes of Practice.[33]

Even where it is a case of consulting with those directly interested in the workings of a self-regulatory system consultation may be sporadic and unstructured. The Williams Report describes the consultation practices of the BBFC up to that time, which it found to be fitful.[34] The explanation it preferred was that formal consultative procedures were necessary, but that there was not sufficient continuing need to keep them in permanent existence. By contrast, the Independent Committee for the Supervision of Telephone Information Services (ICSTIS) has attempted to maintain regular contact with other regulatory bodies, associated industries, the network operators, and service providers. Consumer bodies are not, however, being met with regularly.[35]

Such a patchy record of consultation should not be surprising, given that the ordinary rules of public law do not place much emphasis on consultation. There is of course no general statutory duty to consult before taking decisions, as there is under the American Administrative Procedure Act, and within the common law there will only be such an obligation if there is a duty to act fairly or natural justice applies or, in certain circumstances, if there is a legitimate expectation of consultation. Although these common law duties would apply to self-regulatory organizations, the duty to act fairly and natural justice are not really apt instruments for imposing consultation requirements on what are essentially rule-making proceedings.[36] The idea of legitimate expectations seems more promising but this would only be enforced, apparently, if there was a clear past practice or an express promise.[37] In any event, despite occasional dicta to the contrary, the courts have been reluctant to impose a duty on public bodies to take a consultation exercise seriously.

The difficulties that the lack of such a structure can cause are usefully illustrated if we look at the creation of the Code of Banking Practice. This had its origins in the Jack Report, which recommended substantial new legislation and that the banks and building societies promulgate a Code of

---

[33] Ramsay, 'The Office of Fair Trading', 191.

[34] Williams, *Report*, 33–4.

[35] ICSTIS, *Activity Report 1989–90* (London, 1991).

[36] Although see *R.* v. *Liverpool Corporation ex p. Taxi Fleet* [1972] 2 QB 299, per Lord Denning at 307.

[37] See *Council of Civil Services Unions* v. *Minister for the Civil Service* [1984] 3 All ER 935.

Practice with government ensuring that their action was adequate and timely.[38] In its response,[39] the government rejected the recommendation of major legislation but supported the development of a Code of Practice. The implementation of the Code was to be overseen by the 'independent' committee described above. A draft Code was duly produced in December 1990 and it met with very strong criticism from, among others, the NCC and the Banking Ombudsman. The NCC went as far as to say: 'the Code does not meet the objectives suggested by Professor Jack and confirmed by the Government, in promoting a better relationship between banks and their customers.'[40] After the consultation period, the revised version of the Code showed some important changes. For example, the original draft had proposed that banks might pass personal information about their customers to other companies in the group so that they could inform customers of their services (para. 6.3). The final version says that names and addresses will not be passed, in the absence of express consent (para. 8.1). This seems, in part, to be a response to the objections of the NCC but no reasons for this change are publicly available. Nor were reasons given for rejecting other points that the NCC made, such as advance notification of charges.

We should be clear about the significance of this episode. At one level, the procedure was positive, in that there was a consultation process, including third parties, overseen by a body not directly one of the participants. By contrast, the promulgation and revision of the statements of Insurance Practice have taken place in a manner which seems to offer no room for input for those who were part of neither the industry nor government.[41] There are still deficiencies in the procedure, as we do not know why particular provisions were altered or not, as the case may be. Without knowing the range of arguments for and against, it is impossible to judge the efficacy of the Code. It also becomes clear that you cannot judge the effectiveness of consultation practices in isolation from means of *ex post* accountability and it is to these that I now turn.

Forms of ex post *accountability*

The basic obligation we are concerned with here is that the decision-maker explain and justify the decision that has been taken; in other words, a form of the duty to give reasons. There is, of course, no general duty to give

---

[38] Jack, *Banking Services*, ch. 17.

[39] *Banking Services*, Cm. 1026.

[40] National Consumer Council, *Banking Code of Practice: Response by the National Consumer Council* (London, 1991), 1.

[41] See R. Lewis, 'Insurers' Agreements not to Enforce Strict Legal Rights' (1985) *MLR* 275; Birds. 'Self-Regulation'.

reasons in English law and this is also reflected in the practice of self-regulatory organizations. It is common for the bodies to give reasons where individual grievances are being decided although there is a division between those who put their reasons into the public domain, such as the ASA and ICSTIS, and those who do not, such as the various ombudsmen for the private sector. Rather more rare is the giving of reasons for what might loosely be called 'policy' decisions. For example, when revisions to Codes of Practice are made the reasons for changing them in the particular way chosen, in the light of the arguments presented to the body, are rarely made explicit. We have mentioned the banking Code of Practice above, but could also mention the revisions to the ICSTIS Code of Practice and, generally, OFT-approved Codes of Practice.

Checks

What happens, then, if a person is dissatisfied with a decision of a self-regulatory body and wishes to challenge it? We need to distinguish this situation from the provisions that a self-regulatory body makes for dealing with complaints against its own members which, for convenience, we will deal with first.[42]

There seem, broadly, to be two major models of consumer grievance handling for self-regulatory organizations. The first is the ombudsman model and the second is the conciliation and adjudication model. In the ombudsman model, a consumer will initiate a complaint to an independent body and that body will handle the administration of the complaint. In its pure sense, the ombudsman system is inquisitorial and, importantly, the ombudsman may also have the ability to provide general feedback on the working of the self-regulatory scheme. In the conciliation and arbitration model, the first stage is where the consumer complains to the self-regulatory body, which attempts to promote a settlement. If this is unsuccessful, the complainant is referred to an independent body, often an adjudication scheme run by the Chartered Institute of Arbitrators, where the complaint will be dealt with as a one-off in an adversarial fashion.

These are ideal types and, in practice, elements of both may be combined. For example, the Banking Ombudsman makes substantial use of conciliation and the procedure followed, if this does not work, is actually quite adversarial, although all communication goes through the Ombudsman. Also, the use of the name 'ombudsman' is no guarantee of a

---

[42] Generally see J. Birds and C. Graham, 'Complaints Mechanisms in the Financial Services Industry' (1988) 7 *Civil Justice Quarterly* 313; Birds and Graham, *Complaints against Insurance Companies*; National Consumer Council, *Out of Court* (London, 1991); Office of Fair Trading, *Consumer Redress Mechanisms* (London, 1991).

particular procedure being followed. Thus the ASA and ICSTIS fall on the ombudsman side of the model whilst, notoriously, the various newspaper ombudsmen have been criticized for not being sufficiently independent.[43]

Without going into too much detail there are a number of different practices in this area, each with potentially different effectiveness, and a fair amount of overlap between the schemes with resultant confusion for customers. Again we see a lack of a principled approach compounded by, in this area, the lack of any one government body with responsibility for examining complaints procedures.

Complaints against a self-regulatory body are another matter. It is worth distinguishing between complaints about membership matters and other complaints. If a self-regulatory body operates in such a way that membership of it is economically advantageous to a person then they will desire to become and remain members. In a limited part of this area the courts have been active in devising doctrines to protect the interests of these persons through the use of natural justice.[44] Here is one area where the legal form taken by a body is critical because, although the courts have applied the principles of natural justice to the expulsion of members of contractual associations, they have not applied this principle to limited companies, if the appropriate power is contained in the articles of association.[45] By contrast, where applications to become members are concerned, the courts have been much less strict in imposing requirements of procedural fairness.[46] As we shall see, concern over the limitations of the common law position led to a detailed series of appeal rights under the Financial Services Act. One of the reasons that there are not such detailed rights in other areas, for example, OFT Codes of Practice and the relevant trade associations, is because membership of such associations is not compulsory, unlike the Financial Services Act.

What about the role of the courts more generally in this area? The first problem faced by anyone wishing to challenge decisions of self-regulatory organizations in the courts is the decision in *O'Reilly* v. *Mackman*[47] which laid down, as a general principle, that matters of public law should be decided through the application for judicial review. Given the definition of self-regulatory bodies employed in this essay, the first problem was whether or not they would be seen as sufficiently public to be subject to judicial review. Despite some initial conceptual confusion a clear lead was

[43] See A. Mowbray 'Newspaper Ombudsmen: The British Experience' (1991) *Media Law and Practice* 91.   [44] Note Cotterrell's comments on this point.
[45] See *Andrews* v. *Mitchell* [1905] AC 78; *Weinberger* v. *Inglis* [1919] AC 606; and compare with *Gaiman* v. *National Association for Mental Health* [1971] Ch. 317. For companies the test is merely whether the expulsion is 'bona fide in the best interests of the company'.
[46] See *McInnes* v. *Onslow-Fane* [1978] 1 WLR 1520.
[47] [1983] 2 AC 237. But see now *Roy* v. *Kensington and Chelsea FPC* [1992] 1 All ER 705, which shows a more flexible approach.

established in the *Datafin* case,[48] where the question was whether the Panel, an organization 'without visible means of legal support', that is, non-contractual and non-statutory, was susceptible to judicial review. The Court of Appeal decided that judicial review was available because the Panel was carrying out duties of a 'public' nature and, if it did not carry them out, the government would be forced to provide some legislative framework for these functions. The emphasis in this case was on what might be called a 'functional' test; is the body, regardless of its legal status, carrying out a public duty? This has been extended in later cases to the ASA,[49] a Code of Practice Committee,[50] but not the Jockey Club,[51] the Football Association,[52] nor the Chief Rabbi.[53] This test, and the results in the cases, have been criticized by Pannick, who argues that, if a body has monopoly powers and effectively governs an area of life in the United Kingdom, then the courts should intervene to impose certain minimum standards on the substance and procedure of the decision-making.[54]

This gives an indication that the subject is by no means closed, and that the results of future cases will not be clear-cut. It is possible that these issues will be raised outside the avenue of judicial review as, for example, a recent dispute over the *vires* of the Building Societies Ombudsman was decided by way of originating summons by the agreement of the parties.[55] Furthermore, it is not clear that the courts will apply the same standard of review to self-regulatory bodies as they seem to do with ordinary public bodies. In other words they are likely to be more deferential to the decisions of self-regulatory bodies. There were indications to this effect in the *Datafin* case, and, in the BPI case, in refusing to quash a decision the judge commented that *Datafin* was likely to impose on domestic bodies a standard and code of conduct they were never intended to have.

We should remember that the principles developed by the British courts for judicial review have been developed at a very high level of generality and do not provide much guidance in predictive terms for individual cases. Nor for that matter is it clear that they are applied consistently by the courts.

[48] *R.* v. *Panel on Take-overs and Mergers ex p. Datafin* [1987] 2 WLR 699.
[49] *R.* v. *Advertising Standards Authority ex p. Insurance Services* [1989] SJ 1545.
[50] *R.* v. *Code of Practice Committee of the British Pharmaceutical Industry ex p. Professional Counselling, The Times*, 7 Nov. 1990.
[51] *R.* v. *Disciplinary Committee of the Jockey Club ex p. Massingberd, The Times*, 3 Jan. 1990; *R.* v. *Jockey Club ex p. RAM Racecourses* (1990) 3 Admin. LR 265; and *R.* v. *Disciplinary Committee of the Jockey Club ex p. Aga Khan* [1993] 1 WLR 909.
[52] *R.* v. *Football Association ex p. Football League, The Times*, 22 Aug. 1991; *R.* v. *Football Associaton of Wales ex p. Flint Town UFC* [1991] COD 44.
[53] *R.* v. *Chief Rabbi ex p. Wachmann* [1992] 1 WLR 1036; See similarly *R.* v. *Imam of Bury Park James Masjid ex p. Sulaiman Ali, Independent*, 13 Sept. 1991.
[54] D. Pannick, 'Who is Subject to Judicial Review and in Respect of What?' (1992) PL 1.
[55] *Halifax Building Society and Others* v. *Edell* [1992] Ch. 436. See now also *R.* v. *Insurance Ombudsman Bureau ex p. Aegon Life*, 1993, *unreported*.

External accountability: review of performance

Given that self-regulation is the delegation of public powers to private bodies, often under the threat of statutory intervention, it would be logical for the public authorities to make some arrangements for reviewing the performance of self-regulatory arrangements. The review process does not, however, seem to be institutionalized. There is no equivalent of the National Audit Office, with its link to the Public Accounts Committee or the Audit Commission for local and health authorities. There may be doubts about whether these bodies provide systematic performance appraisal, but, at the minimum, they put the relevant institutional machinery into place. There are no such equivalents in relation to self-regulatory organizations which will also fall outside the scope of the departmental select committees of the House of Commons.

The body which offers the most potential for doing an equivalent job is the Office of Fair Trading. We shall see that it has an important role in relation to financial services but, outside this, its review function seems more sporadic. For example, the OFT recognizes that it must review the Codes of Practice that it has approved and it does engage in periodic reviews of the codes approved.[56] These exercises have covered only a proportion of the twenty or so codes and do not seem to represent a systematic monitoring effort. Indeed the OFT has stated that it will usually only review such a code in response to public concern. The OFT has set out some general criteria that Codes of Practice must meet,[57] which includes a requirement that the trade associations should publish an annual report on the operation of the code, preferably compiled by an independent person or body. Equally, in the advertising sector, although the OFT reviewed the self-regulatory system in 1974 and 1978 it has not done any work since then.

Outside the OFT, review of systems seems to depend more on the demands of the moment than on any institutionalized method of scrutiny. The press is a good example, having been subject to three royal commissions since 1949 and to the Calcutt Committee, of which it was said, 'A minor moral panic lay behind its establishment'.[58] Similarly, the last major review of the BBFC was the Williams Report of 1979, which came

---

[56] Since 1987 it has reviewed glass and glazing, package holidays, footwear, funerals, and furniture and carpets. See OFT Annual Reports 1987–90. For review up to 1986 see NCC, *Self-Regulation*, annex 2.

[57] See *Beeline*, (1991), 24–5.

[58] C. Munro, 'Press Freedom: How the Beast was Tamed' (1991) 54 *MLR* 105. For the most recent developments see *Review of Press Self-Regulation*, Cm. 2135 (1993).

about in the wake of, *inter alia*, the differing standards being applied by the BBFC and certain of the local authorities.[59]

FINANCIAL SERVICES[60]

The Financial Services Act 1986 makes it a crime for any person to carry on investment business[61] in the United Kingdom unless they are either authorized or exempted under the Act. Exempted persons are, among others, the Bank of England, Recognized Investment Exchanges, and Lloyd's. Authorization may be obtained in three main ways, for our purposes. First, through membership of a self-regulating organization (SRO) (section 7); secondly, by certification by a recognized professional body (section 15); and, finally, through authorization by the Securities and Investments Board (SIB).

What are these organizations? Let us begin with the SIB. Under the Financial Services Act the Secretary of State has power to make rules and recognize SROs, among other things. The Secretary of State also has power to transfer certain functions to a designated agency if it meets certain requirements of the Act (section 114). These requirements relate to the constitution of the agency, the arrangements for the discharge of its functions, its means of monitoring and enforcement, the investigation of complaints, the promotion and maintenance of standards, and record-keeping (Schedule 7). Schedule 8 sets out the principles which are applicable to the rules created by the SIB. These functions have duly been transferred to the SIB. This description is a bit misleading, although it follows the structure of the Act, because there was no intention from the beginning of the Secretary of State taking on the major regulatory functions.[62] In fact the SIB was set up in advance of the passing of the legislation even though its only mention in the legislation is in section 114 (2).

The SIB is a company limited by guarantee whose chair and other members of the governing body are appointed by, and removable by, the Secretary of State and the Governor of the Bank of England, acting jointly. The members of the governing body must include persons with experience of the relevant investment business and other persons, including regular users of investment business services or their represent-atives. The composition of the body must be such as to secure a proper

---

[59] G. Robertson, *Obscenity* (London, 1979), 263–5.
[60] Generally see A. Page and R. Ferguson, *Investor Protection* (London, 1992).
[61] This is widely defined in Schedule 1, part 1, as amended.
[62] See *Financial Services in the United Kingdom*, Cmnd. 9432 (1985).

balance between the interests of persons carrying on investment business and the interests of the public (Schedule 7).

The SIB has two primary functions, in so far as we are concerned. First, it is allowed to make rules, statements of principles, and Codes of Practice relating to the conduct of investment business (sections 47A, 48, 63A, 63C) and, secondly, it may recognize SROs for the purposes of the Act. In order to be recognized the SRO must meet the requirements laid down in Schedule 2 of the Act as well as the requirements of section 10. Schedule 2, paragraph 3, specifies that the rules of the SRO governing the carrying on of investment business 'must afford investors protection at least equivalent' to the rules, statements of principle, and Codes of Practice promulgated by the SIB. In addition, the members of the SRO must be 'fit and proper' persons, there must be fair and reasonable provisions for the admission, expulsion, and discipline of members, there must be effective complaints mechanisms, effective monitoring and enforcement of the rules, etc., and the SRO must be able and willing to promote and maintain high standards of integrity and fair dealing in the carrying on of investment business (Schedule 2). The arrangements for the appointment and removal of members of the governing body must be such as to secure a proper balance between the interests of the different members of the organization and between the interests of the organization and the interests of the public which means that there must be a certain number of independent members. Although it is not necessarily obvious from this description, the SROs are to have the major day-to-day burden of regulating investment businesses. There are currently four SROs,[63] which are again companies limited by guarantee, but, unlike the SIB, the source of their power is contractual, not statutory.

This is clearly a complex system, and the above account is a simplified one, so the first question is why did the government opt for a self-regulatory solution in this area, particularly as Professor Gower had provided it with the blueprint for a statutory scheme,[64] run either by the Department of Trade and Industry or by a self-standing commission? The answer given by the two most authoritative commentators links the changes in the regulatory system with the more general changes in the financial services industry.[65] For reasons that we need not discuss, it was

[63] The Securities and Futures Association (SFA), Life Assurance and Unit Trust Regulatory Organization (LAUTRO), Investment Management Regulator Organization (IMRO), and Financial Intermediaries, Managers, and Brokers Regulatory Association (FIMBRA). It is planned that the Personal Investment Authority (PIA) will take over the bulk of FIMBRA and LAUTRO's work.

[64] L. C. B. Gower, *Review of Investor Protection Report: Part 1*, Cmnd. 9125 (London, 1984).

[65] M. Moran, *The Politics of the Financial Services Revolution* (London, 1991); A. Page, 'Financial Services: The Self-Regulatory Alternative?', in Baldwin and McCrudden (eds.), *Regulation and Public Law*.

becoming clear by the early 1980s that the growing internationalization of
the securities industry threatened the important position of London as a
financial centre. Reform was stalled, partly due to internal opposition and
partly due to the pending case by the OFT against the Stock Exchange in
the Restrictive Practices Court. At a crucial point in 1983 the government
came to an agreement with the Stock Exchange that, in return for certain
reforms, the OFT case would be withdrawn (the so-called Goodison–
Parkinson Agreement).[66] This agreement intensified the competitive
struggles in the City and made the creation of a new regulatory framework
a necessity. Gower provided the blueprint but it was significantly altered
by substituting self-regulation for regulation by state agency. Moran points
out that almost all the players favoured this solution, although they had
different perceptions.[67] Neither the DTI nor the Bank of England wanted
the horrifyingly complex task of creating and controlling the details of the
new system. A private institution gave the City interests the hope that they
could control the system. Crucially, as Page has it:

the main advantage of self-regulation is . . . that it is thought less likely than is
governmental regulation to inhibit innovation and international competitiveness
and thus frustrate the goals which the government has set up for the financial
sector.[68]

In so doing the Act, according to Moran,[69] involves a shift towards more
juridification, codification, and institutionalization, which in turn might be
seen to have made the regulatory system somewhat more open. For
example, before making any rules under its transferred powers, the SIB
must publish the proposed rules in such a manner as appears to the agency
to be best calculated to bring them to the attention of the public, allow
representations to be made, and have regard to those representations
(Schedule 9, paragraph 12). Although not an onerous obligation, this is in
line with the standards applied to many public bodies.

   Also, though there are no freedom of information requirements or
related obligations, the SIB is required to present an annual report to the
Secretary of State, who is required to lay that report before Parliament
(section 117). A similar obligation is not, however, placed on the SROs,
who must simply adhere to the Companies Acts requirements for annual
reports.

   The procedures put in place for the resolution of complaints by SIB and
the SROs are particularly interesting. SIB originally wanted one investment
ombudsman but discovered that the Act did not give it the power to insist
on this solution. Instead, each of the SROs has developed its own solution.

---

[66] Moran, *The Politics of the Financial Services Revolution*, 68–79.
[67] Ibid. 73.   [68] Page, 'Financial Services', 309.
[69] Moran, *The Poliics of the Financial Services Revolution*, 79.

Again, we see the division between ombudsmen and conciliation and arbitration models. LAUTRO contracts most of its complaint-handling to the Insurance Ombudsman Bureau, whilst maintaining a separate complaints committee for those members who do not belong to the Insurance Ombudsman Bureau. IMRO attempts in-house conciliation in the first instance but, if this is unsuccessful, the case is referred to the Investment Ombudsman. The SFA and FIMBRA, by contrast, both run conciliation and arbitration schemes. A very interesting part of the SFA's arrangements is that they have created the office of Complaints Commissioner, whose job it is to oversee the working of the SFA's in-house complaint-handling system. Again we can see a distinct lack of a pattern. One of the questions for the future will be, following the Clucas Report which recommended the creation of a new SRO for private investors,[70] covering LAUTRO, FIMBRA, and part of IMRO's jurisdiction, how the different systems will be combined and, hopefully, rationalized.

The situation as regards members complaining against the work of the SROs shows more of a pattern.[71] The reason for this is partly the demands of natural justice, which are explicitly recognized in the SFA's Rule 7-1, which states that the SFA is to have regard to the principles of natural justice in interpreting and applying the rules relating to disciplinary matters. Although the procedure for investigating disciplinary matters differs somewhat from SRO to SRO, all provide that members may appeal against disciplinary decisions to an appeal tribunal. The chair of the tribunal is usually legally qualified, appellants must know the case against them, they may have legal representation, oral hearings, and may cross-examine witnesses. The appeal tribunal will give reasons for their decision. With the exception of the SFA, the same tribunal will deal with appeals against refusal of membership and related matters, for example, imposing special and onerous conditions of membership. This procedure does make it easy for disgruntled appellants to bring an application for judical review and the courts have clearly accepted that the SROs are public bodies for this purpose, although they have not yet overturned any decisions of the SROs.[72]

Finally, let us examine the procedures for reviewing the performance of

[70] Sir Kenneth Clucas, *Report on a Study on a New SRO for the Retail Sector* (London, 1992). See now Personal Investment Authority *The PIA's Approach to Regulation* and *Prospectus* (London, 1994).

[71] For details see FIMBRA Rules, parts 8–9; IMRO Rules, ch. viii; LAUTRO Rules, part 7; SFA Rules, ch. 7. The requirements placed on SIB are found in ch. ix of the Financial Services Act.

[72] See *R. v. FIMBRA ex p. Cochrane, The Times*, 23 June 1989; *Bank of Scotland v. IMRO* 1989 SLT 432; *R. v. Association of Futures Brokers and Dealers ex p. Mordens, Financial Times*, 11 July 1990; *R. v. LAUTRO ex p. Ross* [1992] 1 All ER 422; and Lord Alexander, 'Judicial Review and City Regulators' (1989) 52 *MLR* 640.

these institutions. The first point to mention is the role of the OFT. We have noted that self-regulatory arrangements may raise concerns about anti-competitive practices. Section 119 of the FSA provides that the Secretary of State shall not recognize an SRO unless satisfied that its rules do not, to any significant extent, restrict competition. If they do have this effect, they must not be greater than is necessary for the protection of investors. Before making this decision, the Secretary of State is required to have regard to a report by the Director-General of Fair Trading (section 122) which is limited to the effects on competition. These arrangements apply even though the powers have been delegated to the SIB.

Oversight is otherwise a joint matter for the SIB and, before June 1992, the DTI, whilst since June 1992 it has been the responsibility of the Treasury. The recent transfer of government responsibilities from the DTI to the Treasury raises a series of questions about the future of the regulation of financial services.[73] Since it is still too early to judge the effects of this change, we will concentrate on two other reviews of the regulatory system.

The first occurred early on in the life of the SIB, when the regulated industry began to complain about the costs of regulation and its style, that is, that it was over-legalistic and too bureaucratic. These complaints led to a series of amendments introduced into the FSA by the Companies Act 1989, which have allowed SIB and the SROs to rewrite their rulebooks in such a way that they are more flexible and which give the SROs greater freedom to tailor the rules to their particular circumstances. We can see this as an attempt to move from a traditional rule-bound approach to regulation to one more in keeping with a self-regulatory solution. The other change which is on the future agenda is the outcome of the Clucas Report, which, in light of the financial and regulatory difficulties faced by FIMBRA, examined whether it was possible and desirable to set up a new regulatory agency for investment business done with the private investor. As mentioned above, the conclusion was that this was both possible and desirable and, amid much controversy, this has now been accomplished. Thus it is likely that the details provided in this section will be different in the near future, although the principles will remain the same.

CONCLUSIONS

What conclusions can we draw from our examination of self-regulation in Britain today? We have seen that self-regulation has developed as a partial response to the limitations of *imperium* methods of policy delivery, to use

[73] See *Financial Times*, 24 Apr. 1992.

Cotterrell's term. This is a method of policy implementation which will not disappear and may well, arguably, become increasingly important. What we have seen, however, is a rich variety of arrangements but little evidence of principle or pattern, except in the financial services area, where the Financial Services Act does, albeit in a limited way, impose some sort of order on one sector. Given the unprincipled and pragmatic nature of the British constitution as a whole, this is hardly surprising. In order to give some shape to this area, further reflection is needed on what constitutional norms are relevant and how they ought to be put into operation. Only once this is established can we begin the task of examining the empirical evidence and deciding the relationship of these phenomena with our constitutional ideals. If we do not undertake this challenging exercise, then self-regulation will remain simply a wilderness of single instances.

9

Irrelevant Considerations? The Role of Administrative Law in Determining the Local Connection of Homeless Persons

Ian Loveland

INTRODUCTION

A beneficial implication of recent works emphasizing administrative law's roots in political theory[1] is that the lawyer's traditional concern with the legality rather than the legitimacy of governmental action appears increasingly untenable. While notions of legitimacy have long been informants of leftist critiques of public law theory and practice,[2] the Thatcher administrations's radical policies placed questions about the adequacy of public lawyers' reliance on legality as an analytical tool rather more firmly in the mainstream of academic debate. Legitimacy has been embraced as a macro-concept, concerned with the Jeffersonian precept that government derives 'its just powers from the consent of the governed'. Much recent legislation has been found wanting in this respect, prompting increasing interest in such large-scale constitutional questions as electoral reform, the entrenchment of basic individual rights, and effective decentralization of legislative·and executive power.[3]

The traditionalist perspective argues that public law should eschew such lofty considerations. Its task is merely to evaluate the executive behaviour against a limited and strictly ranked hierarchy of legal norms. Sitting atop that hierarchy is the statute or prerogative power whence the administrative power allegedly derives. Of slightly less authoritative hue is case-law, including both judgments specific to the particular statute concerned, and the general principles of administrative law which apply to a wide range of government activities. Judicial norms over such issues as jurisdiction and

---

[1] See esp. P. Cane, *An Introduction to Administrative Law* (Oxford, 1986); P. Craig, *Public Law and Democracy in Britain and the USA* (Oxford, 1991).

[2] H. Laski, 'Judicial Review of Social Policy in England' (1926) *Harvard LR* 832; I. Jennings, 'Courts and Administrative Law: The Experience of English Housing Legislation' (1935) *Harvard LR* 426.

[3] See e.g. the collection of essays in P. McAuslan and J. McEldowney (eds.), *Law, Legitimacy and the Constitution* (London, 1985), and J. Jowell and D. Oliver (eds.), *The Changing Constitution* (Oxford, 1985).

procedural fairness are themselves highly complex constructs, and the difficulty of predicting the enthusiasm with which reviewing courts will perform their role as constitutional policemen is heightened when one considers that judicial review may accord much weight in theory (and determinative influence in practice) to 'non-legal' sources of authority, such as administrative circulars or resolutions of the House of Commons.[4] Added complications ensue when implementation of discretion-laden legislation is entrusted to elected local authorities, whose traditional, if only conventional, constitutional role has been to express political pluralism and pursue policy innovation within the governmental process.[5]

The visibility of such considerations within administrative law's recipe for lawful government evinces a judical concern with a micro-contextual search for extra-statutory sources of legitimacy within the bounds of autonomy granted by legislative rules. However, the courts' adequacy as evaluators of executive behaviour is compromised by the narrowness with which they define the extent of micro-contextual legitimacy. Proceeding in parallel with the macro-legitimacy debates has been a substantial body of socio-legal work charting how the implementation of legislation contravenes statutory and judical constraints.[6] Such 'realist' critiques cogently undermine the administrative law's traditionally formalist approach by demonstrating that government decision-makers take a far more expansive view than the courts of factors which 'legitimize' executive behaviour.

Thus corporate decisions over staffing levels, employee quality, and training provision manifestly affect an organization's capacity to discharge statutory obligations in legally sophisticated ways; intra-organizational industrial relations disputes, or a desire to maintain 'good' relations with other bodies, may also wield considerable influence over decision-making behaviour, as may the extent to which organizational culture permits administrators to express personal political beliefs in their job.[7] The irresistible inference emerging from such studies is that the policy objectives underlying legislation which is politically contentious, loosely drafted, implemented by politically and organizationally heterogeneous bodies, and ineffectively policed by intrusive external constraints may be severely compromised by various anti-legal subtexts which enjoy appreciable

---

[4] *R.* v. *SOSE ex p. Nottinghamshire County Council* [1986] AC 240: *R* v. *SOSE ex p. LB Hammersmith and Fulham* [1990] 3 All ER 589.

[5] J. Sharpe, 'The Theory and Value of Local Government' (1970) *Political Studies* 154; M. Loughlin *Local Government in the Modern State* (1986), chs. 1, 9.

[6] K. Hawkins, *Environment and Enforcement* (Oxford, 1984); D. Cook, *Rich Law, Poor Law* (Milton Keynes, 1989); J. Jowell, 'The Limits of Law in Urban Planning' (1977) *Current Legal Problems* 63; B. Hutter, *The Reasonable Arm of the Law* (Oxford, 1988).

[7] M. Hill 'The Exercise of Discretion in the National Assistance Board' (1969) *Public Administration* 59.

legitimacy in the administrative arena. This chapter examines administrative law's micro-level failure to understand the realities of the administrative process through an empirical account of the implementation by three local authorities of legislation which possesses both great legal complexity and uncertain constitutional legitimacy, namely Part III of the Housing Act 1985.

THE HOUSING ACT 1985, PART III

The Housing (Homeless Persons) Bill was presented to Parliament as a private member's bill in 1976 by Stephen Ross, Liberal MP for the Isle of Wight. Homelessness had enjoyed a high political profile throughout the previous decade, following the television programme *Cathy Come Home* and the emergence of the housing pressure group Shelter. While recognizing the inadequacy of existing legislation (the National Assistance Act 1948) which obliged local councils to assist homeless persons, the Heath government did not feel the problem merited legislative reform. Rather the D.o.E. and DHSS issued a joint circular (18/74) urging local authorities to assume considerably expanded responsibilities towards homeless people. As they were contained in a circular, the government's preferences were not legally binding. Since many councils lacked the capacity and/or the desire to accommodate more homeless people, the circular was widely ignored.[8] The 1974–9 Labour government's intention to put Circular 18/74 on a statutory footing was shelved following the OPEC oil crisis,[9] although the government subsequently offered tacit support when Ross adopted the D.o.E.'s proposed Bill as a private member's measure.

This Bill sought to impose on local authorities an absolute rehousing duty towards families with children, the elderly, and the severely ill/disabled. In so doing, the Bill marked a distinct break with the post-war tradition of affording councils virtually unfettered autonomy in the allocation and management of their housing stock.[10] The proposed legislation was vigorously opposed by some Conservative MPs and local authorities. Their disquiet evidently rested less on the Bill's unconventional approach to central/local relations than on a concern that their areas would be overwhelmed by 'undeserving' poor people seeking to enforce their newly

---

[8] A. Arden, *Homeless Persons: The Housing Act 1985 Part III* (London, 1988), ch. 1.

[9] L. Thompson, *An Act of Compromise* (London, 1987) ch. 12.

[10] See I. Loveland, 'Legal Rights and Political Realities: Governmental Responses to Homelessness in Britain' (1991) 16 *Law and Social Inquiry* 249. For the courts' (indulgent) approach see especially *Shelley* v. *London County Council* [1948] 2 All ER 898 and *Bristol District Council* v. *Clark* [1975] 1 WLR 1.

granted 'rights' to council housing.[11] Had that been the Act's ultimate objective, further questions would have arisen concerning its consitutional legitimacy, given that popular support for universalistic welfare provision has been highly selective in post-war Britain. Only the National Health Service, elementary and secondary schooling, and old age pensions have consistently attracted the approval of a majority of citizens: non-contributory cash benefits and subsidized public housing have had a particularly tenuous hold on popular affection.[12] In the event, the Labour government's then precarious parliamentary majority resulted in a significant dilution of the Bill's initial intent. Stephen Ross and the D.o.E. steered an uneasy middle way between a restrictive Conservative opposition orchestrated by Hugh Rossi, and a liberally inclined grouping of Labour back-benchers led by Robin Cook.

As well as provoking intense substantive controversy, the Bill's passage was dogged by accusations of procedural illegitimacy.[13] Its end product, however, presented applicants with what has been termed an 'obstacle race'. This race has three preliminary stages. Applicants must be 'homeless', a notion defined in the narrow sense of legal rights of occupancy rather than the more expansive sense of poor-quality or unsuitable existing accommodation.[14] Applicants must also be in 'priority need', a criterion which excludes most childless people below retirement age from any entitlement to permanent rehousing.[15] A third barrier to rehousing is raised by provisions concerning 'intentional homelessness'. This removes entitlement from applicants whom the local authority adjudges homeless as a result of deliberate acts or omissions—for example following eviction for rent arrears or abandonment of housing in which they had a legal right to remain.[16]

All three tests were ultimately drafted in language which afforded administering authorities significant discretion. Labour MPs favouring more expansive provision have warned that such formulas would place applicants 'at the mercy of petty bureaucrats', and permit councils whose political sympathies did not extend to homeless people lawfully to avoid

---

[11] The most celebrated comment belongs to William Rees-Davies, MP for Thanet: 'it is the view of [my] local authority as well as my own that the Bill, unamended, is a charter for the rent dodger, for the scrounger, and for the encouragement of the homeleaver' (HC Deb., 18 Feb. 1977, col. 972).

[12] Administrative lawyers who incline to be political theorists may have to get used to drawing on opinion poll data; on these specific points see P. Taylor-Gooby, *Public Opinion, Ideology and State Welfare* (London, 1985), ch. x, and the sources cited therein.

[13] Conservative MPs considered the Bill was *de facto* a government measure, and that the D.o.E. was cynically taking advantage of procedural benefits enjoyed by private members' bills to sneak the measure through (HC Deb., 20 May 1977, col. 957-8).

[14] s. 58. (The Act is now contained in Part III of the Housing Act 1985: all citations are to this Act.)   [15] s. 59.   [16] s. 60.

rehousing obligations.[17] The D.o.E. sought to assuage such concerns by producing a Code of Guidance alerting authorities to the spirit in which the government hoped the letter of the law would be applied, and to which councils would be obliged to have regard.[18] Although much of the Code's language did indeed express Labour back-benchers' preferences, the MPs themselves were sceptical about its probable impact, suggesting that, as was the case with Circular 18/74, its advice would be ignored by hostile authorities.

Recent Audit Commission statistics reveal that approximately 50 per cent of applicants fail to clear one or more of the statutory obstacles,[19] which suggests that the filter mechanisms introduced by opposition MPs to protect local authorities from 'unmeritorious' applications have had appreciable effect. Although the Act affords councils considerable discretion in how their rehousing responsibilities to entitled applicants are discharged, it appears that almost all applicants are allocated secure tenancies in council flats or houses. However, in certain circumstances, local authorities may avoid permanent rehousing duties by transferring their responsibility to another council. The so-called 'local connection' provision, contained in section 67 of the Act, is this chapter's primary empirical focus.

LOCAL CONNECTION: THE LEGAL CONCEPT

The duties owed to homeless persons under the National Assistance Act 1948 were imposed simply on the authority where the application was made;[20] there was no scope for responsibility to be transferred elsewhere. However, despite the perfect clarity of the law, a conventional practice grew up whereby housing was provided by the council to whom the entitled person was most closely connected.[21] Applicants linked to several areas were often made the object of inter-authority squabbles: the authority to which an application was made might seek to refer it to another council, a course of action which, unsurprisingly, the second authority frequently resisted.[22] The original 1977 Bill restated the 1948 provisions. Rehousing duties were imposed on the council to which applicants applied. This outraged some Conservative MPs and local authorities, who argued that

---

[17] HC Deb., 8 July 1977, col. 1663.   [18] s. 71.

[19] The Audit Commission, *Housing the Homeless: The Local Authority Role* (London, 1988), 8.   [20] s. 24 (2).

[21] Arden, *Homeless Persons*, ch. 1: Shelter, *The Grief Report* (London, 1972), 190–226.

[22] Arden, *Homeless Persons*, 74: Association of District Councils, *Homelessness: A Review of the Legislation* (London, 1988), 4.

their pretty seaside or suburban town would act as magnets for itinerant 'scroungers'.[23]

Some Conservative MPs took pains to identify Irish citizens as a potential problem. William Rees-Davies alerted the Commons to 'the beach scrounger . . . often an Irish building labourer', who would inflict himself and his family on seaside councils after having spent all his money on holiday; Hugh Rossi feared that the Act would be used to subsidize 'the Paddy O'Connors of this world'.[24] Had resort towns been overrun by 'scoungers' following enactment of the Bill, most applicants undoubtedly would have been found not to be homeless, or not in priority need, or to have become homeless intentionally. Nevertheless, fear of invasion afflicted many Conservative authorities, and the threat that MPs from those areas might oppose the Bill induced its sponsors to make a further concession. Should an applicant entitled to accommodation have no 'local connection' with the authority she initially approached, but be so connected with another council, the second authority would be obliged to rehouse her.

The criteria for establishing a local connection derive from an elongated hierarchy of sources. Section 67 activates the concept only when four conditions are met. First that the initial ('notifying') authority has concluded that the applicant is homeless, has a priority need, did not become homeless intentionally, and is therefore entitled to permanent rehousing. Secondly that the applicant has no local connection with the notifying authority. Thirdly that such a connection exists with another (the 'notified') authority. And fourthly that the applicant would not be at risk of domestic violence should she return to that other council's area. In formal terms therefore consideration of the local connection issue is to be the final stage of an authority's decision-making process, initiated only after decisions as to the prior obstacles of homelessness, priority need, and intentionality have been made in the applicant's favour by the notifying authority.

The Code of Guidance stressed that the local connection test was a threshold requirement.[25] Any local connection which an applicant had with the authority she approached would make that council responsible for securing permanent rehousing, even if the applicant had an equal or greater connection with one or more other authorities. Arden observes that the threshold test was expressly introduced 'to end "shuttling" homeless persons between different authorities, each alleging there was "greater connection" with the other'.[26] However the Bill's Report stage

---

[23] Per Hugh Rossi MP, HC Deb., 8 July 1977, col. 1611.
[24] Ibid., 8 July 1977, col. 1658; ibid., 20 May 1977, col. 963.
[25] At para. 2.22.   [26] Arden, *Homeless Persons*, 85.

suggests that the Conservative MPs backing the amendment had quite different intentions, namely 'to enable the authority to which the application is made to look into the circumstances, and if it finds that the applicant has a *greater tie with another authority*, to notify the other authority that the person is its responsibility' (emphasis added).[27] The 'threshold' test appears to have been inadvertently introduced by a drafting amendment at the Report stage in the Lords.[28] The discretion-laden nature of much of the legislation indicates that its terms were frequently an uncomfortable compromise, designed to placate irreconcilable opposing camps. But the drafting of section 61 appeared simply to prevent local authorities producing the result for which MPs assumed the Bill had provided.

Establishing a local connection: a mix of sources

Section 61 (1) provides that a local connection arises (1) if an applicant is, or in the past was normally, resident in that district, and that residence is or was of his own choice, or (2) if he is employed in that district, or (3) because of family associations, or (4) because of special circumstances.

MPs had frequently accepted that such definitional imprecision would be fleshed out by the D.o.E. Code. However, the Act provided that referral questions 'shall be determined by agreement between the notifying authority and the notified authority'.[29] This led to the production of a Local Authority Agreement (LAA), negotiated by the Association of Metropolitan Authorities, the Association of District Councils (ADC), and the London Boroughs' Association. The LAA noted that section 61 contained much scope for argument, which only the courts could authoritatively resolve. But the LAA hoped its provisions would foster a negotiatory rather than juridified approach to dispute avoidance and settlement.[30]

The LAA emphasized that determining a local connection was not a question of degree: 'the Act makes it clear that if a household has any local connection in the receiving authority's own area, then that authority will be responsible, even though the household may be thought to have a greater local connection in another area'.[31] It also provided councils with a fuller definition of section 61.[32] 'Normal residence' would result from occupancy

---

[27] Per Hugh Rossi MP, HC Deb., 8 July 1977, col. 1620.
[28] HL Deb., 27 July 1977, cols. 986–7.   [29] s. 67 (4).
[30] If disputes could not be avoided, the LAA offered an arbitration mechanism which it hoped would render court proceedings unnecessary; LAA para. 1.2; s. 67 (5); LAA para. 6. The arbitration procedure was given statutory force by the Housing (Homeless Persons) (Appropriate Arrangements) Order 1978, SI no. 69, and the Housing (Homeless Persons) (Appropriate Arrangements) (no. 2) Order 1978, SI no. 661.   [31] At para. 2.7.
[32] All references in this paragraph are to the LAA para. 2.5.

of a dwelling within an authority's area for six of the past twelve months, or three of the past five years. 'Employment' would be sufficient if 'not of a casual nature'. Family associations would be satisfied by parents, children, or siblings resident in the area for five years; more distant relatives would suffice only in 'exceptional circumstances'. The Agreement suggested that 'special circumstances' might apply to military personnel or applicants returning to the area where they had previously lived for long periods. This contradicted parliamentary intent, which had been concerned primarily with labour mobility: 'the question of special circumstances is meant to relate to work. It relates to someone moving into an area to take a job but whose normal place of residence might be elsewhere.'[33]

The LAA appeared to have achieved its primary objective; a 1988 ADC study reported that it 'has worked well, authorities adhere to the guidelines and there are relatively few disputes between them'.[34] The frequency and subject-matter of disagreements aired through the arbitration system confirm this point; most arguments centre on whether unusual facts fit within LAA criteria rather than on the legitimacy of the criteria themselves.[35]

The Agreement also emphasized that section 61's four-stage test and its own guidance were devices enabling an authority to defend a decision that an applicant lacked a local connection; councils may find that applicants have a local connection with their area on any ground they choose.[36] However, the LAA did not stress the converse point, namely that councils seeking to avoid rehousing obligations might reject statutory and Agreement criteria as too generous, and subsequently defend their own interpretation of local connection in arbitration or judicial proceedings.

That councils might do so was confirmed by the House of Lords in *In Re Betts*.[37] *Betts* held that section 61's four tests were subcategories of a broader statutory concept of local connection. The House of Lords concluded that the LAA offered an 'eminently sensible' interpretation of that wider concept, but it was no more than a relevant consideration; councils should have regard to it, but they need not follow its advice.

The Act permitted 'notified' authorities to challenge whether referred applicants did indeed have a local connection with their area, but did not allow those councils to challenge the notifying authority's conclusions on homelessness, priority need, or non-intentionality. In *R. v. Slough BC ex parte Ealing LBC*,[38] the Court of Appeal confirmed that the consequence

---

[33] Per Stephen Ross MP, HC Deb., 27 July 1977, col. 871.

[34] ADC, *Homelessness*, 7.

[35] Digests of decisions made under the arbitration process are published by the London Borough's Association.   [36] Para. 2.7.   [37] [1983] 2 AC 613.

[38] [1981] QB 801.

of this omission was that notified authorities favouring restrictive interpretation of the three 'obstacles' must rehouse applicants properly referred
by councils adopting a more expansive approach to those provisions. This
judgment had two undesirable consequences for councils antagonistic
towards the Act. First, a locally connected applicant could sidestep a
restrictive authority's interpretation of homelessness or intentionality by
approaching a generous authority with whom she had no local connection.
Having established the applicant's rehousing entitlement, the generous
authority would then refer her to the restrictive council. A second, even
less palatable, possibility was that an applicant found not homeless or
intentionally homeless by the first authority could then approach a
generous council with which she was not locally connected. This council
might establish entitlement on the same facts that were not accepted by the
first authority. A subsequent referral would oblige the first authority to
rehouse an applicant they themselves had specifically rejected. As the
Court of Appeal stressed, section 67 made both hypotheses legally
incontestable.

These so-called 'merry go-round'[39] cases intensified a local authority
concern that had been aroused by *R. v. Hillingdon London Borough
Council ex parte Streeting*,[40] where the Court of Appeal held that foreign
applicants, lacking ties to any council in Britain, were the responsibility of
the authority they initially approached. The leaders of Hillingdon council
(then Conservative controlled) seemingly rejected the legitimacy of both
the statute and the courts, announcing that 'We will be looking for every
way to avoid our obligations to house these people . . . We were elected by
local people to house Hillingdon residents.'[41]

Turning law into practice: an overview

Despite the dire warnings offered by the Bill's parliamentary opponents,
recent D.o.E. studies suggest there are very few local connection cases
relative to total Part III applications: the 1989 *Review of the Homelessness
Legislation* reported that section 67 was invoked in fewer than 1 per cent of
homeless acceptances.[42] A 1988 D.o.E. survey recorded that 33 per cent of
councils did not invoke section 67 at all in the 1985/6 financial year; over 90
per cent used it fewer than ten times.[43] The D.o.E. survey indicates that

---

[39] Ibid., per Shaw LJ. [40] [1980] 3 All ER 413.
[41] *The Times*, 11 July 1980, cited in P. Robson and P. Watchman, 'The Homeless Persons
Obstacle Race'., (1980) *Journal of Social Welfare Law* 65.
[42] Para. 16.
[43] D.o.E., *Responding to Homelessness: Local Authority Policy and Practice* (London,
1988), tables 27–9.

the local connection provisions do not provoke a worrying degree of inter-authority dispute. Similarly Niner's 1989 study of nine authorities recorded that all claimed to follow LAA recommendations.[44]

However, a 1988 ADC adopted a less complimentary position. The ADC recommended that 'normal residence' be extended to twelve months, observing that 'the residential qualification is being abused because the six months period can include the whole holiday season and could leave seaside authorities with obligations to rehouse casual workers and visitors'.[45] The ADC did not quantify such 'abuse'. It also seems to misinterpret both the legislation and the Agreement. The LAA suggests that casual employment would not create a local connection, and also provides that occupancy of holiday accommodation would not count towards residency qualifications.[46] It seems unlikely that any court (or LAA arbitrator) would not apply such 'eminently sensible' tests to deny local connection claims to visitors or casual workers.

Nevertheless the ADC's distaste for section 61 is evident, and is reinforced by suggestions that a local connection arising through employment should be negated by residence in a nearby authority, and that siblings should no longer constitute a family connection.[47] The D.o.E.'s 1989 *Review of the Homelessness Legislation* similarly made no attempt to quantify the scale of the 'abuse' suffered by supposed 'magnet' areas. But despite the D.o.E.'s aforementioned conclusion that section 67 was relevant to fewer than 15 per cent of acceptances, the *Review* promised that the government would shortly take steps 'to moderate undue demands on the most heavily burdened areas'.[48] However, the ADC's most interesting proposal was that an applicant connected with more than one authority should be rehoused by the council with whom she 'has the strongest connection'.[49] This amendment would restore Conservative back-benchers' initial, unenacted intention, and suggests that there is a strong sublegislative current of opinion among local authorities which accords considerable legitimacy to the 'greater local connection' argument which, in blatant contradiction of statutory provisions, authoritatively structured inter-council relations between 1948 and 1977. This inference is reinforced by Niner's observation that several authorities were systematic-ally ignoring the section 67 procedures by simply advising non-locally connected applicants to apply elsewhere.[50] Quite why a council might do this, and the implications such behaviour has for the lawful implementation of the Act, are the issues addressed below.

---

[44] P. Niner, *Homelessness in Nine Local Authorities* (London, 1989), 34–5.
[45] ADC, *Homelessness*, 8.   [46] At paras. 2.5 (iii) and 2.5 (i) respectively.
[47] ADC, *Homelessness*, 8.   [48] Niner, *Homelessness*, 22.
[49] ADC, *Homelessness*, 8.   [50] At 34.

IN THE FIELD: IMPLEMENTING THE ACT

The following data are drawn from fieldwork conducted in three authorities between 1988 and 1991. Eastern, a New Town near London, was hung during the early stages of fieldwork, and thereafter passed (briefly) into Labour control. Its housing was predominantly owner-occupied (and expensive), with a substantial but shrinking public sector, most of which was controlled by the Commission for New Towns rather than the council. Officers in Eastern's homeless persons unit (HPU) felt that the lack of clear political control had paralysed formulation of housing policy, and councillors had made no clear recommendations concerning the interpretation of Part III criteria. Left largely to its own devices, the HPU had adopted a fairly generous approach to the legislation. Since demand for rehousing greatly outstripped supply, this substantive generosity had forced the council to place a large and growing number of applicants in bed and breakfast accommodation in neighbouring authorities.[51]

Midland is a solidly Labour-controlled industrial city which suffered high unemployment during the 1980s. Unlike Eastern, Midland has a large private rented sector, and when fieldwork began it also had a surplus of difficult-to-let council housing where most part iii applicants were accommodated. The city's councillors were active in formulating the broad sweep of housing policy, but had traditionally shown little interest in the minutiae of part iii decision-making, which was undertaken by officers in the council's Housing Centre.

Western is an authority created in 1974, neatly split into a rural suburb of a major city and several large public-sector overspill estates built in the 1950s and 1960s. Traditionally a solidly Conservative authority, the Conservative majority had almost disappeared by 1990. Conservative councillors displayed little interest in or knowledge of the homelessness legislation. This was illustrative of a more pervasive officer dominance of the council's housing policy: the Director of Housing characterized his task as 'trying to run a middle-of-the-road housing policy in a right wing Tory borough', an objective which in the main he felt he achieved.

Unlike either Eastern or Midland, Western encouraged its officers to gain professional housing qualifications, and laid considerable emphasis on training, promotion, and structured career progression. Officers in Eastern felt more rigorous training was desirable, but considered their work-loads were too heavy for additional training time to be allocated. Midland felt

[51] For a more detailed analysis of Eastern see I. Loveland, 'Administrative Law, Administrative Processes, and the Housing of Homeless Persons' (1991) 10 *Journal of Social Welfare and Family Law* 4.

such expertise was unnecessary, given that it had a constant supply of difficult-to-let properties which could be allocated in cases involving uncertainty over an applicant's entitlement. All councils were alike, however, in having experienced an appreciable rise in homeless applications and a significant decline in their available housing stock between 1985 and 1989. None of the three authorities studied was in any sense a 'magnet' area. Although the councils did not keep precise statistics recording the number of non-locally connected applicants who approached them, officers in all authorities felt that the issue was of minor quantitative importance. In a qualitative sense, however, it could prove to be a particularly problematic issue.

Decision-making in Eastern Borough Council

Eastern's officers generally handle local connection cases without formal section 67 referrals; telephoning the 'notified authority' to say an applicant is coming is usually sufficient. This informal mechanism is employed as the first step in the inquiry process; if an applicant clearly has no local connection with Eastern, and equally clearly has one elsewhere, investigations concerning homelessness, priority need, and intentionality are dispensed with.

For an applicant, this reversal of the statutory process may have certain advantages; it may for example mean she is rehoused more quickly. But it also has possible disadvantages. Eastern interpreted homelessness, priority need, and intentionality in a fairly generous manner.[52] If the statutory process is followed, Eastern would establish the applicant's status *vis-à-vis* those three criteria before section 67 is invoked. Consequently an authority favouring restrictive interpretations would, in theory, be bound by Eastern's more liberal views.[53]

Eastern's officers evidently did not appreciate that their procedural short cut might undermine an applicant's prospects of securing permanent accommodation if she was informally transferred elsewhere. The mechanism is obviously open to accusations of overriding applicants' (procedural) rights for reasons of administrative expediency, but this is countered by the reciprocity inherent in the procedure: Eastern's officers were quite content to undertake the full inquiry process concerning applications transferred to Eastern in this extra-statutory fashion. The HPU found local connection

---

[52] Ibid.
[53] In *R.* v. *London Borough of Newham ex p. London Borough of Tower Hamlets*, reported in *Guardian*, 13 Mar. 1990, it was held that the original authority's decision as to intentionality was a relevant consideration of which a second council should take account before referring an applicant back to the original authority.

cases problematic only if the notifying authority's behaviour fell between the two stools of fully respecting or entirely ignoring statutory investigation requirements. Eastern's officers felt that some authorities used referrals in cases with ambiguous factual or legal features to spare themselves time-consuming investigation, and/or to avoid reaching restrictive decisions, without having to shoulder the obligation of rehousing the persons concerned. The HPU only encounters this situation infrequently; but these few occasions are often the cause of appreciable aggravation.

Applicants E/LC1 left Eastern in 1986 for Northern Ireland. In 1988 the HPU received a section 67 notice from a Cornish authority, stating that the applicants had left Northern Ireland because of sectarian harassment, taken a six-month holiday let in Cornwall, and were about to be evicted. The Cornish authority found them unintentionally homeless and in priority need, but decided they had no local connection and so referred them to Eastern. The HPU accepted that the original authority's local connection decision was defensible. However, officers were much annoyed by that authority's complete failure to investigate both why the applicants had left Northern Ireland, and the legality of their eviction from the holiday let; either situation might have warranted an intentionality finding. Recalling a phone conversation with the Cornish authority's homelessness section, an HPU officer thought its failure to make inquiries reprehensible: 'They've not done all their work on this. I said "Why have they got to get out?" He said, "Oh I don't know." I said, "have you got any proof that they're in fear of violence?" He said "No. That's not up to me." '

The HPU's legally well-founded indignation arose because such investigation was undoubtedly 'up to' the Cornish officer, precisely because Eastern was not legally competent to make such decisions itself. Since the council's approach to intentionality is not particularly harsh, officers were not aggrieved at the prospect of adopting a generous interpretation of the individual case *per se*; their irritation arose because nobody had considered whether such generosity was justified.

Similarly, applicants E/IHoo7's approach to Eastern was rejected because their homelessness was adjudged intentional. They then applied to an East Anglian authority with which they had no local connection. Without contacting Eastern's HPU, this authority found the applicants unintentionally homeless and in priority need. The applicants had claimed local connections with both Eastern and a London borough, and in accordance with their preferences had been referred via section 67 to the latter authority.[54] This council subsequently contacted Eastern's HPU to establish why the applicants had left their accommodation in Eastern.

[54] An authority is not bound to respect an applicant's preferences in such circumstances, but the LAA (at para. 3.6) recommends they should be accorded some weight.

HPU officers were appalled at the sloppiness of the East Anglian officer's behaviour, which they considered to be incompatible with the standards of professional competence and integrity upon which the effective functioning of the informal local connection procedures relied. As one officer put it, in slightly more graphic terms: 'She made a right prat of herself. You always get in touch with the places where they've been to see if they've made an application there.'

Incompetence and expediency are not the sole obstacles to the informal referral process. A small Conservative authority adjoining Eastern employs only one homeless persons officer. HPU officers were of the opinion that this person was neither willing nor able to subscribe to notions of professional competence and reciprocity. He was characterized as 'Horrible! A shithead! He tries to worm his way out of everything.' Relations were particularly strained by case E/LC3. The applicant, a long-term resident in the neighbouring authority, was a young mentally handicapped man who moved into lodgings in Eastern. After two months,[55] he had fallen into arrears and faced eviction. His home council's homeless persons officer told him that the authority had no accommodation or advice to offer, and that he should apply to Eastern.

The HPU was unhappy with, but not surprised by, its neighbour's obvious failure to discharge its legal obligations. Nevertheless officers accepted the application, conferred with the applicant's social worker and landlord, and subsequently found him unintentionally homeless and in priority need. They then invoked section 67 to transfer the resulting rehousing obligation to their neighbour. The response was not unexpected. The applicant's file recorded that the notified authority's officer's response was both intransigent and legally incompetent:

refused to act on telephone advice and accept a referral, on the basis that we had not actually asked Social Services to confirm that he was ESN, and anyway he didn't accept that even if he is mentally handicapped [that] this is sufficient to find 'vulnerability'. I suggested he couldn't argue with our assessment if we're referring—said he proposed to go to arbitration. Not the most helpful response from a neighbour! Said if we wanted to view as homeless/priority up to us to secure temporary tenancy.

The case was 'temporarily' settled following Social Service and HPU intercession with the (then) DHSS and the applicant's landlord. But officers expected to see the applicant again soon, when he would have established a local connection; and the neighbouring authority would successfully have 'wormed its way out' of its rehousing responsibility.

---

[55] The LAA (at para. 2.5) suggests that a local connection would be established by six months' residence in the last twelve, or three years during the past five; criteria which this applicant clearly failed to meet.

However, Eastern's officers found its neighbour's politically uncooperative stance less irksome than the incompetence of the other councils mentioned above because it was entirely predictable, and could thus be built into the HPU's decision-making processes.

Decision-making in Western Borough Council

For Western's officers, an adjacent authority's failure to apply section 67 accurately was a more persistent, if less acute, source of irritation. Western borders Central, one of England's largest cities, and is to some degree a commuter suburb for its larger neighbour. Many of Western's residents work in Central, or have family members living there, and so would have a local connection with both authorities. In such circumstances the legislation clearly imposes any rehousing obligation on the council applicants initially approach. As noted above, the provisions of the 1977 Act were couched in terms that apparently precluded the inter-authority squabbles which accompanied implementation of the National Assistance Act. However, Central had apparently failed to understand the legal position.

Western frequently received 'referrals' from Central which stated that applicants had a 'greater local connection' with Western than with Central. These 'referrals' operated very informally; Central did not issue a section 67 notice, and rarely investigated homelessness, intentionality, or priority need. Officers thought that Central's problem was rooted in ignorance rather than malice. Central had decentralized its housing functions to over twenty Neighbourhood Offices. Western's officers assume that the intermittent appearance of 'greater connection' cases derive from new, untrained staff arriving at a particular Neighbourhood Office and assuming immediate, sole, and legally inept responsibility for homelessness decisions. One senior officer recalled somewhat incredulously: 'I had one report from their Housing Adviser that said "My knowledge of the law is very hazy here but I think I can refer them to you." That was the actual report sent to us!' After some months on the job, and several indignant phone calls from Western's officers, Central's new employees begin to implement the Act correctly. But with over twenty offices, Central always has someone new in post.

Western's officers doubted that they could stop the problem recurring. They did not consider the LAA arbitration process an appropriate mechanism for challenging their neighbour's foibles. As one explained; 'That puts the punter in a "piggy in the middle" situation—something we avoid. I take the view that we accept them . . . I'm not going to have people kicked backwards and forwards.'

Western's officers pursued individual cases with Central's Neighbourhood Offices on an *ad hoc* basis, but doubted that Central's behaviour posed a sufficient problem to require a formal approach from the Director of Housing to his Central counterpart.

Although Western's offices adopt the same informal short cut as Eastern's HPU in respect of applicants whose local connection is with Central, cases which involve referral further afield are investigated and a formal section 67 notice issued: officers do not consider administrative expediency a good enough reason to expose applicants to other authorities's potentially unlawful and restrictive decisions on homelessness, priority need, or intentionality.

Western's officers, like employees in Eastern's HPU, regard other authorities' overt incompetence as a professional failing. However, they do not view Central's shortcomings as indicative of an anti-homeless bias. Central is a Labour-controlled council with huge housing resources; it also has a reputation for interpreting part iii generously, and for accepting non-priority need or intentionally homeless applicants through its ordinary waiting list. Western's officers therefore have no qualms about bypassing section 67 if Central is the applicant's final destination.

That Central's inexpert interpretation of section 61 causes Western merely a procedural irritation, rather than the significant substantive problem that other councils' similar ineptitude poses in Eastern is due in part to Central's readiness to atone for its mistakes by offering properties to future Western applicants. Central does not try to 'worm its way out' of its responsibilities—it simply does not always understand what those responsibilities are. Some of Western' officers also found Central's confusion could occasionally work to Western's advantage. Officers produced a little rough justice by informing applicants with a dual connection that they might have an entitlement to rehousing with either authority, and that the choice of where the apply was theirs to make.

With the exception of relations with Central, and despite occasional aberrant decisions, Western's officers do not find interpretation and application of section 61 tests unduly problematic, but generally make considerable efforts to ensure that solutions are legally defensible. Applicant 1W/LC1 sought to establish a local connection through a daughter involuntarily detained in a local psychiatric hospital since 1982. The interviewing officer had not faced a similar problem before. Thorough perusal of the LAA did not provide her with an answer, and consulting first Andrew Arden's textbook, then the Code, and finally the Act itself left her none the wiser. While section 61 (3) informed her that an *applicant herself* did not acquire a local connection through involuntary detention, it made no reference to the involuntary detention of a family member. The housing adviser subsequently discussed the case with her colleague, and they hesitantly concluded that a local connection would arise under section 61 (1) (*d*)'s 'special circumstances'. Officers presented this case as illustrative of a general predisposition to 'stretch' the legislation to support generous decisions. From an applicant's perspective, that substantive predisposition is probably the most important element of the decision-making equation. But the point of interest to administrative lawyers is perhaps the hierarchy of authority which officers constructed for the governmental information sources available. In descending order of importance they were the LAA, the Code and then the Act; the ostensibly authoritative analysis of section 61 provided by the House of Lords in *In Re Betts* played no part at all in the officers' decision-making.

Except in cases involving Central, Western's officers approach the Local Authority Agreement not as an 'eminently sensible' *interpretation* of the Act; but as the effective determinant of the 'legal' response to most situations. In routine cases its criteria are applied automatically; in more difficult cases it is the primary point of reference. The procedures followed in the third authority, Midland, reveal a markedly different picture.

Decision-making in Midland Borough Council

Data from Midland indicate that the 'most closely connected' version of local connection continues to structure councils' implementation of the Act. Applicant MID/LC1, his wife, and their two small children left a Sunderland council tenancy to seek work in Midland. The applicant's father was a Midland resident (and so gave them, per the LAA, a local connection), but could not accommodate them. After a night in their car, the family made a homeless application to Midland, where an officer advised them to 'report as homeless in the North-East as he was not our responsibility'. A similar outcome occurred in case MID/LC2. The applicant had relinquished her London council tenancy following threats of violence from her husband, and returned with her child to her parents' home in Midland. She maintained that she was not prepared to return to London under any circumstances. While the applicant was obviously in priority need and had a local connection with Midland through her parents' long-term residency, the facts of the case suggest that investigation would be necessary to determine the questions of homelessness and intentionality. However, the interviewing officer adopted a more peremptory approach. 'Advised that under Homeless Persons Act [*sic*] we would refer her back to London as she is their responsibility and even then they may class her as intentional as she terminated tenancy rather than approaching them to see if they could transfer to another part of the borough.'

Midland's confusion over section 61 is not confined to junior employees. Applicant MID/LC3, a 23-year-old pregnant woman with a young child, had spent the first twenty years of her life in Midland, where her parents still lived. On marrying she moved to London, but returned to Midland when the relationship broke down. The interviewing officer's notes record that she 'Discussed case with [Manager] who advised not our responsibility under the Homeless Persons Act [*sic*] and we'd refer her back to London (disputable as she has a family connection). However she can register on the waiting list in the normal way and await turn.'

Misunderstanding section 61 did not always lead to substantively indefensible decisions. File notes for applicant MID/LC6 record that she and her three children approached the Housing Centre following violence from her husband:

Going through divorce. Baby from this marriage. Husband wants baby. Threatening to snatch child. Last Sunday husband beat up applicant and also hit baby. Came back tonight threatening to petrol bomb house. Injunction against husband. A states GP has record of bruising. Solicitor aware of situation . . . Police confirmed that they were in attendance and that damage had been done by estranged husband.

Midland placed the applicant in a bed and breakfast hotel overnight while seeking a permanent solution. The response adopted was to issue a section 67 referral notice to the Norfolk authority where the applicant's parents were resident. Since the applicant was also locally connected to Midland, a section 67 notice could not lawfully be issued, but, as the Norfolk council was willing to house the applicant, the end result was clearly satisfactory to all parties concerned.

In an isolated case, one might wonder if the way in which a decision is produced is important if its contents are both expedient and lawful. But it may be rash to assume that procedural irregularities always 'turn out right in the end'. Midland's misconstruction of section 61 also extends beyond the 'most closely connected' scenario. Unlike Western and Eastern, Midland does receive a small but regular stream of applications from citizens of Eire. As Eire is a member of the EEC, such applicants are entitled to Part III rehousing if they satisfy the Act's eligibility criteria. It is, however, quite likely that non-British EEC nationals will not have a local connection with any housing authority. As the *Streeting* case made clear any rehousing obligation would therefore fall on the council to which the application was made; and as Hillingdon's reaction to *Streeting* made equally clear, some authorities were less than enthusiastic about the demands this would place upon their stock and their administrators.

Midlands does not allow Eire citizens to impinge appreciably on its officers' time or its dwindling housing supply. The local connection provisions appear to be used quite erroneously, but entirely effectively, to rebut applications from Irish citizens lacking a connection with any housing authority. Thus when applicants MID/LC[e]1 and their two young children arrived at Midland's Housing Centre, having left Ireland to look for work,

they met with a brusque reception: 'Advised applicants not our responsibility and the best we could arrange would be a travel warrant back to
Ireland. Gave general advice re hostel/B&B etc.'

As habitually occurred in Eastern, and sporadically in Western,
Midland's officers often appeared to make local connection their first point
of reference when dealing with non-Midland residents. Applicant MID/
LC[e]2, a 62-year-old Eire citizen, had left Ireland to live with his son and
girlfriend. When the son's relationship with his partner broke down, the
applicant was required to leave the couple's flat. It is quite plausible that
Midland would not have been obliged to house the applicant on the
grounds that he was not in priority need,[56] but this preliminary point was
not addressed. Rather the officer's initial and only point of reference was
to the local connection provisions, which were again incorrectly construed
as supporting the conclusion that the applicant was not connected with
Midland. In contrast the officer deciding case MID/LC[e]3 went through
the investigatory process in the 'correct' order. Having found the applicant
homeless and in priority need, the officer considered that a finding of
intentional homelessness might be possible. She did not pursue this
further, however; point 4 in her notes recorded that the applicant had no
local connection and therefore was not entitled to accommodation.

CONCLUSION

The case-studies have recorded a lucid example of pervasive subversion of
statutory requirements in Midland, and a not infrequent predisposition in
Eastern's HPU to sidestep legal constraints. Only in Western does
decision-making proceed in broad, but not perfect, conformity to legal
requirements. From this vantage-point it seems that administrative reality
bears little resemblance to prescriptive legality. But while one may
conclude that the councils' decision-making processes are in varying
degrees unlawful, the question as to whether they are therefore also
illegitimate is far less straightforward. For if one begins to contextualize
administrative behaviour in the three authorities studied, it appears that it
is the Act's legal form rather than its practical (unlawful) application that is
pathological. In both the micro- and macro-contexts, systemically *ultra
vires* decision-making makes considerable sense.

Awareness of the controversies surrounding the passage of the 1977 Act
might lead one to assume that councils would flout the local connection
requirements simply to safeguard their housing stock from 'undeserving'

---

[56] The applicant may have been in priority need by virtue of being 'vulnerable as a result of
old age' (s. 59 (1) (*c*)).

applicants. However, that consideration appears to have limited relevance in either Eastern or Midland, both of which have different internally generated reasons for contravening legal requirements. In Midland, using referral as the first rather than last stage of the investigatory process, and misinterpreting its substantive content, produces appreciable savings in administrators' time. Legalistic requirements are administratively expensive in two senses. At an individuated level, investigation of homelessness, priority need, and intentionality may consume considerable time and effort, whereas the search for a local connection can be completed in minutes, particularly if officers' vision is bounded by simplistic and incorrect criteria. Legal competence is also expensive on a systemic level, in so far as it commits an organization to significant investment either in high-quality staff and training, or in the design and maintenance of sophisticated quality control mechanisms which ensure that decisions received expert scrutiny before being communicated to applicants. Midland's failure to adopt either course is quite consistent with traditional approaches to the recruitment and training of public housing administrators: council house management is a distinctly 'unprofessional' occupation. Drawing on data collected in a postal survey,[57] Davies and Niner record that barely 7 per cent of local authority housing staff had *any* professional qualification, with only 3.7 per cent being accredited members of the Institute of Housing.[58] The survey charts higher rates of educational and professional qualifications as samples among higher tiers of the organizational structure; professional qualifications were held by 4 per cent of officers with purely 'administrative'[59] duties, 17 per cent of supervisory staff, 33 per cent of policy-making managerial staff, and 47 per cent of non-policy-making managers.[60] It should therefore come as no surprise that Part III decisions made by junior officers may lack even a tenuous grip on legal acceptability. It may surprise administrative lawyers that Davies and Niner's survey accorded so little importance to legal competence that questions about legal training and qualifications were not even asked. When placed in its occupational context, therefore, Midland's behaviour is readily understood.

While Eastern also takes short cuts, its readiness to assume full investigative duties regarding applicants referred in a similarly unlawful manner by other authorities suggests that saving administrative time is not the reason for its *ultra vires* behaviour. While Eastern's errors may seem obvious to public lawyers, they are perhaps less so to housing administrators. Until 1977, a council's control over allocation of its housing was

---

[57] P. Niner and M. Davies, *Housing Work, Housing Workers and Education and Training for the Housing Service* (London, 1987).   [58] Ibid. 64–6.
[59] The concept is unfortunately not defined.

effectively untrammelled by legal rules.[61] With the exception of race relations legislation, the notion that citizens had enforceable legal 'rights' in the allocation of council housing was a concept which had neither a statutory or common law foundation until the 1977 Act appeared. It was therefore almost impossible for allocation practices to overstep legal boundaries, a state of affairs which made legal training unnecessary.[62] The homelessness legislation ostensibly curtailed councils' distributive autonomy by identifying certain individuals whom authorities were obliged to house. However, by couching entitlement in such discretionary criteria as homelessness, priority need, and intentionality, the Act effectively gave much of that control back. In general terms, the Act's contents represented a desperate compromise which obviously could and would be manipulated by antagonistic local authorities. In contrast, the local connection provisions—albeit more by accident than by design—virtually eliminated a council's control over housing allocation by delegating the crucial stages of Part III decision-making to another authority. As such, they entirely contradicted both decades of theory and practice in council house management, and the overall schema of the homelessness legislation itself. Consequently, when one considers that Eastern's disregard of sections 61 and 67 enhances stock control both for itself and for other authorities, one can understand why HPU officers might consider their approach to local connection issues to be 'correct'.

Western therefore appears as an odd man out, in so far as it evidently assumes that conformity to legal norms is an intrinsically desirable feature of the administrative process, irrespective of those norms's potential dysfunctional impact on other organizational goals. Such a hierarchy of authority evidently corresponds quite closely to lawyerly ideals. But while this ordering may seem absolute for administrative lawyers, it is a rather more relativistic concept in Western's administrative reality. Western's implementation of Part III indicates that non-legal objectives such as fostering careerism among junior officers may generate corporate concerns which adherence to legalism can reinforce rather than undermine. Displaying legal competence is a useful vehicle for officers seeking promotion, for example. It may also serve an effective defensive purpose for senior managers concerned that their 'middle of the road housing policy' might one day be questioned by 'right wing Tory' councillors. But even in Western, legalism can be sacrificed unwittingly when individual decisions demand a sophisticated rather than rudimentary degree of legal expertise. And it is on occasion knowingly discarded in pursuit of the

---

[60] Davies and Niner, *Housing Work*, table 6.5.

[61] *Shelley* v. *London County Council* [1949] AC 56; *Bristol District Council* v. *Clark* [1975] 3 All ER 976.

[62] This argument is developed at greater length in Loveland, 'Legal Rights and Political Realities'.

avowedly *ultra vires* consideration of maintaining an approximate parity in the council's relations with its neighbour.

Nor did any of the three authorities' homelessness officers find their internally generated rationality on local connection decision-making significantly compromised by external constraints, whether individuated or systemic. The legally competent and combative applicant was rarely seen in any of the councils, and never in relation to local connection decisions. Neither had councillors, as constitutional propriety might suggest they should, set clear *intra vires* policy guidelines within which the administrative process took place.

The steady accumulation of empirical studies which highlight appreciable gaps between legal formality and bureaucratic reality presents administrative lawyers with a precisely defined dilemma. Should they continue with efforts to force their square legal pegs into round administrative holes, thereby creating for themselves an ever more sophisticated set of formal rules which have ever less applicability to the administrators they purportedly control? Or should they instead recognize that meaningful legal control of administrative discretion demands that they begin to fashion a dialectical relationship between a top-down value system rooted in legal principle and a bottom-up rationality drawn from bureaucratic practice? Jerry Mashaw began his celebrated study of administrative decision-making in the American social security system by suggesting that 'the normative structures created by legislation and by judicial decisionmaking are often, if not usually removed from the concrete experience of bureaucratic implementation'.[63] If such normative structures are to become a relevant consideration at the sharp end of the contemporary government process, it would seem that their builders might sensibly lay their foundations on a rather more empirically stable base.

[63] *Bureaucratic Justice* (New Haven, Conn., 1983), 11.

This chapter draws on material contained in chapter eight of a longer study to be published by OUP in 1994, *Housing Homeless Persons: Administrative Law and the Administrative Process*.

10

The Influence of European Union Law upon United Kingdom Administration

David Williams

The United Kingdom joined the European Communities in 1973, under the internal authority of the European Communities Act 1972, giving effect to the ratification of the relevant Community Treaties by authority of the Royal Prerogative. Since 1973, Community law has formed part of the law of the several parts of the United Kingdom. With the merger of the Communities into one Community, the adoption of the aim of a Single European Market under the Single European Act 1985, the transformation into the European Union,[1] and a signalled advance under the terms of the Treaty of European Union towards eventual economic and monetary union, legal change has oustripped the administrative processes that are designed to handle it.

The aim of this chapter is to explore the effect of our membership of the Union on the administration of governmental functions in this country, the problems that Union law has created for the process of administration, and the solutions that are appearing. The argument that is advanced is that some areas of our administration are now subject to rules, principles, and standards of administrative law, as well as of substantive law, which derive their force and content from Union law rather than United Kingdom law. It is argued that this can be true of any area of administration operating laws of, or based on, the Union legal order. This observation applies as much to procedural laws and principles as it does to substantive law. The discussion notes that this change has confronted government officials with new problems for which they have no precedent and for which they must therefore find new solutions and new procedures. The argument observes that the administrative laws and procedures explored in this book may be modified or even superseded where the laws being administered are part of

---

[1] Known erroneously in the United Kingdom for several years as '1992', this took effect in large measure from 1 Jan. 1993 under Art. 8a of the European Ecomonic Treaty of 1957 (now renumbered as Art. 7a of the retitled European Community Treaty (ECT), since ratification of the Treaty of European Union (TEU). The TEU came into effect on 1 Nov. 1993. It also renamed the EC as the European Union, EU, which title and abbreviation are used in this text.

the Union legal order. It concludes that the process of adjusting to the European Union legal order is itself a dynamic both influencing and impelling reform of United Kingdom administrative law.

The argument as stated above is couched in words that carry such heavy alternative meanings that they may serve to confuse. The reference is to 'United Kingdom law' and the 'Union', whilst the writer and so many others have been conditioned to talking about 'English law' in the context of another union—the customs and legal union of 1707 between England and Scotland. Whilst the analogy may tempt, it is not the purpose of this discussion to make an issue of language. My purpose is to examine areas of law which are truly United Kingdom law because it is there that the pressures of the European Union will, it is suggested, prove greatest.[2]

ADMINISTERING TAX AND SOCIAL SECURITY

The chapter does not attempt to survey the whole of the administration of law in England and Wales in exploring its argument. For the reason just stated, it undertakes a more modest task of exploring two areas of administration of United Kingdom law which are affected by the United Kingdom's Union obligations. The first of these areas is taxation, taken to include the administration of customs duties. The second area is that of administration of social security. United Kingdom tax laws are the same throughout the kingdom,[3] whilst social security laws are separately enacted

---

[2] A recital of the areas of law which are, for one reason or another, national law rather than separate laws of the separate countries of our nation sounds like a list of areas of European Union competence. Those areas where English law most differs from Scottish law—family law, criminal law, land law, court procedures—are the areas that European Union law least affects.

[3] The main direct taxes (income tax, corporation tax, and capital gains tax) are imposed by the Income and Corporation Taxes Act 1988, read with each year's Finance Act. The courts have insisted on imposing English law on Scotland wherever necessary to ensure an even interpretation of tax law. See *IRC* v. *Glasgow Police Athletic Association* [1953] AC 380, where the House of Lords imposed the English law of charities on Scotland for income tax purposes. Their Lordships' reasoning is worth considering in the context of the wider discussion of this chapter. The main indirect tax is the value added tax, for which the United Kingdom authority is the Value Added Tax Act 1983. Whilst differences between England and Scotland have emerged (see e.g. *Lord Advocate* v. *Johnson* [1985] STC 527), they have been eclipsed by the need for both systems to ensure that their interpretations of the law are consistent with the Union obligations. See e.g. the way the House of Lords dealt with the meaning of contractual 'consideration' in *Apple and Pear Development Council* v. *Customs and Excise Commissioners* [1986] STC 192, which went to the European Court of Justice as Case 102/86, reported at [1988] STC 221. Customs duties are now covered by the Community Customs Code, Council Regulation 2913/92 of 12 Oct. 1992 (*OJ* (1992), 1302/1), which is directly applicable and therefore needs no legislation in the United Kingdom. Nor has it been re-enacted, although it grants a right of both administrative appeal and judicial appeal which does not otherwise exist: Art 243 (coming into effect in 1995 in the United Kingdom and in 1994 elsewhere).

for Great Britain and for Northern Ireland, but in almost identical form.[4]

The first of the two areas is the concern of two government departments: HM Customs and Excise (Customs), the oldest of all central government departments, and the Board of Inland Revenue (the Revenue). Both are subject to control not by departmental ministers but by ministers in HM Treasury. Both departments are under the charge of commissioners who are full-time civil servants and who do not answer directly to Parliament, but whose rights and responsibilities are (or, at least, were) regulated entirely by Acts of Parliament. Their authority extends throughout the kingdom.

The other area is the concern of the Department of Social Security (DSS), a separate government department since it was divided from the former conjoint Department of Health and Social Security. It is under the charge of its own Secretary of State. Much of the work of social security formerly performed directly by the DSS is now performed by two separate executive agencies, the Benefits Agency and the Contributions Agency. The powers of the DSS and the agencies are laid down by Act of Parliament. Their power extends to Great Britain, with a separate administrative structure in Northern Ireland. One minor aspect of social security law, unemployment benefit, is within the scope of the Deparment of Employment, working in conjunction with the DSS.

Both areas are therefore administered directly by central government throughout the kingdom. The first level of appeal, to tribunals, is also common to all parts of the kingdom. Two forms of tribunal are involved: the General and Special Commissioners of Income Tax and the value added tax tribunals for taxation, and the tribunals run by the Independent Tribunal Service (particularly. the social security appeal tribunals and disability appeal tribunals) together with the appellate Social Security Commissioners for social security law.

UNION LAW IN THE UNITED KINGDOM

A significant part of substantive United Kingdom law concerning both tax and social security is now either Union law operating directly in the United Kingdom, or the United Kingdom variant of a Union obligation. These obligations derive from four sources of Union law:

- Treaty provisions;
- regulations;

---

[4] The British laws were reconsolidated into the Social Security Contributions and Benefits Act 1992 (1992, ch. 4) and the Social Security Administration Act 1992 (1992, ch. 5). The parallel Northern Ireland measures are 1992, ch. 7 and 1992, ch. 8.

- directives;
- European Court judgments.

Only the terms of regulations are, by virtue of the EC Treaty, directly applicable, that is, take effect automatically as part of the law of Member States without legislative intervention by those states, and notwithstanding national legislation to the contrary.[5] The Court's judgments have a similar effect.[6] The European Court has, in addition, made some provisions of the Treaties and of directives directly effective, that is, has ruled that individual provisions, if their terms are sufficiently clear and precise, and if certain other conditions are met, take effect directly in the law of the Member States notwithstanding that the Member State has failed to comply wih the obligation to provide implementing legislation, and notwithstanding national legislation to the contrary.[7] It follows that government officials are required by Community law to pay attention to all four sources of Community law as productive of obligations operating internally.

In connection with the laws relating to taxation, Union law is of major significance. A primary aim of the European Economic Community Treaty (Treaty of Rome) in 1957 was the creation of a full customs union between the Member States. That union now operates for all twelve Member States. The EC Treaty has removed the competence of all Member States to impose their own customs duties (or any equivalent taxes on imports or exports). It has, instead, created and imposed a common customs regime.[8] Most of the details of the regime, in so far as they are not imposed in the Treaties, are laid down by regulations directly applicable in all Member States without further legislation. Although a few measures have been implemented by directives, the largest part of customs law requires no legislative action by Member States.[9]

Union law is of considerable significance to all forms of indirect taxation, most notably value added tax (VAT). Excise duties are also affected in fundamental ways by Union obligations. In connection with these taxes, the regime established is based on general principles expressed as obligations in the EC Treaty,[10] and finds its detail in various Council

---

[5] EC Treaty, Art. 189.

[6] Art. 5 of the EC Treaty obliges Member States to give effect to European Court judgments.

[7] See S. Weatherill and P. Beaumont, *EC Law* (London, 1993), ch. 11, 'Direct Effect of Community Law', for a recent account of this development.

[8] See ibid., ch. 13, for a full account.

[9] The extent of the invasion of 'our' law by Union law in this area is concealed because of the extent to which United Kingdom law has been left on the statute book. The massive Customs and Excise Management Act 1979 remains firmly in place, although large parts of it are, for customs purposes, a 'dead letter' (the description is that of a senior officer of Customs privately to the writer).   [10] Art. 95–9.

directives.[11] In contrast with the customs regime (with which, in practice, this regime overlaps), most Community rules formally require national legislative action. However, the Court of Justice has ruled that many of the key rules of VAT are directly effective, and therefore prevail over conflicting national rules. In the United Kingdom the value added tax was introduced by primary legislation, the Value Added Tax Act 1983 being the current consolidation. This, and relevant provisions of the annual Finance Acts, may therefore be overridden by Union legal requirements. As chancellors have acknowledged in more than one budget speech, United Kingdom policy with regard to VAT is subject to significant Union constraints.[12]

Direct taxes are less affected by Community rules, by the 'French Package' of the Mergers Directive, the Parent-Subsidiary Directive, and the draft Arbitrtion Convention[13] does have internal effects in ways which conflict with the United Kingdom's corporation tax laws. It also has an effect on our bilateral treaty arrangements with other states both within and without the Union. Here the chief potential influence of the Union legislation is that is may override action taken or which could be taken by the Crown under the prerogative treaty-making powers.

The involvement of Union law in social security matters is of a different nature again. In this case, based on general provisions in the EC Treaty, the main obligation inherited by the Department of Social Security is to ensure that the rules governing the various social security contributions and benefits do not infringe the equal treatment provisions of the Union: both equal treatment of British and other Union citizens, and equal treatment between men and women. In contrast with the effect of Union law on our taxes, here the effect is more akin to that of a binding statement of human rights in a constitution. This has been important because the British system traditionally distinguished in a number of ways between male and female contributors and beneficiaries. In addition, relevant common administrative procedures have been laid down by regulation for dealing with co-ordination of social security systems between the Member States of the EU.

---

[11] For a detailed recent account see A. J. Easson, *Taxation in the European Community* (London, 1993), ch. 3, 4.

[12] Most dramatic is perhaps the restriction on the rates of tax that Member States may levy since the acceptance of the amendments to Art. 12 of the EC Sixth VAT Directive (Directive 77/388) by Directive 92/111 (*OJ* (1992), L384/47). It is under that Directive that the United Kingdom Parliament decision to subject heating fuel to VAT (through the Finance Act 1993) becomes irreversible once it takes effect: see Art. 12 (3) (*b*).

[13] Respectively Directive 90/434, Directive 90/435, and the convention published in draft as 90/436, all of 23 July 1990, *OJ* (1990), L225. For a full account see Easson, *Taxation in the European Community*, ch. 5.

THE PROBLEM OF LEGISLATING UNION PROVISIONS

As this brief survey makes clear, one problem confronting officials of the two government tax departments for the first time because of the Union is that of advising ministers and instructing draftsmen to legislate for what might be termed 'alien' tax laws. Taxation is, traditionally, an intensely national activity in the United Kingdom as in many other states. The assumption is that the taxes to be imposed in any year are those chosen by the government of the day, and endorsed by the House of Commons, without any outside interference.

Because of the tight control over the House of Commons by the executive on tax matters, the assumption of the policy units in the Treasury and the tax departments has been that they instruct the draftsmen on the policies they and their ministers have accepted, and the same team may well both instruct officials generally on how to administer the law, and also provide guidance to the public on how the law effects them. There is a continuity throughout which allows government to implement the law it asks Parliament to approve, subject only to judicial decision.

The task of implementing a Union legislative requirement confronts policy units with a completely different challenge. It may require them to seek legislation for something with which they do not agree. This occurred at the time the United Kingdom entered the Communities, and had to accept as part of the obligations on entry the adoption of VAT to replace purchase tax and selective employment tax. Attempts were made to mitigate the shock to the British system by a series of derogations from EC law, and by a series of approximations of British law to Union obligations, but some of those have come unstuck since.[14] The likelihood of major new initiatives in taxation being passed without British agreement is low, because of the veto built into the Union voting procedures on taxation matters,[15] but on minor points this may not protect the integrity of the British system.

At the technical level, this new source of obligations presents new kinds of practical difficulty. It may be that a Union obligation is designed primarily from, say, the French legal system and does not work well in the British context. It may even be that the British officials do not understand the purpose or scope of Union provisions. One example of difficulties being caused here arose with the recent direct tax Mergers Directive.[16] For

---

[14] Most dramatically in the value added tax tribunal decision in *Merseyside Cablevision* [1987] VATTR 134, where the tribunal chairman stopped just a little short of ruling the entire registration scheme for VAT to be illegal. The scheme was substantially amended in the next Finance Act. There was no appeal from the judgment.

[15] Art. 100*a*, EC Treaty.   [16] See n. 13 above.

the purposes of this directive, a merger is 'an operation whereby one or more companies, on being dissolved without going into liquidation, transfer all their assets'[17] in a number of specific ways. This definition is a direct translation into English of the text of the 1969 Commisison draft in French, and reflects a procedure which was assumed to be normal in France and other Union states, but which was, in the literal sense, impossible under English corporate procedures.[18] This confronted officials with a quandary because, while advice from the Department of Trade and Industry was to the effect that the procedure was impossible in English law, and therefore could not be implemented, simultaneous advice from other sources indicated that procedures were possible, and that a 'Communautaire' approach to the provisions suggested that enabling legislation should be enacted, a sentiment echoed by Commission officials. Advice from elsewhere in government prevailed. It was unofficially accepted that there was a risk that this advice might possibly prove to be out of line with an eventual ruling by the European Court. In practice, such a ruling seems unlikely.

Whilst the circumstances of adoption of the Mergers Directive were exceptional, in that a political decision was taken to implement a directive in the twelve Member States which derived from a draft prepared when six of those states were not members of the EC, it emphasizes the need for national officials to work with the drafts of Union legal texts, and to compare notes both with Commission staff and with their opposite numbers in other national governments if they are to have a full working understanding of the legislation that they will in due course be asked to administer.

A CHALLENGE TO PREROGATIVE POWERS

A separate aspect of the effect of Union provision for our tax laws arises in connection with the treaty provision we use to deal with double taxation. Under the authority of section 788 of the 1988 Income and Corporation Taxes Act, the government may, by Order in Council, incorporate into United Kingdom law double taxation agreements concluded with other states with a view to dealing with clashes between the tax systems of the UK and the other state. An Order in Council has effect, under the section, notwithstanding anything in any enactment, and a double taxation agreement therefore overrides the internal provisions of our tax laws.

---

[17] Directive 90/434, Art. 2, first indent.
[18] For a discussion see D. W. Williams, 'The British Reaction to the French Package', [1991] *Intertax* 208–10.

Union law also has effect notwithstanding anything in any enactment.[19] Does Union law also override the double taxation agreements? There are two issues here. The first is whether the topics covered by a double taxation agreement are within the scope of Union law. If they are not, clearly the issue does not arise. If they are within the scope, then the point arises whether Union law can override the terms of an international obligation agreed by the United Kingdom with another state.

It is not clearly accepted by everyone that the EC Treaty does reach to these agreements.[20] But if it does, it would seem clear that the principles of Union law such as the national treatment rule[21] must be applied to treaties as to internal legislation. Failure by a Member State to observe these principles may leave the provisions open to challenge.

COMPLYING WITH UNION PRINCIPLES AND RULES

A related problem, again unprecedented in British experience, has arisen in the social security field. This is the need to ensure that both legislative proposals and the administration of legislation occur within the guiding principles of Union law. For example, it is not permissible under Union principles to discriminate on grounds of gender in the application of the social security system (save for an express provision protecting the different ages for claiming state retirement pension of men and women).[22] Since the effect of this principle became clear, and was accepted, moves have been made quietly to ensure that the British system complies with Union obligations. There was, however, a significant period during which British legislation failed fully to reflect this principle and consequently officials were required to enforce discriminatory provisions. The most

[19] Under s. 2 of the European Communities Act 1972.

[20] The only express mention in the EC Treaty is in Art. 220, which merely requires Member States to negotiate with a view to concluding such agreements. There is no express Union involvement. For an argument that Union law is involved see the opinion of Advocate-General Darmon in Case C-330/91, *R*. v. *IRC ex p, Commerzbank* [193] STC 605, at 613. The Court, in giving judgment, stepped round this issue.

[21] Art. 6 of the EC Treaty laying down the general principle that Member States must not discriminate between Union citizens on grounds of nationality. This is applied to companies by Art. 58.

[22] Council Directive 79/7 of 19 Dec. 1978 makes provision for the equal treatment of men and women in matters of social security. For a full account, see Weatheril and Beaumont, *EC Law*, ch. 20. The validity of differing periods of payment of contribution, because of different pensionable ages, for men and women in the United Kingdom was disputed before the European Court of Justice in Case C-9/91, *R*. v. *Secretary of State ex p. Equal Opportunities Commission* [1992] 3 All ER 577. The Court found that the express authority to have differing pensionable ages included implicitly also authority to make differing contribution arrangements. The Court did not deal with the fact that part of the contribution of each contributor also pays for benefits which are not age-linked.

significant example was the entitlement (or, rather, lack of entitlement) of a housewife to claim invalid care allowance for looking after an elderly relative because separate rules provided, in a restrictive way, for a housewife's claim, as compared with the entitlements available to other claimants. In due course this was ruled to be a breach of Community principles and the rules were replaced.[23] In the interim, benefit was refused to many claimants who claimed, as a results of a campaign by a lobbying group, on the basis of the illegality of the national rules.

Officials were here placed in the position of enforcing rules which they had good reason to believe were invalid, but which they were required to enforce through what appeared to be a lack of political will to alter the system until the clash could not be avoided. None the less, this clash was different from one to which administrators and their political masters have become used in both the tax and the social security fields. Unlike clashes within the United Kingdom systems, this one could not be dealt with by action from Parliament, except to tidy up the inconsistencies.

The problem of clashing legalities is one which has confronted officials in Customs on a number of occasions in dealing with VAT. It is also a problem that is difficult to handle for those who are conditioned only to the omnipotence of Parliament. VAT is imposed, according to Westminster and its ministers, by virtue of the Value Added Tax Act 1983, as amended. But VAT is imposed, according to Union law, by the Sixth VAT Directive and other relevant Union measures, most of which have direct effect. There were (and still are) a number of points on which the UK VAT is out of line with Union VAT. This places the British civil servant in a quandary which is again unprecedented. If British statute law is followed, then result x arises from a taxable activity. If Union law applies, then result y arises. Should the official apply result x or y?

Intriguingly, both the British rules and the Union rules provide the same answer in the first instance. Result x must be applied. For national reasons, the sovereignty of Parliament supplies the authority, subject to tortuous arguments about the relative effects of the European Communities Act 1972 as it interacts with the Value Added Tax Act 1983. Union law provides the answer x, but it does so because it provides that a national authority is estopped from denying that its national legislation is not in accordance with Union obligations. For officials to use answer y would be for them to admit that their government is in breach of Union law.[24]

If a taxpayer demands answer y in preference to answer x, the legal

---

[23] Case 150/85, *Drake* v. *Chief Adjudication Officer* [1986] 3 All ER 65, where the European Court of Justice held that the relevant legislation (s. 37 of the Social Security Act 1975) was in breach of Directive 79/7 because, *inter alia*, it placed married women living with their husbands at a disadvantage.

[24] See, for a full discussion, Weatherill and Beaumont, *EC Law*, ch. 11.

position changes. The availability of two answers means that the matter is one where, prima facie, there is no clear answer to the relevant legal questions, and therefore the European Court has the ultimate say. But what if, despite their being unable to say so, the officials accept that answer *x* is not valid? In that case, but not before, they will presumably accept the result that the taxpayer demands without contesting its validity. In so doing, they are implicitly accepting the European Union bases of the laws they administer.

Herein lies another problem. Once officials accept the principle that our law is a manifestation of Union law (as, say, Customs officials have done with regard to some parts of VAT law), do they have any legal basis for not accepting the full extent of the Union content—at least, in cases where the law is clear? If, say, they were given political instructions to ignore Union legal requirements that were clear, on the basis that British law to another effect was also clear, whom should they obey? Whatever the politics of the situation, has the minister any legal basis for requiring his officials to ignore clear Union law? If he has no such basis, what is the administrative effect of his requirement, and what consequences follow from this? How far can the procedures of English administrative law, in so far as they relate to errors of law, or to non-enforcement of law for ulterior motives, be used to control such actions?

'IT ISN'T GOING TO GO AWAY'

Each of these problems present ministers and their advisers with a new experience, the irreversible legal decision. Close observers of judicial activity in both tax and social security are well used to seeing judges 'getting it wrong.' A judge who finds against the administration on a point of, say, social security entitlement presents the administration with a decision which the administration may regard as a minor problem. The judge may, or may not, be right in the logic of the judical argument, but judges cannot prevail over the will of Parliament. If the judical answer is inexpedient, it will be reversed by legislation or (in the case of social security) ministerial regulation. Tax cases in the House of Lords were not infrequently in past years based on the interpretation of legal provisions which had been changed to protect the Revenue position before the appeal before the Lords was heard. Sometimes the reversal of the legal position was retrospective; only the one taxpayer who was involved in the litigation might have the previous position preserved.

Such overriding of inconvenient judical reaction is not now always within the competence of ministers. Errors, if that is what they were, cannot now be corrected. This leads to uncertainty, particularly in relation to the financial cost of given provisions. There is therefore no parliamentary escape route from the legal error by the time-honoured method of the Indemnity Act, unless Union law permits it.

THE SIGNIFICANCE OF UNION ADMINISTRATIVE PRINCIPLES

The question of indemnification gives rise to another, under-explored, problem. How far is English administrative law relevant in controlling the administration of Union legal provisions operating on areas of law applied consistently throughout the United Kingdom?

A prior argument suggests that the usual approach to administrative law is now of limited validity in approaching work of government departments such as Customs. The argument can be presented at two levels. The first relates to the specific legal structure within which officials operate. In the case of Customs, the framework law for handling issues of customs duties is no longer the Customs and Excise Management Act 1979—it is the Community Customs Code. The Management Act will still apply to some questions of procedure, such as enforcement of penalties—or will it? It is submitted that this Act must be subject to Union law in the same way as are substantive customs laws. Union laws provides detailed procedures, and statements of rights and obligations, although they are not comprehensive. But, in general, the powers used by customs officers are Union powers. Can we use English administrative procedures, such as judicial review, to control customs officials acting under Union powers?

Here we must present the second level of the argument. Union law must be enforced in a neutral and non-discriminatory way, and subject to any other relevant principles. An attempt to enforce customs laws in a way which contradicts Union law will be invalid. This applies, the argument must run, not only for substantive provisions, and set procedures, but also for the principles on which the administration operates.

For example, how do Engish judges operate the principles of natural justice in this context? The basic argument for the principles of natural justice, outside the contractual context, is that it is the will of Parliament that these principles be observed. Is that relevant to Union law? If officials proceed in a way that the English court finds unexceptionable, but to which the Union court takes exception, how is this fitted into the criteria on which English judges determine natural justice? If, on the contrary, Union law finds as unexceptionable something which the English courts do not like, how is that to be handled?

The argument can also be applied elsewhere. When handling Union laws, the officials ought, the argument must run, to apply Union legal principles. These sometimes reflect French or German legal principles not accepted in English law. For example, the European Court has accepted the principle of proportionality as relevant to the operation of Union law, as with penalties and their enforcement. English law has yet to recognize that principle.

This conundrum has been before the British courts twice recently. In *W. Emmett & Son Ltd.*[25] the appellant company disputed the imposition of a VAT penalty on it, *inter alia*, on the ground that the penalty offended against the principle of proportionality. The chairman heard a full argument on the point. His conclusion, after thorough citation of relevant European Court and United Kingdom decisions, was that 'the doctrine of proportionality is not a part of the law of the United Kingdom.'[26] Having established that, he turned to a second question, namely the effect of Community law on the issue. His conclusion was that 'it seems to us . . . that a taxpayer may attack national legislation if it is legislation which is intended to implement the provisions of a directive which are directly effective . . . and if such national legislation is in breach of basic principles of Community law such as that of proportionality or the citizen's right to the enjoyment of his property'.[27] However, on analysis of the individual provision, the chairman found nothing to offend the relevant principles. Nor did he see reason to refer the matter to the European Court.

The same issue came before Simon Brown J and subsequently the Court of Appeal on appeal from another tribunal decision of Judge Medd in *Customs and Excise Commissioners* v. *P. & O. Steam Navigation Co.*[28] In this case, the taxpayers had wrongly included two invoices in their returns for one month, and as a consequence wrongly excluded them from the following month's return. The error was significant, because it led to a repayment of tax of £335,000 being made a month early. Applying the penalty provisions then operating,[29] the taxpayer was required to pay a penalty of £99,000. This was challenged, *inter alia*, on the basis of the principle of proportionality. Simon Brown J considered the issue in detail. In so doing, he adopted some of the decision in *Emmett*. He concluded:

My inclination . . . is to assume without finally deciding that in circumstances such as arise here the court could indeed strike down national penal legislation simply on

---

[25] (1991) 5 VATTR 456, London VAT Tribunal chaired by the tribunal president, Judge Medd.

[26] Ibid. at 461. For further discussion of proportionality see Ch. 4 above.

[27] Counsel for the Customs and Excise Commissioners did not dispute the relevance of either of these rights in appropriate cases: (1991) 5 VATTR 456, at 462.

[28] [1992] STC 809.

[29] s. 14 of the Finance Act 1988. This imposed a penalty which was in some situations automatic, and which was 30% of the amount of the error. It may be noted that the relevant provision has been twice amended since then to reduce the percentage first to 20 (Finance Act 1991, s. 18), and then to 15 (Finance Act 1992, s. 7).

the ground that it offends the principle of proportionality. That said, however it seems to me that only most exceptionally could the court properly do so. Member states must have the very widest margin of appreciation for determining just what penalties are appropriate to underpin the efficient functioning of the value added tax system operating in their own country.[30]

His conclusion was that the provisions in question did not in any way offend against the principle. Nor could the taxpayer rely on the government's own change of heart[31] to provide evidence of such offending. On reference to the Court of Appeal, the case was found in favour of the taxpayers without reference to the EU law.[32]

THE EXISTENCE OF DUAL STANDARDS

The logic of the above argument leads to an uncomfortable position. Even if courts will be slow to interfere, and even if they prefer to say that Union law is not part of the law of the United Kingdom,[33] at the extreme officials operating Union laws must operate them under Union administrative principles and rules, using Union-provided procedures. In so far as those officials are British officials administering law to those within the jurisdiction of the English administrative courts, the courts should assist the enforcement of Union law.

At the same time, officials operating non-Union rules are subject to the ordinary English administrative principles. Yet it is quite possible that the same officials operating the same laws may at times be acting in a Union-controlled area of legal decision, whilst at other times acting in an area of legal decision subject to review at national level only. Just such problems confront any official concerned with VAT, where to take one specific instance some aspects of the process of registration of a taxpayer for VAT are matters of Union law, whilst others are left to the discretion of national competent authorities. A penalty for the breach of one aspect of the registration procedure would be open to Union review, whilst breaches of other areas would not. The logic of the argument presented is that the official is, say, subject to the principle of proportionality in some of the things he or she does, but not in others.

---

[30] [1992] STC 809, at 821.   [31] See n. 24 above.

[32] Changes in the underlying statutory provisions have since removed the basis of the complaint in the case.

[33] Although it may be doubted he intended this, the logic of the argument of Judge Medd is federalist, in that we are now subject to two orders of law; Union law and United Kingdom law. The latter therefore has gaps in it where the former operates. This is somewhat different from the usual formula that Union law forms part of the United Kingdom law—much as does any other international obligation incorporated into our law.

The reverse argument also requires brief consideration. Should the English courts interfere to impose English principles on the operation of Union legislative provisions? For example, if a customs officer is carrying out the duties required of her or him under Union law, can this be challenged under a procedure available in England and not available as part of Union law? The writer is not aware of a case raising this precise position, though it is possible to suggest that it might happen. For example, judicial review has been used against the tax authorities to ensure fair and consistent administration of taxes.[34] It might be that judicial review could be sought to impose a limit on the powers of the Revenue that could not be imposed on a tax authorities of other states. It could also be that, in the case of a multinational corporation, it therefore found itself treated one way in one state and the opposite way in the other, under the same Union legislation. Is that a matter of concern to the English courts?

CONCLUSION

This brief argument has sought to present some of the unprecedented challenges confronting officials responsible for administering certain areas of national governmental provision as a result of our membership of the European Union. The purpose of the argument is to draw the attention of the reader to the extent to which a full description of the administrative law affecting officials needs to take account of this trend.

The principles and procedures of English administrative law, and of United Kingdom Acts of Parliament setting out powers and duties as well as those presenting substantive provisions, are now of limited relevance to some decisions taken by Crown servants. An account of administrative law which ignores this is incomplete. In the case of the two areas of law used as illustrations in this account, the effect of Union law is now significant. This effect is not only substantive, but it also injects into the administrative process a number of new challenges and also alternative approaches. For example, the rejection of the principle of proportionality from English law is clearly stated.[35] However, we find that it is now accepted that officials, in

---

[34] One recent example is *R.* v. *Inland Revenue Commissioners ex p. Kaye* [1992] STC 581, where the taxpayer challenged the effect on him of the publication of a Statement of Practice on the interpretation of a particular provision. The case discusses the duty to act fairly in the context of tax cases involving avoidance of tax, and in the context of the 'various Charters and Resolutions of Good Behaviour and helpfulness made by the Revenue'.

[35] The arguments against the incorporation of the principle of proportionality, as stated by their Lordships in *R* v. *Secretary of State for the Home Department ex p. Brind* [1991] 2 WLR 588, are rehearsed in the tribunal decision in *Emmett*, n. 25 above. There may, however, be some confusion to the reader in taking the quotations in the tribunal decision as they stand, as they are out of context. The 'European Court' referred to by Lord Ackner is the European

carrying out some of their duties, are bound by the principle, and that, furthermore, it may be deployed to override United Kingdom law. If the principle is of that potency in some parts of the administration of our law, how long may it sensibly remain no part in the handling of other areas of our law? Should the legitimate expectations of United Kingdom citizens or (for it is in the areas commented on here the same thing) Union citizens vary depending on the source of the relevant provision of United Kingdom law on which they seek to rely?

Court of Human Rights, not the European Court of Justice, the Convention being the Convention on Human Rights. This is why it can be argued that the Convention had not been incorporated into the law of the United Kingdom. That, with respect, is a firm basis for the decision in *Brind*, but is not relevant to the decision in *Emmett*. By contrast, the relevant parts of the EC Treaty, including the obligation in Art. 5 to take all appropriate measures resulting from actions taken by Community institutions, have been incorporated into United Kingdom law. That is why, with respect, Judge Medd was wrong in stating that the principle is not part of English law.

11

Tribunal Review of Administrative Decision-Making

Hazel Genn

The use of specialist tribunals to hear appeals against administrative decisions has a long history in this country.[1] Tribunals have historically been viewed as informal, accessible, and efficient substitutes for the ordinary courts, before which aggrieved parties may challenge administrative decisions at little cost and without the need for legal representation. These tribunals are not a *voluntary* alternative to formal court procedures. Tribunals are the primary mechanism provided by Parliament for the resolution of certain grievances against the state, and for some specific disputes between private individuals.[2] The diversion of disputes against a wide range of administrative decisions from the ordinary courts into tribunals has been the result of deliberate choice; and it has been argued[3] that in the early days of the Welfare State this choice was underpinned by philosophical as well as practical considerations. Enthusiasm for tribunals among policy-makers, at least, has led to a substantial growth in their number over the last fifty years. The annual volume of cases disposed of by tribunals currently exceeds a quarter of a million cases, representing some six times the number of contested civil cases disposed of at trial before the High Court and county courts together.[4] As far as the average citizen is concerned, therefore, tribunals are a considerably more important mechanism for the review of administrative decisions than judicial review.

Despite the potential significance of tribunals as scrutinizers of administrative decisions the writers of leading administrative law textbooks appear to have some difficulty in coping with tribunals. They do not seem to fit easily within the framework of standard texts.[5] Discussion of tribunals

---

[1] Although early forms of tribunals were in existence in Tudor times, the origins of the modern tribunal date to the beginning of the 20th century. See below, p. 000.

[2] e.g. matters concerning disputes with government departments about benefits, immigration, release from mental hospitals, etc. can only be heard in tribunals, but in addition employment disputes under the EPCA legislation must be heard in industrial tribunals and disputes concerning child support under the Child Support Act 1991 must be heard in special child support appeal tribunals.

[3] e.g. R. E. Wraith and P. G. Hutchesson, *Administrative Tribunals* (London, 1973); B. Abel-Smith and R. Stevens, *In Search of Justice* (London, 1968).

[4] *Council on Tribunals Annual Report 1992–93*, HC 78 (London, 1993).

[5] An exception is P. Craig, *Administrative Law* (2nd edn. London, 1989).

generally tends to be relegated to a separate chapter which has little theoretical content and which follows a conventional pattern involving, for example: an assertion that tribunals are different from courts; a description of the variety of forms that tribunals take; despair at the hopelessness of attempting any comprehensive categorization or analysis; and a final declaration, on the basis of meagre argument, that tribunals are a 'good thing'.

The purpose of this chapter is to adopt a more critical stance and to challenge some of the traditional claims made for tribunals using material collected in an empirical study of the procedures, decision-making processes, and outcomes in four tribunals.[6] The chapter offers detail about the way that administrative tribunals concerned with welfare benefits and immigration operate in practice, and in so doing considers the limitations of tribunals as an effective check on faulty administrative decision-making. The first sections discuss various justifications for the growth in number and scope of administrative tribunals and their place within the British system of administrative justice. Later sections then present empirical data collected from tribunal case files, observation of tribunal hearings, and interviews with members of tribunals, representatives, and tribunal applicants.

THE GROWTH OF TRIBUNALS

In the UK there are about sixty[7] different types of tribunals and some 2,000 tribunals altogether. The issues covered by tribunals range across such diverse subjects as agriculture and aviation, child support, education, employment, tax matters, transport, and encumbrances over land. Tribunals are supervised on a general basis by the Council on Tribunals,[8] but there is no common procedure followed by these bodies, and no common appeal process or appellate body. Some tribunal decisions are appealable to ministers, and others to courts or other tribunals. Many tribunals are composed of legal and lay members, although some tribunals are comprised of an individual without legal qualifications,[9] and some have

---

[6] H. Genn and Y. Genn, *The Effectiveness of Representation at Tribunals* (London, 1989).

[7] The number of tribunals is growing all the time. Recent new creations are disability appeal tribunals established under the Social Security Administration Act 1992, child support appeal tribunals established under the Child Support Act 1991, parking adjudicators established under the Road Traffic Act 1991.

[8] See the Annual Reports of the Council on Tribunals for descriptions of their activities and for the kinds of recommendations made about procedures and other matters concerning tribunals.

[9] e.g. Traffic Commissioners, General Commissioners of Income Tax.

members with specialist qualifications relevant to the particular jurisdiction. Some tribunals act in a strictly judicial fashion, while others look more broadly at policy considerations. It is, in fact, impossible to provide a simple definition of a tribunal. The label is given to many different kinds of bodies with widely differing functions, and covering a vast range of subject areas including private as well as public law issues. More than twenty years ago the authors of a leading text devoted to tribunals confessed the impossibility of arriving at a satisfactory definition of tribunals: 'it is far from simple to say what a tribunal *is* . . . The very phrase "Administrative Tribunals" which is the title of this book is . . . misleading. In short, the nomenclature of the subject is chaotic.'[10]

One classification of tribunals proposed by Abel-Smith and Stevens suggests that administrative tribunals fall into two broad categories based on function: those that are policy-oriented and those that are court substitutes.[11] Those in the first category represent an extension of ministerial power and may simply comprise an independent administrative agency with responsibility for making regulations, or granting licences.[12] The second category, with which this chapter is concerned, comprises tribunals which are, in effect, court substitutes. They do not have responsibility for making regulations or devising policy, but are required to act as informal courts, reviewing administrative decisions or adjudicating between disputing parties.

Such similarities as there are between court-substitute tribunals tend to reside in the absence of certain features of courts. For example, the absence of complex pre-hearing procedures; the absence of strict rules of evidence; the absence of court robes; the frequent absence of representatives appearing for applicants; and the almost universal absence of legal aid for tribunal hearings.[13] Indeed, it might be argued that the *only* common, unifying aspects of adjudicative institutions that bear the label 'tribunal' concern their superficially distinctive procedures and personnel.

The literature on tribunals reveals a number of plausible explanations for their growth during the twentieth century. The most common accounts of their popularity suggest that a mixture of ideological, practical, and political considerations have been important in their development, but that the exact mix of considerations in any particular case has been variable. No

---

[10] Wraith and Hutchesson, *Administrative Tribunals*, 43.

[11] Abel-Smith and Stevens, *In Search of Justice*.

[12] The Civil Aviation Authority is an example of a policy-oriented tribunal.

[13] Although legal aid is generally not available to fund representation before tribunals, there are some notable exceptions. Legal aid is available for hearings before the Employment Appeal Tribunal (the appellate tier of the industrial tribunals) and the Lands Tribunal. Special schemes also exist for immigration cases, where the UKAS representation service is funded by the Home Office, and in mental health review tribunals representation by panel solicitors is financed through ABWOR (assistance by way of representation).

guiding principle appears to have governed their development. 'The place which any particular tribunal may occupy on the spectrum is determined by various factors, deliberate choice, force of circumstances, accidents of history, parliamentary pressures, and of course, the nature of the issue to be settled. The spectrum itself derives its colours from the interplay of law, policy and administration, rather than from any set of principles.'[14]

Underlying many of the arguments in favour of tribunals are at least two assumptions. First, that court-substitute tribunals are in certain important ways *different* from ordinary courts; and second, that they are somehow *better* for dealing with the matters allocated to them. The bases of these arguments are briefly outlined below. In the following section it will be shown that there is a substantial body of opinion critical of the orthodoxy on administrative tribunals, and an influential school of thought that questions both the principles and practice of such 'informal' forms of justice.

THE JUSTIFICATION FOR THE TRIBUNAL OPTION

Early ideological arguments

The historical roots of modern tribunal go back at least to the beginning of the twentieth century and the genesis of the modern Welfare State with the major social reforms introduced by the Liberal government, such as the Old Age Pensions Act 1908 and the National Insurance Act of 1911.[15] These reforms required the creation of administrative and adjudicative mechanisms on a new and grander scale than had previously existed. A variety of methods were devised to deal with disputes arising from the new entitlements and regulations. The Liberal reformers, in establishing grievance procedures, were at some pains to bypass the ordinary courts and they sought alternative means of settling disputes about benefit.

Some writers suggest that, in the field of industrial relations especially, the decision to bypass the ordinary courts in the early part of the twentieth century stemmed from trade union antagonism towards the courts.[16] This antagonism developed from the perception that judges were unsympathetic to the problems and claims of working people. Abel Smith and Stevens argue that judges were regarded as 'anti-union'. 'While the judges were reluctant to interfere with business associations they had far less compunction about interfering with the activities of trade unions.'[17] As a result, politicians formed the view that courts were not satisfactory forums

---

[14] Wraith and Hutchesson, *Administrative Tribunals*, 249.
[15] Cf. ibid.; Craig, *Administrative Law*.
[16] Wraith and Hutchesson, *Administrative Tribunals*, 36.
[17] Abel-Smith and Stevens, *In Search of Justice*, 111.

for hearing issues 'which raised class interests', and early welfare legislation was deliberately drafted to avoid appeals to the courts. Thus claimants disputing entitlement to National Insurance benefits could appeal to a tribunal which provided a free service to users and in 'front of them legal representation was unnecessary'. The Court of Referees, established to hear disputes concerning unemployment insurance, introduced the 'local tribunal', which was a new concept in British administration. It was a non-legal body which had representatives from the same class as those most likely to be affected by decisions. The mistrust of judges which is thought to have underpinned the shift to tribunals derived not only from a perception of class bias, but also from a sense that their approach to decision-making was too inflexible to deal with disputes that so directly concerned matters of government policy. 'The judging process in many of these areas requires an adaptability which judges are not accustomed to display.'[18]

Constitutional arguments: the law and policy divide

It has also been argued that the subject-matter of tribunal hearings is not appropriate for adjudication in the ordinary courts. This view stems from the distinction drawn between 'policy' questions and 'legal' questions. The former are thought to be the province of the administration and executive, the latter the job of the courts.[19] The distinction involves the constitutional issue of the extent to which the courts are entitled to interfere in the decision-making processes of the executive. The idea that judges might be required to substitute their own decision for that of an administrative decision-maker is contrary to fundamental constitutional principles which require the separation of power between executive and judiciary. Despite the fact that every constitutional lawyer knows that these powers are most imperfectly separated in practice, the endurance of the principle may act as a constraint on the willingness of the judiciary to interfere in what are deemed to be 'policy' matters, thus providing a constitutional justification for diverting appeals against administrative decisions away from the ordinary courts towards specially created tribunals.

The Franks Committee on Administrative Tribunals which carried out a major review of tribunals and reported in 1957 stated that 'tribunals should properly be regarded as machinery provided by Parliament for adjudication rather than as part of the machinery of administration'.[20] None the less, some writers continue to distinguish tribunals on the grounds that the issues brought to tribunals require decisions concerning matters of policy

---

[18] H. Street, *Justice in the Welfare State* (2nd edn. London, 1975), 9.

[19] See Chs. 1 and 3 above for further discussion of these issues.

[20] Franks Committee, *Report of the Committee on Administrative Tribunals and Enquiries*, Cmnd. 218 (London, 1957).

which ought not, or cannot, be decided by judges. This distinction was clearly in the minds of the JUSTICE Committee that carried out a review of administrative law in 1988. The Committee concluded that the role of the court in the administrative law field is essentially 'to supervise the legality of administrative action'. It saw the 'true' role of the courts as being restricted to a review of legality by judges who are unconcerned with the merits of decisions 'in the sense of the[ir] rightness (or wrongness)'. In contrast they visualize tribunals as having a different role which is primarily concerned with the merits of decisions and deciding 'as between citizens and the State, whether an official has dealt correctly with a claim or application.'[21]

Similar distinctions continue to be drawn. For example Cane argues that, while tribunals are primarily concerned with the 'day-to-day administration of government programmes and policies and with the substance of administrative decisions', courts are more concerned with establishing 'the broad legal and constitutional framework within which the business of government is carried on.' Having drawn this distinction he then goes on to suggest that for the activities carried out by the courts 'the more elaborate procedures . . . their specialist legal personnel and their elaborately protected independence from political influence or control, are both necessary and desirable'.[22] It is arguable that these distinctions are somewhat superficially drawn and do not represent realistic descriptions of the work of either tribunals or courts.

Practical arguments

The practical justifications for establishing tribunals tend to rest on two sets of considerations, the first relating to the difficulties of creating new areas of jurisdiction for the ordinary courts (i.e. the volume of cases, the lack of specialization of judges), and the second relating to the supposed positive characteristics of tribunals that render them a preferred option (informality, speed, accessibility, cheapness).

Floodgates and proportionality

Accounts of the advantages of tribunals to the administration of justice tend to focus on two issues. First, that welfare legislation and other social regulation creates the potential for a huge number of disputes that could not be accommodated within the ordinary courts without a vast expansion of personnel and facilities. A second related, and apparently durable, assumption is that the nature of these new areas of dispute would not

---

[21] JUSTICE/All Souls, *Review of Administrative Law in the UK* (London, 1988).
[22] P. Cane, *An Introduction to Administrative Law* (Oxford, 1992), 290.

justify such an expansion of the ordinary courts, and that to attempt to resolve them within the existing court system would result in a dangerous dissipation of judical resources. This argument was propounded in the evidence of the Franks Committee in the 1950s. The Committee quoted the Permanent Secretary to the Lord Chancellor (Sir George Coldstream, KCB):

It is plain . . . that if all the disputes now determined by administrative tribunals had to be transferred to the ordinary courts, such a transfer would necessary involve the creation of a large number of additional Judges, particularly in the County Court . . . many of the disputes in question do not warrant, at least in my judgment, the services of a highly remunerated Judge . . . I believe that it is essential for the administration of justice as a whole that, because the Bench should be of the highest possible quality, any proposals for dilution should be jealously regarded . . . These are some of the reasons why I believe, with others, that the system of administrative tribunals as it has grown up in this country has positively contributed to the preservation of our ordinary judical system.[23]

As the above quotation implies, underlying much of the thinking about the subject-matter of tribunal hearings are assumptions about 'proportionality'. Commentators argue not only that the volume of cases would 'clog up' the administration of justice if they were heard in the ordinary courts,[24] but that the comparatively 'trifling'[25] nature of the claims at issue does not warrant a large investment of resources. A clear statement of the problem in the field of welfare benefits was made by Street in the mid-1970s and has been frequently quoted with approval since: 'What is needed above all else is a cheap and speedy settlement of disputes. For these cases we do not want a Rolls-Royce system of Justice . . . If the average claim to benefit is less than £10 we do not want a judge on a pensionable salary of over £12,000 a year with all the trappings . . . to decide the claim.'[26]

---

[23] Franks Report, para. 39, p. 9. Note that similar arguments were being made in the USA somewhat earlier than this: 'There are certain duties . . . more administrative than judicial, which can properly be performed by an official of lower salary under the direction of a judge . . . Genuine judicial talent is too rare and too valuable to be permitted to wear itself out on details which can as well be done by an assistant' (H. Harley, 'Court Organisation for a Metropolitan District' (1915) 9 *American Political Science Review* 507, quoted in C. Harrington, *Shadow Justice* (Westport, Conn., 1985), 46).

[24] S. A. de Smith and R. Brazier, *Constitutional and Administrative Law* (6th edn. London, 1989), 608: 'Setting up a specialized court, rather than a tribunal, may be to make heavy weather of small issues . . . It would be absurd to make applicants for sickness benefit or supplementary benefits go before a High Court judge; the cost, delay and formality would thwart the objectives of social security schemes and would clog up the general administration of justice.'

[25] P. Birkinshaw, *Grievances, Remedies and the State* (London, 1985), 28: 'For the individuals in dispute with the Department, their claim or grievance is for them often a matter of supreme importance; in the wider context of constitutional decision-making, such tribunals adjudicate on relatively small claims and comparatively trifling issues.'

[26] Street, *Justice in the Welfare State*, 3.

While Street's contention may be true, it is none the less a value judgment which assumes that small claims do not warrant a heavy investment of resources in order to ensure that they are properly and expertly decided. As a society we could decide that claims for benefit *should* be heard by highly trained judges, particularly since there is no logical connection between the amount of money at stake and the complexity of the law governing entitlement to the relevant sum of money. Claims of very low value can be both legally and factually complex.[27] None the less, beneath the contemporary arguments that endorse tribunals lies both the implicit and explicit assumption that disputes concerning, for example, entitlement to welfare benefits and immigration rights constitute relatively trivial matters for which the elaborate paraphernalia of the courts are neither justified nor appropriate. This contention, however, tends to be presented in conjunction with a second: that tribunals have been chosen in preference to courts because of their peculiar 'advantages'.

Procedural advantages

The spreading jurisdiction which has been conferred on tribunals by Parliament might have been conferred on the courts, but the statistics demonstrate that the existing courts would have been totally engulfed by the flood of cases . . . But Parliament's choice of a tribunal in preference to a court has been based on more than a desire to spare the courts from an unsupportable burden. The intention has been that tribunals should be cheap and accessible.[28]

In the early days of the modern tribunal system the intention was that tribunals should provide easy access to specialist adjudicators at no cost to applicants. There was no charge for the initiation of applications to tribunals and no cost for applicants if they lost. The hearings were to be 'informal' and there was an assumption that the informality of proceedings would make it possible for applicants to represent themselves at hearings. Tribunal chairs would take a relatively active role in hearings and adopt flexible procedures. The process was intended to be swift, not bogged down in 'technicality' and not bound by rules of evidence. Since there was perceived to be no need for highly trained judges, the system could be operated relatively inexpensively. Although tribunal chairs would not be of the same calibre as judges, their concentration on specific subject areas would lead to expertise and, presumably, good-quality decision-making. In addition to the presumed advantages of speed and cost it was argued that tribunals could provide a level of expertise that would be unlikely to be

---

[27] The same argument has been made, for example, in relation to personal injury cases; cf. H. Genn, *Hard Bargaining: Out of Court Settlement in Personal Injury Actions* (Oxford, 1987). [28] JUSTICE Report, para. 9.3, p. 212.

available in the ordinary courts. The need for 'specialist' tribunals apparently derives from the complexity of the state regulations which form the subject-matter of many tribunal hearings. At the same time, however, no inconsistency is apparently perceived in expecting claimants to go it alone and argue their cases without representation.

Tribunals were therefore presented as being 'good' for applicants who might often be from among the most disadvantaged groups in society and who, it was assumed, would be overawed and dismayed at the prospect of bringing their case to a court. These attributes of tribunals had evidently been sufficiently well established by 1957 for the Franks Committee to set them out as descriptive characteristics rather than as a set of objectives to be attained by tribunals: '[T]ribunals have certain characteristics which often give them advantages over the courts. These are cheapness, accessibility, freedom from technicality, expedition and expert knowledge of their particular subject.'[29] This description of tribunals has been happily accepted in the literature on tribunals ever since the publication of the Report by the Franks Committee in 1957, despite the fact that the claims have been put to the empirical test on relatively few occasions. Although some of the most up-to-date analyses of tribunals by public lawyers continue to repeat the Franks description,[30] published research on tribunals suggests that in practice tribunals often fail to display the characteristics of which commentators appear so fond.[31]

The arguments then for establishing tribunals to deal with certain categories of dispute rather than giving jurisdiction to the ordinary courts have variously been based on constitutional arguments; allegations of class bias in the courts; practical arguments concerning lack of resources in the courts to handle new and potentially huge case-loads; and finally the positive benefits of tribunals over ordinary courts in terms of their speed, cheapness, informality, and expertise. Most of these justifications for the establishment of tribunals have been criticized either directly by administrative lawyers sceptical of theoretical arguments, or by those who have conducted empirical investigations of tribunals in action.

---

[29] Franks Report, para. 38, p. 9.

[30] For examples see Cane, *Introduction*, 290; de Smith and Brazier, *Constitutional and Administrative Law*, 609.

[31] Cf. e.g. K. Bell, P. Collison, S. Turner, and S. Webber, 'National Insurance Local Tribunals' (1974) 3 *Journal of Social Policy* 289, and (1975) 4 *Journal of Social Policy* 1; R. Lawrence, 'Solicitors and Tribunals' (1980) *Journal of Social Welfare Law* 13; A. Frost and C. Howard, *Representation and Administrative Tribunals* (London, 1977); M. Adler and A. Bradley (eds.), *Justice, Discretion and Poverty: Supplementary Benefit Appeal Tribunals in Britain* (London, 1975); L. Dickens, M. Jones, B. Weekes, and M. Hart, *Dismissed* (Oxford, 1985); J. Peay, *Tribunals on Trial* (Oxford, 1989).

CHALLENGING THE ORTHODOXY

Within the administrative law literature which focuses on the role of
tribunals in administrative justice, there can be found a division between
those commentators who continue to assert the existence of significant
differences between tribunals and courts (e.g. Craig; Cane; JUSTICE),
those who suggest more modest differences (Farmer), and those who think
there is no difference at all (Abel-Smith and Stevens). The criticisms of
tribunals from within administrative law tend not to deal with issues that
require empirical validation, i.e. their cheapness, accessibility or the value
of informality for those who appear before tribunals, but argue on
theoretical grounds and on the basis of the developing body of tribunal
decisions that some of the orthodox claims for tribunals are overstated.

Distinction between law and policy overdone

One criticism of tribunal orthodoxy suggests that the description of
tribunal functions as being concerned with 'policy' matters and courts
being concerned exclusively with 'legal' issues is based on an overstated
and artificial distinction.[32] It is argued that once 'policy' decisions in
individual cases have been reached on the basis of clearly defined rules
(rather than the exercise of discretion[33]) then decisions made 'according to
rule', i.e. according to law, can easily be defined as coming within the
scope of court adjudication. This has been recognized by some commentators and used as a basis for questioning the assertion that tribunals are
dealing with policy issues rather than law. For example: 'With legalization,
policies are transformed into rules that bind the decider. Law is a source of
restraints on authority; this is particularly striking in the case of the
adjudicator, who must not only decide within the *limits* imposed by rules
on his discretion, but is required to justify the outcome of his judgment *by*
authoritative principles.'[34]

The function of many court-substitute administrative tribunals is to
adjudicate on disputes between individuals and the state concerning

---

[32] J. Jowell, 'The Legal Control of Administrative Discretion' (1973) *PL* 178; Abel-Smith
and Stevens, *In Search of Justice*.

[33] The development in social security decision-making provides a perfect example of the
move from discretionary decision-making to decision-making based on complex regulation.
Although decision-making is rarely unconstrained in the welfare benefits field the level of
discretion within the system had, until 1988 at least, been drastically reduced. See Ch. 12
below for a full discussion of administrative decision-making in social security. Cf. also
J. Baldwin, N. Wikeley, and R. Young, *Judging Social Security: The Adjudication of Claims
for Benefit in Britain* (Oxford, 1992).

[34] P. Nonet, *Administrative Justice* (New York, 1969), 246.

entitlements established by rules. In these contexts the job of the tribunal is to decide whether a decision has been made according to rule on the basis of the facts presented before the tribunal. To this extent it is behaving exactly like a court. 'Courts are said to be administering rules of law while tribunals are thought to be administering both law and policy. We would maintain that no such clear line can or should be drawn. Indeed it was the evolution of this myth which helped establish the tribunal system by convincing the judges of the ordinary courts that they were concerned with legal but not with policy questions.'[35]

The analysis of tribunal decision-making and the views of tribunals presented in later sections of this chapter indicate that these clear distinctions are difficult to sustain in practice. The perception of tribunals is that their primary function is to act judicially. Their articulation of the principles that guide decisions concern judicial values of legal accuracy, impartiality, and fairness. This is a view shared by the Judicial Studies Board, which is responsible for the promotion of training within different tribunal systems and geared toward higher standards of adjudication in tribunals. Moreover, the establishment of presidential tribunals systems and the distancing of tribunals from the influence of departments[36] increases the appearance of the independence of tribunal justice, increases the practical independence of tribunals, and gives credibility to the claim that the function of tribunals is primarily 'adjudication' as opposed to 'administration'.

Tribunals just as precedent-bound as courts

One of the claims made for tribunals is that they are more flexible and less technical than courts. However, the notion that a flexible and relaxed approach to tribunal proceedings is carried over to the decision-making process is unrealistic and in any case probably undesirable. Decisions and reasons for decisions are recorded in all tribunals, and in many tribunals, decisions of appellate bodies are binding. SSATs are bound by Commissioners' decisions; immigration adjudicators are bound by the Immigration Appeal Tribunal and are greatly influenced by the substantial number of immigration cases that are heard in the High Court on applications for judicial review. It has been argued[37] that, although tribunals may strive for flexibility in decision making in the early years of their operation, it is almost inevitable that over time principles must emerge and that decision-making becomes constrained in the pursuit of consistency. This inevitability

---

[35] Abel-Smith and Stevens, *In Search of Justice*, 227.
[36] Cf. Ch. 12 below.
[37] Cf. J. A. Farmer, *Tribunals and Government* (London, 1974); Abel-Smith and Stevens, *In Search of Justice*.

stems from basic principles of justice which require consistency, uniformity, and equal treatment. To this extent tribunals are no different from ordinary courts and are bound by similar standards of justice, as Abel-Smith and Stevens point out: 'Properly understood, tribunals are a more modern form of court. In some cases they may have more discretion than the courts . . . conversely the court-substitute tribunals are often as precedent-conscious as, and may even exercise a much narrower discretion than, the ordinary courts.'[38] These doubts about the ability of tribunals to free themselves from the constraints of precedent are clearly supported by the views of tribunals themselves when describing their approach to decision-making. Their views and the impact of the requirement for reasoned, consistent decisions are discussed further below.

The politics of tribunal justice

Other writers have rejected constitutional justifications for the establishment of tribunals and instead suggested that the principal motivation for diverting disputes away from courts and toward tribunals is political. It has been argued that the allocation of certain disputes between citizen and state to informal adjudication procedures is a calculated political action which is intended to deflect attention from oppressive state policies, to protect such policies with a cloak of legitimacy, and to give the impression of the existence of the right to appeal while ensuring that such rights cannot be vindicated. Thus it has been suggested that decisions to establish a right of appeal to tribunals rather than to courts have been based primarily on political and cost considerations, not on the belief that tribunals will provide greater access to justice. This argument has been put most forcefully in this country by Prosser as follows:

The tribunals were not established to make up for defects in the judicial system. The choice was never between appeal to tribunals and appeal to the courts, but between appeal to tribunals and no appeal. Their introduction did not represent an incorporation of the idea of legality into new areas of society for its own sake. The provision of a formal right of appeal . . . was introduced as a counter-measure to political protest and as a means of making oppressive changes in the relief of poverty more palatable by giving a symbolic appearance of legality whilst ensuring that this had no real effect.[39]

The doubts expressed by some British commentators in relation to the political objectives driving the growth of tribunals in the UK during the twentieth century are echoed by modern critics of other kinds of informal

---

[38] Abel-Smith and Stevens, *In Search of Justice*, 228.
[39] T. Prosser, 'Poverty, Ideology and Legality: Supplementary Benefit Appeal Tribunals and their Predecessors' (1977) 4 *British Journal of Law and Society* 39, 44; see also Cane, *Introduction*, 286.

courts. As with tribunals, the most common reasons for establishing informal dispute mechanisms outside the administrative law field have been either that the courts are overburdened, or that the ordinary courts are in some way inappropriate for dealing with certain classes of dispute because their procedures and the cost of bringing cases before them represent an obstacle to free access to justice. Abel, however, has argued that, in the civil justice field at least, the modern trend toward informalism, based on efficiency arguments, represents a 'downgrading' of the problems of the poor and a relegation of their disputes to second-class forms of justice.[40] In his view 'informal' tends to be synonymous with 'inferior'.

Similar arguments have been made more recently in this country in relation to changes in civil justice designed to reallocate cases down the court hierarchy. Sedley has suggested that recent changes to the civil justice system have been driven by the desire to free the courts for international business disputes. 'The inevitable corollary of this process in the present hierarchy of courts and tribunals is that individual claims and rights are marginalised and trivialised. The Lord Chancellor's Department allocates them to courts of often poorer quality, and the appellate courts keep them there by placing jurisprudential blocks on the issues that they throw up.'[41]

The issues that arise from these trenchant attacks on the motives for establishing tribunals are whether tribunals do represent an inferior form of justice within which the ability to vindicate rights and entitlements is a chimera, or whether, in fact, despite some limitations, they provide greater access to administrative justice than could be achieved through the ordinary courts.

The significance of administrative tribunals

Justifications for the historial popularity of tribunals, therefore, have been based on both theoretical and practical considerations. The most likely explanation for the continuing and growing contemporary passion for tribunals is their relatively modest cost to the administration of justice. As government strains to reduce or at least contain public expenditure, efficient alternatives to courts that can adjudicate on disputes without increasing the legal aid bill become more interesting. The attraction of tribunals has always been the fact that they are cheap to run and the theory that cases can be brought relatively easily and without the need for legal representation. The absence of legal representation has several supposed benefits: it increases speed because lawyers are thought to slow down

[40] R. L. Abel, 'The Contradictions of Informal Justice', in R. L. Abel (ed.), *The Politics of Informal Justice* (New York, 1982).
[41] S. Sedley, 'Improving Civil Justice' (1990) *Civil Justice Quarterly* 348.

proceedings; it reduces cost to individuals and especially to the taxpayer, who might otherwise be required to subsidize the service through legal aid; and it prevents creeping 'legalism', which is characterized as the enemy of simplicity. This last supposed benefit is largely tautological since 'simple' procedures are generally only regarded as vital when a prior decision has been taken that representation will not be subsidized.[42]

These considerations have led to a situation in which the primary means for citizens to challenge a wide range of administrative decisions is through tribunals rather than the ordinary courts. The significance of tribunals in terms of the sheer volume of cases dealt with cannot be disputed, although it is astonishing how little academic attention has been directed toward the activities and decision-making in tribunals as compared with judicial review, given the High Court's relatively modest throughput of cases. The significance of tribunal decisions in terms of the impact on future administrative decision-making remains unclear and requires proper investigation.[43] However, the success of tribunals as an effective check on administrative injustice and provider of cheap and efficient justice for tribunal applicants depends on the extent to which, given the state of the law, regulations, and procedure, they can conduct proper reviews of decision-making and reach accurate, consistent, and fair decisions. Some evidence on these issues is provided below.

THE PRACTICE OF TRIBUNAL JUSTICE

Previous empirical studies of tribunals[44] have suggested that, despite procedural informality, there are a number of discrepancies between the theory of how tribunals operate and the practice. For example, research has shown that only a small proportion of those receiving adverse decisions from the government department will actually take the step to process an appeal, despite an automatic right to do so; that despite the supposed accessibility and informality of tribunals the matters to be decided at hearings often involve highly complex rules and case-law; that procedures in some tribunals remain overtly 'adversarial' and often legalistic; and that those who appear unrepresented before tribunals are unable sufficiently to understand the proceedings to participate effectively in the hearing. The cumulative result of these shortcomings is that, in the absence of the conventional 'protections' of formality, such as representation, and strict

---

[42] Cf. R. Lempert and K. Monsma, 'Lawyers and Informal Justice: The Case of a Public Housing Eviction Board' (1988) 51 *Law and Contemporary Problems* 135, for a discussion of this issue.

[43] But for an attempt to explore the issue see Baldwin *et al.*, *Judging Social Security*.

[44] See e.g. the studies cited in n. 31.

rules of evidence, the cases of those appearing before informal tribunals and courts may not be properly ventilated, the law may not be accurately applied, and ultimately justice may not be done. The result may be that citizens with genuine and justified complaints against faulty administrative decision-making cannot obtain redress. Wrong decisions therefore go uncorrected.

The research upon which this chapter is based was designed to look a tribunal processes and to assess the effect of legal and lay representation on the outcome of tribunal hearings. The stimulus for the research came from the continuing debate concerning the extent to which representation increases the likelihood of success at a tribunal hearing and whether legal aid should be extended to tribunals.[45] In the process of making that assessment, the research provided useful insights into the way in which tribunals operate in practice and the difficulties that face unrepresented tribunal applicants. Although the study covered industrial tribunals, mental health review tribunals, social security appeal tribunals, and hearings before immigration adjudicators, the following sections present examples drawn only from material on social security appeals tribunals and hearings before immigration adjudicators.

The Tribunals in the Study

Social security appeals tribunals (SSATs) are the result of the amalgamation of supplementary benefit appeal tribunals and national insurance local tribunals which resulted from the Health and Social Services and Social Security Adjudication Act 1983 and are now governed by the Social Security Administration Act 1992. An SSAT consists of a legally qualified chair appointed by the Lord Chancellor sitting with two lay members appointed by the president of the Independent Tribunal Service. These tribunals have their own system of appeals, which lie to the Social Security Commissioners. There is an automatic right of appeal to an SSAT following an adverse decision by the Department of Social Security about entitlement to benefits. A simple letter requesting an appeal is sufficient to activate the appeal process. Legal aid is not available for applicants to SSATs although both legal and lay representation is permitted before SSATs. In 1992 the number of social security cases decided by SSATs was 75,325.[46]

Immigration adjudictors hear appeals against certain decisions of

---

[45] Demands for the extension of legal aid to tribunals have been made regularly since the Franks Report, which itself recommended that legal aid should be available: the Council on Tribunals Annual Reports; Reports of the Lord Chancellor's Advisory Committee on Legal Aid; the Benson Royal Commission on Legal Services in 1979.

[46] *Council on Tribunals Annual Report 1992–3*, HC 78 (London, 1993).

immigration officers, entry clearance officers, and the Home Secretary taken under the immigration legislation. Adjudicators sit alone, are legally qualified, and are appointed by the Lord Chancellor. Appeals lie to a three-member Immigration Appeal Tribunal. Although legal aid is not available for hearings before immigration adjudicators there is a government-funded specialist representation service (UKAS) which provides no-cost representation to any appellant who requests assistance. The result of this is that the majority of those appearing before adjudicators are represented. In 1992 the number of cases decided by immigration adjudicators was 32,260.[47]

SSATs and immigration hearings are at rather different ends of the procedural informality spectrum. SSATs are among the least court-like of tribunals. Hearings are more informal than other tribunals and chairs are encouraged to adopt an 'enabling' role. Hearings are generally conducted across one or more large tables on the same level with the chair flanked by the two members on one side and the applicant and a presenting officer from the Department of Social Security side by side on the other. Where a representative is present he or she will normally sit between the presenting officer and the claimant. Neither the tribunal chair nor the members wear any special clothing. However, in all the hearings observed, the dress of chairmen and chairwomen tended to be rather formal, as did the clothing of lay members.

Immigration hearings are procedurally more formal than SSAT hearings. Appeals are heard by a lone adjudicator sitting either on a raised platform or at a distance but on the same level as the appellant. Adjudicators tend on the whole to remain formal and aloof, although they take an active part in the proceedings, putting questions to witnesses and asking for clarification. Some adjudicators require witnesses to affirm before giving evidence. The hearings are adversarial to the extent that a Home Office presenting officer is present to put the Home Office case and his or her main function is to cross-examine witnesses. The appellant, or his representative, does not, however, have the same opportunity, since the person responsible for the original refusal is almost never present at the hearing.

Accessibility and the failure to appeal

In order for tribunals to act as a check on administrative decision-making, those who believe that their case has been wrongly decided must take the step of initiating an appeal. In most tribunals, commencement of tribunal proceedings is very simple and cost-free. The initiative must, however, come from the individual whose application has been refused by the

---

[47] *Council on Tribunals Annual Report 1992–3*, HC 78 (London, 1993).

Department. In social security cases, the appeal will be against the decision of a benefit officer. Social security benefit regulations are very complex, and cover a multiplicity of benefits. The regulations are generally recognized as being difficult to use by the relatively low-level administrative officers who are required to make initial decisions on behalf of the Department.[48] When the scheme was first introduced benefit officers had considerable discretion in decisions about entitlement to benefit. However, benefit officers' freedom of choice has been limited by administrative instructions which dictate the way in which discretion should normally be exercised. One of the objectives of the Health and Social Services and Social Security Adjudication Act 1983 was to reduce discretion in the social security system[49] and there have been further recent and significant changes which have reintroduced a large area of discretion which is not subject to appeal (compare Chapter 12 below). However, during the period that the current study was undertaken, the relevant legislation was the 1983 Act.

Adjudication officers' decisions are made on the basis of written information submitted on the appropriate form by claimants. Information will often be followed by AOs requiring further information to assist with the decision-making process. Research by the Department of Health and others has repeatedly indicated a high level of error in the decision-making of adjudication officers.[50] An examination of decision-making by AOs carried out by the Chief Adjudication Officer in 1985/6 discovered that in 101 of 430 appeal submissions examined it was considered that the AO's submission supported an incorrect decision. In seventy-two cases further evidence was received which should have led to the original decision being reviewed and revised. The Report goes on to state: 'The process of review is of course of great value where the making of an appeal produces fresh evidence. But the high revision rate casts doubts on the correctness of the original decisions. My monitors examined 818 cases and found that the original decision in 382 (47%) could not be supported in fact or in law. In 305 cases (37%) the original decision had been based on evidence which was demonstrably inadequate at the time the decision was given. In the remainder, the letter of appeal brought new evidence to light.'[51]

The significance of the poor standard of first-line decision-making for principles of administrative justice becomes clear when one considers the

---

[48] For a good discussion of these issues see Baldwin *et al.*, *Judging Social Security*.

[49] See Ch. 12 below.

[50] See Chief Adjudication Officer, *Annual Report of the Chief Adjudication Officer for 1988/89 on Adjudication Standards* (London, 1990); id., *Annual Report of the Chief Adjudication Officer for 1989/90 on Adjudication Standards* (London, 1991); Baldwin *et al.*, *Judging Social Security*.

[51] Chief Adjudication Officer, *Annual Report of the Chief Adjudication Officer for 1985/86 on Adjudication Standards* (London, 1987), para. 7.9, p. 51.

small proportion of cases in which decisions are challenged. Claimants who are dissatisfied with the decision they receive from the Department about their entitlement to benefit have an automatic right of appeal to a SSAT, and information about the procedure for appeals is given on the form that accompanies the notice of an adverse decision. Despite the large number of adverse decisions dispatched by the DSS and the ease with which an appeal can be initiated, *less than 1 per cent* of claimants receiving nil decisions from the DSS exercise their right of appeal.[52] This prevalent failure to exercise the right to appeal is important in terms of the goals of administrative justice. It demonstrates the very limited overall contribution that tribunals can make as a corrective to inaccurate first-line decision-making.

During the course of our study we attempted to gather some information about this widespread failure to exercise a right of appeal among disappointed benefit claimants. Some clues about why disappointed benefit applicants fail to take advantage of the free right of appeal to a tribunal were obtained from questionnaires that we dispatched as part of our study with a sample of adverse decisions sent out by the Department of Social Security.[53] The questionnaire asked whether, having received the adverse decision from the Department, the claimant would be likely to appeal against the decision. The questionnaire also asked questions about advice obtained prior to submitting the claim and whether any advice had been received, or would be taken, about whether to appeal against the decision. The overwhelming majority of those who return completed questionnaires (85 per cent) stated that they would not appeal to a tribunal. The most frequently cited reason for not intending to appeal was that the claimant did not believe that the decision could be changed. Many of those who returned questionnaires to us assumed that the decision made by the Department must be correct. There were also many expressions of powerlessness to affect departmental decisions. Others said that appealing would be too time consuming, involve too much red tape, or be too distressing.[54]

Examples of reasons for not challenging DSS decisions are as follows.

---

[52] DSS, *Social Security Statistics 1990* (London, 1991).

[53] With the co-operation of the Department of Health, postal questionnaires were included with 1,000 adverse decisions sent out by DSS offices in five regions (London, Leeds, Birmingham, Cardiff, and Surrey). Some 168 questionnaires were returned, representing a response rate of approximately 17%. Since the response was so low (although higher than we had anticipated), the results are presented to illustrate the constraints on appealing and claimants' expressed reasons for not appealing. It is not suggested that this information is conclusive.

[54] A full list of reasons is given in Genn and Genn, *Effectiveness of Representation*.

General confusion

They have made a decision and they leave it at that. I don't understand. It takes too long. They don't explain properly. They use words that nobody understands.

Because they should know how much to give you. That is their job. What is an independent tribunal? I have never heard of this.

I can't win and I haven't a clue where to go.

Powerlessness/conspiracy

Seems pointless. The Government are looking at ways of strangling the poor unemployed people. They've cut the benefits so much. Once you've failed, always failed. I expect the same answer [from a tribunal] as the first time. Why waste time. The DHSS will win every time.

Because they will give the same answer as the DHSS. They seem to work together and get the same result.

They are hell bent on trying not to give any help and the delay between letters is by far too long. They have said No already. What's the use. They think everyone's a State scrounger. You can't beat the system, so I would not bother.

No point. I'm too proud to beg. They will probably say the same as the DHSS, so there is no point in applying. They all work together.

Because they said no once, they will say no again. It is a waste of time and effort.

Stress/trouble

To appeal before a tribunal would be far too stressful in my state of health.

I have given up. I am too depressed to face it.

Being 80 years old and ill I cannot pursue such matters.

I could not face the hassle of a tribunal. I already eat less and only heat one room. Could not bear moving if that was suggested.

Decision must be right

Because I think the DHSS are qualified people and their decision is final.

A decision has been made by authority via the adjudicator who considers I need only £44 per week to live on. I am too old to appeal.

The Government will not allow me any more. The rules are adamant.

Because the law has cut allowances that we used to enjoy. It seems pointless to pursue an argument with a Government that has no regard for pensioners or others. Perhaps they should issue us with cyanide pills.

Satisfied with decision

I am satisfied that the decision is correct.

Because I know Social is right by not giving me maternity allowance.

Because there was nothing wrong with their decision. There is nothing to appeal about.

I think that they have been very fair. There is nothing to appeal against.

After receiving back the completed questionnaires from claimants who had received nil decisions, we carried out tape-recorded follow-up interviews with a small sample of those who had returned questionnaires to us. Evidence from these interviews reinforces the conclusion drawn from questionnaires, that claimants rarely obtain advice when they receive an adverse decision and tend to do nothing more about it. The inaction frequently stems from lack of knowledge and a sense of helplessness. For example.

We really don't know. It's our first time to be in this situation. That's what is so difficult. You just don't know what to do. We don't know how the system works.

I was wondering if there was anybody who could help me. I thought once they made their mind up nothing would change it. I thought when it said there was an independent tribunal that it was just another branch of the DHSS and that they would just stick up for each other. So there was no point. But if there is somebody totally independent, then they won't mind what you say. Do you know who they are?

Although the procedure for initiating appeals is much more straightforward than in ordinary courts, and although there is no cost to the claimant, the number of people requesting appeals represents a tiny fraction of the number of claimants in receipt of adverse decisions.[55] The significance of this pervasive failure to appeal for principles of administrative justice is sharply illustrated by evidence of the number of initial decisions reversed following notice by claimants of an intention to appeal to a tribunal.

Notices of intention to appeal are returned to the local DSS office and, before the tribunal clerk proceeds to arrange for the appeal to be heard by the tribunal, a re-examination of the case will be carried out in order to decide whether the decision which is being appealed ought to be revised. An original determination may be revised if it was based on a mistake as to law; made in ignorance of some material fact; or there has been a relevant change of circumstances since the determination was made.[56] If a new determination is made on review then the appeal 'lapses'. Otherwise, unless the claimant withdraws, the appeal will go before the tribunal. Figures quoted by the DSS indicate that in 1989 31 per cent of income support appeals cleared were disposed of by an adjudication officer revising the original decision.[57] This demonstrates that in up to a third of cases the simple act of requesting an appeal hearing may result in a

[55] For an analysis of similar problems concerning reviews of housing benefit decisions see Roy Sainsbury and Tony Eardley, *Housing Benefit Reviews Final Report* (York, 1991).
[56] See Ch. 12 below.
[57] DSS, *Social Security Statistics 1990*, table H6.01. See Baldwin *et al.*, *Judging Social Security*, for an extended discussion of these issues.

favourable outcome, without the need for a hearing to take place. It also highlights the fallacy of the belief among respondents to our postal questionnaire that there is little hope of original decisions being altered.

The rate at which initial decisions are changed following a request for an appeal provides conclusive evidence of the unreliability of first-line decision-making. A DHSS review of appeals handling carried out in 1987 attempted to analyse the causes of poor-quality initial decision-making and came to the conclusion that as a result of time pressures on staff it was neither possible, nor cost effective, for adjudication officers to treat every case as if it was a potential appeal. It was also apparent that many of the problems on appeals work stemmed from weaknesses in first-tier adjudication, making it necessary to seek information that should have been established when the original decision was under consideration.

Failure by claimants to give comprehensive information at the earliest stages often causes incorrect application of regulations. Interviews that we conducted with social security claimants who had received adverse decisions from the Department provided examples of these problems:

It's so impersonal. There's not even an initial on it, or where it came from. The other thing I find very disturbing is that I think I can say I'm a little bit above the average educationally, but I find it very difficult to fill in their forms and I find the more honest you are with these people the worse off you are.

The problems of inadequate information in social security decision-making are often recognized by presenting officers who are required to put forward the Department's position at appeal hearings. Those we interviewed in the course of our study were often perplexed by the story that emerged at the hearing. They were also occasionally frustrated, being unable to understand why claimants did not give full information to adjudication officers in the first place. For example:

Very often the story that comes out at the hearing is totally different from what was written down . . . The problem is that you don't have all the evidence. That's why our office never dissuades a claimant from appealing . . . Not everyone is good at putting things down on paper. The decisions are not changed because we were wrong, but because there is something that we didn't know. We are not there to save the Government money. We are not judged on our 'savings'. We are just there to see that the money is paid out properly. (SSAT presenting officer)

There is often more information on the appeal letter than we get ourselves. We keep writing to people, but we don't get the information. People don't understand the relevance of the questions. They don't know why we are asking so they don't give the information. The decision we make on the information we have is usually right, but we don't have all the information. (SSAT presenting officer)

The tribunal is drawing out fresh information from the appellant which the DHSS know nothing about and then override the decision. If we had known it could have saved them coming to appeal. (SSAT presenting officer)

It seems then that although the procedure for initiating appeals is much more straightforward than in ordinary courts, and although there is no cost to the claimant, the number of people requesting appeals in SSATs is low in relation to the number of claimants in receipt of adverse decisions. Information from recipients of adverse DSS decisions suggests that failure to exercise the right of appeal results from a belief that it is impossible to get the decision changed, from confusion about the appeal process, or from an unwillingness to undergo the stress of a tribunal hearing. What emerges from the evidence collected about initial decision-making and reviews is that, in some cases at least, the work of SSATs represents an expensive information-gathering exercise that might properly be accomplished at an earlier stage.[58] Cost savings in the investigative activities of DSS adjudication officers lead to unnecessary appeals, as the work of first-line decision-makers is shunted along the decision-making hierarchy to tribunals. In the context of administrative justice the deficiencies of first-line decision-making mean that the appeal process provides an important opportunity for welfare claimants and others affected by adverse decisions from government departments to obtain their entitlement or other request under the relevant regulations. In social security cases, at least, this opportunity is being relinquished by the vast majority of claimants, and in the light of this finding it is clear that justice would be done to the greatest number of claimants by improving the quality of first-line decision-making. However, to the extent that first-tier decisions may contain a relatively high degree of inaccuracy or questionable reasoning, it is for appeal tribunals to make good the shortcomings of the earlier decision-making processes. In order to accomplish this task satisfactorily tribunals must be capable of eliciting the information that is necessary to make an accurate decision; and second, they must correctly apply the relevant regulations to reach an accurate decision. The difficulties in practice of achieving these objectives are examined in the following sections.

Outcome of tribunal hearings

A consideration of the outcome of tribunals' decision-making should be fundamental to an assessment of their value as mechanisms for review of administrative decisions, and a fundamental objective of our research was to analyse success rates in the tribunals studied and to estimate the impact of representation and other factors on the likelihood that applicants would succeed with their tribunal appeals.

In SSATs and immigration hearings large numbers of concluded tribunal case files were studied and relevant data extracted and analysed. Of 1,115 social security appeals cases sampled, 30 per cent had been allowed or

---

[58] Cf. Baldwin *et al.*, *Judging Social Security*.

allowed in part at the hearing of the case, and 70 per cent had been dismissed at the hearing. However, among appeals decided in the absence of the applicant, the dismissal rate was 88 per cent overall. Of the 1,050 immigration cases sampled, 22 per cent had been allowed or allowed in part and 77 per cent had been dismissed. However, among cases which had been decided on the basis of papers and where a full hearing had not been requested, only 2 per cent of cases had been allowed. Of the 728 cases that went to a full hearing before an adjudicator 30 per cent had been allowed.[59]

Outcome figures thus show that on average about one-third of administrative decisions reviewed by tribunals are reversed when there is a full hearing and in SSATs when the applicant attends the hearing. The data also show clearly that those who make appeals and then fail to attend or request a hearing on papers massively reduce the chance that their case will succeed before the tribunal. This is understandable since the absence of the applicant means that new information cannot be provided to the decision-makers and evidence cannot be tested. It is also likely that tribunals will be less likely to undertake a thorough review of the original documentation and the Department's view of the applicant's position in relation to the regulation.

Whether the figures for reversal of decisions are regarded as good or disappointing rather depends on expectations of review mechanisms and beliefs about the quality of initial decision-making. In both SSATs and immigration hearings, cases that are decided by tribunals and adjudicators will have been reviewed internally by the relevant department, albeit cursorily. Thus in each case decided by the tribunal the applicant has had his request or claim denied on two previous occasions by the relevant department. However, given that many initial decisions are based on inadequate information or evidence and that assessments of first-line decision-making suggest that it can be rather weak and inaccurate, one might expect more cases to be allowed following a full hearing and given the opportunity for the tribunal or adjudicator to hear from the applicants themselves, review evidence, and collect further information.

In addition to estimating success and failure rates in the tribunals

---

[59] In SSATs it is possible for an appeal to take place if the applicant is not present at the hearing. In our study some 46% of hearings proceeded on that basis. The low success of such cases has been noted in previous studies and some research has been carried out which provides evidence about why applicants to SSATs frequently fail to attend their hearing. See M. Farrelly, 'The Reasons why Appellants Fail to Attend their Social Security Appeal Hearing' (Ph.D. thesis, Birmingham University, 1989). In immigration cases applicants can ask for their case to be dealt with on the papers by an adjudicator. Among the immigration cases sampled in the study some 29% overall were decided on the papers but there was substantial regional variation and in one area almost one-half of appeals were decided on the basis of the papers alone.

studied, statistical analysis using multiple regression techniques was carried out to assess the effect of various factors relating to the circumstances of the applicant and the circumstances of the hearing on the outcome of cases. In both social security cases and immigration cases the type of case, the type of representation, the geographical location of the hearing, and the identity of the chair or adjudicator had a significant and independent effect on the outcome of cases. Thus in social security cases disqualification from benefit cases were the least likely to succeed and in immigration hearings political asylum cases and deportation cases had the lowest chances of success, holding other factors constant. In both types of tribunals, the presence of a skilled representative significantly and independently increased the likelihood that cases would succeed. In SSATs the presence of a skilled representative could increase the likelihood of succeeding from the average of 30 per cent to about 48 per cent after controlling for other factors. In immigration hearings, the presence of a skilled representative could increase the chance of succeeding from 20 per cent to 38 per cent, holding other factors constant. Another important influence on success was found to be the identity of the adjudicator or tribunal chair. In SSATs the identity of the chair could cause a reduction in the chance of success by as much as 25 per cent. Thus a case that might on average have a 30 per cent chance of winning could be reduced to 5 per cent before certain chairs. Similar effects were found in immigration hearings, where adjudicators had significantly different success rates.

The information collected from tribunal case files thus established that the likelihood of a tribunal deciding in favour of the applicant is significantly increased if the applicant's case is put by a skilled representative. They also showed that, irrespective of the nature of the case, the outcome of cases is affected by whether or not there is a full hearing, who is present at the hearing, who is advocating the case, and who is deciding the case. The following sections attempt to suggest why this should be so by analysing the context within which tribunals take their decisions; the approach that tribunals take to their role; and the problems that face unrepresented applicants.

Procedural informality and complex tribunal decision-making

When the Franks Committee reviewed the operation and functions of administrative tribunals in 1957 they drew attention to the important characteristics which were thought to distinguish tribunals from ordinary courts. These were: cheapness, accessibility, freedom from technicality, expedition, and expert knowledge.[60] In highlighting these characteristics the Franks Report failed to acknowledge the fundamental conflict that

---

[60] Franks Report, 9.

exists between the desire for cheap, quick, informal simple hearings and the requirement of fair, reasoned, and consistent decision-making. There is a profound difficulty, rarely addressed or discussed directly in the literature, in delivering 'simple' justice in the context of complicated statutory provisions that do not lend themselves to negotiated outcomes. Many of the cases that come before tribunals have an 'all or nothing' quality about them. Either a claimant is, according to law, entitled to a benefit or he or she is not. Either a foreign national is, according to law, entitled to remain in the country or he or she is not. There is limited scope for creative or negotiated outcomes. Thus a quick, but not very accurate, tribunal decision may mean that a justified claim to benefit is denied or that an individual is refused entry to the country or forced to leave. In this way a little less accuracy in pursuit of simplicity and speed can render serious injustices which may have a far greater impact on the lives of applicants than many claims in the county court and High Court. The Franks Committee did not articulate how 'freedom from technicality' was to be manifested in practice, and provided no guidance as to whether, and in what circumstances, accuracy and consistency in decision-making could be sacrificed in its achievement. Indeed, the Franks Report provides no guidance on how conflicting objectives are to be resolved in practice and the evidence of our research suggests that, while many tribunals retain a considerable degree of procedural informality as compared with the High Court at least, the *substance* of hearings, in pursuit of legal accuracy, is often highly technical and complex.

Observation of hearings and interviews with participants in tribunals suggests that the overall impact of procedural informality and simplicity in physical surroundings can be overestimated. Irrespective of superficial informality, the decisions of tribunals must be reached on the basis of evidence of the applicant's factual situation within the framework of relevant statutes, regulations, and case-law. The concept of informality does not relieve an applicant from the responsibility of proving his case nor the tribunal from reaching reasoned and consistent decisions. During the course of the study, tribunals, applicants, and representatives who were interviewed tended to feel that bringing cases before tribunals and deciding tribunals cases was a relatively technical business. Some of those interviewed believed that it had always been so, but many tribunal chairs and adjudicators felt that tribunal cases had become more difficult and complex in recent years and felt unhappy about what they saw as growing technicality and 'legalism' in tribunals. What underlies these views is the fact that, done properly, the job of tribunal adjudication is every bit as technical as that of court adjudication. Tribunals are required to scrutinize administrative decisions, and check that they have been made in accordance with regulations and statutory provisions. Most tribunals have an appellate tier whose decisions affect future determinations, and the decisions of all tribunals are subject to judicial review. Tribunals are therefore required to reach accurate decisions by means of demonstrably fair procedures.

When describing their adjudicative functions and their methods of reaching decisions, the process adopted and described by chairs and adjudicators tended to conform to a traditional legal model, i.e. the collection of full information; establishment of relevant facts that can be proved; correct identification and interpretation of legal rules; consideration of relevant case-law; and application of the law to the facts which should, in theory, lead to accurate decisions. Whether or not tribunals, in practice, always follow this model, the technicality of the process presents problems not only for tribunals but also for those who bring their cases before tribunals. The problems for appellants in this respect were summed up by the following quotations from a representative from a tribunal unit and from a chair of an SSAT:

Appellants need a good understanding of the rules if they are going to argue that the rules have been wrongly applied, and they have got to get into the technicalities and the legalistic bits in order to persuade the tribunal to overturn the decision. (Tribunal representation unit)

[Y]ou are dealing with rules and regulations, and a person who is a lawyer or is somebody who deals in that field will be able to know what is required, what evidence is required before the tribunal and will be able to present the facts and the evidence that is essential to his or her case. Consider a person who doesn't know anything about statute law—and we are dealing with statute law. It takes a long time for someone who is not associated with the tribunals or who isn't a lawyer to understand what the regulations mean, what the words mean, and what are the conditions under one regulation or another. (SSAT Chair)

Although the procedure in social security appeals is the most informal of the four tribunals studied, the majority of representatives, and at least two-thirds of the chairs and members interviewed, thought that the regulations were very technical. This was perceived to present problems for appellants, and also for representatives who did not specialize in welfare law. For example:

The process is very complex. I have problems understanding it all, so I don't know how the appellants manage, and I am legally trained. (SSAT chair)

Social security law is very underrated, but it is very finicky and these are people that need help more than any. (SSAT chair)

I don't think that most people understand social security law at all. It is a fiendishly complex area. There is the whole question of precedent. Commissioner's decisions that your average claimant doesn't know exist. They can be totally flummoxed by an argument between the tribunal and say the DHSS presenting officer about the relevance of a particular Commissioner's decision, which in all likelihood they have never heard of, never read, and wouldn't understand if they did read. (Tribunal unit)

Statements about complexity of the regulations were often linked with the issue of advice and representation. Many of the chairs and members interviewed perceived that social security regulations were complex and felt that this posed difficulties for those who appeared before tribunals without advice or representation. Observation of appellants' evident confusion about the significance of regulations to their cases at all, let alone the content of the regulations, supports this view (see below).

Why shouldn't an appellant need representation in a tribunal any more than in a court of law? The machinery and the written material is prepared by the Department and it's the material which we work on. The relevant provisions are all trotted out there, but it may be that they have left something out. We can't be classed as experts by any means. Even a qualified chairman, if he is a part-time chairman, comes here maybe twice a month or only once a month for a few hours and then he goes away for the next four weeks and forgets all about his insurance law. He has other things to occupy his mind. (SSAT chair)

Complaints about the complexity of the law in immigration matters were made forcefully by representatives and adjudicators. There has, indeed, been an enormous growth in reported cases and in applications for judicial review of immigration decisions,[61] and the perception of those interviewed was that the law was often impossible to untangle for adjudicators and representatives, let alone unrepresented appellants. Representatives believed that the relative informality of proceedings at hearings was of no consequence when it came to establishing an entitlement under the immigration rules. They regarded the technicality involved in immigration matters as a direct and inevitable result of the nature of the regulations. The following quotations from representatives vividly express the real-world problems of requiring 'simple' decision-making which is consistent both with complex regulations and with previous decisions. Their views inexorably lead to the problems faced by unrepresented applicants.

It's not lawyers that have made things legalistic, it is the rules and regulations—the law itself that is making it ever more difficult. Appellants on their own are really not viable. They have language and literacy problems. Lawyers cut through the crap. It is after all a legal forum. Tribunals are part of the legal system and necessarily require a legal approach. Tribunals are not 'informal'. Immigration

---

[61] Cf. M. Sunkin, 'What is Happening to Judicial Review?' (1987) 50 *MLR* 433; L. Bridges, M. Sunkin, and G. Meszaros, *Judicial Review in Perspective: An Investigation of Trends in the Use and Operation of the Judicial Review Procedure in England and Wales* (London, 1993); and see Ch. 3 above.

appeals may be relaxed, but the issues are complex and you can't really leave it to appellants to get on with it on their own. They would stand no chance at all. They would answer most questions with 'I don't know'. (Immigration barrister)

A lot of the rules are terribly technical. When one thinks of the issues, the legislation about whether somebody ought to stay here as an overseas student would be fairly simple to draft in a clear and fair way, but they are incredibly complicated. (UKAS)

There is now a complete body of law on immigration and it is not just law at adjudicator and tribunal level. For a variety of reasons immigration law has become one of the largest areas of judical review, and that is partly to do with the inadequacies of the appeal system. So the short answer in my view is that a person without representation is at a complete disadvantage. (Immigration solicitor)

Adjudicators were no less convinced than representatives of the technicality of the law and the difficulties this posed for themselves, for representatives, and for applicants. They were, however, inclined to attribute the increasing technicality of the law to the exertions of lawyers attempting to push at the limits of the regulations in order to succeed on behalf of their clients. For example:

It is all getting very complex now. It is the High Court that is doing it. There is a stack of case-law which a representative has to be familiar with. (Adjudicator)

We have to apply the stated law to the facts, and the stated law includes not just the statute, but of course the case-law, and occasionally, when you have fresh legislation, the adjudicator will have to reach a decision without the benefit of case-law and in those instances it is probable that it will go not just to the Tribunal, but the House of Lords, and even Strasbourg. It is sometimes difficult to reconcile the different decisions of the Tribunal and the superior courts. (Adjudicator)

Those adjudicators who had been sitting for some time suggested that their role had changed over the years and perceived increasing technicality to be a by-product of the removal of discretion. As discretion has been curtailed by regulations, so the decision-making task becomes more difficult— requiring accuracy rather than even-handedness. For example:

It has become rather more formal. I think what was really envisaged was that it would just be a fairly informal hearing before an adjudicator. The Home Office would put their side and the appellant would put his side. I think it was envisaged that there would be far less adherence to normal court procedures at all. It is an unusual procedure anyway. The rules of evidence go out of the window. It is all hearsay evidence. It has become far more legalistic than anyone could ever have expected and that is the truth of the matter. (Adjudicator)

When these appeals were set up, it was all perceived as quick and easy and the appellant could represent themselves. In fact the idea was to have us behave like 'Night Courts'. A bang of the gavel—appeal allowed. But it is nothing like that. It is far more complex and technical. (Adjudicator)

It used to be possible to treat hearings as informal, with little law. Just a question of fact. Now you must appreciate that the Rules involve consideration of issues that are anything but simple. They involve considerations of intention. A large body of law has been formulated on what the Rules mean, but you get lawyers twisting words round and it has become a lovely fruitful source of litigation . . . There has been a proliferation of case reports. Six thousand unpublished tribunal decisions which equal precedents. (Adjudicator)

Immigration adjudicators regard hearings as relatively formal and adversarial, although they feel that they have a right and a duty to take an active part in the proceedings if they believe that they require more information or clarification in order to make their decision. Some adjudicators think that hearings have actually become more adversarial with the reduction in discretion and growing complexity of the law.

[This region] is more adversarial than [elsewhere]. The problem is that the presenting officers here are a pretty tough lot. They are people who will leave no stone unturned. Whereas elsewhere there is more readiness to accept things on each side. They call less evidence and elsewhere many cases go off. The presenting officers here are very thorough. We keep the hearings reasonably informal, but consistent with maintaining a proper atmosphere for giving evidence. (Adjudicator)

Adjudicators perceive that they have the freedom to be flexible about procedure. Although hearings follow a set pattern, this can be interfered with if the adjudicator thinks that it would be appropriate. Rules of evidence are relaxed, and witnesses are allowed to give hearsay evidence, although adjudicators were frequently observed to remark that hearsay evidence carried little weight. Despite the relaxation of procedural rules in comparison with ordinary courts, adjudicators do not, on the whole, regard immigration hearings as informal proceedings. Indeed, they perceive that a relatively high degree of formality is desirable and appropriate:

I think it would be dangerous if we were less formal. I think a certain amount of formality helps to fix the issues and to establish that you are dealing with a set of laws which have to be applied and not just a social security case conference where you've got to make your mind up what is good for the appellant and what isn't. (Adjudicator)

I try and put people at ease if I can, but I think that one can take that too far. You don't want everyone sitting round the table having a cup of tea. It wants to be formal at some stage and I achieve the formality that's necessary by getting them to affirm that they are going to tell the truth. Quite honestly I don't think that it makes a lot of difference as to whether someone tells the truth or not, but this is as much to punctuate the proceedings and it emphasizes that what they are going to say is going to be taken down and form part of the record. (Adjudicator)

These hearings to me always appear exactly like any other civil proceedings. But they are not fully civil. They have got this criminal element in them in spite of the balance of probabilities. There must be a criminal element if the result is to deport you. (Adjudicator)

Adjudicators characterize their function as scrutinizing decisions, and checking that they have been made in accordance with the law. This is not a particularly straightforward procedure, however, since the question of whether a decision is the correct decision in the circumstances often depends on the view taken of the 'intention' of the appellant in making his or her request under the immigration rules. Establishing the true intention behind a request is further complicated by the fact that the appellant may not be in the country and cannot, therefore, be questioned directly:

I think the purpose of immigration hearings is to make certain that decisions are right and in accordance with the law and immigration laws; and the other is to make certain that it seems that the right decision has been taken. The two really go together. (Adjudicator)

The Franks concept of freedom from technicality sits somewhat uneasily with these accounts of the realities of modern tribunal decision-making processes. Freedom from technicality may simply be a quality of unchecked discretionary decision-making which implies the freedom to make inconsistent decisions. Where scope for the exercise of discretion on the part of tribunals has been largely removed, and where the demands of justice require consistency in decision-making, it is arguable that the concept of informality and freedom from technicality are limited to such matters as the atmosphere of proceedings and tribunal documentation. What tends to be pejoratively termed as creeping 'legalism' in tribunals may not, after all, be an unwanted side-effect of the involvement of representatives in tribunal hearings, but, rather, at the very core of the tribunal process. Almost all of the legal and lay representatives interviewed during our study felt strongly that the traditional view of tribunals as 'informal' forums in which appellants and applicants could bring cases without assistance was either no longer true, or had never been true. Their opinions were based largely on perceptions of the complexity of the law, but also on beliefs about the power balance between parties. For example:

I think the truth and reality is that the notion with which tribunals were set up, about being an accessible forum of justice for the ordinary person, has now been overtaken by history and they are adjudicating such complex and legalized areas that it is actually hopeless to think that people are going to get a fair deal, or *feel* that they are getting a fair deal, or feel easy with the deal they get, if they go on their own. (LAG representative)

I don't think that you can have informal tribunals. They are courts. They are perceived as courts by everybody else, apart from some lawyers who distinguish between the court system and the administrative tribunal system. It isn't informal. How could it ever be like that? You have got to make decisions based on a set of rules. Then you are going to have the interpretation of the rules. Then the rules are always going to be subject to getting it wrong in law and judicial review. How can you have an informal tribunal system? (SSAT solicitor)

The conflict between the view that tribunals should be informal and free from technicality, and the requirement for accurate and consistent decisions, poses problems for those who adjudicate tribunal cases and who are attempting to reach their decisions in accordance with complicated regulations, statutes, and case-law. Tribunals feel, or are led to feel, that they should be able to do without representation in this process, but many regard the need for representation as an inevitable consequence of legal complexity. From the point of view of tribunal applicants, informal procedural arrangements do not impinge on the technicality of establishing and proving a case in law, and the veneer of informality presents a trap for those who attempt to proceed with their cases without advice or representation. Although the appearance of procedures in tribunals may be relatively informal, the true content of the proceedings is always 'formal' in the sense that the relevance, meaning, and weight to be given to information provided by applicants is, in theory at least, determined by the law. The decisions of tribunals are taken on the basis of what has been heard or presented in relation to the relevant law and it is through this crucial linkage that procedure influences decision-making. Those who bring cases before tribunals without the assistance of advice or representation are disadvantaged because they may not know what information is relevant to their case, nor which items of evidence might constitute sufficient proof to establish their case. Although unrepresented applicants may welcome the opportunity to tell their story in their own way in tribunal hearings, there is clear evidence that the freedom to 'speak for oneself' is less valuable than it may appear. O'Barr and Conley suggest that without the assistance of representation and without being constrained by formal rules of evidence 'unassisted lay witnesses seldom impart to their narratives the deductive hypothesis-testing structure with which judges are most familiar and often fail to assess responsibility for events in question in the way that the law requires.' The result is that litigants experience satisfaction with the process, but ultimately lose their case.[62] Lempert and Monsma describe this situation as the 'trap of hidden legalism'. In a study of housing eviction tribunals in Hawaii they clearly, and persuasively, identify the limits of procedural informality and the way in which tribunal applicants can be deceived by the appearance of informality. They distinguish between 'procedural' and 'substantive' informality and argue that, if an applicant's 'participation' in tribunal hearings is procedurally

[62] William O'Barr and John M. McConley, 'Litigant Satisfaction versus Legal Adequacy in Small Claims Court Narratives' (1985) 19 *Law and Society Review* 661.

and substantively informal while the tribunal's stance is procedurally informal and substantively legalistic, the applicant will believe that his or her case is being heard in an informal tribunal, but there is in fact a situation of hidden legalism. Lempert and Monsma contrast this situation with the example of settlement conferences in which informality can provide an efficient method of testing who has the better legal case.[63] The interviews conducted with tribunal applicants in our study demonstrate vividly how hidden legalism can trap applicants into appearing at hearings unprepared and failing to provide the tribunal with information and arguments that might establish their entitlement to their claim according to law.

The applicant's perspective

Information from interviews with applicants at hearings showed that the majority had never been involved in an appeal to a tribunal before, and that many had little idea about what appealing meant, little knowledge about the powers of tribunals, vague and unrealistic expectations of the hearing, and little idea of what the possible outcome of their hearing could be. When those appealing to SSATs and immigration adjudicators were asked how they knew that they could have the decision of the Department looked at again, most replied that they had learned about this from the letter sent to them by the relevant department advising them that their original application had been refused. Many did not know what would happen next. Although applicants received a number of documents from tribunal offices in connection with their hearing, the recipients of these documents often found them confusing, and failed to obtain advice about what would happen at the appeal. Unrepresented applicants are not informed in advance about their role in the hearings and what they will have to do in order to persuade a tribunal or adjudicator to allow their case. This basic lack of knowledge constitutes an important and fundamental weakness in the ability of unrepresented tribunal applicants to succeed with cases that may have merit.

In common with most legal claims, a crucial element in success at tribunals is the preparation of the case in terms of collection of information, evidence, and argument on the law. Tribunal applicants may be forgiven for being unable to argue on the law, but they are also impeded by their inability to collect relevant information because they often do not understand that cases must be decided according to regulations and that it is the regulations that determine what is and is not relevant to their case. This common failing is well understood by tribunal representatives, and, indeed, by many tribunal chairs:

---

[63] Lempert and Monsma, 'Lawyers and Informal Justice', 393.

By saying that it is an informal tribunal, it makes it sound as if you can go there and talk your way into something, and that isn't true at all, because the law is not negotiable. The law is what *is* behind and what *should be* behind tribunal decisions and I think probably a lot of unrepresented appellants come up against that. They think, 'Well I've got the gift of the gab. I can go in there and persuade them.' But the rules are the rules and they are stuck with them. (Advice agency)

What lay people don't know or understand are the regulations which actually govern what is going on. If they did read them they would never begin to be able to understand them . . . so they are thrown back effectively on the chairman of the tribunal's goodwill. (Solicitor)

When [applicants] are not represented, either they give a lot of evidence which is quite irrelevant or they don't produce the most relevant evidence to us. (Immigration adjudicator)

Preparation is crucial if a claimant with a potentially winnable case is to be in the best position to succeed with that case. Those without representation are disadvantaged in this respect because they cannot, without advice, know what they must prove, nor what items of evidence might constitute sufficient proof to overturn a departmental decision. The most significant barrier to effective case preparation among unrepresented claimants was felt to be lack of understanding that, in order to succeed with an appeal, claimants must bring themselves within the regulations, and that assertions of fact may require proof. There are also dangers for unrepresented claimants who do attempt to obtain evidence in support of their appeal. They are unable, in the way that a representative might be, to vet the evidence. Representatives stated that, even where the type of evidence needed was clear, it was often difficult to obtain. This was just as true of social security cases as immigration cases. For example:

If it's a medical matter it's very hard, quite often, to get doctors to supply the information you need and in some cases I might have to send someone back twice to his doctor to say: 'Look, I am sorry. The wording on this just doesn't help the case. You've got to ask them again.' You have to explain to them why it is important, why the case will succeed or fail on this particular point. We have got to explain to them the importance of it and make sure that they work on it and get it. (Welfare rights centre)

The need for the right kind of evidence to be obtained and for the evidence to be vetted by representatives was clearly illustrated in one case in which a woman was appealing to a social security appeal tribunal against the refusal of a payment to replace clothing as a result of rapid weight gain. She had asked her doctor to write a letter in support of her appeal. The doctor evidently agreed, and then wrote directly to the tribunal in the following terms:

To whom it may concern
Re: [name of patient]

This patient has requested a note from me to enable her to claim allowance for her clothes. If she ate less sweet food, then she would save money and have no need to buy larger clothes.

Yours faithfully,
[doctor's signature]

The letter undoubtedly contributed to the failure of the claimant's appeal, although she did not know what it contained.

Observation of hearings revealed that, in addition to the difficulties of collecting relevant evidence, appellants often fail to tell a linear story and also have difficulty in remaining objective about their case. If they become upset or angry they are likely to lose the sympathy of the tribunal. Thus, despite the fact that the surroundings are informal, and despite the fact that many chairs are at some pains to put unrepresented appellants at ease, they are frequently at a disadvantage. Representation can avoid these problems by selecting information about the applicant's case that is likely to be most useful to the tribunal and by presenting the arguments without emotion:

I think that they are legalistic hearings on the whole and the claimant, even if they were themselves an advice worker, would benefit from representation, because it is much easier to put somebody else's case than it is to put your own. It is often very difficult for unrepresented appellants to put their case clearly, objectively, and straightforwardly to the tribunal. (CAB)

Applicants were often dismayed at the binding nature of regulations and did not understand why the regulations appeared to be so rigid. Some SSAT applicants had clearly been misled by information from the tribunal stressing 'independence' from the DSS. They interpreted the notion of independence as a tribunal which had complete freedom to make any decision it liked on the basis of the information provided by the claimant, and that it was capable of looking at the case in a different manner from the Department—with 'humanity and sympathy'.

They should bring a bit of humanity or common sense into the thing. All I have heard up until now is section this and subsection that, which are very rigid.

They don't look at you as a person. They have got the rule-book there and they have got to go by the book.

Unless those appealing to tribunals have an appreciation of what is likely to occur, they are at a huge disadvantage. Those who come to hearings without the benefit of advice or representation frequently feel that all they have to do is tell the truth, explain the difficulties of their position, and all will be well. For example:

Knowing that there will be a hearing made me happier, because I can speak to somebody who is prepared to listen. Somebody who is independent, because the Immigration people never gave us a chance to convince them. (Immigration appellant)

In practice, many applicants, both represented and unrepresented, find tribunal hearings intimidating and the procedures formal and difficult to understand. Despite the fact that applicants may have a strong belief in the merits of their case, the atmosphere of hearings and the questioning by tribunals, adjudicators, and presenting officers tend to inhibit applicants. Many of those applicants whom we interviewed after their hearing felt that they had not known how they should have put their case and had not been adequately prepared for what was required of them at the hearing. For example:

I thought I could handle it myself, but I couldn't. Once you're in there you are nervous and you realize you could have been better prepared. It's all so unfamiliar and authoritarian . . . It was very degrading, all your dirty washing is hung out, so to speak. (SSAT appellant)

I needed somebody who knew what they were talking about . . . it would have been different if someone had come who knew how to talk right, with authority . . . it's just degrading.

Even with the benefit of representation, applicants leave the tribunal feeling quite shocked. For example:

If someone had told me what it was going to be like I would have just gone home. No hassle, no questions asked. (immigration appellant)

Applicants also found the language of the tribunal formal and difficult to follow, despite the efforts of tribunal chairs to enable applicants to put their case. Even applicants whose first language is English may encounter serious problems with vocabulary. Members of tribunals who are legally trained and those who are experienced tribunal members are familiar with the vocabulary of the law and technical language. This familiarity is not shared by the average tribunal applicant, who may find the language threatening and may misunderstand the thrust of questions:

I was only answering questions . . . A representative would have been able to say more. He could have spoken up a bit more. There's too much jargon. I was lost by all the legal talk.

I didn't know what to say about the case. I didn't understand the situation. It's very complicated. I didn't have a clue about what was happening. No one explained who was who and what role they played. I didn't understand what was being said.

Although far fewer applicants at immigration hearings appear unrepresented, a substantial minority attended without representation because they did not believe a representative was necessary. This was occasionally the result of failing to realize that they were attending a hearing and thinking, instead, that they were simply going to an interview. For example:

I just got this letter saying that I had to be at [this place] at 10.00 and my case would be heard. I don't know what is going to happen. (Immigration appellant)

It is a common characteristic of most tribunals that those appearing before them do so without representation. Indeed, the design of procedures is supposedly tailored to the needs of unrepresented applicants. None the less, the evidence of our study suggests that unrepresented applicants may be disadvantaged in tribunal hearings because there is an imbalance of power between the parties, because applicants do not understand the law, are often unable to present their cases coherently, and are unaware of the need to furnish the tribunal with evidence of the facts they are asserting. Although it is the job of tribunals to 'compensate' for these disadvantages, representatives, and many tribunals themselves, do not believe that this is possible. These beliefs were largely supported by our observations of tribunal hearings and our statistical analysis of tribunal outcome.

CONCLUSION

there is nothing inherent in the nature of the judicial process that is necessarily complex; nor in the alternative to it that is necessarily simple . . . It is incumbent on all of us who are in a position to control or influence the operation of our judicial system to do what we can to keep the law simple. Historically, conscientious draftsmen of substantive and procedural law have understandably been too often inclined to subordinate clarity to precision . . . The result can be a tangle of statutory provisions that are unintelligible to most of the people affected by them . . . I believe that we should continue to be open to any opportunity to provide informal procedures which lay people can operate themselves without legal assistance.[64]

This chapter has attempted to show that there are considerable limits to the effectiveness of tribunals as a check on administrative decision-making and that these limitations stem at least in part from the design of tribunals and the low levels of representation at tribunals. In order for tribunals to act as an *effective* means of review they must be capable of conducting an accurate and fair review of administrative decisions. This requires time, expertise, and full information. It also requires that those who appear before tribunals are capable of understanding the relevance of regulations and the basis of their entitlement, and can provide relevant information

[64] The Lord Chancellor the Rt. Hon. the Lord Mackay of Clashfern, 'The Administration of Justice: Alternative Dispute Resolution', *Hamlyn Lectures* (London, 1993).

and evidence of facts, largely without the benefit of advice or representation.

Given the weakness of first-line administrative decision-making, tribunals theoretically represent an important means of minimizing administrative injustice. However, evidence collected from recipients of adverse administrative decisions, although not conclusive, suggests that even when a relatively straightforward mechanism exists for review of decisions the opportunity is not taken because those affected may assume that the original decision was 'correct' or that it is unlikely to be changed. Thus, even if tribunal hearings provided perfect conditions for effective review of administrative decisions, they could only ever afford a partial corrective to poor decision-making and administrative injustice. In practice, however, from the perspective of tribunal applicants, the conditions that operate in many tribunals are far from perfect. Despite their conventional characterization as informal, accessible, and non-technical, frequently tribunals are not particularly quick, there is considerable variation in the degrees of informality, and the issues dealt with are highly complex in terms of both the regulations to be applied and the factual situations of applicants. This study of tribunal processes and decision-making has highlighted the complexity of many areas of law with which tribunals must deal and the impact of this complexity on decision-making. Although tribunal procedures are generally more flexible and straightforward than court hearings, the nature of tribunal adjudication means that those who appear before tribunals without representation are often at a disadvantage. The short-comings of tribunals as effective checks on administrative decisions are the result of misdescription of procedures as informal and misconceptions about simple decision-making and the scope for unrepresented applicants to prepare, present, and advocate convincing cases.

The analysis of factors influencing the outcome of tribunal hearings suggests that increased advice and representation for applicants, and improved training and monitoring of tribunals, would be likely to increase the rate at which cases reviewed at tribunal hearings were allowed. This may not, of course, be the desired objective. It has been argued[65] that tribunals were never intended to act as 'effective review mechanisms' and that their primary role is to provide a cloak of legitimacy for unpopular social regulation. If, however, there is a genuine intention that tribunals should provide a check on administrative decision-making, rather than merely providing a forum in which disappointed and disgruntled applicants can let off steam, their deficiencies must be addressed. It is not sufficient to assume or to assert that tribunals operate well. In order to achieve their theoretical objectives and to attain the qualities claimed for tribunals,

---

[65] Prosser, 'Poverty, Ideology and Legality'.

consideration must be given to their procedures and to standards of tribunal adjudication. Finally, and most importantly, explicit attention must be paid to the means by which a balance can be struck between the conflicting demands of procedural simplicity and legal precision, in order to achieve substantive justice.

Sections of this chapter have appeared in H. Genn and Y. Genn *Representation at Tribunals*, Lord Chancellor's Department, London 1989.

12

Internal Reviews and the Weakening of Social Security Claimants' Rights of Appeal

Roy Sainsbury

INTRODUCTION

The development of judicial review is widely recognized as one of the most significant features of modern public law. Yet judicial review is irrelevant to most citizens who wish to challenge the decisions of public bodies. Their grievances are mostly considered in the lower reaches of the judicial hierarchy by a tribunal, or through an administrative review. The literature on tribunals is substantial, reflecting their growth as the mechanism most favoured by governments for providing a means of redress against the decisions of public officials. By contrast, the literature on the structures and practices of internal administrative reviews is extremely small[1] even though far more people will go through such a review than will have their case considered by a tribunal.

In this chapter I will examine the development and growth of internal reviews in an area of public policy which affects all citizens at some stage in their lives—social security. The example of social security is particularly useful since among its thirty or so benefits there are a range of review arrangements which illustrate recent important developments in their use.

I will begin the chapter with a discussion of the defining characteristics of what I will call the *ideal types* of internal reviews and appeals. These will be used to show how internal reviews have, for some social security benefits, moved from being a element of routine administration to constituting the first tier of an appeals structure. Recognizing that internal reviews have

I would like to thank Hazel Genn and Nick Wikeley for their helpful comments on an earlier draft of this chapter.

[1] Notable contributions to the literature on internal reviews within the social security system include R. Coleman, *Supplementary Benefits and the Administrative Review of Administrative Action*, Child Poverty Action Group pamphlet (London, 1970); J. Baldwin, N. Wikeley, and R. Young, *Judging Social Security: The Adjudication of Claims for Benefit in Britain* (Oxford, 1992); G. Dalley and R. Berthoud, *Challenging Discretion* (London, 1992); and T. Eardley and R. Sainsbury, 'Managing Appeals: The Control of Housing Benefit Internal Reviews by Local Authority Officers' (1993) *Journal of Social Policy* 461.

come to occupy the place previously held by tribunals in appeals structures, I wish to argue that, in evaluating their new role, they should be subject to criteria traditionally applied to tribunals. While acknowledging that there is potential for disagreement about the most appropriate measures to be used for evaluation, I will propose that the criteria of speed of decision-making, independence and impartiality, participation by aggrieved citizens, costs, and quality of decision-making are among the most important.

The use of internal reviews as a first-tier appeal is an important shift, the extent of which will be shown in the following section contrasting the mainstream adjudication system (which operates for benefits such as income support, retirement pensions, child benefit, and family credit) with departures from it in the last ten tears or so (for housing benefit, the social fund, disability benefits, and child support).

By comparing these departures from the mainstream with the evaluative criteria, I will reach the conclusion that social security claimants' appeal rights have been weakened by the growth of internal reviews as the first tier of appeal. When reviews become a means of redress they cease to be part of the machinery of administration and become part of the machinery of adjudication. They should therefore be subject to similar criteria to higher forms of adjudication such as tribunals and courts. When a comparison is made using such criteria internal reviews emerge as inferior to tribunals.

APPEALS AND REVIEWS WITHIN THE SOCIAL SECURITY
ADJUDICATION SYSTEM

Social security adjudication

Social security decision-making is often described in terms of its 'adjudication system' established by the Health and Social Services and Social Security Adjudications Act 1983 (HASSASSA). It comprises three independent statutory authorities. At the first tier, most decisions are made by adjudication officers although some (mainly relating to the medical aspects of industrial disablement benefit and severe disablement allowance) are reserved for adjudicating medical practitioners.[2]

At the second tier of adjudication, appeals against the decisions of adjudication officers and medical practitioners are heard by one of the range of social security tribunals (described later in this chapter). The

---

[2] There is also a small class of decisions defined as 'Secretary of State decisions' which fall outside the adjudication system. These are comprehensively described in M. Partington, *Secretary of State's Powers of Adjudication in Social Security Law* (Bristol, 1991).

HASSASSA Act also established an independent 'presidential' organization, called the Independent Tribunal Service since 1991, to administer the appeals system.[3]

At the third tier, the Social Security Commissioners decide cases (on a point of law only) on appeal from either of the tribunals. Beyond this formal adjudication system lies the right of appeal to the ordinary courts.

Appeals and reviews

Appeals and reviews are both mechanisms by which decisions of social security officials can be looked at again and altered if appropriate. Though the position is less clear now, until the early 1980s reviews were primarily an element of routine administration and appeals reserved for claimants wishing to challenge the outcome of their claims.

The rationale for providing administrative reviews was to allow officials a simple and quick means of changing decisions without claimants needing to make a fresh claim or lodge a request for a formal appeal. For most social security benefits a review could only be made when one of the following conditions was met.[4] First, there must have been ignorance of, or a mistake as to, a material fact; or secondly, there must have been a relevant change of circumstances; or thirdly, there must have been a mistake of law. The review provisions can be thought of as being primarily for officials to be able to correct errors and to deal with changes in circumstances. Claimants also have the right to request a review, although they rarely do so. Much more common in practice is the request for an appeal.

A claimant has a right to lodge an appeal against any decision of an adjudication officer of the DSS. (As will be explained later this right is not enjoyed by claimants of housing benefit or disability benefits or by social fund applicants.) An appeal allows a *de novo* consideration of the case by an independent tribunal rather than a review on the restricted grounds described above, although a tribunal may also change decisions on these

---

[3] The presidential organization established by HASSASSA was similar to those already in operation for other tribunals such as industrial tribunals, immigration tribunals, and VAT tribunals. The president is a senior judge appointed by the Lord Chancellor. As well as being responsible for the management to SSATs and MATs, the president also has responsibility for the selection and training of tribunal chairs and members. The rationale behind the presidential system is to remove any direct and obvious link between social security tribunals and the Department, and to concentrate experience and expertise relevant to both types of tribunal.

[4] Social Security (Administration) Act 1992, s. 25 (1) (replacing Social Security Act 1975, s. 104 (1)). For family credit and disability working allowance 'changes in circumstances' are not included as one of the conditions for a review (Social Security (Administration) Act, s. 25 and s. 30 respectively) because an award of these benefits is made for a period of six months during which the award will be fixed.

grounds. If the review arrangements can be thought of as being primarily for administrative use, then the right of appeal is intended as the main mechanism for redressing the grievances of claimants against decisions of the DSS.

. .This does not, however, tell the whole story of what happens when a social security claimant wishes to appeal against a decision of an adjudication officer. Whenever an appeal against the decision of an adjudication officer is made, the case is lodged with the Independent Tribunal Service but at the same time is also scrutinized by an adjudication officer to identify whether there is justification for a review of the original decision (see Chapter 11 above). If the letter of appeal points to a previous error or contains new information which constitutes a change in the claimant's circumstances, adjudication officers will use their powers to review the claim. If the officer can review a decision fully in the claimant's favour then the appeal lapses. If not, an SSAT hearing will be arranged.

There is no clear definition of the difference between reviews and appeals provided in any social security legislation. What we can identify instead is a number of characterstics that are associated with each which allows the construction of two 'ideal types'.[5] The defining characteristics of the ideal type of the 'review' are (1) that it is an internal mechanism carried out by officials of the relevant administrative organization, and (2) that it can be carried out only on limited grounds defined in legislation. The contrasting characteristics of an 'appeal' are (1) that it is a right of claimants to instigate appeal proceedings, (2) that the grounds for appeal are not restricted, and (3) that the appeal is heard by a body independent of the department responsible for making the initial decision.

The adjudication arrangements for the majority of benefits conform closely to these ideal types, whilst the arrangements for housing benefit, the social fund, most disability benefits, and child support depart from them to varying degrees.

The structure of social security appeals established in 1984 was the result of a ten-year evolution which took place in the context of the increasing legalization of social security provisions that commenced in the mid-1970s. It might have been thought at the time that a mould had been set in which future appeal arrangements would naturally be cast. As the subsequent discussions of housing benefit, disability benefits, the social fund, and child support will show, this has not been the case.

---

[5] 'Ideal types' are abstract yet coherent formulations that contain an internal logic to their structural features. They do not purport to describe reality but to provide models which can be used to analyse and understand observable patterns of behaviour.

DEPARTURES FROM THE MAINSTREAM

Housing benefit and council tax benefit

The housing benefit scheme was introduced in 1982 and brought together for the first time in a national framework the numerous arrangements adopted by local authorities to help people with low incomes pay their rent and domestic rate costs.[6] Though described as a 'unified' benefit, housing benefit comprised three distinct elements—rent rebates for council tenants, rent allowances for private tenants, and rate rebates for domestic ratepayers.[7] Since 1982 community charge benefit has replaced the rate rebate element of housing benefit only to be replaced itself by council tax benefit in 1993. The current position is that council tax benefit is separate from housing benefit, which comprises rent rebates and allowances only. Importantly, both benefits are administered by local authorities and not the Department of Social Security.

Despite the changes to housing benefit, the arrangements for hearing appeals have remained largely the same. Claimants wishing to challenge local authorities' decisions on benefit assessments have recourse to a review system. The system has two distinct tiers; an internal administrative review by local authority officers[8] and a further review by either a 'housing benefit review board' or 'council tax review board', both of which comprise local authority councillors.[9] There is no equivalent of the Social Security Commissioners for housing or council tax benefit but decisions of review boards may be challenged by judicial review on a point of law in the High Court or the Court of Session in Scotland. Furthermore there is no separate administrative organization for review boards comparable to the Independent Tribunal Service. Each local authority makes its own arrangements for the appointment and training of review board members and can adopt, within the parameters laid down in regulations, its own procedures for hearings.

The differences between housing and council tax benefits and the mainstream social security adjudication system become more pronounced when we consider that they form part of a national social security system and share many of their eligibility provisions with income support and family credit.

It is worth noting at this point that the decision-making arrangements for

---

[6] Social Security and Housing Benefits Act 1982.

[7] Community charge rebates replaced rate rebates in 1989 in Scotland and in 1990 in England and Wales.

[8] Housing Benefit (General) Regulations 1987, reg. 79 (2).

[9] Ibid., Schedule 7.

housing benefit were the first to introduce the internal review as the first tier of appeal. Much of the explanation for this and the other distinct features of the housing benefit decision-making structure lies in the political context within which housing benefit was introduced. In the passage through Parliament of the Social Security and Housing Benefits Bill the question of appeal rights for aggrieved claimants was raised only late in the committee stage.[10] The debate revolved around the competing arguments of pressure groups such as the Child Poverty Action Group and Shelter, who favoured an independent tribunal, and those representing local authority interests, who argued for appeals to remain an internal responsibility as they had been for rent and rate rebates. The compromise eventually reached favoured local authority interests by combining the existing review powers of local authorities with the traditional tribunal model to form the two-tier structure described above, and by keeping the review arrangements entirely within local authorities. The only concession to the lobby for an independent tribunal was that review boards would have a legal status independent of the authority.[11]

Social fund

The social fund replaced the single payments provisions of the former supplementary benefit scheme in April 1988.[12] The statutory entitlement to payments for items such as furniture, cookers, and refrigerators was largely replaced with a discretionary scheme of loans and grants which would be administered not by statutorily independent adjudication officers but by social fund officers acting within the directions and guidance of the Secretary of State.

Applicants dissatisfied with the decision of a social fund officer can obtain a review of the decision if they apply in writing, giving the grounds for their request. The social fund officer who made the original decision will either grant the application in full or invite the claimant for an interview, at which the decision will be explained. If the social fund officer is still not prepared to change the decision, the case is passed to a senior member of the local office management who will again review the original decision.

Claimants who are still dissatisfied may then request a further review by a social fund inspector. The inspectors have three possible courses of action. They can substitute their own decision, uphold the original

---

[10] For an excellent account of the parliamentary origins of the housing benefit review system, see M. Partington and H. Bolderson, *Housing Benefit Review Procedures: A Preliminary Analysis* (Uxbridge, 1984).

[11] See DHSS, *Reform of Social Security*, vol. ii, Cmnd. 9518 (London, 1985), at para. 3.71.

[12] Social Security Act 1986, ss. 32–5.

decision, or refer the decision back to the social fund officer. There is no right of appeal to the Social Security Commissioner though inspectors' decisions are subject to judicial review. The quality of decision-making by social fund inspectors is monitored by the Social Fund Commissioner, who has a statutory responsibility to report annually to the Secretary of State. Reminiscent of the genesis of housing benefit review boards, the provision of a right of appeal to a social fund inspector was only introduced following the considerable opposition that the original proposals provoked.[13]

These arrangements are as much a departure from the mainstream social security appeals system as the housing benefit review system, but in a very different direction. Rather than interposing the internal review between the initial decision and consideration by a tribunal, the social fund arrangements replace an adjudication system with a hierarchy of reviews. The first review is not only a paper review but includes the offer of an interview to applicants whose decision has not been changed by the social fund officer. But at no stage in the structure is there the opportunity of a hearing before a body comparable to a social security appeal tribunal.

The rationale for using a review system in place of tribunals is set out in the 1985 Green Paper on the reform of social security. The mainstream appeals structure for other social security benefits was rejected on the grounds that it would be inappropriate for reviewing the exercise of judgment by social fund officers. In addition, it was argued that the existing tribunal system could not operate quickly and effectively in making decisions which required a knowledge of local circumstances. The first argument, that a tribunal is not an appropriate forum for reconsidering discretionary decisions, is particularly weak given the historical record of social security tribunals hearing appeals against discretionary decisions (such as extra needs payments under the pre-1980 supplementary benefit scheme). It was, in Fulbrook's words, 'speedily demolished'[14] by the Council on Tribunals in its unprecedented special report on the social fund:[15] 'It is perfectly feasible to have independent appeals against discretionary decisions as shown by the systems which operated before 1980 and by other appeal systems. In some ways it is even more important with discretionary decisions.'[16] If we accept the arguments of the Council on Tribunals, the only remaining valid justification for social fund reviews is their relative speed.

---

[13] Particularly vehement was the Council on Tribunals, who took the unusual step of publishing a special report on the subject: see Council on Tribunals, *Social Security: Abolition of Independent Appeals under the Proposed Social Fund*, Special Report, Cmnd. 9722 (London, 1986). See also Social Security Advisory Committee, *The Draft Social Fund Manual: Report by the Social Security Advisory Committee* (London, 1987).

[14] J. Fulbrook, 'HASSASSA and Judge Byrt: Five Years on', (1989) *Industrial LJ* 177.

[15] Council on Tribunals, *Social Security: Abolition of Independent Appeals under the Proposed Social Fund*, above n. 13.   [16] Ibid., para. 8.

Disability benefits

The structure of disability benefits was subject to major changes in 1992 with the introduction of two new benefits. For people under 65 years of age, disability living allowance replaced two non-contributory, non-means-tested benefits, mobility allowance and attendance allowance. For people over 65 an amended form of attendance allowance has been retained. Disability working allowance is an entirely new benefit, modelled on family credit, designed to help disabled people establish themselves in the labour market by topping up low or part-time earnings.

Initial decisions on the new benefits are taken by adjudication officers. However, at the second tier of adjudication, disability decision-making departs from the mainstream model of an appeal to a tribunal by introducing 'a right to a formal review'.[17] The review is carried out by a different adjudication officer taking into account any new evidence submitted by the claimant.

Claimants who are still dissatisfied at the result of the internal review can appeal to a new tribunal, the disability appeal tribunal (DAT), comprising a legally qualified chair, a medical practitioner, and another person with experience of the needs of disabled people.[18] The Independent Tribunal Service is responsible for the running of the tribunals. As with most other benefits, there is a further right of appeal on a point of law to the Social Security Commissioner and the new tribunal is placed under the jurisdiction of the Council on Tribunals.

The appeal system for the new disability benefits is far closer to the mainstream model than either housing benefit or the social fund. Its one important point of departure is the introduction of the mandatory internal review stage before an appeal to a tribunal may be lodged.

In contrast to the rationale presented for the introduction of social fund reviews, the justification for the arrangements for the new disability benefits appears limited to their relative speed. In the DSS paper on the adjudication arrangements for the new disability benefits, the government proposed 'to introduce a streamlined review system as a second tier of adjudication'.[19] The only difference between this 'streamlined' system and the mainstream adjudication system was to make the internal review a formal stage which claimants must complete prior to a tribunal hearing. It was justified in the following way. 'The advantage of adding this formal review stage is that decisions will be looked at, and changed if they are wrong, very much more quickly than would be possible if the claimant

[17] DSS, *The Way Ahead: Benefits for Disabled People*, Cm. 917 (London, 1990).
[18] Social Security Act 1975, s. 100A (1), inserted by the Disability Living Allowance and Disability Working Allowance Act 1991.
[19] DSS, *Note on Disability Working Allowance* (London, 1990), at para. 6.3.

appealed against the first decision straight to a Social Security Appeal Tribunal.'[20] Behind the rhetoric of 'streamlining', the argument that the new arrangement would be quicker is disingenuous. The mainstream adjudication model, with direct access to a tribunal, still allows DSS adjudication officers to review and change decisions if they are wrong (see Chapter 11 above). The new structure does not in itself guarantee quicker decisions but requires the dissatisfied claimant to appeal twice before receiving an independent hearing.

Child support

The most effective means of providing financial maintenance for children in lone parent families has long presented governments with problems.[21] The arrangements that existed in the late 1980s were a result of incremental policy change over many years. Where a divorce has taken place, the award of maintenance has operated through a High Court and county courts, the magistrates' courts, the Court of Session, and the Sheriff Courts in Scotland, and through the offices of the DSS. This wide diversity of decision-making bodies has resulted in inconsistency in the levels of maintenance awarded.[22] Furthermore, the numbers of lone parents had, by the beginning of the 1990s, risen to over one million,[23] two-thirds of whom were dependent on income support.[24] In 1989 fewer than a quarter who were receiving income support also received child maintenance. The central problem, as the government saw it, was to increase the flow of money from absent parents by ensuring that they honour their obligations to pay maintenance. The government's proposals for achieving this were set out in a White Paper, *Children Come First*, and enacted in the Child Support Act 1991. The most radical change was to transfer the responsibility for deciding maintenance awards from the courts to a new quasi-autonomous government agency, the Child Support Agency. Initial decisions on maintenance, therefore, cease to be a judicial function and instead become administrative. The new arrangements came fully into force in April 1993.

Though maintenance is clearly not a social security benefit, the close link between the two has already been shown. Many absent parents (usually the father) who are responsible for paying maintenance also receive benefits, and many lone parents receive income support. However, because maintenance is treated as income in the calculation of an income support

[20] Ibid., para. 6.4.
[21] See e.g. the Finer Committee, *Report of the Committee on One-Parent Families*, Cmnd. 5629 (London, 1974), and J. Bradshaw and J. Millar, *Lone Parent Families in the UK* (London, 1991).
[22] DSS, *Children Come First*, vol. i, Cm. 1264 (London, 1990), 2.
[23] Bradshaw and Millar, *Lone Parent Families*, 1.
[24] DSS, *Children Come First*, 3.

award, the effect of receiving maintenance has no impact on a lone parent's total income since the benefit is reduced pound for pound as maintenance increases. There has, therefore, been little incentive in the past for lone parents to press for payment of maintenance. Many absent parents have thus become defaulters and the social security system has effectively been picking up the maintenance bill.

The strong links between maintenance and social security are emphasized by the government's consideration at one stage in preparing the Child Support Bill of placing appeals against the decisions of Child Support Agency officials with the existing SSATs (though this was not eventually adopted). However, the debate about the proper location of appeals ranged further than a consideration of SSATs. Reflecting the history of maintenance provisions, there was considerable support for giving aggrieved parties the right of appeal directly to the courts. However, the eventual outcome, which closely parallels the arrangements for the new disability benefits, was the establishment of another new tribunal, the child support appeal tribunal (CSAT), preceded by an internal administrative review by agency officials.[25] Further appeals are decided by the newly constituted Child Support Commissioner. The Independent Tribunal Service is responsible for the running of the tribunals. Both the new tribunal and Commissioner are placed under the jurisdiction of the Council on Tribunals.

The appeal system for child support is analogous to that for the new disability benefits. Its one important point of departure from the mainstream model is the introduction of the mandatory internal review stage before an appeal to a tribunal may be lodged.

In the White Paper introducing the new child support arrangements the section on appeals begins thus: 'There must, of course, be a right of appeal if one of the parties to the assessment believes the decisions to be mistaken. The Government proposes that, in the first instance, the [Child Support] Agency should be required to review its decision and check that the decision has been made accurately.'[26] It is interesting that, in contrast to the social fund and disability benefits, there is no case at all made for reviews in this statement.

COMPARING REVIEWS AND TRIBUNALS

Having reviewed the spread of internal reviews into adjudication structures, I wish to consider how we might compare their claims with those of tribunals to be appropriate first-tier appeals mechanisms.

---

[25] Interestingly, in what appears to be a sop to the family law lobby, the Child Support Act gives the Lord Chancellor the power at any future date of transferring appeals back to the courts.   [26] DSS, *Children Come First*, above n. 22, para. 3.40.

The Franks Committee considered that tribunals had distinct advantages over courts, summarized in the familiar litany of 'cheapness, accessibility, freedom from technicality, expedition and expert knowledge of their particular subject'[27] initially identified twenty-five years earlier by Donoughmore.[28] However, to be acceptable as alternatives to courts, tribunals had also to incorporate some of the principles associated with court proceedings—openness, fairness, and impartiality.

In this section I wish to present a similar analysis of the relative advantages and disadvantages of internal reviews and administrative tribunals as the first tier of an appeals structure. Franks debated whether tribunals are a part of the machinery of administration or part of the machinery for adjudication and firmly concluded that they were the latter.[29] Internal reviews can fall into either category but when they are intended as a means of redress rather than a means of correcting errors or amending benefit awards, they move from the machinery of administration to the machinery of adjudication. There is an argument, therefore, that the standards used to assess their acceptability change accordingly and values such as independence and impartiality become highly salient.

Some of the criteria that I will be using are drawn from Franks, others are drawn from the literature on administrative and procedural justice (which cover similar areas of inquiry).[30] Part of this literature has consciously incorporated the views of participants to appeal hearings and court proceedings. The consumer view is an important perspective but must be treated with caution. Numerous studies of tribunals and courts show that appellants' views are affected by the outcome of their appeal, that they are often not well enough informed to make an objective assessment of their experiences, and that their assessments are often based on low expectations of public bodies.[31] This is certainly not to argue that the views of any group of appellants should be treated lightly or dismissed. While studies have repeatedly shown that unsuccessful appellants are more critical of tribunals, this may not only reflect a reaction against the decision but may also indicate that unsuccessful appellants are more inclined to reflect upon their experience and identify where they were dissatisfied. In

[27] Franks Committee, *Report of the Committee on Administrative Tribunals and Enquiries*, Cmnd. 218 (London, 1957), para. 38.
[28] Donoughmore Committee, *Report of the Committee on Minister's Powers*, Cmd. 4060 (London, 1932). [29] Franks Report, para. 40.
[30] e.g. W. Robson, *Justice and Administrative Law* (London, 1928); P. Nonet, *Administrative Justice* (New York, 1969); J. Thibaut and L. Walker, *Procedural Justice* (Hillsdale, NJ, 1975); J. Mashaw, *Bureaucratic Justice* (New Haven, Conn., 1983); R. Sainsbury, 'Deciding Social Security Claims' (Ph.D. thesis, 1988); E. Lind and T. Tyler, *The Social Psychology of Procedural Justice* (New York, 1988).
[31] e.g. Lind and Tyler, *The Social Psychology of Procedural Justice*; R. Sainsbury, *Survey and Report into the Working of the Medical Appeal Tribunals* (London, 1992); Baldwin *et al.*, *Juding Social Security*.

contrast, successful appellants may be inclined to be more charitable and overlook any shortcomings of their tribunal. Grievances are clearly felt more acutely when the long road to the tribunal or court ends in failure.

I will discuss the relative merits of reviews and tribunals under the headings of speed of decision-making, independence and impartiality, participation, costs, and the quality of decisions.

Speed of decision-making

It is virtually axiomatic that claimants want a quick resolution of their appeals and on this criterion alone reviews have inherent advantages over tribunals. In undertaking a review it is not necessary to prepare comprehensive documents for the parties, nor to organize a date for a hearing that suits tribunal members, appellants, and representatives. Similarly, there is no need to give appellants the statutory ten days' notice that applies, for example, to SSAT and housing benefit review board hearings, nor is time taken up by documents being absorbed by the postal system.

However, the differential between the clearance times of reviews and tribunals does not only depend on these administrative advantages. All appeals are potentially subject to delays outside the control of administrative agencies which have no relation to the appeals system in operation. In a recent study of medical appeal tribunals,[32] it was found that requests by appellants and representatives for postponements of hearings (for reasons such as the unavailabilty of representatives or to have more time to gather additional evidence), and waiting for reports from third parties (usually hospitals, general practitioners, or employers), contributed, on average, an additional three months in deciding the appeal.

An indirect cause of delay, though not an inherent feature of either reviews or tribunal appeals, is a surge in benefit claims which leads to an increase in the number of appeals lodged. In recent years it has been common for imminent changes in social security to generate a temporary rise in claims to take advantage of provisions soon to be lost. For example, in 1980, discretionary extra needs payments payable under the supplementary benefits scheme were replaced by single payments, and in 1987–8 single payments were in turn replaced by the loan-based social fund. On both occasions there was a rise in claims before the changes were implemented. Many claims were unsuccessful and appeals were subsequently lodged. The tribunal system was unable to respond quickly to these increases in demand and backlogs built up. Arguably it would have been easier for a system based on internal review by officials to respond since

---

[32] Sainsbury, *Survey and Report into the Working of the Medical Appeal Tribunals.*

staff could have been moved temporarily from other duties until the backlog was cleared.

Clearance times are undoubtedly influenced by the amount of resources provided by governments to run appeals systems. In theory, as soon as a tribunal has gathered all the relevant information needed for a particular case, a hearing can be arranged. If sufficient resources were allocated to cover the costs of a hearing and to accommodate the tribunal, then it could proceed without delay. In practice, each case will go on a waiting list until resources are available.

There is little doubt that internal reviews are inherently quicker than tribunal hearings. What is also clear however is that crude comparisons between clearance times are misleading because they do not take into account the resources devoted to each, nor the costs that have to be borne to achieve greater expedition (for example, in the reduced opportunities for participation or the loss of some degree of independence).

Independence and impartiality

The question of independence is essentially one about principle. The case for the independence of appeals structures lies in the natural justice tenet *nemo judex in sua causa*, that is, no one should be a judge in their own cause. As a guiding principle it is very powerful, but as a prescription for the design of appeals structures it raises a number of difficulties. Before I discuss some of its implications I want to make a distinction between independence and impartiality since the two are often confused and conflated.

Impartiality implies the absence of bias and prejudice in decision-making. It is not an attribute that can be guaranteed by the structure of an appeals system but must be practised by decision-makers whether they are judges, tribunal members, or officials. In his seminal work on administrative justice, Robson builds up a picture of the impartiality of judges in the following passages:

the judge shall as far as possible deal with the materials before him by categories, treating equally all the separate items within each category. Every purchaser who has been fraudulently deceived as to the goods which he has bought must be treated alike; there must be no discrimination between them on grounds of religion, or personal attractiveness, or wealth, or nationality, or excellence at golf.[33]

What is meant by the impartiality of judges, so far as social matters are concerned, is that they shall not permit their opinions on certain controversial subjects of the day to influence their judgment. The judicial mind is not be deflected by the passions of the moment on social, economic, political or religious questions.[34]

---

[33] Robson, *Justice and Administrative Law*, 264.   [34] Ibid. 309.

The link, and the distinction, beween impartiality and independence is also made by Robson in the same work. 'Impartiality involves various psychological factors . . . but it also requires certain institutional conditions. The first of these is the independence of the judiciary.'[35] The Franks Report does not include independence as one of the principles that it recommended should be present in all tribunals, but its definition of impartiality follows closely the Robson discussion and is effectively a case for independence. As Franks put it: 'impartiality [requires] the freedom of tribunals from the influence, real or apparent, of Departments concerned with the subject matter of their decisions.'[36] The case for independence is clarified later: 'it is important to secure the independence of the personnel of tribunals from the Departments concerned with the subject-matter of their decisions. This is particularly so when a Government Department is a frequent party to the proceedings before a tribunal.'[37] This all seems very clear but some questions remain. How much distance should there be between the relevant government department (or other public body) and the officials who are charged with deciding appeals? When does that distance constitute 'independence'? And at what stage of an appeals structure should it become a consideration?

If we pose the question of what independence means for the social security system the following proposition emerges. Independence is clearly demonstrable if the following five conditions are met: (i) the appellate decision-makers should not have any connection with the department or office responsible for initial decisions; (ii) the relevant department should not appoint the decision-makers; (iii) nor should it train them; (iv) nor provide them with advice or other assistance; (v) nor administer the appeals system.

When we apply these criteria to the existing range of social security appeals structures the results are mixed. When claimants (to most benefits) make an appeal, their case will proceed to a tribunal hearing unless the original decision is overturned in their favour at the review stage. Since 1984, members of SSATs have had no connection with the DSS, whose officials are responsible for initial decisions. SSATs therefore pass the test of independence. Any system of internal administrative review, when it is the first formal stage of appeal, fails all five criteria. Furthermore, housing benefit and council tax review boards also fail all five criteria, though the proposed DATs and CSATs which follow very closely the SSAT model satisfy them all. The position of the social fund is less clear-cut. At the initial internal review stage all five criteria are again failed. However, if we consider the social fund inspectors we find that at their present stage of development there is some claim to limited independence. Social fund

---

[35] Ibid. 41.
[36] Franks Report, para. 42.   [37] Ibid., para. 45.

inspectors are recruited by the Social Fund Commissioner. Although the eventual aim is to recruit new inspectors from outside the DSS, initially they were all seconded from within. The DSS, as the relevant department, does not therefore appoint decision-makers, nor does it administer the system, train inspectors, or provide other assistance. Whilst the social fund inspectors approach some degree of independence, this is not to suggest that they constitute an acceptable alternative to independent tribunals along SSAT lines. There are other points of comparison which will be considered below.

The principle of independence clearly has a powerful influence in the upper reaches of decision-making hierarchies yet has less impact lower down. How far independence is built into appeals structures is ultimately, of course, a political decision. What we appear to be witnessing in the social security system in the last ten years is a willingness to abandon its symbolic and practical advantages and to embrace structures which bow to other principles such as speed and efficiency.

Participation

The opportunity for appellants to participate in proceedings is a defining characteristic of court and tribunal hearings. As such it is not an advantage of one over the other and therefore did not feature in the Franks Report when comparing the two. However, it becomes highly salient when comparing an essentially participatory process (the tribunal hearing) with the characteristically non-participatory internal administrative review.

Participation can, of course, take many forms. It can be in person, before the actual decision-makers, or through a representative. It can be conducted orally or in writing. Apart from the symbolic importance of involving individuals in decision-making, there are instrumental advantages. Appellants have the opportunity of providing additional, or clarifying existing, evidence. In principle the presence of the appellant allows the tribunal to adopt the inquisitorial mode intended for it.[38] Tribunal members have the opportunity of checking information and of eliciting evidence which may not have seemed important or relevant to the appellant. Although not contributing to decision-making, the presence of the appellant also affords the opportunity of providing a more comprehensive explanation of the initial decision than is usually contained in DSS (or local authority) decision letters. Without an appellant present, none of this can take place and, as recent studies have shown, the chances of winning the appeal are reduced.[39]

[38] In practice this opportunity is often lost through appellants failing to attend their tribunal hearing; see Baldwin *et al.*, *Judging Social Security*.

[39] H. Genn and Y. Genn, *The Effectiveness of Representation at Tribunals* (London, 1988); Sainsbury, *Survey and Report*.

Whilst the ideal-type review procedure is entirely internal (for example, in relation to income support, housing benefit, the new disability benefits, and the child support arrangements), the social fund internal review is an interesting hybrid incorporating one feature of the tribunal hearing ideal type. As described earlier, if a social fund officer has made a provisional decision to uphold his or her original assessment, then the claimant must be offered the chance to attend an interview with the officer in the DSS office. At this interview the decision is explained and the applicant offered the chance to present further information. If the officer still wishes to uphold the initial decision, he or she must first get the approval of the relevant member of the office management. This is clearly a form of participation, though more limited than in the tribunal setting, and recent research has shown that it is welcomed by most social fund applicants.[40]

American studies have similarly shown that participation in proceedings is one of the desired features of appeal or court hearings.[41] The value for appellants lies in the opportunity of influencing the eventual outcome, and in the opportunity of presenting their view in their own way ('having their day in court'). Whether the social fund hybrid internal review could serve as a model for other social security benefits will be considered later.

Costs

Much of the argument about the relative costs of courts and tribunals appears to have been based more on assumptions than on hard evidence. The received wisdom has been that tribunals are cheaper than courts. Despite the lack of firm supporting data it is not my intention to challenge this view, which applies equally to tribunals and reviews. Whatever the magnitude of the difference, the nature of reviews renders then inherently cheaper.

The costs of reviews include only the salaries of relatively junior staff and the usual administrative overheads. In contrast, tribunals not only require an administrative hierarchy but must pay tribunal members at least their expenses and often an attendance fee. In addition, appellants can usually claim travel and other expenses.

Though the relative costs of reviews and tribunals will be largely irrelevant to individual appellants, this will rightly be of interest and concern to government. It is all the more striking therefore to find no mention of the relatively low cost of reviews in the published policy

---

[40] Dalley and Berthoud, *Challenging Discretion.*
[41] Lind and Tyler, *The Social Psychology of Procedural Justice*; T. Tyler, 'Procedure or Result: What do Disputants Want from Legal Authorities?', in K. Mackie (ed.), *A Handbook of Dispute Resolution* (London, 1991).

documents of the social fund, disability benefits, and child support appeal arrangements. This silence arouses suspicions. Coupled with the fact that the arguments for reviews that have been put forward are so meagre, it is easy to be left with the feeling that the costs of appeals have loomed larger in debates within Whitehall than other considerations. Reviews are not only attractive because they are inherently cheaper, but also because they can act as a filter (or barrier) to the tribunal, since only the most determined of unsuccessful claimants seem prepared to make a second appeal having failed to secure an award of benefit after their initial claim and again at the review stage.[42]

Quality of review decision-making

A discussion about the quality of decisions made at internal reviews compared with tribunal decisions is fraught with difficulties. The first problem is with a definition of what constitutes high-quality decisions. The second problem is with the empirical evidence (or rather the lack of it) that is available on the quality of decisions. The final difficulty is with interpreting the information that is available—if we find that the review arrangements carried out by one agency produce high-quality decisions, but those in another are inferior, what conclusions can we draw about reviews in general?

The clearest yardstick of decision-making in social security is that used by the Chief Adjudication Officer in his assessment of the standards of adjudication of officers of the DSS and the Department of Employment.[43] The scrutiny of adjudication decisions by CAO monitoring teams is based on whether the *process* of adjudication has been adequate. If an adjudication officer makes a decision based on insufficient evidence, or makes an incorrect finding of fact, or applies the wrong law, or applies the right law incorrectly, or makes an incomplete or inaccurate record of the decision, then, in the jargon of adjudication monitoring, an 'adjudication comment' is raised. An analysis of adjudication comments is presented in the Chief Adjudication Officer's Annual Reports. This narrow and technical method of appraising decision-making is a reflection of the difficulties in assessing as correct or incorrect decisions which rely in varying degrees on the judgment of officials. Whilst this gives a good indication of the standards of the process of adjudication, it cannot necessarily be taken as a proxy measurement of the outcomes of

[42] R. Sainsbury and T. Eardley, *Housing Benefit Reviews: An Evaluation of the Effectiveness of the Review System in Responding to Claimants Dissatisfied with Housing Benefit Decisions*, DSS Research Report Series No. 3 (London, 1991).

[43] See R. Sainsbury, 'The Social Security Chief Adjudication Officer: The First Four Years' (1989) *PL* 323.

adjudication. In other words, the number of 'adjudication comments' does not represent a decision-making 'error rate'.

The adjudication monitoring system applies to lay adjudication on all the benefits administered by the DSS and Department of Employment. However, there is no comparable system for housing benefit, the social fund, and all medical adjudication. Whatever internal monitoring of review decision-making is carried out for management purposes it is not generally made public. Similarly, there is no external scrutiny of the decisions made by SSATs, MATs, DATs, CSATs, or housing benefit and council tax benefit review boards.

The evidence in the CAO's Reports in recent years indicates that review decision-making (following an appeal request) in DSS offices often fails the test of adequate adjudication. In three recent Reports[44] adjudication comments have been made in 46 per cent, 52 per cent, and 32 per cent of the cases where a decision had been reviewed and revised. While no official statistics are available on the standards of housing benefit internal reviews, a recent research study found that many would have failed the criteria of adequate adjudication adopted by the CAO.[45] Similarly, there are no definitive data on the standard of internal reviews of social fund decisions. However, if one takes as an indication the proportion of reviewed decisions that are either changed or referred back to a DSS office on further review by a social fund inspector, then the evidence is not reassuring. The report of the Social Fund Commisioner for 1990–1[46] reveals that only 18 per cent of social fund officers' decisions were upheld by an inspector. By comparison the proportion of decisions upheld by SSATs is approaching 70 per cent. However, it must be remembered that adjudication officers have already overturned in the region of 15 to 20 per cent of decisions at the internal review stage.[47]

The standards of decision-making during internal reviews have attracted the criticism of the Chief Adjudication Officer (for mainstream social security benefits) and independent researchers (for housing benefit). The results of social fund inspectors raise further doubts about the quality of initial reviews in social security offices. Unfortunately there is no information on tribunal decision-making which we can use for comparison.

---

[44] *Annual Report of the Chief Adjudication Officer for 1988/89 on Adjudication Standards* (London, 1990); *Annual Report of the Chief Adjudication Officer for 1989/90 on Adjudication Standards* (London, 1991); *Annual Report of the Chief Adjudication Officer for 1990/91 on Adjudication Standards* (London, 1992).

[45] Sainsbury and Eardley, *Housing Benefit Reviews* above n. 42 at 30.

[46] Social Fund Commissioner, *Annual Report of the Social Fund Commissioner for 1990–91 on the Standards of Reviews by Social Fund Inspectors* (London, 1991).

[47] The figure for 1991 was 16% (DSS, *Social Security Statistics 1991* (London, 1992)).

The results of judicial review of tribunal decisions are not helpful since only appeals on a point of law are admitted.

What can be concluded from the small amount of data that we have is that internal reviews may have the potential of providing high-quality decision-making but have yet to demonstrate that they do. It is not a criticism of the professional standards of DSS or local authority officers to say that tribunals have the better opportunity of meeting the standards (as used by the CAO) of adequate adjudication since they have more time to consider each case, have the benefit of questioning claimants and their representatives in person, and have greater experience of inquisitorial techniques.

DISCUSSION AND CONCLUSION

While there has been a vigorous debate in the past over the use of courts or tribunals to hear appeals (briefly resurrected in the deliberations over child support) and there is currently a similarly robust debate surrounding the growth of judical review, there has been no comparable discussion about the increase in internal reviews as the first stage of appeals systems. It is important to remember that, just as much as judicial review or tribunal hearings, internal reviews are a means of redressing grievances, and, given the large volume of reviews that are carried out in comparison with all higher forms of adjudication, a comparable discussion is both necessary and desirable.

An important question at issue is whether internal reviews or tribunal hearings should form the first formal tier of an appeals system. The answer is neither clear-cut nor obvious and is not aided by the numerous ways in which 'review' has been attached as a label for different activities. Intended primarily as a means by which officials could change decisions without the necessity of an appeal or a fresh claim being made by a claimant, the 'review' has taken on a narrowly defined form which I have called its 'ideal-type' formulation. In contrast the term 'appeal' has become associated with a *de novo* consideration of a case by an independent body of decision-makers. 'Appeal' is therefore associated with both courts and tribunals. Where there has been a policy decision to avoid using tribunals, therefore, we find a reluctance to use the term 'appeal' to describe a claimant's right of seeking redress. The social fund and housing benefit are clear examples of such policies. The invalidity of the distinction is clear if viewed from the claimant's position. It is a very common occurrence for people to claim income support and housing benefit at the same time. If they disagree with their income support assessment they have an immediate right of appeal to an independent SSAT, but if they disagree with their housing benefit decision they can only demand initially an internal review by local authority officials. The claimant is doing the same thing in each case: challenging the decision of a public body administering a social security benefit. To treat one as an 'appeal' and the other as a request for a 'review' has no logical basis and will make no sense to the claimant.[48] As with many other aspects of social security, there has been a top-down approach in which the imperatives of government have prevailed over the interests of claimants. A discourse of claimants' rights begun by Franks has been replaced by a discourse dominated by efficiency and value for money characteristic of Conservative governments of the 1980s.

In this chapter I have tried to clear away some of the obfuscation by identifying the defining characteristics of the ideal-type review and tribunal hearing and by outlining the parameters within which a debate about the proper place of reviews might take place. What emerges from the analysis is a picture of the relative strengths and weaknesses of reviews and tribunal appeals. Reviews in their ideal type offer as advantages over tribunals their speed, and lower costs. Tribunals, again in their ideal type, offer independence and the associated promise of the impartiality of decision-makers, as well as the numerous advantages that accrue from the participation of the appellant. They also encourage greater confidence in their competence as decision-makers through their experience and expertise of adjudication. The choice between reviews and tribunals as the first tier of appeal requires trade-offs to be made between these contrasting advantages. How these trade-offs are resolved depends crucially upon who is making the judgment. It is clear where successive governments have stood in the 1980s and early 1990s; what has been lacking is the incorporation of the preferences of the consumer.

What can be drawn from studies of appeals systems in this country and in America can be summarized by citing Tyler's conclusions from his and others' work on procedural justice.[49] What participants primarily want is to be able to participate in the process, to be treated with respect and dignity, to have an impartial decision-maker look at their case, and to receive a fair outcome. On these criteria tribunal hearings have advantages over internal reviews, even where, as in the social fund, the appellant is allowed a degree of participation in an internal review.

It was noted earlier that reviews have moved between social security administration and adjudication in the past decade. This transition of internal reviews has seemingly taken place unnoticed and without the necessary debate about their proper place in decision-making structures.

---

[48] e.g. Dalley and Berthoud, *Challenging Discretion*, found that people using the social fund review procedures wanted a reassessment of their needs and were not challenging the conduct or behaviour of social fund officers.

[49] Tyler, 'Procedure or Result: What do Disputants Want from Legal Authorities?' in K. Mackie (ed.), *A Handbook of Dispute Resolution*.

Internal reviews are now occupying the position previously held by tribunals. It is surprising, therefore that the tribunal watchdog, the Council on Tribunals, has found nothing wrong in principle with this development.[50]

The conclusion from the analysis presented in this chapter is that internal reviews best serve the interests of social security claimants when they form part of the administration of benefits and not part of the formal appeal arrangements. The current range of appeals structures is riddled with inconsistencies for which there is no visible justification. The introduction of internal reviews as a first tier of appeal has already weakened the ability of housing benefit claimants and social fund applicants to obtain redress of their grievances against social security authorities. Claimants of the new disability benefits and those subject to the decisions of the Child Support Agency are now beginning to experience similar disadvantages.

[50] See Council on Tribunals, *Annual Report for 1990/91* (London, 1991), para. 3.26. The Council has been concentrating its attention on the equally worrying development of *replacing* tribunals by reviews, in contrast to adding them as an initial extra tier.

13

The Ombudsmen:
Remedies for Misinformation

Paul Brown

INTRODUCTION

The ombudsmen

In 1967 Britain obtained its first ombudsman, more properly known as the Parliamentary Commissioner for Administration. His brief then, as now, was to investigate complaints from members of the public who claimed to have 'sustained injustice in consequence of maladministration' in any action taken by or on behalf of a government department, being 'action taken in the exercise of the administrative functions of that department'.[1] Central to the creation of the Commissioner's office was the belief that there were many situations where administrative incompetence or error could result in hardship to citizens, but might nevertheless not be susceptible to review by the courts. Some other avenue for redress was therefore required.

As his name suggests, the PCA is primarily concerned with the administration of central government. In 1974 the need for a local government equivalent was met with the creation of the Commissioner for Local Administration.[2] Since their inception, both ombudsmen have enjoyed considerable success. In spite of this, there has been comparatively little research into their work. This chapter sets out to redress that imbalance. It does so by reference to a particular type of complaint made to the ombudsmen, namely where a citizen has been misled by information given to him or her by a government body. In particular it looks at the sort of complaint which the common law would attempt to resolve by reference to principles of estoppel. This area has been chosen primarily because it raises problems to which the courts have as yet produced no satisfactory answer. In this sense, in addition to demonstrating the work of the ombudsmen, this chapter may also help to illustrate the thesis that administrative law does not begin and end with judicial review.

This chapter originally formed part of the author's Ph.D. dissertation at the University of Cambridge, 1989.

[1] Parliamentary Commissioner Act 1967, s. 5 (1) (a.).
[2] Local Government Act 1974, ss. 23–4.

Misleading information: the basic problem

As one commentator has recently observed:

In the context of our contemporary society, it is inevitable that a great deal of sought after information is located within government departments, particularly where they are responsible for generating the detailed provisions that govern today's numerous administrative programmes. Therefore, a vital element of the relationship between citizens and the state concerns the nature of the obligation on the latter to provide advice to citizens regarding matters falling within the competence and expertise of those departments.[3]

For the purposes of this chapter, what is important is not merely the obligation to give advice, but the obligation to ensure that the advice given is correct. Government departments may misunderstand or misrepresent the law. They may give advice which was accurate at the time, but which ceases to be so following a change in the law or in policy. Where individuals have been led to rely on the advice they have received, it may seem fundamentally unfair if the advising authority is allowed to turn around and go back on what it has said before.

In private law, an answer to this sort of problem would be to invoke the doctrine of estoppel, so as to prevent the representor from going back on his word. As between private individuals who are free to order their affairs as they choose, this is not unreasonable. But public authorities are not free agents. Their powers are strictly defined, and their decisions and actions affect a wider general public. If their representations imply the legitimacy of a state of affairs which is prohibited by statute, can estoppel override the terms of the statute? If an official has a discretion to be exercised in the public interest, can that wider interest be ignored where it conflicts with a promise which has been made to some individual? What if an official has no authority to give the advice at all? Or if government policy has changed? In such situations, is it desirable, or even legally possible, to say that the assurances cannot be denied? There is a conflict here between the right of the individual to rely on what he has been told; and the broader demands of the public interest and the *ultra vires* rule.

In the courts, that conflict has produced a confused body of case-law. Some judges have been moved by the potential unfairness to the individual to allow estoppel to operate.[4] Others have held that the doctrine cannot be

---

[3] A. Mowbray, 'A Right to Official Advice: The Parliamentary Commissioner's Perspective' [1990] *PL* 68.

[4] See e.g.*Robertson* v. *Minister of Pensions* [1949] 1 KB 227; *Falmouth Boat Construction* v. *Howell* [1950] 1 All ER 538 (CA); *Wells* v. *Westminster for Housing and Local Government* [1967] 1 WLR 1000; *Lever Finance Ltd.* v. *Westminster (City) London Borough Council* [1971] 1 QB 222; *Gowa* v. *Attorney. General, The Times*, 27 Dec. 1984 (CA).

allowed to fetter the exercise of a discretion,[5] or that it cannot prevent an authority from exercising a statutory duty.[6] The cases reveal such an unbridgeable gap between the individual equity of the private law remedy, and the very deep theoretical objections to its application to public bodies, that de Smith has concluded, 'There is no consensus of judicial or academic opinion as to the circumstances in which unauthorized or erroneous assurances given by public bodies or public officials to members of the public may acquire binding force by creating an estoppel.'[7]

Inherent in this problem is the all or nothing nature of estoppel, where the representation is either fulfilled (with whatever consequences that might have) or the reliant party walks away empty-handed. In the courts, the possible half-way house of a remedy in damages is, despite calls for its wider availability, at present only available in an action for negligent misrepresentation. This is not always an easy path where changes of policy or the interpretation of complex legislation are concerned. But if the courts have no solution, there were early suggestions that the ombudsmen might do better.[8] It is now possible, with the benefit of almost twenty-five years of investigations, to assess the extent to which that hope has been fulfilled.

THE CASEWORK OF THE OMBUDSMEN

The cases discussed in this chapter have been taken from the reports of the CLA from March 1981 to July 1988, and from those of the PCA from 1967 up until November 1991. The subject-matter of the complaints varies widely from loss of a benefit or grant to the loss of citizenship, amenity, or livelihood. Some of these losses are more easily compensated than others: cases involving promises of money are relatively easily resolved, but a promise not to demolish a row of historic houses is impossible to enforce if these have already been knocked down.[9] The following analysis looks at some of the different types of complaints investigated by the ombudsmen, and the remedies recommended in each.

In analysing these complaints, it is important to remember that the jurisdiction of both ombudsmen is limited to cases of 'maladministration'.[10] The general effect of this is to confine the scope of investigations to the

---

[5] *Southend on Sea* v. *Hodgson (Wickford) Ltd.* [1962] 1 QB 416; *Brooks and Burton Ltd.* v. *Secretary of State for the Environment* (1976) 35 P. & CR 27; *Western Fish Products Ltd.* v. *Penwith District Council* [1981] 2 All ER 204.

[6] *Maritime Electric Co. Ltd.* v. *General Dairies Ltd.* [1937] AC 610; *Howell* v. *Falmouth Boat Construction Ltd.* [1951] AC 837 (HL).

[7] S. A. de Smith, *Judicial Review of Administrative Action* (3rd edn. London, 1973), at 89.

[8] see B. Schwartz and H. W. R. Wade, *Legal Control of Government* (Oxford, 1972), at 66.   [9] As in Case No. C. 245/1, HC 138 (1969/70), at 71.

[10] Parliamentary Commissioner Act, s. 5; Local Government Act 1974, s. 26 (1).

administrative procedures adopted by a government body. Maladministration has nothing to do with the nature, quality, or reasonableness of a decision,[11] and, as a general rule, neither the PCA nor the CLA will examine the merits of a decision, or the policies which underlie it.[12]

Cases of financial detriment

A significant number of the complaints received by the ombudsmen involve erroneous statements by government officials that the complainant was entitled to some form of financial assistance from the government body. The types of benefit promised vary widely, but the problem caused is usually the same: in the belief that he or she is entitled to the benefit, the complainant has increased his or her level of expenditure, only to be told when the mistake is discovered that the benefit cannot be paid or, if already paid, must be recovered. Although the complainant was never legally entitled to the money, denial of the right to it in such circumstances can cause considerable hardship. As Abbott CJ noted in *Skyring* v. *Greenwood*:[13]

It is of great importance to any man . . . that [he] should not be led to suppose that [his] annual income is greater than it really is. Every prudent man accommodates his mode of living to what he supposes to be his income; it therefore works a great prejudice to any man if, after having had credit given to him in account of certain sums, and having been allowed to draw on his agent on the faith that those sums belonged to him, he may be called upon to pay them back.

This is particularly so in the case of subsistence allowances such as unemployment and supplementary benefit, where recipients are unlikely to have any other savings available to meet the demand.

As a general rule, once satisfied that a complainant has spent money in reliance on past receipt of an award, or on a promise that money will be paid, the ombudsmen have been happy to recommend that compensation be paid.

The extent to which these decisions contravene statute or amount to a fetter on discretion varies. In some cases, the departmental advice has actually led the complainant to forego a benefit to which he or she was entitled, and the ombudsman has recommended that the benefit be paid.[14]

---

[11] *R.* v. *Commission for Local Administration ex p. Eastleigh Borough Council* [1988] 3 WLR 113; *R.* v. *Commission for Local Administration ex p. Croydon (London) Borough Council* [1989] 1 All ER 1033.

[12] Although the PCA recognizes an exception to this where a decision is 'so thoroughly bad in quality' that he can infer that there must have been maladministration in its taking: HC 350 (1967–8). See also R. Gregory and P. Hutchesson, *The Parliamentary Ombudsman: A Study in the Control of Administrative Action* 313 ff.

[13] (1825) 4 B. & C. 281, at 289, 107 ER 1064, at 1067.

[14] Case No. C. 256/B, HC 116 (1971/2), at 72; Case No. 3A/440/77, HC 524 (1977/8), at 263; Case No. C. 202/83, HC 388 (1983/4), at 23; Case No. C. 238/85, HC 312 (1986/7), at 87;

Elsewhere, the PCA has gone further, to endorse claims which would never have been permissible under department policy;[15] or under regulations[16] or statute.[17] So, for example, a pregnant woman who went to join her husband in Australia, having been incorrectly advised that maternity allowance was payable in respect of periods spent abroad, received an extra-statutory payment equivalent to the allowance to which she would have been entitled had she not gone.

It is important to note that, in all of these case, the remedy has not been a requirement that the promise be fulfilled, but a recommendation that compensation be paid for the loss suffered. In many cases, the effect of this has been the same: where money equal to the amount of the grant has been spent, the complainant's reliance loss is the same as his expectation loss, and his compensation has been the full amount which was promised. However, in some cases there is a difference. A typical example is the homeowner who has mistakenly been promised an improvement grant towards the cost of building and materials for work on his home, but who has not got beyond commissioning an architect to draw up plans before the promise is withdrawn. The CLA's recommendation in such cases has generally been limited to compensation for the money paid out in architect's fees.[18] The wider expectations of money for the cost of construction remain unfulfilled.

Case No. C. 80/84, HC 150 (1984/5), at 53; Case No. C. 114/85, HC 336 (1985/6) at 107; Case No. C473/89, HC 548 (1989/90), at 75; Case No. 467/89, HC 638 (1989/90), at 16; Case No. C622/89, HC 360 (1990/1), at 54; Case No. C221/90, HC 195 (1991/2), at 36. See also Inv. 87/B/171, 27 Nov. 1987.

[15] See Case No. C. 188/83, HC 190 (1983/4), at 94: weekly child-minding allowance paid for duration of a College of Adult Education course, contrary to Treasury policy; Case No. C. 640/68, HC 138 (1969/70), at 137: farmer paid investment grant for plant and machinery not covered by Board of Trade policy (see also Case No. C. 1004/80, HC 150 (1982/3), at 50); Case No. C. 752/82, HC 190 (1983/4), at 190: student grant paid for an extra year, and similar cases addressed to the CLA: Inv. 262/C/82, 8 Dec. 1982; Inv. 202/J/83, 11 July 1984; Inv. 1353/C/85, 10 Sept. 1985; Inv. 86/A/1241, 6 July 1988; cf. Inv. 375/S/81, 25 Feb. 1982.

[16] Case No. C. 170/85, HC 184 (1985/6), at 78.

[17] Case No. C. 155/67, HC 134 (1967/8), at 44; Case No. C. 370/B, HC 116 (1971/2), at 157; Case No. C. 143/G, HC 490 (1971/2), at 126: unemployement, maternity, and sickness benefit paid in respect of period spent overseas, cf. Case No. C.416/T, HC 170 (1974) at 31, where an apology was given, but no mention was made of any other remedy. See also Case No. C. 346/81, HC 327 (1981/2), at 69: training course expenses well in excess of statutory limit paid; Case No. C. 516/80, HC 395 (1980/1), at 27: Job Release Allowance paid to a person whose age technically excluded him from the scheme after he had retired early; Case No. C. 307/K, HC 46 (1976/7), at 41; Case No. C. 243/T, HC 281 (1974), at 17; and comments in Case No. C. 463/T, HC 281 (1974), at 30: Employment Transfer Scheme allowances paid to workers who did not qualify, but had moved home in the belief that they did; Case No. C. 217/83, HC 548 (1983/4), at 40; Case No. C. 701/84, HC 536 (1985/6), at 30; and the very similar response of the CLA in Inv. 235/C/81, 10 Nov. 1981; Inv. 178/J/82, 31 May 1983.

[18] Inv. 513/C/82, 12 Jan. 1983, cf. Inv. 600/C/81, 24 Mar. 1981, where the Commissioner decided that, since the complainant had subsequently elected to carry out all the work at his own expense, he had had the benefit of the architect's plans, and an apology was the only

This distinction between reliance and expectation loss has also been central to a line of cases concerning payment into the national insurance scheme. Payment of national insurance contributions is a condition precedent to eligibility to receive retirement pension, which is payable in graduated amounts depending on the number of contributions paid during a person's working life. Two particular problems arise out of the scheme which are of interest for present purposes. First, representations are sometimes made by the DHSS that cessation of contribution payments will not affect entitlement to a pension or other benefit, when it will actually result in a reduced pension. Secondly, contributors are sometimes told that continued payment will secure or improve their entitlement to a pension, when in fact it will not. The two are essentially different in that cessation of payment may legally disqualify someone who would otherwise have qualified. To this extent the departmental advice has affected the contributor's legal rights. In contrast, continued payment will only raise expectations of eligibility, but will not affect the legal position, which is that there was at all material times a statutory bar to entitlement. The Department can be criticized for building up unfounded hopes, but not for causing the contributor to act to his legal detriment.

The PCA's response to the cessation of payments cases is that, if the blame for the loss of legal entitlement lies at the door of the DHSS, the complainant ought not to be the one to suffer for it. However, rather than demanding payment of the promised benefit notwithstanding the absence of the required contributions, the PCA has sought a compromise in the form of an arrangement whereby the contributor is allowed to make a late payment of contributions, and the Department then pays the benefit.[19] The result is, as far as is possible, a return to the situation as it would have been were it not for the misrepresentation. This requires concessions from both sides—from the DHSS in waiving the time limit, and from the complainant in agreeing to pay the arrears. The rationale as the PCA sees it is that there is no provision for a complainant to be credited with contributions that have not in fact been made, and to do so would place one person in a better position than others who have been correctly informed.[20] None the less, the solution does preclude the Department from enforcing the time bar on payment.

redress required. Cf. Inv. 189/Y/84, 22 Nov. 1984, and the cases where the full repairs had already been done, or had reached such a stage that it was impractical to call a halt; Inv. 93/S/82 30 Nov. 1982; Inv. 899/C/82, 22 Sept. 1983; Inv. 563/J/83, 24 Aug. 1984; Inv. 27/C/85, 4 Nov. 1985; Inv. 200/C/85, 24 Feb. 1986. Compensation for the loss here was equivalent to payment of the grant.

[19] Case No. C. 563/J, HC 37 (1975/6), at 116; Case No. C. 225/V, HC 496 (1975/6), at 114; Case No. C. 3A/994/78, HC 211 (1979/80), at 97; Case No. C. 541/81, HC 312 (1982/3), at 37. In similar vein, see Case no. C. 606/86, HC 103 (1987/8), at 18; Case No. C526/88, HC 151 (1989/90), at 69.   [20] Case No. C. 563/J.

In the majority of cases this works well, but there are situations in which it breaks down. Where complainants have been advised that they need not pay further contributions, they are more likely to have spent the contribution money than to have set the money aside in case there has been a mistake. Consequently, they may later find it impossible to pay the arrears. The problem is heightened if payment of several years' contributions is required in one lump sum, or if the mistake is not discovered until the complainant has retired, and is living on a lower income.

Surprisingly, this argument has not often been pressed on the PCA.[21] In one case where it was, the complainant was faced with the need to pay £955 in contribution arrears in order to restore her pension to the full rate. She pointed out that she was struggling on a limited income, and had spent the money which would otherwise have been set aside for national insurance. After giving the claim detailed consideration, the DHSS agreed to grant the woman a pension at the full rate, and to pay nearly £1,900 in arrears, without setting this off against the contributions she ought properly to have made.

In the cessation of payment cases, the complaint is essentially twofold: firstly, an expectation has been created but not fulfilled, and secondly, a legal right has been lost as a result of the official error. The complainant's reliance loss and expectation loss are exactly the same. This may be contrasted with the second type of case referred to above, where complainants have been encouraged to make national insurance contributions in the mistaken belief that this will enhance their pension entitlement.

In these cases, the PCA has been content to accept the DHSS policy, which is to pay out only if there was an official misdirection or a failure to give advice at a time when it would still have been possible for the complainant to satisfy the test for qualification.[22] The argument is that, because there was never any legal entitlement to the benefit at the crucial time, it cannot be said that the Department has caused the benefit to be lost. Indeed, to fulfil the promise would be to place any claimant in a better position than if he had been given correct information.[23] The only true detriment is the loss of the money paid out in pointless contributions. This the PCA has usually requested the Department to refund,[24] but in no case of this kind

---

[21] Case No. C. 547/84, HC 324 (1984/5), at 45. The complainant in Case No. C. 894/67, HC 129 (1968/9) raised a similar complaint, but was only able to obtain permission to continue paying contributions into the first year of receiving her pension.

[22] Case No. C. 412/G, HC 290 (1972/3) at 106; Case No. C. 30/T, HC 42 (1973/4), at 90; Case No. C. 438/V, HC 259 (1975/6) at 89; Case No. C. 650/K, HC 528 (1976/7), at 37; Case No. C. 454/77, HC 126 (1977/8), at 140.

[23] Case No. C. 702/J, HC 529 (1974/5), at 88.

[24] Except where the complainant has used his contribution to obtain some other benefit (e.g. unemployment benefit): Case No. C. 454/77, HC 126 (1977/8), at 105.

has he been prepared to recommend that the complainant's expectations be fulfilled.

Again, the essence of this approach is to restore the situation as nearly as possible to the *status quo ante*. However, there are cases where the demonstrable detriment goes beyond payment of unnecessary contributions, and where a simple refund is insufficient. Most people approaching pensionable age will regulate their savings and spending according to the pension they expect to receive, and, once retirement is reached, their capacity to correct a mistake is drastically reduced, if not completely eliminated. The distinction between loss of a pension to which the complainant was legally entitled, and the discovery that there was never any real entitlement, then becomes noticeably thin. Two cases which illustrate this involve women who had been led to expect a higher rate of pension than was their legal entitlement, but who were able to show that, but for this advice, they would have used the money paid into national insurance to purchase pensions under alternative private schemes.[25]

In both cases the PCA and the Department were sensitive to the fact that complainants had lost more than just the unnecessary contributions. In one case[26] the Department agreed to an *ex gratia* payment of £500, representing the difference between what the alternative pension would have yielded and what the complainant would have had to pay for it. In the other, compensation was fixed at a sum which the Department calculated as the amount now required to purchase an annuity which would put the complainant in the same position as that which she would have enjoyed had she used her national insurance contributions to pay into an alternative scheme. Of the two solutions, the second is preferable—as the complainant in the first case was at pains to point out, a pension would have been inflation proofed, whereas the lump sum was not.

Hence both the PCA and the CLA have tried to put complainants in the position they would have occupied if they had been correctly advised at the outset. In so doing, they have sought a middle road between individual hardship and the requirements of statute or departmental policy. While many of the complainants will have walked away with less than they had been led to expect, the ombudsmen's general approach has been to ensure they do not suffer from incorrect advice. In some cases, this has effectively resulted in fulfilment of the promise, but if that has happened, it is only because that was the measure of the complainant's reliance loss.

These results are in stark contrast to the approach taken by the courts. As the passage cited earlier from *Skyring* v. *Greenwood* reveals, the potential hardship caused by over-payments is well recognized by the

---

[25] Case No. C. 335/80, HC 250 (1980/1), at 32; Case No. C. 541/81, HC 312 (1982/3), at 37; cf. Case No. C. 221/J, HC 241 (1974/5), at 117.

[26] Case No. C. 335/80.

courts when dealing with private debts.[27] When dealing with the payments made from public funds, however, the courts have been less sympathetic. In a leading case[28] the Minister of Railways had been empowered by statute to pay the appellants a sum of money from the Public Works Fund. Payment was contingent upon the conclusion of a lease agreement between the appellants and a third party. In fact the lease was never granted, but the sum was paid, and the question arose whether the government could recover the money. The Privy Council advised that it could. As the Act had provided that the sum would only be payable on a condition which was not actually fulfilled,

[t]he payment was accordingly an illegal one which no merely executive ratification . . . could divest of its illegal character. For it has been a principle of the British Constitution now for more than two centuries . . . that no money can be taken out of the consolidated fund into which the revenues of the State have been paid, excepting under a distinct authorisation from Parliament itself. The days are long gone by in which the Crown or its servants, apart from Parliament, could give such an authorisation or ratify an improper payment. Any payment out of the consolidated fund made without Parliamentary authority is simply illegal and ultra vires, and may be recovered by the Government if it can, as here, be traced.[29]

Hence, in the eyes of the Court, the statute overrode any individual hardship.

A further significant difference between the ombudsmen and the courts is the broad view the former have been able to take of what amounts to 'loss' or detriment.[30] This is illustrated in a group of complaints involving parents whose choice of secondary school for their children had been influenced by the local council policy on the provision of free transport for school children.[31] Some families gave up personal preferences in order to comply with the guidelines laid down for the issue of bus passes, only to

---

[27] See *Skyring* v. *Greenwood* (1825) 4 B. & C. 281, 107 ER 1064, cited above.

[28] *Auckland Harbour Board* v. *R.* [1924] AC 318. See also *Maritime Electric Co. Ltd* v. *General Dairies Ltd.* [1937] AC 610. For general discussion, see R. Pagone, 'Estoppel in Public Law: Theory, Fact and Fiction', (1984) 7 *UNSWLJ* 267.

[29] Per Viscount Haldane for the Privy Council, at 326–7. In *Commonwealth of Australia* v. *Burns* [1971] VR 825, Newton J intepreted Viscount Haldane's use of 'tracing' as a reference not to the equitable or proprietary sense of the word, but to the possibility of tracing the identity of the recipient. English cases on *Auckland Harbour Board* are scant, although see *R.* v. *Blenkinsop* [1892] 1 QB 43. However, the principle has both Canadian and Australian authority to support it: *R.* v. *The Toronto Terminals Railways Co.* [1948] Exch. CR 563; *Commonwealth of Australia* v. *Burns* [1971] VR 825; *Attorney-General* v. *Gray* [1977] 1 NSWLR 406 (cf. *Commonwealth of Australia* v. *Crothall Hospital Services (Aust.) Ltd.* (1981) 36 ALR 567).

[30] See especially Case No. C. 665/84, HC 590 (1984/5), at 46, for a broad view of financial loss.

[31] Inv. 380/440/441/442/J/84; 594/925/L/84, 12 June 1985. See also Inv. 852/L/84, 19 Nov. 1985, and No. 458/S/80, 13 Aug. 1981. In the latter investigation, the CLA left it to the council to decide whether or not to issue the pass, but indicated that he hoped that they would.

have their council later withdraw the offer of assistance. Their complaints to the CLA were upheld. The CLA acknowledged that it was the council's responsibility to determine policy, and that they had the right to change it, but felt that 'when they do so, it is good administration to ensure that the change is made and announced in sufficient time to allow those affected by the policy to take it into account in reaching their decision'.[32]

In these cases, the parents had not been given the opportunity to make their decision in the full knowledge of their rights, and this constituted maladministration. The CLA concluded that the council should apologize and stand by the assurance they had given by providing bus passes to the children in question throughout the remainder of their school lives.

This may be contrasted with the decision in *Rootkin* v. *Kent County Council*,[33] where the Court of Appeal declined to enforce a local authority's promise of a school travel allowance, even though this had influenced the plaintiff's choice of school for her daughter. Among other reasons, it was held that no detriment had been suffered. The plaintiff argued that, if the grant was not forthcoming, she would have to find another school for her child, as she could not afford the bus fares herself. In spite of recognizing that 'children do not like being uprooted from one school to another', Lawton LJ concluded that the case was 'a very long way from the kind of situation where there is prejudice such as to bring into operation the doctrine of estoppel'. This narrow approach to questions of detriment rides uncomfortably alongside the breadth of subject-matter over which public authorities may be asked to give advice.

Licences, permissions, and similar guarantees

Whereas in cases of promised financial assistance the public interest manifests itself only in a broad concern that public funds are not misapplied, cases involving permissions and licences can raise a more direct conflict between the interests of the individual and those of the public. Grants or purported grants of planning permission have a direct effect upon neighbouring residents. Licences to drive or to run public transport affect the safety of passengers and other road users. These competing interests raise particular problems for the ombudsmen. Three particular areas will be considered here: planning permission, housing, and television licensing.

Planning permission

More than any other area, it is the field of planning law which has troubled

---

[32] Inv. 380/440/441/442/J/84; 594/925/L/84, 12 June 1985, para. 24.
[33] [1981] 2 All ER 227.

the courts in terms of the inadequacy of existing remedies for non-negligent misrepresentation. The reasons for this can be illustrated by reference to two cases. The first is *Level Finance* v. *Westminster (City) London Borough Council*,[34] in which the plaintiffs had obtained permission to build fourteen houses on a site, in accordance with a detailed plan. They later decided to vary the plan by moving the line of one of the houses. The defendant's planning officer was consulted on the revised drawings, and led the plaintiffs to believe that the alterations were not material, and therefore that no further permission was required. The plaintiff proceeded to build the houses, only to have the authority decide that the alterations were material, that consent should have been obtained, and that further construction should not be allowed. The Court of Appeal found for the plaintiff. Lord Denning MR stated: 'if an officer, acting within the scope of his ostensible authority, makes a representation on which another acts, then a public authority may be bound by it, just as much as a private concern would be.'[35]

As between the council and the developer, this result may seem fair. However, as Megaw LJ pointed out in a later case: 'To permit the estoppel no doubt avoided an injustice to the plaintiffs. But it also may fairly be regarded as having caused an injustice to one or more members of the public, the owners of adjacent houses who would be adversely affected by this wrong and careless decision of the planning officer that the modifications were not material.'[36] In this latter case, the plaintiffs claimed to have been advised by the local authority's planning officer that a site owned by them had existing use rights, and consequently that they did not require planning permission to develop the land. After they had begun to erect new buildings, the authority decided that permission should have been sought, and that, had it been sought, it would not have been granted. On this occasion, the Court of Appeal sided with the local authority. Estoppel could not be raised to prevent the exercise of the council's discretion to grant permission, or to prevent or excuse the performance of its duty to take into account representations by members of the public.

In neither *Lever Finance* nor *Western Fish* is the result satisfactory. In the former, the public was forced to accept an undesirable development. In the latter, the developer was left out of pocket. Is there a middle road? The investigations of the ombudsmen suggest that there is. The CLA's general approach to the problem is well laid out in a passage from a report on a complaint that a property owner had been misled into believing that planning permission was not required for the erection of a stable block in his garden:

[34] [1971] 1 QB 222.   [35] [1971] QB, at 230.
[36] *Western Fish Products Ltd.* v. *Penwith District Council* [1981] 2 All ER 204, at 221.

In certain circumstances an authority might be 'estopped' from taking enforcement action if an officer makes a representation that the planning permission is not required for a particular development. I am not suggesting that this is necessarily such a case. What is required, however, is not that planning permission should be granted, because this might lead to injustice to innocent third parties . . but that Mr. Brown should be compensated for his losses. These are the cost of the erection of the stables . . . the cost of their removal and also the cost of any damage inevitably caused when the stables were dismantled.[37]

This recognizes both the hardship caused to the property owner if he is required to remove the construction, and the injustice to the public if it is not removed. The solution is not the all or nothing of estoppel, but a remedy in damages. The complainant is compensated for the money he has wasted, and so is put back in the position he would have enjoyed had he been correctly advised at the outset.[38]

The only situation in which the CLA has been prepared to recommend that a developer be allowed to go ahead with his project, notwithstanding the opposition of the local council and the objections of neighbours, involved a complainant who actually had a legal right to develop the property, but lost it as a result of official misinformation.[39] The complainant had wanted to build a garage and bedroom extension on to his home. Due to a loophole in the planning regulations, planning permission for both would almost certainly have been obtained provided the garage was built first. If the two were built together, then neither would have been permissible. The complainant wanted to minimize his costs by laying the foundations for the whole proposal at the same time. He was advised by his local authority that there was no objection to this, but was afterwards told that it was an unauthorized development.

[37] Inv. 926/Y/84, 22 Jan. 1986, para. 15. See also Inv. 240/H/80, 29 Dec. 1981; Inv. 6/Y/84, 5 Nov. 1984; Inv. 351/S/80, 1 July 1981.

[38] Similar recommendations have been made in cases where complainants have been encouraged by the local authority to make applications for planning permission, have incurred the cost of making those applications, but have had the applications refused. In these cases, compensation is limited to the cost of making the abortive application: Case No. C. 226/67, HC 134 (1967/8), at 46; Case No. C. 357/B, HC 490 (1971/2), at 73; Case No. C. 441/G, HC 290 (1972/3), at 83; investigations 67/J/82, 9 Mar. 1983; 775/J/81, 15 Aug. 1983; 810/J/82, 28 Dec. 1983; 89/J/83, 11 July 1984; 189/Y/84, 22 Nov. 1984; 1192/A/85, 7 Jan. 1987. Cf. the approach of the courts, as in *Rockhold Ltd.* v. *Secretary of State for the Environment* (1986) JPL 130. Where complainants have been encouraged to purchase land at a price which reflects the benefit of planning permission, which is either not granted, or is later removed, compensation may also include the difference in the value of the land: Inv. 755/C/85, 23 Sept. 1986. See also the PCA's report in Case No. C. 257/G, HC 290 (1972/3), at 57.

[39] Inv. 172/H/81, 16 Apr. 1982.

The Commissioner found that there had been maladministration causing injustice.[40] When the authority had first advised on the matter, it would still have been possible for the complainant to arrange matters so as to comply with the law, and there was every reason to suppose that planning permission for the bedroom extension would have been granted had a proper application been made.

The point of this is that the authority had actually deprived the complainant of something which he could legitimately have enjoyed, irrespective of any conflicting public interest. The CLA report suggests that if the law has not protected the public interest, then the ombudsman will not consider it either, but will ask that the complainant be given back that which he has lost, namely the right to do with his property as the law would have allowed.

Housing

In the planning cases it has usually been possible to quantify the complainant's loss. Compensation was therefore a practical solution. However, in other areas it it less easy to put a price on the injustice to the complainant. One such is the field of housing.

The CLA has received a number of complaints from citizens who have vacated their homes on the strength of council assurances. Three investigations involve councils who, in pursuit of plans to redevelop an area, had compulsorily purchased the necessary land, promising that, once the area had been redeveloped, the council would operate a 'return to area' policy giving existing residents first priority in the allocation of the new housing.[41] These complainants argued that resistance to the council's compulsory purchase order had been reduced by the promise. In a fourth case, the complainant had been promised that he would be allowed to return to his house once certain repairs had been carried out.[42] The complainant said that he would not have moved were it not for the council assurance.

When none of the promises were fulfilled, the CLA concluded that the council action amounted to maladministration. In one of the 'return to area' cases, the Commissioner noted that, although the council was perfectly entitled to alter its housing allocation policy, the 'return to area' promise had not only been made to the resident, but had also formed part of the submission made to the Secretary of State when seeking his approval

---

[40] See also Inv. 749/J/82, 15 Dec. 1983, where the complainant was told that his planning permission was valid for five years, when it was in fact valid for only three. This information was not received until after the shorter period had elapsed, and construction could no longer proceed.

[41] Inv. 529/S/81, 28 Sept. 1982; Inv. 696/S/80, 23 May 1983; Inv. 0391/C/86, 5 Nov. 1987.

[42] Inv. 86/C/1247, 23 Nov. 1987.

for the CPO. There was therefore a commitment to abide by the statements, and that commitment should be met by offering the complainants rehousing in the area 'at the earliest opportunity'.[43] A remedy in the repairs case was more difficult, since the complainant's old house had been allocated to a third party in the interim. However, the complainant indicated that he would be happy with a house on the same road, and the CLA therefore recommended that he be given the 'highest priority' for a move back to his old street, and that the council pay all the reasonable costs of the move.

Housing cases raise particular difficulties for the Ombudsman because of the limited resources and competing claims with which many councils must deal. The CLA has not been insensitive to this, and in two of the 'return to area' complaints[44] the Commissioner was prepared to accept an undertaking to return the complainants after three priority categories (statutorily overcrowded families, families from clearance areas, and high-priority medical cases) had been housed. However, these urgent cases aside, it was not acceptable for councils to give higher priority to other parties. Although it might seem that this deprives councils of the power to provide housing where it sees the greatest need, in fact this is not so. As the Commissioner has pointed out, families which are returned to their former area in accordance with the council's promise will vacate other houses which can be relet.[45]

Television licensing

Not all licensing decisions involve such a clear-cut public interest as the planning and housing cases. One area in which the public interest is less obvious is television licensing. This gave rise to a number of complaints to the PCA in 1975, following an announcement by the Home Secretary in January of that year that as of April 1975 licence fees for television sets would be increased. In the intervening period some 26,000 viewers, having licences which were still valid, took out new licences at the old rate, thus savings themselves the excess. This loophole was well advertised, yet the Home Office did nothing to indicate disapproval until the Post Office, as licensing authority for the Home Office, demanded that viewers pay the difference between the new and old fees, or else have their licences revoked. The Home Office acknowledged that it was not illegal to hold overlapping licences, but said that the Secretary of State had a discretion to revoke any licence, and was not duty bound to issue a licence where one was already in force.

---

[43] See also Inv. 529/S/81, 28 Sept. 1982. The complaint has still not been satisfactorily remedied.

[44] Inv. 529/S/81, 28 Sept. 1982; Inv. 696/S/80, 23 May 1983.

[45] Inv. 529/S/81.

The PCA was heavily critical of the decision, and particularly of the failure to contradict newspaper articles publicizing the loophole.[46] 'In my view it is quite unfair that a licence-holder, who may quite reasonably believe that the holding of a second licence is not illegal, should not be given advance warning that the Government intended to use powers they are advised they have to deprive him of a second one if he obtains it.'[47] In spite of this, the PCA noted that the vast majority of viewers had not availed themselves of the chance to obtain a 'cheap' licence, and agreed with the Home Office that: 'these people would . . . have a legitimate grievance if a minority . . . were allowed to escape the clear intention that they should, following the expiry of their existing licences, pay the announced higher fees. The holders of overlapping licences are clearly not being put in any worse position by the Home Office proposals than this majority.'[48] Therefore, though he deplored the administrative short-comings, he did not feel entitled to question the arrangements in principle.

Interestingly, the complainants's objection in the television licence case was eventually met by challenge in the courts. In *Congreve* v. *Home Office*[49] the Court of Appeal unanimously held the purported revocation of licences invalid, on the basis that the Home Secretary's discretion to revoke was not absolute but had to be exercised for proper purposes, which did not include the extraction of higher fees. As Lord Denning MR succinctly put it, 'Want of money is no reason for revoking a licence.'[50] As to the PCA's concern that other viewers who had paid the full fee would have a justifiable grievance if a minority succeeded in obtaining a cheap licence, Lord Denning was not convinced. If anything, he thought the very converse was so. 'They might only say "Good luck to them. We wish we had done the same." '[51]

It is significant that the basis of the Court of Appeal's decision was *Wednesbury* unreasonableness rather than any sort of reliance or estoppel. Although the complainants had lost an expected advantage, until the Court of Appeal held the overlapping licences lawful, it could not have been said that they had lost any legal right or interest. This is ultimately the reason behind the PCA's refusal to recommend a remedy: it was not that he could find no maladministration, but that he could find no injustice which that maladministration had caused.

Procedural promises

There is now a substantial body of judicial authority for the proposition that public authorities should abide by their undertakings as to the

---

[46] HC 680 (1974/5).
[47] Ibid., at 15.
[48] Ibid., at 17–18.
[49] [1976] 1 QB 629.
[50] Ibid., at 652.
[51] Ibid.

procedure they will follow in reaching a decision.[52] By and large, the ombudsmen have also supported the idea that procedural promises should be fulfilled; but have shown themselves markedly weaker than the courts in their preparedness or ability to enforce this.

The general preference for following the promised procedure is illustrated in a complaint arising from the proposals for a new national park in Wales.[53] A group of associations which supported the scheme had been given an unqualified assurance that a public inquiry would be held if there were significant objections to it, and this had been reinforced by an answer to a Parliamentary Question. In the event, the Secretary of State for Wales received so many objections that he decided to abandon the project without a public inquiry.

His defence when challenged on the point was twofold. Firstly, he was not legally required to hold an inquiry; and secondly, he did not see that any new evidence could have been offered which was not in the written objections. The PCA none the less felt that the associations had a justifiable grievance. While he sympathized with the Secretary's reluctance to hold an expensive and time-consuming investigation which would serve no purpose, he felt that it would have been only fair to explain this position to the complainants and give them the opportunity to put forward any further representations such as they might have deployed at the inquiry. Had this been done, they would not have been left with so acute a feeling that they were being denied a proper hearing.

Beyond giving the associations the satisfaction of knowing that their complaint was justified the report does not go. The indications are that the PCA was not prepared to question the Secretary's opinion that the decision would have been the same, and, if pressed, would have declined to intervene on these grounds. This point was made explicit in other similar cases.[54] Underlying this is the argument that, if the decision would have been the same, the complainant has not suffered any injustice. However, this involves an assumption that the official assertion (that the outcome would have been the same) is correct. Although at times the courts have made similar assumptions and exercised their discretion to decline a remedy,[55] this has usually be criticized,[56] and the tendency is far less

[52] Leading cases are *R.* v. *Liverpool Corporation ex p. Liverpool Taxi Owners' Association [1972] 2 All ER 589; Attorney-General for Hong Kong* v. *Ng Yuen Shiu* [1983] 2 All ER 346; *R* v. *Secretary of State for the Home Department ex p. Khan* [1985] 1 All ER 40.

[53] Case No. C. 162/V, HC 259 (1975/6), at 185.

[54] Case No. C. 56/T, HC 406 (1972/3), at 68; Case No. C. 415/67, HC 134 (1967/8), at 21; *The Sale of Wisley Airfield*, HC 322 (1980/1); Case No. C. 429/84, HC 184 (1985/6), at 43; Inv. 86/B/751, 19 Oct. 1987; Inv. 396/C/80, 9 May 1981.

[55] e.g. *Glynn* v. *Keele University* [1971] 1 WLR 487; *Malloch* v. *Aberdeen Corporation* [1971] 1 WLR 1578, at 1595.

[56] See e.g. H. W. R. Wade, *Administrative Law* (6th edn. Oxford, 1988), 533–4.

marked than in the decisions of the PCA. The courts will generally not attempt to second guess the outcome of a case had the procedural defect not existed, but will insist that the matter be tried for itself. The PCA has no power to direct such a course of action, or to quash the existing decision. The difference is significant.

In other cases the PCA's failure to provide a remedy is due to factors beyond his control, as in two instances in which public interest groups had been promised an inquiry before buildings of historic value were demolished, only to find that the buildings had been knocked down without inviting representations, or even advising that an inquiry would not be held.[57] Restoration of the status quo was clearly impossible, and the only redress available was an apology. The PCA's investigations are not well suited to anything other than a post-mortem in this sort of complaint, which might have been better dealt with by seeking interim injunctions in the courts at an earlier stage in the case.

Hence, the general conclusion offered in respect of procedural promises is that these are not complaints with which the PCA is particularly well equipped to deal. In particular, the time taken by the PCA's investigations is such that circumstances may well have changed irrevocably by the time a conclusion is reached. Little can then be done by way of recompense, save extract an apology. Also, restricted to intervening where there has been maladministration, the PCA has been unwilling or unable to question the government body in their assertion that the decision would have been the same. The courts have been less ready to make this assumption, preferring to find out by quashing the initial decision and starting afresh.

Agreements to contract

In the private sector, contractual negotiations always carry with them an element of speculation. Expenditure incurred in the expectation that the negotiations will be successful is a natural part of the risk attendant upon a commercial venture. Arguably, there is no reason why this should be any different if one of the negotiating parties happens to be a public body: any loss should still lie on the party sustaining it. In spite of this, both the PCA and the CLA have tended to the view that good administration requires public bodies not to mislead would-be contracting parties in the course of negotiations. A government department or local authority is expected to act as a model businessman, and breach of what is only a 'gentleman's agreement' may amount to maladministration.[58]

[57] Case No. C. 245/L, HC 138 (1969/70), at 71; Case No. C. 676/78, HC 799 (1979/80), at 15; See also Case No. C. 6/808/K, HC 246 (1977/8), at 268, with respect to road construction; and Case No. 4/36/77, HC 664 (1977/8), with respect to the sale of a country estate for industrial purposes; Case No. 443/90, HC 195 (1991/2), at 13.

[58] Inv. 216/L/85, 9 Dec. 1985.

The result is not that the Ombudsman will demand fulfilment of the contract (although this has sometimes happened), but that he will insist on compensation for loss incurred through having been 'led up the garden path'. This recognizes that, while a council or department may need to back out of negotiations for a contract which is no longer considered prudent, and while the council is perfectly within its legal rights to withdraw, there is a strong moral obligation not to do so without recognizing the damage that withdrawal will inflict. As the CLA observed in one case:

The Council are entitled to change their mind, particularly in the face of representations from their citizens. A consequence of their doing so on this transaction has been that the company found they had incurred expenditure made abortive by the Council's decision. The Council have argued that they have no legal obligation to reimburse costs arising from abortive negotiations. I do not dispute that view. My concern however, is not just with whether the Council have complied with the law, but with whether they have maintained an acceptable standard of public administration. That standard requires the Council to ensure that those who have acted in good faith on the basis of one decision of the Council should suffer no consequential loss if the Council change their minds.[59]

Only rarely has the Ombudsman has been prepared to recommend that the initial agreement be completed.[60] One such case involved a company which had sold land to the local authority for highway development, on the strength of an undertaking that the authority would sell it back to the company if the highway proposals were abandoned. This occurred in 1975 but, due to public opposition to the use to which the company wished to put the land, the council refused to transfer the land back. However, those public objections had been fully canvassed when the company had applied for planning permission for the land. The local authority had initially refused the application, but permission was granted after a full public inquiry on an appeal to the Secretary of State. In these circumstances, the CLA considered that the authority was morally bound to honour its undertaking to sell the land. The basis of this conclusion appears to have been that the council decision had been reached on the basis of improper considerations: that the council were using their contractual powers to circumvent the company's successful appeal on the planning issue. In other words, although there was a conflict between the interests of the public and those of the company, that conflict had already been resolved in the company's favour by the Secretary of State. As such, there was no reason why the promise should not be honoured.

The general trend in these cases is therefore well in line with that in the

---

[59] Inv. 1085/C/85, 2 Dec. 1985. See also Inv. 290/C/82, 21 June 1983; Inv. 87/C-141, 18 Jan 1988.

[60] Case No. C. 252/82, HC 84 (1983/4), at 110; Inv. 114/C/80, 21 July 1982 (Second Rep.).

other categories discussed above. Recognizing the public interest against holding the authority to its word, the ombudsmen have generally been content with compensation. Only where the conflict of interests has been resolved in the complainant's favour by a body expressly recognized as competent to make this assessment has either the CLA or PCA been prepared to require the contract to be completed on the terms initially agreed. The result is fair to both complainants and public alike.

THE INLAND REVENUE: A CASE-STUDY

Although the ombudsmen are primarily concerned with individual complaints, their work may also have a broader effect in improving administrative practices generally. In this context, the PCA has derived considerable assistance from a Parliamentary Select Committee which was set up to monitor his office. Almost from its inception, the Select Committee adopted the practice of calling ministers and government officials before it to account for any departmental policy of which the PCA had been critical, or for any refusal to take the action he recommended. The Inland Revenue, as one of the main subjects of complaint reaching the PCA, is one area in which over the years, with the backing of the Select Committee, he has succeeded in bringing about a significant change in attitudes and policies.[61]

One of the most frequent complaints made to the PCA comes from taxpayers whose tax payments have been incorrectly assessed by the Inland Revenue over a period of years, so as to produce an accumulated arrear so large that they cannot now afford to pay it. These people do not dispute the amount of their liability, but simply argue that, had they been taxed properly in the first place, the amount could have been paid without difficulty. Instead they say they have spent the money and should not have to pay the price for the Department's miscalculations.

Errors of this sort usually arise from the use by the Inland Revenue of the wrong PAYE code, or an incorrect grant of tax allowances, leading to insufficient tax being deducted. Such mistakes are almost inevitable in a system where taxpayers' circumstances are continually changing as they change jobs, receive wage increases, or become eligible for additional benefits such as pensions. It takes the Department time to adjust to these changes, and it should therefore come as no surprise if in any given year there is a discrepancy between the amount collected and the amount due. Hence, a complaint that the Inland Revenue is asking for the payment of arrears for a year just ended is unlikely to receive much sympathy. The

---

[61] See generally Gregory and Hutchesson, *The Parliamentary Ombudsman*, ch. 13.

problems arise when this amount is not detected at the end of the relevant tax year, and is carried over from one year into another so that the arrear steadily grows. How much time can the Department reasonably claim before it must be bound by its own assessment?

That question is largely answered by statute, which specifically allows the Inland Revenue to go back six years in making its assessments.[62] This limitation period, in itself a statutory bar against claims after six years, by implication would appear to rule out any possibility of relief before then. This has certainly been the view taken by the Inland Revenue, and it is not one with which the PCA was initially willing to quarrel. While, as a general rule, this still holds true, the PCA has gradually managed to push back the Department's reluctance to waive arrears which have arisen through its own error.

From 1967 until 1971, although critical of the maladministration which led to the accumulation of arrears, the PCA was not prepared to question the Inland Revenue's insistence on collecting the money. This was due largely to the application of two principles: first, that the complainant suffered no detriment, since he was being asked to pay no more than the tax properly due;[63] and second, that waiving the tax was contrary to the clear intent of the statute: 'the Inland Revenue are . . . bound by the law of the land to collect arrears of tax,'[64] and 'since the Department have statutory powers to claim arrears for six years, the complainant's claim is against the provisions of legislation'.[65] These were matters which the PCA did not feel able to question. The argument might have been raised that the Revenue's entitlement to go back six years should not apply where it had all along been in possession of the relevant information, but had failed to use it, but this was not something which the PCA was disposed to accept: 'The Department have a duty to collect tax which is legally due, even where . . . they are responsible for the errors which have contributed to an underpayment.'[66]

That stance was strengthened by the fact that the Department had power to go back indefinitely in cases where the taxpayer was suspected of fraud, implying that the power to go back six years could be exercised notwithstanding the absence of *mala fides* on the part of the taxpayer. None the less, the situation was undoubtedly capable of causing hardship.

Fortunately, small concession though it was, even in this period the Inland Revenue did not pursue its policy of recovery with complete relentlessness. Sir Arnold France, chairman of the Board of Inland

---

[62] Taxes and Management Act 1970, s. 43.
[63] Case No. C. 1009/68, HC 138 (1969/70), at 90.
[64] Case No. C. 179/67, HC 134 (1967/8), at 35.
[65] Case No. C. 516/L, HC 138 (1969/70), at 109.
[66] Case No. C. 568/S, HC 587 (1971/2), at 216.

Revenue, in answer to questions put to him by the Parliamentary Select Committee pointed out that, although there was no stautory power to excuse payment on the grounds of hardship, this was done (as it had been for a 'very long time') with Parliament's approval, as an extra-statutory concession.[67] However, whereas other departments, such as Customs and Excise, would make *ex gratia* payments on grounds of equity, without regard to the degree of hardship or immediate loss,[68] the Inland Revenue would only exercise their discretion in cases of absolute hardship. Sir Arnold admitted that what the Department meant by absolute hardship was 'sheer poverty'.[69]

The Select Committee concluded that this was too narrow an approach, and recommended a review of the Department's policy for awarding *ex gratia* or compensatory payments. The resulting government *Observations on the First Report from the Select Committee*[70] concurred, and a new practice was brought into effect on 14 July 1971 with the result that, where a taxpayer had not been informed of an underpayment within twelve months of the end of the tax year in which it arose, provided the taxpayer's income and savings did not exceed certain prescribed limits, the Inland Revenue would grant remission if the arrears had arisen through the Department's failure to make proper or timely use of information supplied by the taxpayer. In imposing income and investment restrictions on eligibility for relief, the White Paper was still employing a notion of hardship, but this was substantially more relaxed than the absolute hardship formerly required by the Department. In the White Paper's own language, it was a doctrine of 'comparative' hardship.

Once the effects of the White Paper began to be felt, there was a significant increase in the number of complainants who succeeded in obtaining a partial or complete remission of their taxes. Between 1971 and 1977, £7.4 million was remitted under the terms of the White Paper.[71] None the less there were still many who were being denied relief. Although these were arguably those taxpayers who could afford to pay anyway, the government was often slow to update the income and investment levels. Also the income criteria made no reference to factors such as impending retirement, or the number of dependents, which could substantially alter the relevance of the fixed levels to the question of hardship.

In 1979 these deficiencies led the PCA to challenge the arrangements. In

[67] First Report for 1970/1, HC 240.

[68] For examples of concessions by Customs and Excise, see Case No. C. 503/L, HC 138 (1969/70), at 18; and Case No. C. 207/K, HC 223 (1976/7), at 16; both involving waiver of the tax payable on importing vehicles into the UK. See also Case No. C. 515/G, HC 290 (1972/3), at 8; and the 'Snakebite' case, HC 135 (1986/7), noted in *The Times*, 30 Jan. 1987.

[69] Report of the Select Committee (May 1969).

[70] Cmnd. 4729 (1971); hereafter referred to as 'the White Paper'.

[71] First Report of the Select Committee on the PCA (1979/80), at p. viii.

his Annual Report for that year, speaking of the collection of arrears, he observed that 'such demands can be a serious burden, particularly on retired pensioners who seemed, as a group, to be especially susceptible to these [official] errors. And it seemed to me that the way in which the terms of the White Paper . . . were being applied needed urgent review.'[72] Looking back on the tax cases involving official error which had been investigated by the PCA since July 1971, he noted that eighty-six of the 120 complainants had been pensioners, and that, of these, seventy-six of the errors involved simple failures to make proper coding arrangements. The PCA was also critical of the failure to keep the income limits of the White Paper in pace with wage inflation, but stated that even this would not be enough:

It seems to me that anyone who has conducted himself in the belief that he has certain financial resources legitimately available is put to inconvenience, possibly serious embarrassment, if he subsequently discovers that the money is not in fact his to spend, but was owing to the Exchequer—even if he is not particularly impoverished. To decide that there is a financial point beyond which such inconvenience or embarrassment ceases to matter seems to me to be unreasonable and arbitrary.[73]

It was no answer to 'tell [a taxpayer] that he is so wealthy that no injustice has been done to him or that he has anyway had the benefit of the unpaid tax. For almost certainly, he would not have taken the benefit if he had realized that the money was not his to keep, and, if he has spent it, he would not have done so—sometimes irrevocably—had he known it was repayable.'[74] Even further, 'some account should be taken of the degree of vexation to which a taxpayer has been subjected'.[75]

This reflects a far broader view of detriment than the stringent 'loss of a legal right' which characterized the earlier tax cases. It also appears to abandon the idea of comparative hardship in favour of the view that any deteriment should prima facie be compensated.

The PCA's comments were studied by the Select Committee, which agreed with many of the criticisms, and recommended (1) that the basis on which the maximum income levels are calculated be altered, with the effect that these levels be raised; (2) that the operation of the income levels be tapered, so people would not be disadvantaged by the existing rigid stratification; (3) that a token remission of 10 per cent be made available to taxpayers with incomes above the upper limits, as compensation for inconvenience (a (considerably higher) income level was set on this, beyond which point the Committee agreed with the Inland Revenue that the taxpayer could be presumed to have had the use of the money owed

---

[72] HC 402 (1979/80), at 14.   [73] Ibid., at 16.
[74] First Report of the Select Committee on the PCA, at p. x.   [75] Ibid.

and to have derived some advantage from it, in which case this was compensation enough); and (4) that pensioners receive special treatment, due to the difficulties they face in having to adjust to a level of income below that which they had previously enjoyed. The recommendation was that the first £2,000 of a pensioner's income be ignored in applying the income limits.[76]

On 20 March 1981, the government announced changes which effectively implemented all these recommendations. The result today is still a system which relies on ideas of comparative hardship, but this is a considerable advance on the policy as it stood in 1967.[77] Significantly, the changes have come about not through the PCA's intervention in any particular case, but through his ability to make recommendations, based on an overall impression of the complaints reaching him. By this method, and with the backing of his Select Committee, he has been able to establish new administrative practices for dealing with cases of departmental error.

In contrast, although the courts have recognized that the Inland Revenue has a discretion to waive taxes, the cases generally reveal a marked reluctance on the part of the judiciary to compel the exercise of the discretion against the terms of the statute.[78] As Lord Templeman observed, the primary duty of the tax department is to collect and not to forgive taxes. In *Vestey* v. *Inland Revenue Commissioners (No. 2)*, Watson J went even further, and indicated that, however desirable it might be from the point of equity, the exercise of an extra-statutory discretion was in danger of being held invalid as an attempt to claim a dispensing power, contrary to the Bill of Rights.[79] These cases suggest that the changes which the PCA has been able to bring about would still be awaited if the courts were the only avenue of redress.

MISCELLANEOUS POINTS

Problems with changes of policy

In most of the cases discussed thus far, the cause of the complaint has been a simple mistake made by the government body. A more difficult problem arises in cases where official policies have changed after the advice has been given. Because the concept of maladministration does not permit the

---

[76] Ibid., HC 406/261.

[77] The precise terms of the concession are still being refined: see Annual Report (1991), HC 347, p. 13.

[78] See for example, *R.* v. *Inland Revenue Commission ex p. Preston* [1985] 2 WLR 836; *R.* v. *Board of Inland Revenue ex p. MFK Underwriting Agencies* [1990] 1 All ER 91.

[79] [1979] 2 All ER 225, at 233.

ombudsmen to question the rights or wrongs of the policy, or to question the need to change it, this is potentially a source of hardship which the ombudsmen cannot remedy.[80] In practice the problem has been circumvented by a willingness to demand that consideration be given to the plight of any party who might be caught by the change, before it is introduced. Failure to look at cases 'in the pipeline' can itself amount to maladministration.[81] The CLA's general stance in this sort of case is explained by Dr Yardley in his Annual Report for 1984/5:

Councils as political bodies make political decisions; they are entitled to change their policies, and will often do so, especially when the political control of the council alters. However, when such changes do take place, the Council must in my view have regard to the continuing interests of persons who have acted in reliance upon or pursuance of the old policies. Of course some will be disappointed in the change of policy, as where some prospective 'benefit' has been withdrawn. No-one is entitled to expect such benefits always to be on offer, but if any persons have taken action in reasonable reliance on previous policies, and because of the change have necessarily incurred abortive expenses or professional costs, or have irrevocably changed their circumstances, good administration demands either that they should be excluded from the change in policy or that they be compensated for their loss or expense.[82]

However, where consideration has been given to pipeline cases, and the Department has decided to proceed regardless, the ombudsmen are powerless to assist.[83]

A note on fault

A significant feature of the ombudsmen's decisions is that maladministration is broad enough to include non-negligent mistakes by a public official. The point is made most clearly in an investigation by the PCA involving an incorrect DHSS interpretation of a reciprocal EEC agreement on entitlement to pension. The PCA was satisfied that the Department had not been negligent in arriving at its interpretation, but did not see this as absolving them of responsibilty. As he pointed out, 'They did after all get it wrong.'[84] Again, in a case involving misrepresentations made by Customs, the PCA said that he was

conscious of the possibility that, in law, no claim for damages made by an importer would lie against Customs—it being arguable that no duty of care is owed by them

---

[80] See e.g. Case No. C/460/87, HC 151 (1989/90), at 41.
[81] Inv. 529/C/81, 15 May 1982; Inv. 1014/C-82, 13 Sept. 1983. See also the bus pass cases, discussed above.   [82] CLA Annual Report (1984/5), at 5.
[83] Case No. C. 726/K, HC 413 (1976/7) at 287; Case No. C. 569/V, HC 259 (1975/6), at 185 and Case No. C. 379/68, HC 138 (1969/70), at 127.
[84] Case No. C. 494/83, HC 150 (1984/5).

to the individual importer . . . in respect of their surveillance responsibilities. But I am not a court of law . . . Rather, it is my duty to afford equitable relief against that injustice which may not be remediable at law but which in a particular case is shown to have flowed directly from the maladministrative act or omission of a government department.[85]

Though this is not necessarily strict liability, it would clearly impose responsibility where tort law would not. As such, it allows the ombudsmen to remedy injustices which are beyond the reach of the courts.

The nature of the relief granted

No analysis of the work of the ombudsmen would be complete without some observation on the effectiveness of their recommendations. Neither the PCA nor the CLA has power to compel an authority to implement any remedy they consider desirable; their power is simply to recommend. Even if the authority accepts the force of their criticisms, there is still no legal entitlement to compensation. The PCA has said that, where a government body agrees to a scheme for compensation, it has an obligation of 'public morality and common sense'[86] to make all reasonable practical arrangements to ensure that all for whom the scheme was designed have a reasonable opportunity to know and avail themselves of it, but he has not questioned a departmental insistence that repayment is *ex gratia*, that the decision to introduce any compensation scheme is a discretionary act of policy, and that refusal to pay in any particular case is not a breach of any legal obligation.[87]

For the most part, central government bodies have been happy to accept a finding of maladministration made against them, and to remedy the situation in a manner agreeable to the PCA. In local government the CLA has met with greater opposition to its recommendations and 'there remains a hard core of resistance in some local authorities which for various reasons take the view that in the cases concerned they have acted rightly, and that the Local Ombudsman's findings do not persuade them to the contrary'.[88]

On average, between 5 and 6.5 per cent of the complaints which the CLA upholds are not resolved in a manner with which the Commissioner is satisfied.[89] Where a local authority does not co-operate, the CLA has power to issue a second report, but the value of this is questionable, since

---

[85] Case No. C. 356/82, HC 84 (1983/4), at 6. [86] HC 247 (1978/9), at 2.
[87] Ibid.
[88] D. Yardley, 'Local Ombudsmen in England: Recent Trends and Developments' [1983] PL 522.
[89] The figure of 5% comes from the CLA Annual Report (1987/8). That of 6.5% is taken from the Select Committee for the PCA, Third Report (1985/6), HC 448: 'Local Government Cases: Enforcement of Remedies'; and the JUSTICE Report *Administrative Justice: Some Necessary Reforms* (Oxford, 1988), at 115.

three out of four second reports fail to produce any change of heart.[90] This
obduracy on the part of local government has been a source of growing
concern, both within the Commission and among commentators. As Dr
Yardley has observed:

The Local Ombudsman system relies for its efficacy on the willing acceptance of the
umpire's decision even if it is not liked. Bearing in mind that over 70% of all
complaints made to me are in one way or another resolved in the Council's favour,
and that Councils are very reasonably content to accept such findings and to expect
the complainants to do likewise, it is quite unacceptable that any Council should
ignore or reject any finding which happens to be adverse.[91]

The CLA has been reluctant to suggest that steps be taken to make its
decisions binding on councils, but has noted that: 'unless the attitude of a
small minority of authorities changes, there is a bound to be increased
pressure for compulsion to ensure effective remedies are quickly given for
injustices revealed after thorough and objective investigation.'[92] In its
survey of the first five years of the CLA, JUSTICE recommended that
complainants be given the power to take enforcement action in a court of
law.[93]

The main argument against this is that it elevates the ombudsmen's
investigation into an adversarial contest which will alienate the authority, as
JUSTICE recognized in the context of the PCA in its report *Administrative
Law: Some Necessary Reforms*:

perhaps the conclusive objection to any attempt to integrate the PCA with the
court system is the fact that the PCA gets the support and co-operation of
departments precisely because he operates outside the regime of the courts of law.
If the PCA came to be regarded as the investigatory arm of the court we believe
that the whole atmosphere would change and that departments would act strictly in
accordance with their legal obligations and disclose only such documents as were
discoverable at law.[94]

---

[90] JUSTICE, *Administrative Justice*, at 115.
[91] CLA Annual Report (1982/3), 51. See the similar remarks of H. B. McKenzie Johnston
at 57, and of the Baroness Serota in the Annual Report for 1979/80, at 43.
[92] CLA Annual Report (1982/3), 7.
[93] p. 40 f. The recommendation is repeated in the latest survey, *Administrative Justice:
Some Necessry Reforms*, 128. An alternative suggestion was made by the Select Committee
on the PCA, which recommended in 1986 that its own powers be extended to allow it to
summon recalcitrant local authorities in the same way as it called ministers to account: HC
448 (1985/6). See also C. Himsworth, 'Parliamentary Teeth for Local Ombudsmen' [1986] PL
546. The CLA noted the suggestion, but doubted whether it would have the desired effect:
CLA Annual Report (1986/7), 31. JUSTICE concluded that 'the spectre of political contests
being fought between local councillors and a Parliamentary Committee over local issues is an
unattractive one', and that supervision by the Select Committee 'is likely to be so hazardous
that it should only be adopted if there is no better answer to hand': *Administrative Justice*,
126–7.   [94] *Administrative Justice*, 104.

This is equally true of local authorities, and for this reason the CLA has generally opposed court enforceability. None the less, the local ombudsmen have indicated that, unless there is some marked improvement in the voluntary acceptance of their decisions, they too would support legislative change for the enforcement of remedies.[95]

The present solution is a less radical form of coercion, based upon local publicity. The Local Government and Housing Act 1989[96] requires local authorities who fail to provide a satisfactory remedy to place an account of their action, together with a statement from a local ombudsman, in local newspapers at their own expense.[97] The chairman of the CLA, Dr Yardley, has indicated that he regards this as a better solution than enforcement in the courts.[98]

Although regrettable, the 'failures' of the CLA are a minority of complaints. However, the indications are that the problem is somewhat worse where the complaint involves questions of detrimental reliance. Of the forty-six complaints to the CLA referenced in this chapter, eleven have not been satisfactorily remedied. This represents 24 per cent, a figure significantly higher than the more general 6.5 per cent failure rate. This must reduce the usefulness of the CLA as an alternative means of redressing problems in this field.

CONCLUSION

The courts' approach to the problem of reliance on official misinformation has centred on attempts to apply the doctrine of estoppel, which dictates that the initial representation cannot be denied, so that everything which comes after it must fall. This immediately poses problems where the initial representation was *ultra vires*, or was contrary to the public interest. The court is then forced to choose between conflicting demands of justice for the public, and justice for the individual. In contrast, the response of the PCA and the CLA has been shaped by the concept of maladministration. Where the authority has good reason to change its mind, it is in the initial representation rather than the revised decision that the maladministration lies. The question then is not whether to enforce the misrepresentation, but how to compensate the loss which has flowed from it.

The solution is to recommend, wherever possible, that the complainant

---

[95] Annual Report (1984/5), 53. The Representative Body disagreed, and stated that 'the right solution was to act by persuasion'. However, the Widdicombe Committee accepted the CLA's concerns, and recommended judicial enforcement: *The Conduct of Local Authority Business*, Cmnd. 9797 (1986).

[96] s. 26 (1), inserting s. 31 (2D)–(2G) into the local Government Act 1974.

[97] s. 18.   [98] Author's interview with Dr Yardley.

be returned to the position he would have enjoyed had he been correctly advised from the outset. Where he has relied upon the representation, this entails compensating him to the extent of his reliance, but not to the extent of his expectation. There are cases, such as those concerning the promise of lump sum payments, where the complainant may have relied to the full extent of the promise. Compensation then is effectively the same as realizing the promise, and the remedy may be tantamount to an estoppel. This is however coincidental, and the only reason why complainants are fortunate in having the promise fulfilled is because it is impossible to distinguish what they were promised from what they have lost.

There are also situations where what is lost is the legitimate opportunity to obtain a substantive benefit, such as planning permission or a pension. Where this is the case, the ombudsmen have been prepared to go beyond financial reparation, and to recommend that the benefit itself should be provided. In redressing the loss of such a right, the PCA will require the injured party to comply with the legal requirements as far as is possible. In the national insurance context, for example, complainants will still be asked to pay the statutory contributions, albeit that the time limit on payment is waived. Only where the complainant has so disadvantaged himself that full compliance with the statutory requirements is impossible will the Ombudsman be prepared to recommend waiving the rules.

The net result of this is a solution which simultaneously respects the broader needs of administration to correct its own mistakes, and recognizes that correction should not be at the expense of those who have acted in reliance on the earlier incorrect advice. The redress of individual grievances in this fashion may gradually lead to changes in the overall policy and practice of the departments and authorities concerned. In this way, investigations into individual complaints may inure for the benefit of all who deal with the public body.

This is not to say that the ombudsmen are a panacea for all cases of misrepresentation. This chapter has also outlined areas in which the ombudsmen have been less successful. At times the maladministration limit on their jurisdiction has caused them to hold back from questioning an authority's decision where a court might have been more ready to intervene. Particular problems have arisen in complaints involving procedural promises, where the ombudsmen lack the power to order a stay of the government action until the merits of the complaint have been determined. In these cases also, recourse to the courts might have been more appropriate. These failures should not detract from the very real achievements of both the PCA and CLA. Rather, they should be seen as a reflection of the broader thesis that administrative law and government action must be viewed as a whole, where no single body or process provides all the answers.

Bibliography

ABEL, R. L. (1982) 'The Contradictions of Informal Justice', in R. L. Abel (ed.) *The Politics of Informal Justice.*

ABEL-SMITH, B., and STEVENS, R. (1968) *In Search of Justice.*

ACKNER, LORD (1987) 'Judicial Review: Judicial Creativity at its Best', 61 *Australian Law Journal* 442.

ADINOLFI, A. (1988) 'The Implementation of Social Policy Directives through Collective Agreements', 25 *CMLR* 291.

ADLER, M. and BRADLEY, A. (eds.) (1975) *Justice, Discretion and Poverty: Supplementary Benefit Appeal Tribunals in Britain.*

AKEHURST, M. B. (1982) 'Revocation of Administrative Decisions', *Public Law* 613.

ALEXANDER, LORD (1989) 'Judicial Review and City Regulators', 52 *Modern Law Review* 640.

ALLAN, T. S. R. (1985) 'The Limits of Parliamentary Sovereignty', *Public Law* 614.

—— (1988) 'Pragmatism and Theory in Public Law', 104 *Law Quarterly Review* 422.

ARDEN, A. (1988) *Homeless Persons: The Housing Act 1985 Part III.*

ARNULL, A. (1991) 'What Shall We Do on Sunday', 16 *ELR* 112.

ARROWSMITH, S. (1990) 'Judicial Review and the Contractual Powers of Public Authorities', 106 *Law Quarterly Review* 277.

ARTHURS, H. W. (1985) *Without the Law: Administrative Justice and Legal Pluralism in Nineteenth-Century England.*

ASIMOV, M. (1983) 'Delegated Legislation: United States and United Kingdom', 3 *Oxford JLS* 253.

Association of District Councils (1988) *Homelessness: A Review of the Legislation.*

AUSTIN, J. (1847) 'Centralization' 85 *Edinburgh Review* 221.

—— (1955 edn.) *The Province of Jurisprudence Determined.*

BAILEY, S., JONES, B., and MOWBRAY, A. (eds.) (1992) *Cases and Materials on Administrative Law.*

BALDWIN, J., WIKELEY, N., and YOUNG, R. (1992) *Judging Social Security: The Adjudication of Claims for Benefit in Britain.*

BALDWIN, R. (1978) 'A British Independent Regulatory Agency and the "Skytrain" Decision', *Public Law* 57.

—— (1987) 'Why Accountability', 27 *British Journal of Criminology* 97.

—— (1990) 'Why Rules Don't Work', 53 *Modern Law Review* 321.

—— (forthcoming) *Rules and Government.*

—— and DAINTITH, T. (eds.) (1992) *Harmonization and Hazard: Regulating Workplace Health and Safety in the European Community.*

—— and HAWKINS, K. (1984) 'Discretionary Justice: Davis Reconsidered', *Public Law* 570.

—— and HORNE, D. (1986) 'Expectations in a Joyless Landscape', 49 *Modern Law Review* 685.

—— and HOUGHTON, J. (1986) 'Circular Arguments: The Status and Legitimacy of Administrative Rules', *Public Law* 239.

—— and MCCRUDDEN, C. (eds.) (1987) *Regulation and Public Law*.

BARBER, B. (1984) *Strong Democracy: Participatory Politics for a New Age.*

BAYLES, M. (1987) *Principles of Law: A Normative Analysis.*

—— (1990) *Procedural Justice: Allocating to Individuals.*

BEATSON, J. (1979) 'Legislative Control of Administrative Rule-Making: Lessons from the British Experience?', 12 *Cornell Int. LJ* 199.

—— (1987) 'Public and Private in English Administrative Law', 103 *Law Quarterly Review* 34.

BEETHAM, D. (1991) *The Legitimation of Power.*

BELL, K., COLLISON, P., TURNER, S., and WEBBER, S. (1974) 'National Insurance Local Tribunals', 3 *Journal of Social Policy* 289 and 4 *Journal of Social Policy* 1.

BELOFF, M. (1988) 'The Boundaries of Judicial Review', in J. Jowell and D. Oliver (eds.) *New Directions in Judicial Review.*

—— and ELIAS, P. (1992) 'Natural Justice and Fairness: The Audi Alteram Partem Rule', in M. Supperstone and J. Goudie (eds.) *Judicial Review.*

BENTHAM, J. (1981) *A Treatise on Judicial Evidence* ed. M. Dumont.

BIEBER, R., DEHOUSSE, R., PINDER, J., and WEILER, J. (1988) 'Back to the Future: Policy Strategy and Tactics of the White Paper on the Creation of a Single European Market', in R. Bieber *et al.* (eds.) *92: One European Market.*

BIRDS, J. (1987) 'Self-Regulation and Insurance Contracts', in F. Rose (ed.) *New Foundations for Insurance Law.*

—— and GRAHAM, C. (1988) 'Complaints Mechanisms in the Financial Services Industry', 7 *Civil Justice Quarterly* 313.

—— —— (1992) *Complaints against Insurance Companies.*

BIRKINSHAW, P. (1982) 'Homelessness and the Law: The Effects and Response to Legislation', 5 *Urban Law and Policy* 255.

—— (1985) *Grievances, Remedies and the State.*

—— HARDEN, I., and LEWIS, N. (1990) *Government by Moonlight: The Hybrid Parts of the State.*

BLACK, D. J. (1971) 'The Social Organisation of Arrest', 23 *Stanford Law Review* 1087.

BLANKENBURG, E. (1984) 'The Poverty of Evolutionism: A Critique of Teubner's Case for "Reflexive Law"', 18 *Law and Society Review* 273.

BLOM-COOPER, L. (1984) 'Lawyers and Public Administrators: Separate and Un-equal', *Public Law* 215.

BOYLE, A. E. (1984) 'Administrative Justice, Judicial Review and the Right to a Fair Hearing under the European Convention on Human Rights', *Public Law* 89.

—— (1984) 'Reforming Administrative Law', *Public Law* 521.

BRADLEY, A. W. (1987) 'Comment', *Public Law* 485.

—— (1987) 'Social Security and the Right to a Fair Hearing', *Public Law* 3.

—— (1992) 'Administrative Justice and Judicial Review: Taking Tribunals Seriously?', [1992] *Public Law* 185.

—— (1992) 'Sachsenhausen, Barlow Clowes—and then?', *Public Law* 353.

—— and EWING, K. D. (1993) *Constitutional and Administrative Law* (11th edn.).

BRADSHAW, J. (1969) 'From Discretion to Rules: The Experience of Family Fund', in M. Adler and S. Asquith (eds.) *Discretion and Welfare.*

—— and MILLAR, J. (1991) *Lone Parent Families in the UK.*

BREYER, G., and STEWART, R. (1992) *Administrative Law and Regulatory Policy* (3rd edn.)

BREYER, S. (1979) 'Analysing Regulatory Failure: Mismatches, Less-Restrictive Alternatives and Reform', *Harvard Law Review* 549.

—— (1982) *Regulation and its Reform.*

BRIDGES, L., GAME, C., LOMAS, D., McBRIDGE, J., and RANSON, S. (1987) *Legality and Local Politics.*

—— SUNKIN, M., and MESZAROS, G. (1993) *Judicial Review in Perspective: An Investigation of Trends in the Use and Operation of the Judicial Review Procedure in England and Wales.*

BROWNE-WILKINSON, LORD (1992) 'The Infiltration of a Bill of Rights', *Public Law* 397.

CANE, P. (1992) *An Introduction to Administrative Law* (2nd edn.).

CAPPELLETTI, M. (1989) *The Judicial Process in Comparative Perspective.*

—— *et al.* (eds.) (1976) *Integration through Law.*

CARRANTA, R. (1993) 'Government Liability After Francovich', 52 *CLJ* 272.

CARROLL, A. (1991) 'The Gulf Crisis and the Ghost of *Liversidge* v. *Anderson*', 5 *Immigration and Nationality Law and Practice* 72.

CHAYES, A. (1982) 'The Supreme Court: 1981 Term-Foreword: Public Law Litigation and the Burger Court', 96 *Harvard Law Review* 4.

CHESLER, R. D. (1983) 'Imagery of Community, Ideology of Authority: The Moral Reasoning of Chief Justice Burger', 18 *Harvard Civil Rights—Civil Liberties Law Review* 457.

Chief Adjudication Officer (1987) *Annual Report of the Chief Adjudication Officer for 1985/86 on Adjudication Standards.*

—— (1990) *Annual Report of the Chief Adjudication Officer for 1988/89 on Adjudication Standards.*

—— (1991) *Annual Report of the Chief Adjudication Officer for 1989/90 on Adjudication Standards.*

—— (1992) *Annual Report of the Chief Adjudication Officer for 1990/91 on Adjudication Standards.*

CLUCAS, K. (1992) *Report on a Study on a New SRO for the Retail Sector.*

COLEMAN, R. (1970) *Supplementary Benefits and the Administrative Review of Administrative Action.*

COLLINS, H. (1986) 'Democracy and Adjudication', in N. MacCormick and P. Birks (eds.) *The Legal Mind: Essays for Tony Honoré.*

COOK, D. (1989) *Rich Law, Poor Law.*

COOPER, P. (1985) 'Conflict or Constructive Tension: The Changing Relationship of Judges and Administrators', 45 *Public Administration Review* 643.

COTTERRELL, R. (1989) *The Politics of Jurisprudence.*

—— (1990) 'Law's Images of Community and Imperium', in S. S. Silbey and A. Sarat (eds.) *Studies in Law, Politics and Society: A Research Annual.*

—— (forthcoming 1994) *Law's Community: Legal Theory in Sociological Perspective.*

Council on Tribunals (1986) *Social Security: Abolition of Independent Appeals under the Proposed Social Fund*, Cmnd. 9722.
—— (1991) *Annual Report 1990–1*.
—— (1993) *Annual Report 1992–3*.
CRAIG, P. (1989) *Administrative Law* (2nd edn.).
—— (1990) *Public Law and Democracy in the United Kingdom and the United States of America*.
—— (1992) 'Legitimate Expectations: A Conceptual Analysis', 108 *Law Quarterly Review* 79.
CRANSTON, R. (1984) *Consumer Law*.
—— (1985) *Legal Foundations of the Welfare State*.
—— (1987) *Law, Government and Public Policy*.
DAINTITH, T. C. (ed.) (1988) *Law as an Instrument of Economic Policy: Comparative and Critical Approaches*.
—— (1989) 'A Regulatory Space Agency?', 9 *Oxford JLS* 534.
—— (1989) 'The Executive Power Today: Bargaining and Economic Control', in J. Jowell and D. Oliver (eds.) *The Changing Constitution* (2nd edn.).
—— (1991) 'Political Programmes and the Content of the Constitution', in W. Finnie, C. Himsworth and N. Walker (eds.) *Edinburgh Essays in Public Law*.
DALLEY, G., and BERTHOUD, R. (1992) *Challenging Discretion*.
DAVIS, K. C. (1969) *Discretionary Justice*.
DE BURCA, D. (1992) 'Giving Effect to EC Directives', 55 *Modern Law Review* 215.
DE SMITH, S. A. (1973) *Judicial Review of Administrative Action* (3rd edn.).
—— and BRAZIER, R. (1989) *Constitutional and Administrative Law* (6th edn.).
Department of Health and Social Security (1985) *Reform of Social Security*, Vol. 2, Cmnd. 9518.
Department of Social Security (1990) *Social Security Statistics 1990*.
—— (1990) *Note on Disability Working Allowance*.
—— (1990) *The Way Ahead: Benefits for Disabled People*, Cmnd. 917.
—— (1990) *Children Come First*, Cmnd. 1264.
DICKENS, L., JONES, M., WEEKES, B., and HART, M. (1985) *Dismissed*.
DICEY, A. V. (1959) *An Introduction to the Study of the Law of the Constitution* (10th edn.).
DIGNAN, J. (1983) 'Policy-Making, Local Authorities and the Courts; The GLC Fares' Case', 99 *Law Quarterly Review* 605.
DIVER, C. S. (1983) 'The Optimum Precision of Administrative Rules', 93 *Yale Law Journal* 65.
Donoughmore Committee (1932) *Report of the Committee on Minister's Powers*, Cmnd. 4060.
DWORKIN, R. (1971) 'Philosophy and the Critique of Law', in R. P. Wolff (ed.) *The Rule of Law*.
—— (1977) *Taking Rights Seriously*.
—— (1984) *A Matter of Principle*.
—— (1986) *Law's Empire*.
—— (1989) 'Liberal Community', 77 *California Law Review* 479.
EARDLEY, T. (1991) *Housing Benefit Reviews Final Report*.
—— and SAINSBURY, R. (1993) 'Managing Appeals: The Control of Housing

Benefit Internal Reviews by Local Authority Officers', *Journal of Social Policy* 461.

EASSON, A. J. (1993) *Taxation in the European Community*.

ELIAS, P., and BELOFF, M. (1992) 'Procedural Rules and Consultation', in M. Supperstone and J. Goudie (eds.) *Judicial Review*.

ELY, J. H. (1980) *Democracy and Distrust: A Theory of Judicial Review*.

EMERY, C. T., and SMYTHE, B. (1986) *Judicial Review*.

EMILIOU, N. (1992) 'Subsidiarity: An Effective Barrier against the Enterprises of Ambition?', 55 *ELR* 383.

EVANS, J. (1990) *De Smith's Judicial Review of Administrative Action* (4th edn.).

FARMER, J. A. (1974) *Tribunals and Government*.

FARRELLY, M. (1989) *The Reasons Why Appellants Fail to Attend their Social Security Appeal Hearing*.

FELDMAN, D. (1990) 'Public Law Values in the House of Lords', 106 *Law Quarterly Review* 246.

—— (1992) 'Review, Appeal and Jurisdictional Confusion', 108 *Law Quarterly Review* 45.

Finer Committee (1974) *Report of the Committee on One-Parent Families*, Cmnd. 5629.

FINNIS, J. (1980) *Natural Law and Natural Rights*.

FORREST, R., and MURIES, A. (1985) *An Unreasonable Act? Central–Local Government Conflict and the Housing Act 1980*.

FORSYTH, C. (1988) 'The Provenance and Protection of Legitimate Expectations', 47 *CLR* 238.

FOULKES, D. (1990) *Administrative Law* (7th edn.).

Franks Committee (1957) *Report of the Committee on Administrative Tribunals and Inquiries*, Cmnd. 218.

FREDMAN, S., and MORRIS, G. (1991) 'Public or Private? State Employees and Judicial Review', 107 *Law Quarterly Review* 298.

FREEDMAN, J. (1978) *Crisis and Legitimacy*.

FROST, A., and HOWARD, C. (1977) *Representation and Administrative Tribunals*.

FRUG, G. E. (1984) 'The Ideology of Democracy in American Law', 97 *Harvard Law Review* 1277.

FULBROOK, J. (1989) 'HASSASSA and Judge Byrt: Five Years On', *Industrial Law Journal* 177.

FULLER, L. L. (1940) *The Law in Quest of Itself*.

—— (1946) 'Reason and Fiat in Case Law' 59 *Harvard Law Review* 376.

GALLIGAN, D. J. (1986) 'Rights, Discretion and Procedures', in D. Galligan and C. Sampford (eds.) *Law, Rights and the Welfare State*.

—— (1986) *Discretionary Powers: A Legal Study of Official Discretion*.

GANZ, G. (1972) 'Allocation of Decision-Making Functions', *Public Law* 215.

—— (1987) *Quasi-Legislation: Recent Developments in Secondary Legislation*.

GENN, H. (1987) *Hard Bargaining: Out of Court Settlement in Personal Injury Actions*.

—— and GENN, Y. (1989) *The Effectiveness of Representation at Tribunals*.

GIBBONS, T. (1991) *Regulating the Media*.

GOWER, L. C. B. (1984) *Review of Investor Protection Report: Part 1*, Cmnd. 9125.

GRAVELLS, N. (1993) 'European Community Law in the English Courts', *Public Law* 44.

GREGORY, R., and HUTCHESSON, P. (1975) *The Parliamentary Ombudsman: A Study in the Control of Administrative Action.*

GRIFFITH, J. (1985) 'Judicial Decision Making in Public Law', *Public Law* 564. ·

—— (1993) *Judicial Politics since 1920.*

HALL, A. N., and TODD, R. K. (1981) 'Administrative Review Before the AAT: A Fresh Approach to Dispute Resolution', 12 *Federal LR* 71 and 95.

HAMILTON, R. W. (1972) 'Procedures for the Adoption of Rules of General Supplicability: The Need for Procedural Innovation in Administrative Rule-Making', 60 *California Law Review* 1976.

HARDEN, I. (1990) 'Regulated Autonomy and the Concept of "Public" and "Private" ', 3 *European Yearbook in the Sociology of Law.*

—— (1991) 'The Constitution and its Discontents', 21 *British Journal of Political Science* 489.

—— (1992) *The Contracting State.*

—— and LEWIS, N. (1986) *The Noble Lie: The British Constitution and the Rule of Law.*

HARLEY, H. (1915) 'Court Organisation for a Metropolitan District', 9 *American Political Science Review* 507.

HARLOW, C. (1976) 'Administrative Reaction to Judicial Review', *Public Law* 116.

—— (1990) 'The Justice/All Souls Review: Don Quixote to the Rescue', 10 *Oxford JLS* 85.

—— (1992) 'A Community of Interest? Making the Most of European Law', 55 *Modern Law Review* 331.

—— Harlow, C., and RAWLINGS, R. (1984) *Law and Administration.*

—— —— (1992) *Pressure Through the Law.*

HARRINGTON, C. (1985) *Shadow Justice.*

HARRIS, M. (1989) 'The Courts and the Cabinet: Unfastening the Buckle?', *Public Law* 251.

HART, H. L. A. (1961) *The Concept of Law.*

—— (1983) *Essays in Jurisprudence and Philosophy.*

HAWKINS, K. (1984) *Environment and Enforcement.*

—— (1986) 'On Legal Decision-Making', 42/4 *Washington and Lee* 1161.

—— (ed.) (1993) *The Uses of Discretion.*

HAYHURST, J. D., and WALLINGTON, P. (1988) 'The Parliamentary Scrutiny of Delegated Legislation', *Public Law* 547.

HENNESSEY, P. (1989) *Whitehall.*

HEPPLE, B. (1990) 'The Implementation of the Community Charter of Fundamental Social Rights', 53 *Modern Law Review* 643.

HILL, M. (1969) 'The Exercise of Discretion in the National Assistance Board', *Public Administration* 59.

HIMSWORTH, C. (1986) 'Parliamentary Teeth for Local Ombudsmen', *Public Law* 546.

HIRST, P. and JONES, P. (1987) 'The Critical Resources of Estabished Jurisprudence', 14 *Journal of Law and Society* 21.

HOLLIS, M. (1977) *Models of Man.*

HOOD, C. (1976) *The Limits of Administration*.
—— (1983) *The Tools of Government*.
—— (1986) *Administrative Analysis: An Introduction to Rules, Enforcement and Organisations*.
—— (1988) *Dwelling on the Threshold: Critical Essays on Modern Legal Thought*.
HUTTER, B. (1988) *The Reasonable Arm of the Law*?
ICSTIS (1991) *Activity Report 1989–90*.
IPPR (1991) *The Constitution of the United Kingdom*.
JACK, R. (1990) *Banking Services: Law and Practice*, Cmnd. 1026.
JAFFE, L. (1968) 'The Citizen as Litigant in Public Actions: The Non-Hohfeldian or Ideological Plaintiff', 116 *University of Pennsylvania Law Review* 1033.
JENNINGS, I. (1935) 'Courts and Administrative Law: The Experience of English Housing Legislation', *Harvard Law Review* 246.
JERGESEN (1978) 'The Legal Requirement of Consultation', *Public Law* 290.
JOHNSON, N. (1977) *In Search of the Constitution*.
JONES, B. L. (1989) *Garner's Administrative Law* (7th edn.).
JONES, T. H. (1990) 'Mistake of Fact in Administrative Law', *Public Law* 507.
JOWELL, J. (1973) 'The Legal Control of Administrative Discretion', *Public Law* 178.
—— (1975) *Law and Bureaucracy*.
—— (1977) 'The Limits of Law in Urban Planning', *Current Legal Problems* 63.
—— (1991) 'The Take-Over Panel: Autonomy, Flexibility and Legality', *Public Law* 149.
—— and LESTER, A. (1987) 'Beyond *Wednesbury*: Substantive Principles of Administrative Law', *Public Law* 368.
—— —— (1988) 'Proportionality: Neither Novel nor Dangerous', in J. Jowell and D. Oliver (eds.) *New Directions in Judicial Review*.
JUSTICE (1961) *The Citizen and the Administration*.
JUSTICE/All Souls (1988) *Administrative law: Some Necessary Reforms*.
KERRY, M. (1986) 'Administrative Law and Judicial Review: The Practical Effects of Development Over the Last 25 Years on Administration in Central Government', 64 *Public Administration* 163.
KIRBY, M. (1980) 'Administrative Review on the Merits: The Right or Preferable Decision', 6 *Monash University Law Review* 171.
—— (1981) 'Administrative Review: Beyond the Frontier Marked Policy', 12 *Federal LR* 121.
LACEY, N. (1993) 'The Jurisprudence of Discretion: Escaping the Legal Paradigm', in K. Hawkins (ed.) *The Uses of Discretion*.
LANDIS, J. M. (1938) *The Administrative Process*.
LASKI, H. (1926) 'Judicial Review of Social Policy in England', *Harvard Law Review* 832.
Law Commission (1976) *Remedies in Administrative Law*, Cmnd. 6407.
—— (1993) *Administrative Law: Judicial Review and Statutory Appeals*, Consultation Paper No. 126.
LAWRENCE, R. (1980) 'Solicitors and Tribunals', *Journal of Social Welfare Law* 13.
LAWS, J. G. M. (1989) 'The Ghost in the Machine: Principles in Public Law', *Public Law* 27.

LAWS, J. (1993) 'Is the High Court the Guardian of Fundamental Constitutional Rights?', *Public Law* 59.

LE SUEUR, A., and SUNKIN, M. (1992) 'Applications for Judicial Review: The Requirement of Leave', *Public Law* 102.

LEMPERT, R., and MONSMA, K. (1988) 'Lawyers and Informal Justice: The Case of a Public Housing Eviction Board', 51 *Law and Contemporary Problems* 135.

LEWIS, C. (1992) 'The Exhaustion of Alternative Remedies in Administrative Law', 51 *Cambridge Law Journal* 138.

—— and MOORE, S. (1993) 'Duties, Directives and Damages in European Community Law', *Public Law* 151.

LEWIS, N. (1989) 'Regulating Non-Governmental Bodies', in J. Jowell and D. Oliver (eds.) *The Changing Constitution* (2nd edn.).

LEWIS, R. (1985) 'Insurers' Agreements not to Enforce Strict Legal Rights', *Modern Law Review* 275.

LIND, E., and TYLER, T. (1988) *The Social Psychology of Procedural Justice*.

LODGE, J. (1989) *The European Community and the Challenge of the Future*.

LOUGHLIN, M. (1978) 'Procedural Fairness: A Study of the Crisis in Administrative Law Theory', 28 *University of Toronto Law Review* 215.

—— (1986) *Local Government in the Modern State*.

—— (1992) *Public Law and Political Theory*.

LOVELAND, I. (1991) 'Administrative Law, Administrative Processes, and the Housing of Homeless Persons: A View from the Sharp End', 10 *Journal of Social Welfare and Family Law* 4.

—— (1991) 'Legal Rights and Political Realities: Governmental Responses to Homelessness in Britain', 16 *Law and Social Inquiry* 249.

LOWE, N., and WOODROFFE, G. (1991) *Consumer Law and Practice*.

MCAUSLAN, P. (1980) *The Ideologies of Planning Law*.

—— (1983) 'Administrative Law, Collective Consumption and Judicial Policy', 46 *Modern Law Review* 1.

—— (1988) 'Administrative Justice: A Necessary Report?', *Public Law* 215.

—— (1988) 'Public Law and Public Choice', 51 *Modern Law Review* 681.

—— and MCELDOWNEY, J. (1985) 'Legitimacy and the Constitution: The Dissonance Between Theory and Practice', in P. McAuslan and J. McEldowney (eds.) (1985) *Law, Legitimacy and the Constitution*.

—— —— (eds.) (1985) *Law, Legitimacy and the Constitution*.

MCBARNET, D., and WHELAN, C. (1991) 'The Elusive Spirit of the Law: Formalism and the Struggle for Legal Control', 54 *Modern Law Review* 848.

MACCORMICK, N. (1993) 'Beyond the Sovereign State', 56 *Modern law Review* 1.

MACDONALD, R. (1979) 'Judicial Review and Procedural Fairness in Administrative Law: I', 25 *McGill LJ* 520.

MCGEE, A., and WEATHERILL, S. (1990) 'The Evaluation of the Single Market: Harmonisation or Liberalisation?', 53 *Modern Law Review* 578.

MACKAY, LORD (1993) 'The Administration of Justice: Alternative Dispute Resolution', *Hamlyn Lectures*.

MAHER, G. (1986) 'Natural Justice as Fairness', in N. MacCormick and P. Birks (eds.) *The Legal Mind: Essays for Tony Honoré*.

MARSHALL, G. (1961) 'Justiciability', in A. Guest (ed.) *Oxford Essays in Jurisprudence*.

MARSHAW, J. (1981) 'Administrative Due Process: The Quest for a Dignitary Theory', 61 *Boston University law Review* 885.

—— (1983) *Bureaucratic Justice: Managing Social Security Disability Claims*.

—— (1987) 'Dignitary Process: A Political Psychology of Liberal Democratic Citizenship', 39 *University of Florida Law Review* 433.

MEGARRY, R. E. (1944) 'Administrative Quasi-Legislation', 60 *Law Quarterly Review* 125.

METCALFE, L., and RICHARDS, S. (1990) *Improving Public Management* (2nd edn.).

MIDDLEMAS, K. (1979) *Politics in Industrial Society*.

MIERS, D., and PAGE, A. (1990) *Legislation*.

MORAN, M. (1991) *The Politics of the Financial Services Revolution*.

MOWBRAY, A. (1990) 'A Right to Official Advice: The Parliamentary Commissioner's Perspective', *Public Law* 68.

—— (1991) 'Newspaper Ombudsmen: The British Experience', *Media Law and Practice* 91.

MUNRO, C. (1991) 'Press Freedom: How the Beast was Tamed', 54 *Modern Law Review* 105.

National Consumer Council (1986) *Self-Regulation*.

—— (1991) *Out of Court*.

NEAL, A. C. (1990) 'The European Framework Directive on the Health and Safety of Workers: Challenges for the United Kingdom', 6 *Int. J. of Comp. Lab. Law and Ind. Relns.* 80.

NEWTON, L. (1976) 'The Rule of Law and the Appeal to Community Standards', 21 *American Journal of Jurisprudence* 95.

NIELSEN, R., and SZYSZCZAK, E. (1993) *The Social Dimension of the European Community* (2nd edn.).

NINER, P. (1989) *Homelessness in Nine Local Authorities*.

—— and DAVIES, M. (1987) *Housing Work, Housing Workers and Education and Training for the Housing Service*.

NONET, P. (1969) *Administrative Justice*.

O'BARR, W., and McCONLEY, J. M. (1985) 19 *Law and Society Review* 661.

Office of Fair Trading (1978) *Review of the UK Self-Regulatory System of Advertising Control*.

—— (1990) *Estate Agency*.

—— (1991) *Consumer Redress Mechanisms*.

OLIVER, D. (1987) 'Is the *Ultra Vires* Rule the Basis of Judicial Review?', *Public Law* 543.

—— (1988) 'The Courts and the Policy Making Process', in J. Jowell and D. Oliver (eds.) *New Directions in Judicial Review*.

—— (1991) *Government in the United Kingdom: The Search for Accountability, Effectiveness and Citizenship*.

OSBORNE, G. (1982) 'Inquisitorial Procedure in the ATT', 13 *Federal LR* 150.

PAGE, A. (1987) 'Financial Services: The Self-Regulatory Alternative?' in R. Baldwin and C. McCrudden (eds.) *Regulation and Public Law*.

—— and FERGUSON, R. (1992) *Investor Protection*.

PAGONE, R. (1984) 'Estoppel in Public Law: Theory, Fact and Fiction', 7 *UNSWLJ* 267.

PANNICK, D. (1982) 'The Law Lords and the Needs of Contemporary Society', 53 *Political Quarterly* 318.

—— (1992) 'Who is Subject to Judicial Review and in Respect of What?', *Public Law* 1.

PARTINGTON, M. (1991) *Secretary of State's Powers of Adjudication in Social Security Law.*

—— and BOLDERSON, H. (1984) *Housing Benefit Review Procedures: A Preliminary Analysis.*

PEAY, J. (1989) *Tribunals on Trial.*

PELKMANS, J. (1986–7) 'The New Approach to Technical Harmonisation and Standardisation', 25 *JCMS* 249.

PENNOCK, J., and CHAPMAN, J. (eds.) (1975) *Participation in Politics.*

PINCOFFS, E. (1977) 'Due Process, Fraternity, and a Kantian Injunction', in J. Pennock and J. Chapman (eds.) *Due Process NOMOS 18.*

POGGI, G. (1978) *The Development of the Modern State.*

POLLITT, C., and HARRISON, S. (1992) *Handbook of Public Services Management.*

POSTEMA, G. J. (1986) *Bentham and the Common Law Tradition.*

POUND, R. (1942) *Social Control Through Law.*

PROSSER, T. (1977) 'Poverty, Ideology and Legality: Supplementary Benefit Appeal Tribunals and their Predecessors', 4 *British Journal of Law and Society* 39.

—— (1982) 'Towards a Critical Public Law', 9 *Journal of Law and Society* 1.

—— (1985) 'Democratisation, Accountability and Institutional Design: Reflections on Public Law', in P. McAuslan and J. McEldowney (eds.) *Law, Legitimacy and Constitution.*

RAMSAY, I. (1987) 'The Office of Fair Trading: Policing the Consumer Marketplace', in R. Baldwin and C. McCrudden (eds.) *Regulation and Public Law.*

RAWLINGS, R. (1990) 'The MP's Complaints Service', 53 *MLR* 149.

RAWLS, J. (1987) 'The Base Liberties and their Priority', in S. McMurrin (ed.) *Liberty, Equality and the Law.*

RAZ, J. (1986) *The Morality of Freedom.*

REICH, C. (1964) 'The New Property', 73 *Yale Law Journal* 778.

REICH, N. (1988) *Reflexive Law and Reflexive Legal Theory: Reflections on Post-Modernism in Legal Theory.*

REINER, R. (1992) *The Politics of the Police* (2nd edn.).

REISS, A. J. (jun.) (1990) 'Book Review of Discretionary Justice', 68 *Michigan Law Review* 994.

RICHARDSON, G. (1986) 'The Duty to Give Reasons: Potential and Practice', *Public Law* 437.

—— (1993) *Law, Process and Custody: Prisoners and Patients.*

ROBERTSON, G. (1979) *Obscenity.*

ROBSON, P. and WATCHMAN, P. (1980) 'The Homeless Persons Obstacle Race', *International Journal of Social Welfare Law* 65.

ROBSON, W. A. (1951) *Justice and Administrative Law: A Study of the British Constitution.*

ROSENBLOOM, D. (1987) 'Public Administrators and the Judiciary: The "New Partnership" ', 47 *Public Administration Review* 75.

ROSS, M. (1993) 'Beyond Francovich', 56 *Modern Law Review* 55.

RUBIN, E. L. (1989) 'Law and Administration in the Administrative State', 89 *Col. LR* 369.

SAINSBURY, R. (1988) *Deciding Social Security Claims*.

—— (1989) 'The Social Security Chief Adjudication Officer: The First Four Years', *Public Law* 323.

—— (1992) *Survey and Report into the Working of the Medical Appeal Tribunals*.

—— (1993) 'Administrative Justice: Discretion and Procedure in Social Security Decision-Making', in K. Hawkins (ed.) *The Uses of Discretion*.

—— and EARDLEY, T. (1991) *Housing Benefit Reviews: An Evaluation of the Effectiveness of the Review System in Responding to Claimants Dissatisfied with Housing Benefit Decisions*.

SAPHIRE, R. (1978) 'Specifying Due Process Values: Towards a More Responsive Approach to Procedural Protection', 127 *University of Pennsylvania Law Review* 111.

SAWYER, G. (1963) 'Political Questions', 15 *University of Toronto Law Journal* 49.

SCARMAN, LORD (1990) 'The Development of Administrative Law: Obstacles and Opportunities', *Public Law* 490.

SCHEIDER, C. E. (1992) 'Discretion and Rules: A Lawyer's View', in K. Hawkins (ed.) *The Uses of Discretion*.

SCHIEMANN, K. (1990) 'Locus Standi', *Public Law* 342.

SCHUCK, P. (1983) 'Comment', 92 *Yale Law Journal* 1602.

SCHWARTZ, B. (1987) *Lions over the Throne: The Judicial Revolution in English Administrative Law*.

—— and WADE, H. W. R. (1972) *Legal Control of Government*.

SEDLEY, S. (1990) 'Improving Civil Justice', *Civil Justice Quarterly* 384.

Select Committee for the PCA (1985/6) *Third Report*.

SHARPE, J. (1970) 'The Theory and Value of Local Government', *Political Studies* 154.

SIEDENTOP, H., and ZILLER, J. (eds.) *Making European Policies Work: The Implementation of Community Legislation in the Member States*.

Social Democratic Party (1984) *Taming Leviathan: Towards Fairer Administration*.

Social Fund Commissioner (1991) *Annual Report of the Social Fund Commissioner for 1990–91 on the Standards of Reviews by Social Fund Inspectors*.

Social Security Advisory Committee (1987) *The Draft Social Fund Manual: Report by the Social Security Advisory Committee*.

STEINER, J. (1992) 'Coming to Terms with EEC Directives', 55 *Modern Law Review* 215.

STEWART, G., LEE, R., and STEWARD, J. (1986) 'The Case of the Board and Lodgings Regulations', 13 *Journal of Law and Society* 371.

STEWART, R. B. (1975) 'The Reformation of American Administrative Law', 88 *Harvard Law Review* 1667.

—— (1983) 'Regulation in a Liberal State: The Role of Non-Commodity Values', 92 *Yale Law Journal* 1357.

STREET, H. (1975) *Justice in the Welfare State* (2nd edn.).

SUNKIN, M. (1987) 'What is Happening to Judicial Review?' 50 *Modern Law Review* 433.

—— (1991) 'The Judicial Review Case Load, 1987–89', *Public Law* 940.

—— BRIDGES, L., and MESZAROS, G. (1993) *Judicial Review in Perspective*.

—— and LE SUEUR, A. (1991) 'Can Government Control Judicial Review?', [1991] *Current Legal Problems* 161.

SUPPERSTONE, M., and GOUDIE, J. (eds.) (1992) *Judicial Review*.

SYNDER, F. (1993) 'The Effectiveness of European Community Law: Institutions, Processes, Tools and Techniques', 56 *Modern Law Review* 19.

SZYSCZAK, E. (1990) 'Sovereignty: Crisis, Compliance, Confusion, Complacency?', 15 *ELR* 480.

—— (1992) 'European Community Law: New Remedies, New Directions', 55 *MLR* 690.

TAGGART, M. (ed.) (1986) *Judicial Review of Administrative Action in the 1980s*.

TAYLOR, I., and POPHAM, G. (1989) *An Introduction to Public Sector Management*.

TAYLOR-GOOBY, P. (1985) *Public Opinion, Ideology and State Welfare*.

TEUBNER, G. (1983) 'Substantive and Reflexive Elements in Modern Law', 17 *Law and Society Review* 239.

THIBAUT, J., and WALKER, L. (1975) *Procedural Justice*.

THOMPSON, L. (1987) *An Act of Compromise*.

TRIBE, L. (1985) *Constitutional Crisis*.

TWINING, W. (1985) *Theories of Evidence: Bentham and Wigmore*.

—— and MIERS, D. (1991) *How to do Things with Rules* (3rd edn.).

TYLER, T. (1991) 'Procedure or Result: What do Disputants Want from Legal Authorities?', in K. Mackie (ed.) *A Handbook of Dispute Resolution*.

VAN ALSTYNE (1977) 'Cracks in "The New Property": Adjudicative Due Process in the Administrative State', 62 *Cornell Law Review* 445.

WADE, H. W. R. (1980) *Constitutional Fundamentals*.

—— (1988) *Administrative Law* (6th edn.).

WALKER, N. (1991) 'The Middle Ground in Public Law', in W. Finnie, C. Himsworth, and N. Walker (eds.) *Edinburgh Essays in Public Law*.

WEATHERILL, S. (1992) *Cases and Materials on EEC Law*.

—— and BEAUMONT, P. (1993) *EC Law*.

Widdicombe Committee (1986) *The Conduct of Local Authority Business*, Cmnd 9797.

WIDGOR, D. (1974) *Roscoe Pound: Philosopher of Law*.

WILLIAMS, B. (1979) *Report of the Committee on Obscenity and Film Censorship*, Cmnd. 7772.

WILLIAMS, D. (1986) 'Justiciability and the Control of Discretionary Power', in M. Taggart (ed.) *Judicial Review of Administrative Action in the 1980s*.

WILLIAMS, D. W. (1991) 'The British Reaction to the French Package', *Intertax* 208.

WILLIAMS, S. (1990) 'Sovereignty and Accountability in the European Community', 61 *Political Quarterly* 299.

WOOLF, H. (1986) 'Public Law–Private Law: Why the Divide?', *Public Law* 220.

—— (1992) 'Judicial Review: A Possible Programme for Reform', *Public Law* 221.

WRAITH, R. E., and HUTCHESSON, P. G. (1973) *Administrative Tribunals*.

YARDLEY, D. (1983) 'Local Ombudsmen in England: Recent Trends and Developments', *Public Law* 522.

ZANDER, M. (1989) *The Law Making Process*.

ZINES, L. (1991) *Constitutional Change in the Commonwealth*.

Subject Index